THE
ENGLISH TEACHER'S
COMPANION

A Complete Guide to Classroom, Curriculum, and the Profession

Jim Burke

BOYNTON/COOK PUBLISHERS
Heinemann
Portsmouth, NH

Boynton/Cook Publishers, Inc.
A subsidiary of Reed Elsevier Inc.
361 Hanover Street
Portsmouth, NH 03801–3912
http://www.boyntoncook.com

Offices and agents throughout the world

© 1999 by Jim Burke

The author and publisher wish to thank those who have generously given permission to reprint borrowed material:

Excerpt from "Natural Inspiration" by Joan Ryan. From *San Francisco Chronicle*, June 11, 1997. © San Francisco Chronicle. Reprinted with permission.

Excerpt from "Fall" by Jimmy Santiago Baca. From *Black Mesa Poems*. Copyright © 1989 by Jimmy Santiago Baca. Reprinted by permission of New Directions Publishing Corp.

Library of Congress Cataloging-in-Publication Data
Burke, Jim, 1961–
    The English teacher's companion : a complete guide to classroom, curriculum, and the profession / Jim Burke.
      p. cm.
    Includes bibliographical references and index.
    ISBN 0-86709-475-3
    1. English philology—Study and teaching—Handbooks, manuals, etc.   I. Title.
PE65.B87   1999   98-51101
428'.0071'2—dc21   CIP

Editor: Lois Bridges
Production: Abigail M. Heim
Cover design: Judy Arisman
Manufacturing: Louise Richardson

Printed in the United States of America on acid-free paper
03 02 01   RRD   6 7 8 9 10

CONTENTS

FOREWORD
HOLDING OPEN THE DOOR

Fran Claggett

Teaching, of course, is holding open
the door and staying out of the way.

So begins the poem "Not Academic" by Marie Ponsot.[1] And so begin my thoughts as I reflect on Jim Burke's comprehensive companion to teachers who are opening and holding open the doors through which our students enter into the classrooms we create for them.

Every once in a while, about once a decade, a book comes along that makes me wonder, "However in the world did I get along without this book?" Whether you are a first-year teacher, a veteran like me, a mid-career professional like the author, or an administrator who wants to understand more about what is often the most visible and controversial department in the school, you will find in *The English Teacher's Companion* insights and questions, lesson plans and theories, practical how-to guides and checklists alongside the musings of the reflective practitioner.

In his introduction, Burke writes, "The table of contents for this book reads like a syllabus for a course we never graduate from, because our work never stands still." This book never stands still either. It moves from moment to moment, defining, explaining, questioning, referring, elaborating. All the things that good teachers do, Jim does for us. We sit in on his classroom, share the epiphanies, feel the tragedies, experience the day-to-day tedium that sometimes, no matter how creative we've been, how informed, how caring, simply overtakes our students, sweeping us along with it. But we don't quit, because on the next page is another possibility, another resource for us to try, another Internet connection to offer the kids.

The design of the book enables you to find your way around very sensibly. Moving from the foundations of teaching and learning, Burke takes us through the "standard fare," literally providing us with the standards that undergird the current curriculum. We see Burke's students engaged in all facets of "English"—reading, writing, vocabulary, grammar (yes, grammar!). We work through the process of composing a curriculum. We join Burke in dealing, once again, with the complexities of assessment.

---

1. From *The Dark Green* (Alfred A. Knopf, Inc.) reprinted in *Audits of Meaning* (Heinemann).

"Standard" fare is followed by a section that will be of tremendous value to all teachers who are coping with the new literacies. Those of us who began teaching with ditto masters are guided into a comfort zone of digital and media literacy. *The English Teacher's Companion* helped me delve more deeply into Internet references. I've been a bit backward in this regard, only recently spending the time it takes to track down interesting references that might be useful to students as well as teachers. But my "companion" has done much of the work for me, pointing the way. Following up on an Internet address is a bit like the old days of getting loose in the college library "stacks," where I usually forgot what I was originally researching and ended up mesmerized by a tangentially related exploration. And that is one of the joys of libraries and Internet sources, following one's bent and finding what we didn't know we were looking for.

One of the facts of life for English teachers is that if we are doing our job, we are going to have to deal with the big issues—cultural differences, gender, race, ethics. We deal with them in the classroom, in the Board room, on the telephone, in the principal's office. *The English Teacher's Companion* addresses and discusses how to think about and deal with these critical issues in a forthright, non-inflammatory way. This section of the book would be extremely valuable to use as the basis for department or school-wide discussions of such issues.

By the time you finish this book, you know the author as you know few of your colleagues. Jim Burke is the teacher that you wish you had had in your junior year. He is the teacher that you wish taught next door to you so you could run over and share a poem your student just wrote. He is the teacher who should have been your mentor for the first five years of your career. Perhaps most of all, he is the teacher you wish you could hang around with after classes, have a cup of coffee with, and listen to explain why you shouldn't give up on your sixth-period kids.

Having reached the time in my professional life when I spend more time with teachers than I do with students, I found myself revisiting my own history as a teacher as I read *The English Teacher's Companion*. "We are what we imagine," N. Scott Momaday said in "The Man Made of Words."[2] "Our best destiny is to imagine, at least completely, who and what, and that we are." Reading Jim Burke's *The English Teacher's Companion*, I am reminded over and over again of what it has meant for me to imagine myself, to be and to have been, in many senses of the phrase, both an English teacher and an English teacher's companion.

---

2. Lecture printed in *The Remembered Earth*, ed. by Geary Hobson, University of New Mexico Press, Albuquerque, 1990.

ACKNOWLEDGMENTS

If it is difficult to know a man, find out with whom he associates. You will then know him.

—Yugoslavian proverb

This book would not exist if it were not for my editor Lois Bridges. She saw in me and my work what I could not, asking me simply to write about what I do. She is the ultimate companion to any writer, and a wonderful friend.

Sam Intrator, a doctoral candidate from Stanford, walked into my room in October, days after I agreed to write this book. He stayed the rest of the year to study my class and talked with me all year long about teaching and learning. His relentless efforts on behalf of this book, my fourth-period class, and my own learning are blessings for which I will always be grateful.

Without my students, whose numbers now amount to some fifteen hundred after ten years of teaching, I am nowhere. My students have always been and will always be my most important teachers and the source of my deepest joy as a teacher.

I would like to thank the following people who read and, through their comments, improved the book in those ways or areas indicated: Arthur Applebee, University at Albany, State University of New York: History chapter and timelines; Ed Amrhein, director of Admissions, Antioch College: writing letters of recommendation and college application essays; Jerry Arrigoni, principal, Burlingame High School: for patience and encouragement during the year I wrote this book while teaching full-time; Sheridan Blau, University of California at Santa Barbara and president of National Council of Teachers of English: for guidance and encouragement at crucial points; Sandy Briggs, Burlingame High School: for help with ESL strategies and guidance these last few years that has helped me be able to write this book; the Burlingame High School English Department: for daily lessons about teaching, life, and friendship, with special thanks to Jimi Baloian, Jackie Estes, and Linda McLaughlin for their support; the following board members of the California Association of Teachers of English, for lessons about politics, the profession, and the practice of teaching English: Bob Chapman, Pat Cipriano, Dianne Lucas, Punky Fristrom, Bonnie Erikson, Bob Infantino, Ken Lane, Don Mayfield, Akiko Morimoto, and Vince Piro; Rebekah Caplan, English Language Arts director, Oakland Unified School District: Ethnicity; Elaine Caret: Student Teaching, Gender, and Assessment chapters and for many years of conversation about teaching and books; the Castro Valley High School English Department: for the many lessons they taught me during my first years; CATENet: for the amazing community you have helped me create and the remarkable help you provided to every query I sent out—you embody what it means to be professional English teachers; Fran Claggett, Sonoma State University and New Standards Project: How to Read a Poem, Curriculum, and Thinking chapters, and for her teaching and support these past years; John Christgau, retired English teacher and novelist: for permission to use the Principles of an Essay and his example as a teacher; Leila Christenbury, author of *Making the Journey: Being and Becoming a Teacher of English Language Arts*: for permission to use her Dense Question strategy; Pete Feely at NCTE: support and resources; Frank Firpo, the man with whom I teach the freshman English–Social Studies program, for all he has taught me these many years about bridging our disciplines; Richard Foley, California Curriculum and Assessment Commission: Assessment and Law chapters, and for his professional guidance these many years; Karen Frazzini, Burlingame High School: Special Needs; Sue Glick, Burlingame High School: Service Learning; Jeff Golub, University of South Florida: Technology; Amy Haire, English teacher, Hillsdale High School: Student Teaching and Gender; Carol Jago, Santa Monica High School: for years worth of influential conversations that informed so much of my teaching and writing, and for her friendship; Michael Kamil, Stanford University: Reading; Diane Levin, California Department of Education: guidance and lessons in the politics of English education; Catharine Lucas, California State University at San Francisco: for all she taught me about teaching and writing; Alice Parker, director of Special Education, California Department of Education: Students with Special Needs, and for her daughter, Martha Montgomery who, as a student in my class, taught me more than most about teaching; Kyoko Sato, professor of English Education at California State University at Northridge: New Teacher chapter; Jim and Kathleen Strickland, Slippery Rock University: Assessment and general encouragement; Nancy Lester: Student Teaching, Assessment, Teaching and Learning, Gender chapters, and for the time and intelligence Nancy offered at crucial moments; Paul Mariani, University of Massachusetts at Amherst: Poetry; Miles Myers, former executive director, National Council of Teachers of English: Law and Profession chapters, and for years of guidance and his example of what it means to be a professional; Mark Philips, California State University at San Francisco: Media Literacy, and for his early confidence in what I could accomplish; Steve Poling: for years of conversations that gave shape to ideas in this book; Linda Reif, author of _Seeking Diversity: Language Arts with Adolescents_: for permission to use her Life Graph assignment; MaryAnn Rodgers: for inspiring the idea of reflections and activities at each chapter's end; Regie Routman: for help with the Introduction, Law, and Profession chapters, and for her guidance and encouragement during the writing of this book; Sheldon Smith, director of technology, San Luis Obispo County Office of Education: Technology; Bob Simola, teacher Paso Robles High School: Technology; Vicki Spandel, Northwest Regional Education Labs and author of _Creating Writers_ for permission to use portions of the Six Trait Writing Rubric.

Thanks to the following publishers for providing permission to use excerpts from the following authors: Joan Ryan, "Natural Inspiration," is reprinted by permission of the _San Francisco Chronicle_; Jimmy Santiago Baca, "Fall," from _Black Mesa Poems_ (copyright © 1989 by Jimmy Santiago Baca) is reprinted by permission of New Directions Publishing Corporation.

Heinemann has been supportive from the beginning, but I am particularly grateful for help and encouragement from the following: Janine Duggan, editorial assistant; Mike Gibbons, general manager; Abby Heim, production supervisor; Melissa Dobson, copyeditor; Lisa Luedeke, acquisitions editor; and Leigh Peake, editorial director.

At the end of the year in which I wrote this book, three of my most important mentors—Bill Robinson of San Francisco State University, Pat Hanlon of Lowell High School, and Bill Clawson of Santa Monica High School—retired after a combined career of over one hundred years teaching English. I thank them for all they taught me.

Finally, to my wife, Susan, and our sons, Evan and Whitman. The fact that this book is, in part, dedicated to them cannot possibly compensate them for all they endured throughout the last year. There are no words for the daily grace and blessings these three people bring to my life. Their support and encouragement throughout the writing of this book sustained me.

INTRODUCTION
LEARNING TO EMBRACE

I teach high school English, just like you do. Every day I leave my house in San Francisco and drive down to a lovely school in a small town named Burlingame, where I've made my home with the hundreds of kids I've taught. Room 82 is a special place; I am reminded of this each morning as I enter the hall and see the different students squatting around my door, books cradled on their knees while they munch bagels and drink coffee, something I would never have thought to drink at that age. Then again, these kids work harder in a week than I did in all four years of high school combined.

Of course, not all my students arrive at school at seven o'clock to study and help each other. In fact, most of my students are just waking up at that hour. Mine is a school made up of many communities, because it draws from the whole peninsula south of San Francisco. This means that my American Literature class, for example, has kids whose parents could buy the school and others who clean the houses of their classmates. It also means that I have students who could read *The Color Purple* in a weekend, and others who won't even try, who will watch the video, search the Web, consult their trusted friend Cliffs Notes.

This is why I love English, though. Just like poets charge our senses by taking different words and rubbing them together to see what fires they can make, so do I like to watch what happens in my classes, where one student writes about his friends in prison and the girl next to him writes about her daddy the judge who put them there. When we add stories to the mix, when we start talking about " 'Mericans," as Sandra Cisneros calls us, and what such words mean, kids' heads start shaking and nodding, and pretty soon we have an actual conversation going on in the classroom, a conversation that might carry out into the halls and follow them through the day and continue when they get home and keep talking—to their parents, or to friends on-line, or to me through their journals.

The English Teacher's Companion strives to help you create such a community in your classroom by offering you ways to organize your curriculum around such essential conversations; it also provides practical methods to create the necessary intellectual and emotional environments in your class that will allow such important discussions to take place. Sometimes English asks us to juggle so much so fast that new teachers wonder how they can possibly do it all, let alone do it well.

These organizational and instructional challenges have fascinated me from the beginning of my career. The solutions I outline in this book grew out of my own classroom experience and personal reflection. I'd love to say you can plug-n-play them, just open this book and go to a particular page and solve whatever problem drove you to seek guidance. This book *does* offer concrete advice. Scanning through, you will see many pictures and bulleted lists that offer examples and activities to help you teach better tomorrow.

However, this book is based on the fact that we only improve if we embrace and reflect on our errors. To this end you will find, at each chapter's end, "Reflections," which are meant to be used for your own personal writing, or as class assignments for a college course. In addition to these topics, each chapter ends with an activity and a recommended text or texts that I hope will provide further insight into the chapter's main idea.

This book, anchored in standards as it is, aspires to achieve the same level of thoughtfulness that I reach for every day in my classes. The table of contents for this book reads like a syllabus for a course we never graduate from, because our work never stands still: we teach in the midst of complexity and uncertainty every day. When my sixth period convenes, and I find all the wonderful lessons that worked so well before disintegrating in my hands, I find it exciting, rather like live theater: What will happen? Will we rise above our fatigue and frustration today and walk out of class as interested as did those in a previous class period?

This book recognizes, in fact it embraces, the inherent complexity of our enterprise. What else can I do when the poem that elicited immediate deep discussion in fourth period puts students to sleep in fifth—that is, until Frank asks whether it's true that you can cut your nose off and still smell things. Then he continues, actually linking his observations about the poem (Marge Piercy's "Barbie Doll," in which a girl commits suicide because she is not beautiful in the eyes of her peers) to how he was treated when he first came to the United States. It's an opening and we take it, writing and talking, listening and thinking as we go.

When the bell rings and they stumble out of class, homework assigned, I measure my success—and theirs—by Tony's conclusion that the poem was "hella sick," by which he means very good and interesting. It's not the measure of success I learned when I was in college, but then again the theories I heard in college didn't always take into consideration the practice of the real class. *The English Teacher's Companion* offers a solid bridge between those worlds of theory and practice, built as it is on the foundations of what works to help teachers develop in their students those literacies essential to success in life.

My love of literature lives alongside my commitment to the world of work our students must enter. To deny the importance of either of these would ignore what my own experiences have taught me. My father dropped out of high school when he was seventeen, but prospered in the printing business because he developed the skills and literacies he needed to succeed. My involvement with educational reform has further convinced me that these different worlds can live alongside each other, even complement each other. Finally, my experiences teaching special education, learning to speak Arabic and live in a culture different from my own, working with students in advanced and remedial classes, have convinced me that there are ways to reach and succeed with all our students.

I feel as though I have spent the past twenty years preparing to write this book. I hope that it will help you succeed with the type of student I was (very bad) and the type of student I have since become (as evidenced by this book). Every article I have written now seems a draft that led me deeper into these issues and trends, the practice and problems of teaching English in high school. Every opportunity I've enjoyed reminds me now of Rilke's notion that everything is a preparation for that one love we will come to accept as our true blessing. My students are and have always been my greatest blessing in this work; what they, as well as my colleagues, have taught me fills this book. They have been my companions these many years, teaching me what they need as writers, how they read, what matters to them most as people. It is now my turn to be your companion, to help you as I am able by sharing with you what I know about teaching English.

Welcome to the conversation.

Jim Burke
San Francisco
1998

CHAPTER 1

AUGUST
DREAMS AND REALITIES

It's late August when the dreams begin again, each one signaling summer's end and school's beginning. Each dream is a variation on the same theme: the combined exhilaration and anxiety that accompany each new school year. In most of them I end up in strange and mostly embarrassing situations, all of which amount to the way we would feel if we found ourselves standing naked in front of a class of typical American high school students.

Then that last week in August I rise, make a pot of coffee, and get out the bag that I imagine will finally accommodate the complex needs of an English teacher. I put on some music—something calming—and reach for the file trays in which I piled up all my ideas the previous year, thinking that they would be ideal for the coming year. They are newspaper articles with hastily scribbled ideas in their jagged margins, such as "Use as a topic for journal" or "Use as idea for project on trends in society." They are the hopeful notes of someone who believes that next year I will do it better, get it right. These notes are like a compost pile in which my ideas transform themselves into other ideas that, down the line, may amount to a great experience for my students. In late August, before the year has begun, I need something to react to, something to fill my head, to "prime the pump" after the calm months of summer.

By evening on that first day, I have usually spent more hours at the computer in my home office than I have all summer combined. A battered green folder holds a thin sheaf of pages clipped together, bright Post-it notes stuck to each set marked with the number of copies needed and such directions as "find Soto poem to include also." In the morning, having had yet another "teacher dream," I rise early and shoulder my bag, kissing my wife and two sons—who spent the previous day at the zoo so that I could get down to work—and drive off to the dark English office, where I find nearly three months of mail slumped on my desk and a colony of ants feeding on the remnants of the last cup of coffee I drank back in June.

Across the hall I find my room sunk in shadows and full of absence for all the missing voices of students. The halls outside are polished but lonesome; schools seem sad without the children who attend them. The walls of my classroom stare back at me, conspicuously bare after the summer school classes. I walk back to the office and put on some coffee, opening a pound of the good stuff given as a gift by Roushig, a graduating senior whose parents own a local café. The smell of the coffee reminds me of Roushig, of June, of graduation when, after I had worked with her for weeks to prepare her graduation speech, she began to cry after three words, crying harder as the audience's applause grew louder. I smile to think of those who are now gone and those who will take their places in the year ahead.

I unlock the humble computer lab I built up over the last few years and roll out my computer, wheeling it into my classroom. I dig out a CD of Pablo Casals playing Bach's *Suites for*

Unaccompanied Cello and pop it into the computer to play it. I open the windows and survey the lawns, where months before, my students performed *Romeo and Juliet*. I search for the combination to the lock I put on my room's closet door; unable to find it, I hunt down some lock cutters and snap it off to get at my supplies and books.

By the time I have returned the cutters, the coffee is ready and I begin the annual ritual of creating my room, but only after finding the lock combination conspicuously taped to my filing cabinet. I teach in an old school, a majestic building so evocative of high school that a number of movies, most recently *Dangerous Minds*, have been filmed there. My room just barely accommodates the thirty-five desks I need for my students. I note that over the summer the section of the floor that had rotted because of a roof leak was fixed, though poorly. A large hump now swells under a couple of desks and the tiles fail to match. I find little graffiti and think gratefully that the summer school teacher must have been engaging and diligent. By the time the Bach CD is over and I have put on the Billie Holiday, I have started to put up my pictures of students and posters of authors and their books. The white walls soon come to life with images from countries we study, books or authors we read. The biography of my classes and students unfolds as I staple the hundreds of pictures to the wall to honor what they did and, when I see a photograph of Michael, who died in a car accident on his way to school, to remember that they were here for a short time before disappearing off into that vast mobile country of ours.

Around lunch time I begin to hear other cars pulling up to the building. The school band is already out practicing their marching in the parking lot. I hear footfalls in the halls. Meanwhile, I have sorted through at least five pounds of mail to find three phone messages and two envelopes worth keeping.

By the time I leave later that afternoon, I have turned in my course outlines, my first few assignments, and some materials for the other members of the English department on performance standards. The bag I came with now bulges with nearly a dozen books I hope to swim around in, trusting that somewhere in them I will find the ideas I need to improve my classes. I am buoyed by optimism as I consider the blank canvas of the year ahead and all its possibilities, for what moves me most about teaching is the extent to which it is, in the end, a creative act.

CHAPTER 2

THINKING ABOUT TEACHING AND LEARNING

In her classroom our speculations ranged the world. She breathed curiosity into us, so that each morning we came to her carrying new truths, new facts, new ideas, cupped and shielded in our hands like captured fireflies. When she went away, a sadness came over us. But the light did not go out. She had written her signature upon us: the literature of the teacher who writes on children's minds. Many teachers have taught me soon forgotten things but only a few like her created in me a new direction, a new hunger, a new attitude. I suppose to a large extent I am the unsigned manuscript of that teacher. What deathless power lies in the hands of such a person.

John Steinbeck, "A Former Teacher"

Good teaching challenges students to know and to care that they know, to help them know not only *what* they know but *how* they know it. Listening once to a recording of opera singer Maria Callas's "master classes," I was struck by what she helped the fledgling singers find in themselves; whereas she could have showcased her own talent—they sold tickets to the classes so people could watch her teach—she used her own voice only to help her students find theirs, stopping just when the diva in her could have dominated. One witness to her teaching wrote, "She treated her students as if they shared her own sense of dedication. Once, when a student began making excuses for some mistakes, Callas cut her off, by raising a hand and saying, 'Hush—and sing.' When another student tried to explain why she couldn't sing all of the trills in a piece, Callas interrupted her with 'I'm sure you can, if you try hard enough' " (Thomason 1997). Callas's approach illustrates a central question posed in *Making Connections: Teaching and the Human Brain*: "How [does one] teach for expertise from the very beginning, when a person's still a novice?" (Caine and Caine 1994).

The Four Components of Effective Teaching and Learning

I have learned other languages (Arabic and French), mastered sports (tennis), and become a competent user of computers and other technologies. These experiences have helped me, after reflecting on them, better understand how to learn and how to teach. Subsequent conversations with teachers and reading about the nature of teaching and learning helped me arrive at four components of good teaching:

- Construction
- Occupation
- Negotiation
- Conversation

Construction

All effective education involves making things. We make sense of our world by acquiring the language we need to describe it to ourselves and others. We make connections between what we see and what we read, between where we've been and where we're going, to help us understand the relationship between them. And, in the English class, we make various texts in different styles using a range of media to make meaning and, at the same time, demonstrate our understanding. When students' learning is built on such foundations, they become active participants in their own education. It is not enough, however, to just make things: we must follow poet John Ciardi's advice and ask not what but *how* a poem means. This is what some brain researchers call the "active processing of experience" (Caine and Caine 1994).

In *The Dialogic Curriculum: Teaching and Learning in a Multicultural Society* (1995), Patricia Lambert Stock describes an inner-city teacher who extended a "curricular invitation designed to initiate dialogue" to study what was important to her students—to their own lives—by having them assemble an anthology of writings on the subject from various authors. At the same time, the students wrote their own stories, which eventually became part of the anthology. Such independent learning challenges the teacher to redefine his or her role; having provided the opportunity or placed students at some personal or intellectual crossroads, the teacher must then get out of the way to allow room for the inevitable learning. The teacher then becomes a mentor to whom the student comes for guidance and focused teaching in the context of that student's own learning.

We sometimes resist the value and importance of fun, too often feeling insulted by the idea that we should be providing "edutainment," competing with MTV for students' attention. But "creativity is inherently joyful, challenging, and absorbing. It introduces laughter into what would otherwise be tedium. It engages attention and imagination and, when skillfully facilitated, it enhances communication" (Caine and Caine 1994). On one occasion, my students were assigned Philip Levine's "What Work Is," a poem they read as part of our discussion about the Great Depression and characters in Steinbeck's *Cannery Row*. The next day, I gave them an envelope full of words and asked them to construct a poem using them. Eventually most students realized the words came from Levine's poem. This activity allowed us, among other things, to talk about how you can build different meanings out of the same words. We then copied down the poems they "built" and put them up on the walls for others to appreciate. We also posted them to our classroom Web site as a way of publishing them for a larger audience. Here is one example:

> What you don't know
> does not hide knowledge
> wasted hours waiting to work
> because stubbornness is suddenly ahead of you

blurring your vision with simple words
an obvious presence of young failing minds
flooding a night with sad refusal.
—ALLEGRA, ZACH, NICKOLA, SED

Sarah Ivester, one of my seniors, reminds us that it is not enough to make a curriculum: "The first thing [teachers] have to see is that it's the government that makes us come to school but it's the teacher who makes us want to learn." Sarah's comment points to perhaps the most important things we make in our classrooms: a community of learners, and the relationship between these learners and what we ask them to learn. The obvious joy my students felt while creating and reading poems like the preceding one made my day—and theirs. Eight months later, asked to remember what seemed an important moment during the year, Allegra Azzopardi, one of my juniors, said the poem she had composed for the *Cannery Row* discussion signaled to her that more was going on in her mind than she had previously realized.

What *construction* looks like in the English class. Construction is exemplified by:

- manipulating words to effect changes in their meaning
- constructing, deconstructing, or reconstructing texts to better understand how they work and what they mean
- creating a classroom environment that is conducive to an active, participatory classroom that might better be called a "workshop," since students are "building" understanding and "making" meaning
- giving students the tools (i.e., reading, writing, speaking, thinking) and the knowledge of how to use those tools to construct meaning for themselves
- providing students with the blueprints for what you want them to accomplish and requiring them to have to figure out how to do it as they go

Allegra, Zach, and Nikola working on their poem in the library

Occupation

Effective education involves occupation. Construction—of a class, of knowledge, of relationships, of meaning, of a story—implies occupation in both senses of the word: to work and to inhabit. For the word *occupation*, you find such definitions as "to hold or possess" and "to engage, employ" (*American Heritage Dictionary*, 3d ed.). Reflecting for a moment on contemporary usage, we hear students speak of being "into" something or dismiss something because they are "not into it."

Everything teachers do prepares—or should prepare—students for the work their lives will ask of them. In today's world this means, for example, teaching them to read a variety of texts such as they will encounter as employees, parents, home owners, or citizens. Former secretary of labor Lynn Martin wrote, "More than half of our young people leave school without the knowledge or foundation required to find and hold a good job" (U.S. Department of Labor 1991). Whether or not this statistic is true, we do need to prepare our students to do what the world will ask of them when they graduate.

We also speak, however, of inhabiting—through art and stories—an imaginative space. We think in terms of getting kids to imagine themselves occupying certain jobs, but also of envisioning themselves inside sentences, where they roll up their sleeves and look closer at meaning, nuance, character, style. Indeed, *inhibit* and *inhabit* derive from the same Indo-European root, which suggests that through inhabiting different roles—writer, speaker, reader, performer—students will lose their inhibitions. Students in my freshman class, for example, put William Golding on trial each year, charging him with libel against humanity. Some of them take on the role of characters from the book while others adopt roles such as lawyers and expert witnesses who are called to testify (in character) in the trial. Students undergo a remarkable transformation as they inhabit these roles, their costumes forcing them to think and act in ways that help them to understand the book better and to discover new aspects of themselves. After hearing the final verdict in one of the trials, fourteen-year-old Megan Cleveland, who played the author of *Lord of the Flies*, wrote: "As I sat in the middle of the courtroom, I waited to hear the verdict of my character, William Golding. The foreman stood and I held my breath. 'We the jury find the defendant guilty.' My fellow classmates went up in cheers and my stomach churned with embarrassment. How could they have found me guilty? William Golding had done nothing wrong. At that moment visions of the trial, the past week of my life, came flooding back in order to try to justify the verdict."

This Atticus Finch curriculum of "walking around in another's shoes" has profound implications for our increasingly diverse and complicated society. I once read an essay in which a man passionately argued that writer Bharati Mukherjee, originally from a Brahmin caste family in India, had no business writing novels about Indian people from lower castes. Some time later, I read something that challenged this position, that asked, How can we understand what is different from ourselves—or, to put it another way, that we are not different—if we cannot imagine what another person's life is like, how it feels to be that person?

Occupation therefore involves imagination. In my senior class one year, students were asked to draw a "roundtable of influence," seating at the table their mentors or those who had had an impact on their lives. After coming up with the names, students had to write about themselves from one mentor's perspective in order to explore what this person saw in them. This proved all the more important for the fact that many kids resisted looking at themselves critically; Lauren, however, effectively inhabited the role of her grandfather, reflecting on why he loved her so dearly:

> I love my granddaughter, Lauren. I love all my grandchildren very much but there is something about Lauren. When Lauren was a baby and she cried, I'd go hold her and sing to her and it worked

Judge Reno DeRanieri and bailiff Rebecca Chappell in action during the
trial of William Golding, author of Lord of the Flies

like a charm. As she grew up, I liked to watch her play. She'd still take naps with me and I'd still sing to her and she'd still fall asleep. I used to love to rub her cheeks because they were so soft. I'd tell her how beautiful she was all the time. My wife would say, "That's your girl." Anything I said, Lauren would listen. She'd sit with me in the mornings and drink coffee with me. She always liked my coffee better than grandma's because I put sugar in it. Every time I saw her, I got showered with hugs and kisses and "I love you, Papas." And Lauren loved my stories. No matter how stupid they were, she loved them. She wanted to be told over and over about my stories as a boy when I met my wife and about the war. She wants to hear it all.

The drama of one's own life and the opportunity English presents to explore that drama through the examination of one's own and others' stories fosters a dramatic space. Herbert Kohl (1998), reflecting on his early years of teaching kids from "junkie's paradise," writes that he "discovered the power of rooting learning in what students know outside of school, of tying what I teach to what they understand of their own lives and experience." Karina Vela, one of my seniors, wrote about such connections. Karina got off to a slow start when she was a sophomore in my class a few years before. Several weeks before getting accepted into a four-year college, she wrote, "Good teachers are those who when I was screwing up in school cared enough about me to talk to me about it. Those are the ones I respect. Also, they assign work that makes me *think* about myself, about my life, and about the direction my life is going. I like in English class when teachers make us compare ourselves to the characters in books that we are reading. They help me think about things by discussing these ideas and stories."

Occupation challenges us to remember, however, that what we teach must be anchored in the world. Senior Steve Naylor explains that his version of a good teacher is "one who is able to teach without going by the book. They must bring their experiences to the classroom and share them with their students because it's a true 'real life' experience."

What *occupation* looks like in the English class.   To foster occupation, teachers can do the following:

- Have students arrange to shadow someone at work for a day in order to see not only what their job demands, but what life is like for someone engaged in that kind of employment.

- Use a short excerpt from a film, turning off the sound while students write a running interior monologue from one character's perspective; perform these as "reader's theater" for the class, discussing why students think the characters were thinking these things.
- Have students trade journals with each other and respond to each other's responses through a written conversation about some idea or text; this helps students inhabit another's mind and see things a different way.
- Read aloud: as a poet said once, the poet, by forcing you to read and breathe (literally) a certain way through their arrangement of words is actually occupying your body during the reading of the poem.
- Have students write graduation speeches weeks before June as rehearsal for ending their school days and as a means of getting unmotivated students to envision being at graduation, seeing their proud parents, hearing the principal call out their name as they step onto the stage. Tell students to reflect on all they have learned as they address the freshman class who, according to the assignment, has come to listen to their older peers.

Negotiation

Effective education involves negotiation. Our aim is to give students—through skills, knowledge, capacity—power; moreover, such learning is "a matter of awakening and empowering today's young people to name, to reflect, to imagine, and to act with more and more concrete responsibility in an increasingly multifarious world" (Greene 1998). *Negotiation* challenges those teachers who see the class as "their" class. Freshman Shanna Girard reminds us that by inviting students to share and think about their lives, the English class necessarily becomes a communal space where students must assume control. If we refuse to see the students as partners in their education, many will resist us; thus each party involved negotiates their relationship with the other. Such negotiations are informed by the teacher's expectations, the student's culture and needs, and the school's standards. These transactions are *part of the curriculum*, what Linda Darling-Hammond (1997) calls "democracy *as* education."

When possible, I invite students to enter into negotiations not only about *what* they will do but *how* they will do it. This means providing meaningful options within the confines of a larger assignment. But it also allows students to argue that they've discussed a particular story or poem long enough, and feel the need to move on. Though it may sound risky to some, I feel compelled to find out what students are willing to learn about; to ignore this aspect of the negotiation is to deny they have the power to opt out.

No other finding is more significant, however, than that of the relationship between what a teacher knows about their field and how this knowledge affects student performance. Linda Darling-Hammond found this "teacher knowledge," or what others have called "wisdom of practice," to be the most consistent and significant predictor of academic achievement. It is clear to students when a teacher "knows their stuff." It is also crucial to the intellectual negotiations: students won't enter into "talks" with teachers they don't respect. Such doubts about the teacher's knowledge undermine the teacher's credibility in the students' eyes. Senior David Getchel underscores the truth of this notion: "The one thing I notice about the teachers I remember and love is that they love their subject. When you stand in front of the class don't think we will ignore you or block you out. But one of the things you cannot do is try to stuff things down our throats. Instead, tempt us from across the room with the flavors and sweet smells of your subject and your love for it. Because you might think teaching is what you are here for but in reality you are helping us teach ourselves."

Those who can teach themselves have power. Philosophers of literacy such as Rexford Brown (1993) and Lisa Delpit (1995) remind us that the skills to negotiate with the world determine the power and place of our students in the world. Good teaching initiates students—all students—into what Lisa Delpit calls "the culture of power." She identifies five aspects of power:

1. Issues of power are enacted in classrooms.
2. There are codes or rules for participating in power; that is, there is a "culture of power."
3. The rules of the culture of power are a reflection of the rules of the culture of those who have power.
4. If you are not already a participant in the culture of power, being told explicitly the rules of that culture makes acquiring power easier.
5. Those with power are frequently least aware of—or least willing to acknowledge—its existence. Those with less power are often most aware of its existence.

Delpit's ideas add an important perspective to the idea of negotiation, for it seems to be a culturally bound notion. Not all students see the classroom as an appropriate "bargaining table" where power is shared. Delpit quotes one man talking about the expectations African American students bring to their relationships with teachers:

> We had fun in her class, but she was mean. I can remember she used to say, "Tell me what's in the story, Wayne." She pushed, she used to get on me and push me to know. She made us learn. We had to get in the books. There was this tall guy and he tried to take her on, but she was in charge of that class and she didn't let anyone run her. I still have that book we used in her class. It has a bunch of stories in it. I just read one on Coca-Cola again the other day. (Delpit 1995)

This is the difference great teachers make in the lives of their students: they help them learn to make connections between what they encounter and what they know in order to provide a context for that student's learning. But you cannot accomplish this easily if you do not know your students.

What *negotiation* looks like in the English class.   When a classroom values neogitation, the following things are evident:

- Students have choices about what and how they study in class.
- Students choose, when possible, to demonstrate their knowledge in one of several different ways or media.
- Students play an active role in their own assessment and grading in the class.
- The teacher yields to the class members when they clearly indicate their need to discuss some aspect of the text or subject at hand.
- The community of the class recognizes that relationships are negotiations which are based on respect and compromise.

Conversation

All effective education is a conversation. You get to know your students, and help your students to know you, by allowing meaningful conversations to occur. These conversations involve different constituents: students, parents, the texts, the tradition into which students are being initiated, and the community at large. As Arthur Applebee (1996) writes, "The notion that learners are to construct their own understandings leads in turn to new ways of thinking about the role of the teacher, and has generated such now-familiar terms as scaffolding, reciprocal teaching, apprenticeship, and mentoring. From our present perspective, this previous work on instruction provides new and more powerful ways of thinking about how students can best be helped to enter into important domains for conversation. Only in conversation guided by others will students develop the tacit knowledge necessary to participate on their own."

These conversations require serious thought and complex analysis of increasingly difficult texts and ideas. It is also true that we will have students in our classes who will necessarily find such work difficult. In such situations, it is helpful to keep in mind what freshman Lilly Lichaa once wrote to a student teacher: "Patience is the biggest virtue in teaching. Without teachers being patient with me, I think I would feel extremely frustrated and I wouldn't want to do my work because of that frustration. With patience, teachers appear wonderful and kindhearted, qualities that make kids wish to learn."

In *From Communication to Curriculum*, Douglas Barnes (1992) emphasizes again and again the importance of talking as a means of learning, thinking, preparing. Though I share Barnes's conviction in the value of talking, *conversation* means more; it refers to *what* we should be talking about and *how* we should be talking about it. In many respects, the three other components of effective teaching all involve conversation. Barnes elaborates, writing "that curriculum should be treated as composed of meaningful activities; and that amongst these activities are those we call communication. Not only is talking and writing a major means by which people learn, but what they learn can often hardly be distinguished from the ability to communicate it. Learning to communicate is at the heart of education."

What *conversation* looks like in the English class.   Conversation can take on any of the following forms:

- a symposium or roundtable discussion of a story or idea
- small-group discussion about a focused topic on which all must ultimately achieve consensus (e.g., "What does it mean to be an American?")
- correspondence with legislators or other community leaders about a law that affects teens
- letters to the editor of the newspaper to which students submit their writing about a current issue or event that is important to them
- bulletin boards where students post their work
- conferences with individuals and small groups to discuss their work and ideas
- on-line exchanges via the Internet about cultures, ideas, books
- talks with parents who read and respond to their child's work (e.g., their son's portfolio)
- interviews with people about topics that relate to the curriculum

The Continuum of Performance

It is so easy and safe to sit here in my study at home and talk about teaching and learning; the laboratory of my mind is an ideal place where all works as imagined. But every time I start teaching some new unit I've spent weeks creating, I quickly remember how complicated and messy the process is. It helps me to think about this complexity in terms of a continuum of performance; this model allows me to understand why many performances—mine, students', or colleagues'—sometimes need time to mature. Figure 2.1 illustrates the process of revision we all experience as we move away from our initial insecurity or failure toward greater competence or even mastery. The model helps provide a context for my own failures and transforms them into learning that helps me move toward the excellence I seek.

Endnote: What It Means to Be a Master Teacher

It seems appropriate that I should end by celebrating what it means to be not just a good teacher but a true master. I close this chapter with the following excerpt from an article about a legendary high school English teacher named Cap Lavin. *San Francisco Chronicle* columnist Joan Ryan wrote the following column on the occasion of Lavin's retirement after forty-three years of teaching high school English:

> When Ellen Strempek arrived each day for Cap Lavin's Advanced Placement English class, she never knew what was waiting. Sometimes Mr. Lavin would have Blossom Dearie on the turntable, sometimes Ashkenazy playing Chopin, sometimes Ella Fitzgerald. On the walls, there were photographs of Chartres Cathedral and basketball player Bill Russell, all part of a quiltwork of literary quotations, *New Yorker* cartoons and magazine articles that covered the walls.
>
> In his tennis shorts and golf shirt, he looked like the athlete he is, tall and lanky and slightly bow-legged. But he taught like his brain was on fire, his thoughts skipping among half-finished sentences as new thoughts ignited.
>
> For 43 years, most of them at Drake High School in San Anselmo, his classroom was like slipping into a timeless chamber where disintegrating academic standards and adolescent indifference had no foothold. In his room, droopy-drawered teenagers connected Wallace Stevens poems to their own lives. They met Defoe and Milton and Bernard Malamud. Some, like Strempek, were inspired to become English teachers themselves. Others, like novelist Molly Giles and poet Linda Gregg, went on to write.

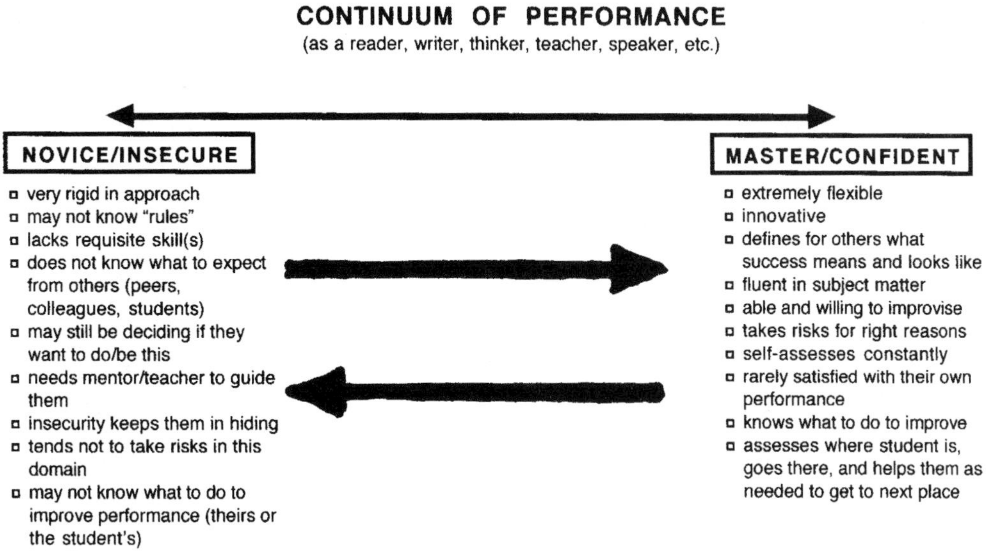

CONTINUUM OF PERFORMANCE
(as a reader, writer, thinker, teacher, speaker, etc.)

NOVICE/INSECURE

- very rigid in approach
- may not know "rules"
- lacks requisite skill(s)
- does not know what to expect from others (peers, colleagues, students)
- may still be deciding if they want to do/be this
- needs mentor/teacher to guide them
- insecurity keeps them in hiding
- tends not to take risks in this domain
- may not know what to do to improve performance (theirs or the student's)

MASTER/CONFIDENT

- extremely flexible
- innovative
- defines for others what success means and looks like
- fluent in subject matter
- able and willing to improvise
- takes risks for right reasons
- self-assesses constantly
- rarely satisfied with their own performance
- knows what to do to improve
- assesses where student is, goes there, and helps them as needed to get to next place

Figure 2.1

At age 67, the best teacher many Marin County kids ever had is retiring. Today is Cap Lavin's last day.

He is leaving teaching for the same reason he entered it: To figure things out. In other words, to read.

"I feel truly composed when I read," Lavin said the other day during a break from classes at Drake. "It's the way you get when you return to a familiar neighborhood. You know that expression: 'I feel like myself'? That's what it is. It's the heightened and sharpened sensibilities that come from trying to understand the world."

The demands of teaching don't leave enough time to read all the books stacked around the Ross home where he and his wife, Mary, raised six children. He wants to read lots of poetry. He says he hasn't read all of Jane Austen. He never read Shakespeare's *A Winter's Tale*. He wants to return to Spanish philosopher Ortega y Gasset. That said, he has been such a voracious reader—even with his teaching schedule—that friends and former students are always asking, "What have you read? Can you give me a list?" Nothing makes him happier than pressing books into willing hands.

It doesn't matter so much that Lavin has published 19 books or that he helped start the Bay Area Writing Project with UC Berkeley, which spawned 200 similar projects around the country. The magic has always been in Room 417 at Drake High.

"The scope of what we studied ranged from Aristotelian logic to the history of jazz, from the tragedy of *Hamlet* to the gentle irony of E. B. White, from the exquisite elegance of T. S. Eliot to the equally exquisite backhand of Bill Tilden," Strempek wrote in recommending Lavin for Marin County Teacher of the Year in 1984.

Many of his pictures and quotations are off the walls already as he packs up more than 40 years of teaching. Shelves are still stacked with photocopied poems and short stories he hands out to students who might enjoy them. He asks if I know the French word, *flaneur*. "It basically means 'stroll,' " he says. "That's what I'm going to do. Observe and walk. Go back to Ninth and 10th and Irving, near the park. I'll go to the parts of the city that aren't rushed, the way it was in the '40s and '50s."

Before I leave, he hands me a slim, battered book with a binding held together with tape. It's poetry by Gerard Manley Hopkins. "Ever read him?" he asks. "Oh, you'll love him. Go ahead. Borrow it. Let me know." (Ryan 1997)

REFLECTION

Think of all the teachers you have had throughout your educational career. Take time to think or write about what it was they did that made them so great; perhaps you can remember a specific moment when you realized a particular teacher had something extra that made them great. What was it?

ACTIVITY

Watch either *Stand and Deliver* or *Dead Poets Society*. Both movies are about inspiring teachers. As you watch, pay attention to what it is that they do as teachers, and how their students respond.

RECOMMENDATION

Making Connections: Teaching and the Human Brain, Renate Numella Caine and Geoffrey Caine (Addison-Wesley 1994). This book stands above all others, providing a summary of research and examples to help illustrate these findings.

CHAPTER 3

A MODERN PROFILE OF ADULT LITERACY

The following profile grew out of a conversation with various adults who talked with me about the work they do. Listening to them, particularly to those who ran their own businesses, reflect on the range of skills they needed to hold professional jobs, I marveled at their different literacies. The implications for teachers challenged me to reevaluate what I teach and assume my students need to know and be able to do. I've found this profile helpful when talking with other teachers and students. My students are astounded to realize the ways they will need to use what they are learning.

The Profile

Gary designs and installs gardens in a suburban town in northern California where he grew up. Rising early, he reads the newspaper, checking the real estate section first to see if there are any new developments listed. If there were, he would schedule an appointment with the developer to present his vision (via his portfolio) for the new property. Gary runs his own business out of his home, a small but attractive house he rents near the campus where his wife works; their daughter, who is in first grade, attends an elementary school around the corner.

By eight o'clock Gary has penciled in all his jobs, meetings, purchases to make, banking to do, and other business. He carries an assortment of tools necessary to run his small business: a pager, a cellular phone, a PalmPilot PDA (personal digital assistant), which contains his client and job information, and a laptop computer for making presentations to clients, keeping his accounts, and using the Internet to check on different work-related business such as orders and jobs. Having designed his own Web site for Change of Seasons (the name of his business), he is able to monitor new job prospects while in the field by checking his e-mail periodically, thanks to the wireless modems which have recently become so affordable and dependable.

After installing new plum saplings for a woman in his old neighborhood, Gary heads home, where he washes up, prepares for a meeting with prospective clients, and eats lunch. He has already met with this couple once to hear their landscaping needs. Based on their ideas and his own, he has translated their thoughts into a drawing on his CAD program and estimated the project's total cost. Because he was in theater in college, Gary is very comfortable talking in front of people. When he meets with Mr. and Mrs. Kaplan, he is relaxed, articulate, and confident, because is he thoroughly prepared. Over coffee, as the different 3-D screens fade in and out on his laptop, they talk about the ideas Gary drew up, each one richly detailed, showing what their new yard would look like. The last screen fades to what resembles a page from an old fairy tale. An elegant but easily readable text slowly scrolls up while soft music plays on the laptop and Gary's voice-over begins:

> Once upon a time there was a secret garden. A rusted key hanging from a weathered timber post invites entry through an old iron gate. A tricolor brick path meanders into a garden bursting with color and passion. A vine-covered arbor, shrouded in sheet ivory curtains, contains a private dining area for two. Water trickles from an iron pump. Light bounces like moonbeams from leaf to brick. Whosoever enters this garden shall live happily ever after . . .

The Kaplans are visibly moved by the intimacy of the world Gary has imagined for them. They agree to sign the contracts he drew up the previous night. After he leaves his new clients, Gary stops by the library to pick up several books to help him with his research for another project, and a few other books for his daughter.

When he gets home, he immediately retreats to his office—which is also his and his wife's bedroom—where he spends a few hours negotiating with a man for day workers (in a halting Spanish). He finishes a new advertisement for the local free newspaper, which he then faxes to the publication. He updates his books, recording the latest debits and credits. Before his wife and daughter get home, he hurries down to the bank, where he uses the ATM to do his banking. Using the automated system reduces his expenses; it is, however, confusing at times because of the different accounts he must manage. His bank has just opened a Starbucks off the lobby as an experiment in customer service and, having a little extra time, Gary steps inside to have a cup of coffee and read the afternoon *Union*. He checks on the performance of a few stocks he bought long ago, then he scans the want ads, looking for good deals on tools for his business. He circles an ad for a chain saw and cement mixer which he decides he will call on later.

That night, after reading his daughter the books he brought home from the library (they had been recommended on the *Parents Magazine* Web site he visited the night before), he looks through some books for ideas about Japanese gardens, during which time he finds a poem translated by Kenneth Rexroth about the rock gardens in Kyoto. He writes the poem down for possible use in a future presentation. Before turning in, he checks his favorite news source on the Net: the Drudge Report. Today's information strikes him as somehow impossible; his critical sense tells him not to trust Matt Drudge's remarks about Microsoft; and, indeed, by morning he will find that Drudge was wrong and is now being sued—again.

Tired, Gary shuffles off to bed, where he and his wife, Nancy, who was reading Lucy Calkins's *Raising Lifelong Learners: A Parents' Guide*, watch the late-night news, which features a story about new legislation that could hurt small businesses. Gary is too tired to worry, but knows he must rise in the morning and investigate this matter and its implications for his business. In the meantime, it is time to sleep.

Endnote

Everything you have just read is true, even if it didn't all happen. This is the world we live in, the world our students enter, the world we must somehow prepare them for while they are in high school. Gary is a friend of mine, and most of what I narrated above accurately describes his life. He utilizes just about every possible literacy in existence, nearly all of which he had to learn on his own. In the course of a typical day, he:

- reads a wide range of texts, many of which are technical (manuals, directions, product descriptions, contracts, newspapers, books)

- speaks publicly to different audiences (clients whose income levels range from lower middle class to affluent)
- uses a range of tools to accomplish different tasks (computers, power tools, fax machines, hand tools)
- communicates through different media (visual, written, spoken, electronic)
- manages various financial transactions with institutions and accounting programs on his computer
- listens to what clients want and then translates their desires into concrete images
- conducts sometimes extensive research for different products, projects, or jobs in order to make the best use of his time, money, and talent
- designs advertisements, Web pages, projects
- draws up and negotiates legal contracts with clients
- estimates and submits bids for jobs which must be competitive and accurate while insuring his profit margin
- teaches—laborers, his daughter, or neighborhood kids who sometimes come over when they see him working in his garage

Obviously Gary is exceptional. For instance, the garden story and its accompanying drawings won a local award and were reproduced in the town's glossy magazine, something which provided welcome exposure and future work. However, like most people, he works long hours in order to make enough to sustain his family. His wife must work. He must keep his office in their bedroom because he doesn't make enough yet to buy or rent a larger house. Yet he is a man whose learning and skills give him the power to live as he chooses and to do work he enjoys after spending years developing his different abilities. He exemplifies what it means to be a fully literate adult in our modern society.

REFLECTION

Write your own narrative (or list, if you are pressed for time) of the different literacies you use in the course of a day. Do you come up with any that are not included in Gary's profile? Where did you learn these different skills? What difference do these abilities make in your life?

ACTIVITY

Reread the profile; as you go through, make a list of the different specific literacies you see included. Then put a check next to the ones that students learn about and practice in the course of your English class during a typical school year. You could also have your students do the same exercise and follow that up with a class discussion.

RECOMMENDATION

Changing Our Minds: Negotiating English and Literacy, Miles Myers (NCTE 1996). Myers offers a remarkable overview of literacy in the past and present, focusing on implications for educators. His definition of literacy includes a broad range of texts and intellectual tools.

CHAPTER 4

TEACHING READING
THE CONTINUUM OF POSSIBILITIES

In every literate society, learning to read is something of an initiation, a ritualized passage out of a state of dependency and rudimentary communication. The child learning to read is admitted into the communal memory by way of books, and thereby becomes acquainted with a common past which he or she renews, to a greater or lesser degree, in every reading.

—**Alberto Manguel,** *A History of Reading*

We read to know we are not alone.

—**C. S. Lewis**

A book must be the ax for the frozen sea within us.

—**Franz Kafka**

My father worked at the California Office of State Printing for thirty-eight years. I grew up hearing about books, about printing, about page layout, about documents. When the state legislature was in session, my father would be gone into the night, working with others to create the drafts of the laws written that day. Later on, when he supervised the operation, he would be called in the middle of the night by printers who wanted my father's advice about problems inherent in creating a history textbook or a government report. It was an era during which men could advance by native intelligence and diligence; by the time my father ran things he had to hire people from universities to do work he had been able to teach himself in the simpler days, and the chief officer of the printing plant was a woman.

In his last years, computers having fundamentally changed the printing business, my father oversaw the transition from mechanical to desktop publishing. The old light tables and stripping knives were replaced by mice and high-speed computers. Men who had been able to learn by trial and error or a quick demonstration suddenly had to learn how to use complicated computers and software programs. The men received massive binders with different production protocols, manuals for each program, each machine, each printer and scanner.

When he came home at day's end, my father read the newspaper. On other occasions, he might read the repair manual for one of our cars or the Austin Healy we started to restore together. Years later, nearing retirement, he would sit in front of the computer reading on-line documents to learn how to use America Online or the manual for another computer program.

He did not come home and curl up with a novel; though, like many, he would occasionally enjoy the popular detective novel or a book like Mario Puzo's *The Godfather*. If he had work to do at home, it involved reading reports, minutes from meetings, or procedural documents; when it came to writing, he wrote memos, employee evaluations, and reports for various state divisions. By the time he retired in 1994, the amount and types of reading his job required were too much for him. An era had passed into history: no longer could a willing seventeen-year-old boy take a job with a company and rise to the top.

Our world changed with the advent of the personal computer, with the Internet, with television, with the expansion of corporate culture and its training manuals filled with standardization procedures. The world demands that we read more: contracts, directions, rules, applications, and other informational documents. This change became startlingly apparent to me one day while I sat in Starbucks having a cup of coffee. Looking around the café, I noticed two young women in Starbucks aprons, each of whom had two three-inch-thick binders, complete with laser-printed tabs and indexes. They were navigating their way between the two complicated texts, the pages of which contained a combination of marginal information, graphs, diagrams, and words. When I asked them if they had to read all *that* just to make me a latté and serve me a scone, they each rolled their eyes and sighed yes.

How prepared are our students to do such reading? Our society and the workplace demand more reading than ever; National Assessment of Educational Progress (NAEP) reading scores and recent findings by Jeff McQuillan (1998) suggest students overall are reading at least as well as they did in the past. Yet our own experience in the classroom tells us that students need to read much better if they are to prosper. In an era of film adaptations, Cliffs Notes, and the Internet, I worry that students will learn how *not to read* a book better than they learn *how* to read one. We sort through a growing number of documents that fill our mailboxes every day— complicated prospectuses of investment programs, retirement programs, health insurance systems, contracts, manuals, service agreements, and newsletters. Kids need specific reading skills if they are to move through both the world and these texts with the confidence and skill we know they need. The profile of adult literacy given in Chapter 3 clearly illustrates how sophisticated the demands are and what our students must be ready to do. The narrative of my father's experience with literacy shows how quickly these changes have occurred.

Evolving Notions of Literacy

Our notions of literacy have evolved dramatically as reflected in the last few pages. The traditional literacies of my father's era—the ability to read and write—have been replaced by notions of literacy that recognize the complexity of today's world and anticipate the changes the future will necessarily bring. Judith A. Langer (1991) has suggested that we understand literacies as "the ability to think and reason like a literate person, *within a particular society.*" Langer's crucial point is that our definition of *literate* changes as our culture does. In this chapter, I try to examine some of these changes and discuss their implications for our students and our teaching so that all our students can have "a larger collection of tools to which they can distribute intellectual problems" (Myers 1996). In *Changing Our Minds: Negotiating English and Literacy*, Miles Myers recognizes a powerful set of literacy tools that we must provide our students through our English curriculum, the most basic skill of all being interpretation. Myers affirms that our students must be able to interpret in order to cope with and master "the increased information diversity in [our] civic life." This is all too true in California, for example, where the ballot initiative process can require voters to decide on dozens of crucial civic policies and projects. Students will arrive at these "interpretations" through different types of "negotiations" with ideas, people, tools, and traditions to produce a functional understanding of the text at hand.

Content Standards: Samples from California, the NCTE, and IRA

Many English teachers across America involved themselves in the ultimate professional study group beginning in the early 1990s. The National Council of Teachers of English (NCTE) and the International Reading Association (IRA) were awarded federal contracts to develop standards for what students in English classes should know and be able to do. NCTE elected to directly involve classroom teachers in the process by establishing regional networks and local discussion groups to draft these standards. Not everyone in the profession supports the idea of standards, of course, and for reasons that I understand (see Susan Ohanian's book *One Size Fits Few: The Folly of Education Standards*, Heinemann 1999); but standards offer us a starting place to consider what, for example, the components of an effective reading program are and what readers should be able to do.

The following examples of reading content standards come from California's Academic Standards Commission. They seem typical of most documents I see emerging; they also draw heavily on the performance standards of the New Standards, which I will discuss in the next section. Content standards identify what students should learn, whereas performance standards describe what they must do to demonstrate their mastery of the content standards. Here are California's high school reading content standards to which California teachers are now held accountable:

1. *Word Analysis and Systematic Vocabulary Development:* Students determine the meaning of, and use accurately, new words encountered in reading materials by applying their knowledge of word sources in British and ancient literature.

2. *Reading Comprehension (Focus on Informational Materials):* Students read and understand grade level appropriate material and produce evidence by analyzing the organization patterns, arguments and positions advanced. The quality and complexity of the materials to be read are illustrated in the California Reading List. In addition, by grade 12, students read two million words annually on their own (as measured by the number of books or pages read or minutes of daily reading), including classic and contemporary literature as well as magazines, newspapers, and on-line materials.

3. *Literary Response and Analysis:* Students read and respond to historically or culturally significant works of American, British, and world literature and provide evidence of comprehension by conducting in-depth analyses of recurrent patterns and themes. The quality and complexity of the materials to be read are illustrated in the California Reading List. (California Academic Standards Commission 1998)

The NCTE/IRA standards complement these governmental standards by demonstrating what the teaching profession thought that educators needed to accomplish in the area of reading:

Standard 1. Students read a wide range of print and nonprint text to build an understanding of texts, of themselves, and of the cultures of the United States and the world, to acquire new information; to respond to the needs and demands of society and the workplace; and for personal fulfillment. Among these texts are fiction and nonfiction, classic and contemporary works.

Standard 2. Students read a wide range of literature from many periods in many genres to build an understanding of the many dimensions (e.g., philosophical, ethical, aesthetic) of human experience.

Standard 3. Students apply a wide range of strategies to comprehend, interpret, evaluate, and appreciate texts. They draw on their prior experience, their interactions with other readers and writers, their knowledge of word meaning and of other texts, their work identification strategies, and their understanding of textual features (e.g., sound-letter correspondence, sentence structure, context, graphics). (NCTE/IRA 1996)

Performance Standards: The New Standards Project

New Standards, headed by Marc Tucker at the National Center on Education and the Economy, offers the closest thing to a set of national standards we have. Their performance standards in English Language Arts are influencing districts and states throughout the country, several of which are asking New Standards to develop end-of-course examinations to assess whether students have mastered the standards. I welcome the idea of standards myself; it makes sense that everyone should know what to expect and what to accomplish. One reason the AP test has always been lauded is that it provides clear standards for what students should know and be able to do, and assesses students using a test that has clearly established criteria that students can know ahead of time.

The New Standards high school performance standards identify what students should be able to do in the area of reading:

a) The student reads at least 25 books or book equivalents each year. The quality and complexity of the materials to be read are illustrated in the sample reading list. The materials should include traditional and contemporary literature (both fiction and non-fiction) as well as magazines, newspapers, textbooks, and on-line materials. Such reading should represent a diverse collection of material from at least three different literary forms and from at least five different writers.

b) The student reads and comprehends at least four books (or book equivalents) about one issue or subject, or four books by a single writer, or four books in one genre, and produces evidence of reading that:
  • makes and supports warranted and responsible assertions about the texts;
  • supports assertions with elaborated and convincing evidence;
  • draws the texts together to compare and contrast themes, characters, and ideas;
  • makes perceptive and well developed connections;
  • evaluates writing strategies and elements of the author's craft.

c) The student reads and comprehends informational materials to develop understanding and expertise and produces written or oral work that:
  • restates or summarizes information;
  • relates new information to prior knowledge and experience;
  • extends ideas;
  • makes connections to related topics or information.

d) The student reads aloud, accurately (in the range of 85–90%), familiar material of the quality and complexity illustrated in the sample reading list, and in a way that makes meaning clear to listeners by:

- self correcting when subsequent reading indicates an earlier miscue;
- using a range of cueing systems, e.g., phonics and context clues, to determine pronunciation and meanings;
- reading with a rhythm, flow, and meter that sounds like everyday speech. (Tucker and Codding 1998)

These different standards give us a range of objectives and issues to consider, but they don't easily translate into what we should do in our classes. Most of us read these documents and see the value in them. We reflexively translate them into our own experience to determine what we already do that would satisfy a particular standard. I don't think I would have found them helpful as a new teacher, however. They remind me too much of the district curriculum binder they gave me at my first teaching assignment; it told me all the books we had to teach and all the other skills I was to develop in students. But I fell asleep wondering how to do it and woke up to wonder the same, until more experienced teachers in my department agreed to meet with me and show me what they did.

Teaching a Range of Texts

Nearly all of these standards documents talk about the need for students to be able to read a range of texts—not just literary texts. They do not advocate that we rip up the current curriculum; they are, however, suggesting that the curriculum be more balanced to reflect the types of reading we encounter and which I have divided into four categories:

- functional/expository
- narrative
- dramatic
- poetic

A curriculum consisting of these different texts necessitates significant changes in other areas, most notably writing, since the study of how texts work invites the study of how they are made. If, for example, we are to teach students how to read functional documents, we must teach those elements that shape the form and function of such documents. As mentioned earlier, learning can only be deep and sustained when it is constructed, linked through manipulations of the material itself. Thus teachers wanting their students to fully grasp the ideas and skills inherent in the reading task must integrate writing into the task, since these two abilities develop simultaneously, one supporting and extending the other (Smith 1982). We don't always assign our students functional types of reading (or writing)—pamphlets, executive summaries, formal letters—which is odd, given that our own experience tells us that such documents are essential to our personal and professional lives. The era of standards into which we are now moving demands that we find ways to make room for them.

I don't mean to privilege one genre over any other; in fact, they should grow out of each other, since each text—functional, narrative, dramatic, and poetic—offers a different route through the terrain the class is exploring. Arthur Applebee's emphasis on conversation provides the most compelling argument for the use of a range of texts. The junior English class having a sustained discussion about the American character and how it was developed, for example, *must* include in its readings journals, letters, essays, poems, and, of course, novels if their study is to be complete. Each text offers information in a different way and serves a different purpose. Nor is there any set order to their use so long as an underlying logic determines the sequence, and the teacher explains how these different texts work as they are introduced. Such opportunities provide the best occasion to teach what, for example, a letter is and how it works, to address what the letter can accomplish that other forms of writing cannot. Here is the chance for students to use writing not only to improve their general skills but to master a particular form.

Teaching Functional/Expository Texts: The Literature of Daily Life

As the earlier example of the Starbucks' training manuals shows, we have entered into a new era of reading. Desktop publishing inspired dramatic changes in the complexity of our documents; this graphic sophistication poses a number of challenges to readers. Between different fonts, bullets, boxes, sidebars, and images, the reader encounters a visual collage that often resists simple reading. If you've seen a recent history textbook, you know what I am talking about. Most pages look like a freeze-frame from a music video. But textbooks are not the only functional documents I have in mind here. Consider, instead, these examples of texts that we encounter daily in our lives:

- manuals
- contracts
- pamphlets
- Web pages
- letters
- memos

In addition to these documents, there are the more traditional expository forms:

> Expository writing is far and away the most common mode of expression. We write exposition not only in college; most writing [and reading] required in professional life is expository—in business, in teaching, in technology and science, in law and medicine. When social workers deliver papers, when geologists make reports, when hospital officials release information on new diagnostic equipment, when marketing managers report on the activities of their competition, they write expository prose. Newspapers, brochures, and guidebooks are all exposition. (Hall and Birkerts 1994)

If you've read a typical contract or looked closely at an issue of *Time* magazine lately, you know how much attention they can require of the reader. What's more, some of these documents are often among the most consequential reading we do: nothing happens if I can't understand a Joseph Conrad short story, but I can suffer financial penalties if I sign a contract that I shouldn't have.

This isn't the place to go into depth about how to teach students to read official documents. I will, however, offer an example from my junior class to show one way of doing it. As part of a larger unit on California's culture, during which time our class studied the state's history and literature, I asked student teams to develop an informational pamphlet on California.

To teach them how such documents worked, I brought in dozens of examples from different businesses. The workers at Noah's Bagels and Starbucks must have thought I really liked their products when they saw me walking out with handfuls of their slick pamphlets. And the school nurse and Career Center director gave me equally curious looks as I pilfered brochures on colleges and sexually transmitted diseases from their pamphlet racks. I asked each group to deconstruct the components of these documents, analyzing the function, for example, of certain design components. We talked about how companies want the customer to read their pamphlets—as an enticement to buy their products. We talked about how such documents were designed to be read: in the time it takes to stand in line and get a cup of coffee. We talked about word choice, tone, and sentence structure; we also discussed how these affect the way we read and respond to persuasive commercial texts.

To illustrate my earlier suggestion that students can best understand how different texts work by creating them—ideally by using computers—the students made their own. Figures 4.1 and 4.2 are an example (which also nicely demonstrate one of the project's integrated objectives: to improve students' ability to use computers to create different types of documents).

When appropriate, I bring in other types of expository documents that my students learn to read by studying how they function. In Chapter 15, for example, you will find a one-page grant my students wrote. To write their grant they studied examples of other grants. We looked at how such a document is read by the audience that receives it. Chapter 13 details other types of functional reading that our class does when, for example, we use the Internet. Certain design

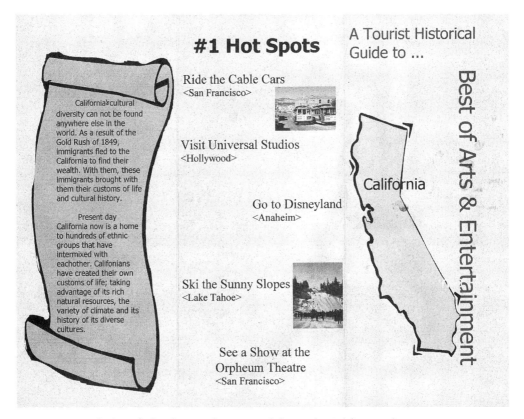

Figure 4.1   *Side One of a brochure students created during the California culture unit*

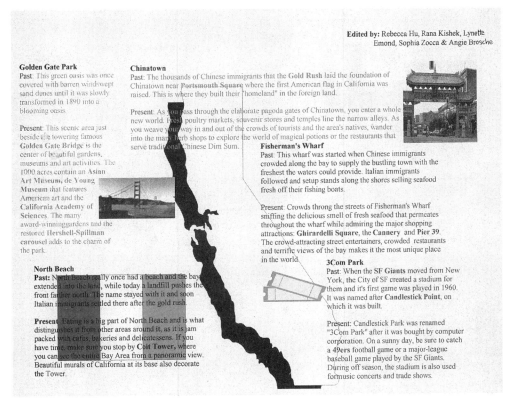

Golden Gate Park

Past: This green oasis was once covered with barren windswept sand dunes until it was slowly transformed in 1890 into a blooming oasis.

Present: This scenic area just beside the towering famous **Golden Gate Bridge** is the center of beautiful gardens, museums and art activities. The 1000 acres contain an **Asian Art Museum, de Young Museum** that features American art and the **California Academy of Sciences**. The many award-winning gardens and the restored Hershell-Spillman carousel adds to the charm of the park.

North Beach

Past: North Beach really once had a beach and the bay extended into the land, while today a landfill pushes the front farther north. The name stayed with it and soon Italian immigrants settled there after the gold rush.

Present: Eating is a big part of North Beach and is what distinguishes it from other areas around it, as it is jam packed with cafes, bakeries and delicatessens. If you have time, make sure you stop by **Coit Tower**, where you can see the entire Bay Area from a panoramic view. Beautiful murals of California at its base also decorate the Tower.

Chinatown

Past: The thousands of Chinese immigrants that the **Gold Rush** laid the foundation of Chinatown near **Portsmouth Square** where the first American flag in California was raised. This is where they built their "homeland" in the foreign land.

Present: As you pass through the elaborate pagoda gates of Chinatown, you enter a whole new world. Fresh poultry markets, souvenir stores and temples line the narrow alleys. As you weave your way in and out of the crowds of tourists and the area's natives, wander into the many herb shops to explore the world of magical potions or the restaurants that serve traditional Chinese Dim Sum.

Fisherman's Wharf

Past: This wharf was started when Chinese immigrants crowded along the bay to supply the bustling town with the freshest waters could provide. Italian immigrants followed and setup stands along the shores selling seafood fresh off their fishing boats.

Present: Crowds throng the streets of Fisherman's Wharf sniffing the delicious smell of fresh seafood that permeates throughout the wharf while admiring the major shopping attractions: **Ghirardelli Square**, the **Cannery** and **Pier 39**. The crowd-attracting street entertainers, crowded restaurants and terrific views of the bay makes it the most unique place in the world.

3Com Park

Past: When the **SF Giants** moved from New York, the City of SF created a stadium for them and it's first game was played in 1960. It was named after **Candlestick Point**, on which it was built.

Present: Candlestick Park was renamed "3Com Park" after it was bought by computer corporation. On a sunny day, be sure to catch a 49ers football game or a major-league baseball game played by the SF Giants. During off season, the stadium is also used for music concerts and trade shows.

Figure 4.2   *Side Two of the same brochure*

and textual features, if not properly read, can mean the difference between believing the Holocaust did and did not happen (see the example of Arthur Butz's Web page in Chapter 13). Finally, students who must write a formal letter to an official as part of my freshman United Nations Project are given sample letters to study as exemplars. We discuss how to read for tone, emphasis, and organization; these ideas prepare students to incorporate such components into their own letters. Here are some other functional and expository texts we read, accompanied by a brief note about how I use them in my class:

- *Teen Driving Law legislative bill.* As part of a sustained "conversation" about independence, we read and examined the language of legislation that would change the laws for teenage drivers. We also read various articles and editorials about the bill.

- *Magazine articles on race.* During our reading of *Adventures of Huckleberry Finn* we read a range of supplemental expository texts to balance our discussion of race. *The New Yorker* had, the previous year, put out a special issue on race in America that represented various perspectives.

- *Expository essays as exemplars.* While studying the traditional rhetorical modes of writing—argumentative, informative, reflective, analytical—we read a range of examples from professional writers. I tend to use short (two- to three-page) essays so we can put them on overheads or make copies to annotate for closer, more analytical reading. We read these to study style, voice, and structure. We also read to determine the main idea, the effectiveness of the argument and its supporting examples. We do this kind of reading throughout the year as part of larger units (see the Dictionary of the American Mind assignment on pages 162–163 as an example) but also to prepare for district and state tests.

- *Newspaper articles*. Newspaper articles offer timely supplements to the larger reading curriculum. I bring them in as I find them. For example, while reading *Lord of the Flies*, I can always count on reading about some current, beastly incident that involves kids. I bring these articles in and use them for discussions or journal topics. Since all major newspapers are now on the World Wide Web, teachers and students can often search a paper's archives for articles on a wide range of related topics.

- *Texts from other classes*. For those teachers who are trying to integrate their English cur- riculum with that of other disciplines, it is important to keep course textbooks in mind. In my English–Social Studies collaborative, I and the Social Studies teacher have copies of each others' books and follow each other's curriculum so we can integrate our read- ings. Thus the assignment for English might be to read a few chapters of Alan Paton's *Cry, the Beloved Country* and the Social Studies assignment might be to read Nelson Mandela's inaugural address. If we are really on the ball, we might integrate the stu- dents' homework, asking them, for example, to compare what Nelson Mandela said in his speech with what John Kumalo said in the novel.

Teaching Narrative Texts: A Study in the Novel's Complexity

We don't read a novel the same way that we read a menu or a newspaper. But how does our reading differ across genre or from author to author? What about a memoir or a novel like Willa Cather's *My Antonia*: Do we read these differently than we do a novel like Fitzgerald's *The Great Gatsby*? And if we don't read them the same way, how *do* we read them? Narratives, along with all other texts, con- form to a continuum of complexity (Figure 4.3) that depends on both the features of the particular text and the capacities of the reader. This notion of complexity is crucial when we consider not just what our students read but the order in which they read. We must carefully scaffold and sequence their reading so that we develop their ability to successfully read a series of increasingly challenging stories. If we begin with Amy Tan's *The Joy Luck Club*, a novel that offers few stylistic or vocabulary difficulties, we might hope that our students would, by the end of the unit, be able to read Maxine Hong Kingston's *The Woman Warrior*, a memoir that dramatically stretches the boundaries of that genre, offering a complicated story made up of folktales, personal narrative, and reflection, and written in a dense, powerful prose style that swings between real and imagined worlds.

It is no easy task to teach students to move along this continuum from simple under- standing to confident interpretation of multiple texts. I am reminded of a junior who came into class one day with a long note from his girlfriend. He kept taking it out to reread it. When the class divided into groups, his team went across the hall, where I later found him conferring with different members in his group about this "text" from his girlfriend. I overheard him several times asking both boys and girls, "What do you think she *really* means by that word, though? And what about the way she says things, her whole tone!?" I don't think I've ever seen a text so scrutinized on so many levels. I like to think that he figured out, if not what the note meant, then at least how to respond to it properly, since I saw him and his girlfriend walking hand-in- hand down the hall the next day.

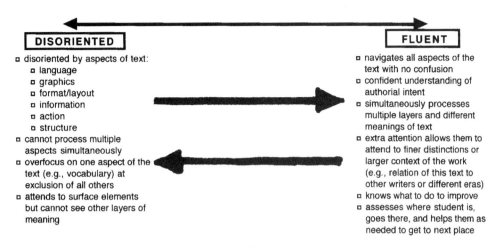

Figure 4.3   *The teacher helps students master different texts' complexities.*

"Narrative" texts include both nonfiction (e.g., memoir, personal essays, biography) and fiction (e.g., novels and short stories). There are many objectives appropriate to the reading of any narrative, but right now I am concerned with improving students' ability to read these texts, since they dominate the English curriculum as it is currently conceived. Most state and district English language arts frameworks, as well as the different standards documents, focus on two primary objectives in the area of reading literature: appreciation (of specific works, our cultural heritage, "fine literature," and different genres of fiction) and formal understanding of how such texts work.

Reading for Appreciation

Kids come to school appreciating stories. It's what some of us, despite our best intentions, do to these stories that causes so much trouble for kids. Film critic Pauline Kael allegedly told a convention of English teachers that if they planned to do to film what they had done to literature, then please leave it alone. This is a troubling comment to hear, since I believe, as Ms. Kael's columns prove, that deep appreciation of any artistic work comes through critically viewing or reading it. Perhaps what she means is that we sometimes diminish the sheer power of the stories by taking them apart, as if that were the reason we read them in the first place. I like what one of my juniors, Rana Kishek, wrote, because it captures what we appreciate about stories:

> There is a story line behind everything and everyone. When you ask your great grandmother what it was like growing up, she tells you about her childhood first, then her teenage years, and on to when she got married, etc., all in a story line. Nothing is out of order. She tells it like an author would write a story, from beginning to end, not all jumbled up. It's just the same when we read about the past of Burlingame; they began to tell you about the man who founded it, who he was, what he did, etc. As we kept on reading, the story kept itself in chronological order. The way we're raised, we're taught how to relate everything to a story. When we watch movies, you never just focus on one time frame of someone or something's life, but instead, you focus on a wide span of time, so it's better understood by the people. Since we're so used to relating everything to stories, it's hard for most people just to sit there and read about a specific time in history in a history book instead of reading a

short story of how it was from beginning to end. But that's not all that helps most of us to concentrate when we read; the fact that we're interested in it or that it relates to modern times or us personally, also plays a big part in our attention span. Undoubtedly, if you like it or you can relate to it, you'll just as easily understand it.

Sandra Mallia, a junior in the same class, wrote, "Usually I don't like to read but if it's a book on something I can relate to I usually have a better interest in the book. When I read, I usually put myself in the story. I make up characters' faces and the setting. I can't read something I don't understand or don't have any interest in. Stories that are true (life stories) are the books that I enjoy."

Stories—whether fiction or nonfiction—have the power to change us in ways that information cannot. They challenge, they demand, they inspire, they threaten. That's why Alice Walker's stories—"Blue" and "Roselilly"—sparked the public debate they did when they and a few other stories considered "dangerous" appeared on the California Learning Assessment System's English test in the mid-1990s. If stories didn't have power, Jesus Christ would have amounted to little more than a man with a few good tricks in his carpenter's belt; instead, stories about him inspired people to change their lives.

I include Jesus specifically—without meaning to exclude any other culture's stories—because the idea of stories raises what for many is also a significant dilemma in our society: the role of morals, ethics, and values in the class (see Chapter 19 for further discussion). In *The Book of Virtues for Young People*, William Bennett (1996) writes that "we need to spend some time thinking about the truly important questions, too, the ones that lead to *better* living." In *The Discipline of Hope: Learning from a Lifetime of Teaching*, Herbert Kohl (1998), reflected on the role that stories play in our classrooms:

> A few years ago, during a visit to a high school, I sat in on a class discussion on violence in the school. The discussion was loud and animated. Every student had a story to tell and there was a lot of competition for attention. The teacher, in order to focus the discussion, silenced the class and made a plea for the students to tell their stories briefly and "get to the point." He did it in order to be able to fit the discussion into the fifty-minute period they had together and to be able to come to some conclusion before the bell. However, instead of focusing the class discussion, the students fell silent. The stories they had to tell were their point. They wanted a moment to share their distress in a personal and intimate way. They wanted to be heard, not to summarize. And they and their teacher knew that the only sensible conclusion to the discussion would have been to continue it to the next time and let it take up the space in the curriculum that the seriousness of the issue demanded.

How then do we develop in our students this appreciation of stories? We provide substantial opportunities for students to read books of their choosing. How else will they read the twenty-five books a year required by the New Standards Project if we don't turn them loose to read what they want? Many things can be done to foster an environment of appreciation.

- Create a strong in-class library that includes different kinds of books. (See Chapter 25 for suggestions about how to set up and manage a classroom library.)
- Allow students choice in what they read. During a unit on California culture, for example, my students read at least two books of their choosing by California authors or about California. On other occasions, I ask them to read the autobiography or biography of someone who made what they feel is an important contribution to society.
- Organize the class into "book clubs." These groups then discuss what kind of book they want to read, perhaps soliciting the guidance of the teacher or librarian, then check it

out or buy it. When the book clubs meet during designated class time, the teacher monitors the discussions, asking questions that grow out of the students' search for personal meaning and comprehension. The teacher also asks why they like the book and what it is allowing them to discuss. This approach to reading turns the students into teachers as they tell the instructor things about a book that he or she may not know.

- Talk about the stories instead of the writing. Discussions about what Esperanza does and what she is like invite students to eventually consider the structure of Sandra Cisneros's *The House on Mango Street*, for example. Maxine Hong Kingston talks about the Chinese tradition of "talking story," a tradition that is similar to the Native American tradition of sitting in a circle and telling a story. Connecting texts to our own lives means being able to say things like, "When Esperanza goes into that old antique shop, it reminded me of this place in my neighborhood when I was growing up." Such opportunities help students appreciate what the stories accomplish: we read these stories for the conversations they let us have. When I surveyed kids about our reading of *Huckleberry Finn*, some said they didn't like the book at all, but loved the discussions the book enabled us to have.
- Translate the stories into dramatic or artistic events—e.g., monologues, plays, collages, the Neighborhood or Life Graphs (see Chapter 9). These activities draw the students into the story and, through the constant sharing in groups, at home, or with the full class, allow them to enjoy it. Stories, after all, create communities within the classroom and help us to not only appreciate each other but ourselves.

Though it frustrates us, we must accept that not all our students will love the books we require them to read. Some students dismiss books just because they don't want to be told what to read. So we must provide them room for their own reading in our classes. I sometimes forget how powerful an opportunity this can be for students. This past year one of my students was so excited about Jess Mowry's novel *Way Past Cool* that he literally ran into the English office at lunch to tell me that he had read the first one hundred pages the night before. Of course I was excited, but I don't think it showed enough. Ken said, "No, you don't understand, Mr. B., I haven't actually read a book in school since [Jerry Spinelli's] *Maniac McGee* years ago! This book is awesome!" Reactions like this are powerful because Ken will infect others with his enthusiasm. Other students will think, "If Ken liked it, I'm sure I will, since he hates books more than I do!"

It's worth noting, however, that I was only able to recommend Mowry's book to Ken because I knew him well enough to suspect he would like it. I sensed Rachel Zangrillo would love Jeffrey Masson's book *When Elephants Weep: The Emotional Lives of Animals* because she always told me about her different pets. I told Vance to read Cormac McCarthy's *All the Pretty Horses*, which, because he had reading difficulties, I found for him on tape. Vance appreciated the story so much that, while listening to it on the way to school in his car, he decided to follow the main character John Grady Cole's example of leaving home, and kept right on driving until he got to Los Angeles eight hours later. Though I was glad he enjoyed the story, I appreciated the fact that he didn't tell his parents that it was because of me that he went on this sudden adventure.

Lord of the Flies: *Levels of Understanding*

There are many ways to approach the teaching of a novel. I found novels the hardest part of my work when I began teaching. Since my background was writing, reading proved a challenge to me early on. I wasn't sure what I was supposed to accomplish with books, nor did I know how long to spend on the subject. The following vignette at least provides a sense of what is involved in teaching a novel. Other strategies for teaching reading will follow later in this chapter.

Establish a frame.   I always have to stop myself when my students and I are walking back to class from the book room with a new book; I remind myself that I cannot just send them off to start reading without talking to them about how to approach this particular book. Thus when we begin a new text, I ask myself and my students some of the following questions to get us thinking in the right direction:

- Why are we reading this book?
- What genre is it and what do we need to know about this form to be able to read the book successfully?
- What is the historical context in which the text was written?
- What do we need to know—about the writer, the historical period, the subject matter—before we begin reading the book?
- What is the book's larger framework or context (e.g., what is happening back in England during the course of *Lord of the Flies*)?
- What are my objectives for the students and what specific standard(s) do these objectives satisfy?
- How can I best measure their progress toward these standards/objectives at different points during the course of our study?
- How does this text relate to those that came before it and those that will follow it?
- What question is the course currently trying to answer and how does this particular text contribute to that conversation or inquiry?
- Which students will have a hard time with this book; why; and what can I do to see that they succeed with it?

Discuss the title.   I always come dangerously close to forgetting what is often the most helpful way into a book: discussing its title. Not every title yields the same depth and quality of discussion, but talking about the name of the book answers one of the first questions we generally have as we pick it up (i.e., what is this book about?).

In the weeks preceding our discussion of *Lord of the Flies* in freshmen English, we did substantial work as part of an integrated English–Social Studies program to prepare students for the novel. Before we began reading the text, we looked at the title of Golding's book to try to find what context it offered us. By the end of our brainstorming session, the class had generated a set of observations and notes (see Figure 4.4) about the title; during the discussion, they created a rich context which would allow them to start reading the book successfully. I asked them questions like "What are the most important words in the title?" "What else could that word refer to?" "What if you changed words like *Flies* or *Lord* into numbers: What is the numerical value of *Lord*?" "What are some of the themes you see emerging as we discuss this title?" "What do you expect this book to be about, based on what we have said about the title?"

Carefully examine the opening paragraph(s) and chapter.   By the end of Chapter 1 (thirty pages) of *Lord of the Flies*, a number of reading issues arise. Golding is an English author, writing in 1954. Certain spellings (e.g., tyres, honour) are "British" and thus confuse young American readers. Such momentary confusion is easily cleared up. More difficult are idiomatic uses of words (e.g., "you're not half bad") or such phonetic spellings as "ass-mar" (for asthma). Some kids will work through these independently; others begin to trip over them and lose confidence

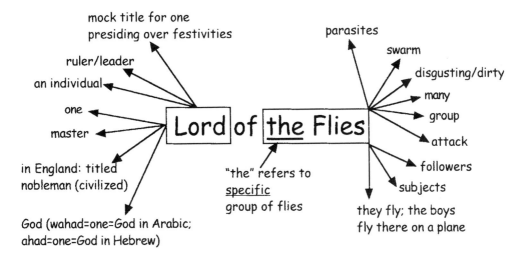

Possible themes based on title brainstorming: power, fear, civilized/uncivilized, religion/faith, violence.

Figure 4.4   *Sample brainstorm of* Lord of the Flies *title and its meanings*

in their ability to comprehend the text. A variation on usage arises in this book that immediately challenges the readers: Golding refers only to the "fair boy" and "fat boy" throughout the first few pages when alluding to the characters we will come to know as Ralph and Piggy. He uses the word *fair* ten times by the end of the second page and the phrase *fat boy* twelve times by the end of the third page.

Obviously you cannot hold the student by the hand throughout the reading of an entire book. You must, however, explicate such textual details as the use of language, the introduction of characters, the format of the text (e.g., extra space between paragraphs, symbols used to divide segments of the text, or in the case of some authors, alternative ways of indicating that a character is speaking—via dashes or quotation marks, for example). In this respect, you are teaching the student how to read each particular text according to its specific details; eventually, when the student has encountered enough texts, he or she will be able to understand what the writer is doing and determine the meaning on their own. Also, with such words as Golding's *fair*, the reader must be helped to realize that the writer's conspicuous use of such a word in lieu of a name signals some greater meaning. Clearly to a writer like Golding there is a purpose behind such repetition; if we miss it, we run the risk of misreading the text and failing to grasp the writer's intended meaning. At such a juncture, I always have someone look up the word *fair* while the class brainstorms possible or known meanings and tests these against the use of the word in the actual text.

Golding will, in subsequent pages, make allusions to events that are both ambiguous and historical. He will make reference to a war and a bombing, but not anchor it in historical time; therefore kids that assume the book is set during World War II do not understand why Golding is intentionally vague about the matter. The atomic bomb is a historical marker, one requiring certain cultural knowledge on the students' part if they are to understand the references. The teacher must bring in the historical and cultural information students need to navigate their way through the different allusions and thereby construct a sound understanding of where the boys are, how they got there, and what their situation is.

Use a variety of activities to explore the book's meaning and structure.   Over the course of the ensuing weeks, my students will do the following assignments, which are representative but not inclusive of all we do during this period of time:

- Watch a documentary of the Stanford Prison Experiment. In the late 1960s, Stanford psychologist Philip Zimbardo created a "prison" in the basement at Stanford to study how becoming either a prisoner or a guard would affect one's behavior. Within two days one "prisoner" had to be removed from the experiment due to a near breakdown and within five days the "guards" had grown so abusive that the psychologists could not let the study continue.

- Make masks that represent aspects of ourselves or human nature in general (see Chapter 9 for an example). Have students write an explanation of what their mask represents and share this as part of a general class discussion on masks and their effect on human behavior.

- Examine the use of symbols in the text. We first draw the island as described by Golding, focusing on the repeated use of the word *scar* to describe the damage the crashing plane did to the jungle.

- Study personification by looking carefully at how Golding describes the landscape, the way darkness "crawls," the fire "devours," the "creepers" move.

- Discuss how Golding creates and evokes character in the boys and how their characters evolve as the story unfolds. The study of character involves looking at word choice, dialogue, actions, gestures, motivations, and changes in the psychology of the boys.

- Study the intentional uses of ambiguity in the novel. Why, for example, does Golding not specifically refer to World War II?

- Analyze Golding's use of storytelling techniques, comparing the novel to a fable, for example, to see if this helps students see deeper into the story and the structure of the novel.

- Watch the film *Au Revoir Les Enfants* and compare the private Catholic all-boys school depicted in the film to the island portrayed in Golding's novel.

- Keep character journals throughout our reading of the novel. Students are asked to keep a journal as if they were, for example, Piggy, writing in his voice, about what he thinks, feels, sees throughout the story. The assignment also holds students accountable for their reading and forces them to engage with the text while allowing them to put forward a more creative response. By this point in the year, they have done lots of dialectical journals and response logs, and need something different that still provokes thought.

- Create a CyberGuide (Web site) for the novel, following the template and requirements provided by the San Diego County Office of Education Language Arts homepage, which hosts dozens of such CyberGuides. This option is done in lieu of a character journal.

- Hold regular roundtables and small-group discussions on different aspects of the novel or connections between the English and Social Studies classes, where they are concurrently studying human nature through the writings of different thinkers.

- Assign groups a character—among which the island itself is included, since it is treated as a character by Golding—to teach the class about. Their presentations lead into class discussion, which the presenting group then facilitates as part of the assignment. I

> monitor students' participation and assess the level of their understanding as revealed through their remarks.
> - Close the unit with the infamous Golding Trial, a simulation lasting several weeks in which Golding, charged with libel against humanity, is prosecuted by the cast of characters from his own novel and a long list of historical figures and thinkers whose ideas students have been studying in their Social Studies class. (See Chapter 2 for more information about this idea.)

The novel serves as a rite of passage into the careful study of literature as well as into students' own society. Throughout our reading of the novel, students read a series of poems thematically related to the book. Moreover, we work on sentence structure, focusing on subordinating conjunctions, which serve as the basis for small writing assignments like this one: "Choose two poems from the packet provided and, after explaining what they are about, compare what they say about human nature to what Golding says about it. In your paper please be sure to use at least five subordinating conjunctions to help you more effectively compare and contrast your ideas."

Teaching Dramatic Texts: Shakespearean Vignette

When I was in graduate school, I took a Shakespeare course that made me love the plays but fear them more than a bit, too. My first paper (on *Hamlet*) came back with a giant "SO WHAT?!" inked across the page. I wondered if the professor had gone out to buy a bigger red marker just for my paper, so huge was his "remark." After a few initial flops teaching Shakespeare, I learned that nothing scares students nor gives them a greater sense of achievement than having successfully read—and, ideally, performed—a Shakespeare play. They know he is the top of the mark, the point of reference. What ultimately convinced me that anyone could do Shakespeare, however, was the documentary a friend of mine made about a fourth-grade class in Berkeley that put on a full performance of *A Midsummer Night's Dream*. I figured that if these little kids could do it, so could my big kids. And so they have.

I happen to be blessed with a lovely park with massive oak trees right next to my school; when we put on plays, we get out and give ourselves room to act out and speak up. I focus here on Shakespeare because, though these ideas will help you teach other dramatic texts as well, it is Shakespeare that challenges us most as teachers and readers. Following are some of the most helpful strategies I use to teach my students how to read the plays.

Prepare them to read Shakespeare. I don't mean that you should take a week or two to study Elizabethan theater or history. What students need is a framework for the play; as my father-in-law used to say, "If you don't read the *TV Guide* to find out what the movie's about, how will you be able to follow it?" I help them create this foundation by using each of the following techniques, though not always at the same time and not with all plays:

- Provide them with a brief summary of the play. You can find these in Charles Boyce's *Shakespeare A to Z*, and Norrie Epstein's *The Friendly Shakespeare*, or in any of the teacher editions of the plays (I prefer the Cambridge Shakespeare series).
- Watch a film version of the play first. This allows students to get the story in their head so that they can concentrate in their reading more on language and characterization.
- Acclimate them to Shakespeare's language. Have them read a group of sonnets. Typically

I have them do this in a group, giving each team a different sonnet copied onto a transparency so that they can mark it up and present their reading to the class.

Dramatize the plays.   Plays were written to be heard, spoken, and seen. You can use any number of the following techniques to have students enact the play:

- Divide the play into parts. I often have a group take one act, then, after they read it, create their own script for their performance. They can keep it Shakespearean or adapt it into other styles. Either option helps them better read the play, because they have to understand it in order to revise it. Some go onto the Internet to download the text of their act or scene; this has the advantage of allowing them to adapt and revise their script into a format that works best for them. When the group is finished performing, they must write a critical analysis of their portion of the play, examining its importance to the larger story of the play. This last assignment is essential, as it asks students to keep the entire play in their heads instead of reducing it to just one piece.
- Perform it as "reader's theater." This approach focuses on dramatic reading. You can assign readings to individuals—e.g., one of Hamlet's soliloquies—then follow up the performance with interpretive discussions. You can also assign a reading to a group—e.g., the fight scene between Romeo and Tybalt. You might keep the readers in front of the class after they are done and allow students to ask them questions about what they think Mercutio means, for example, when he says "A plague on both your houses."
- Read the play in groups and discuss it as you go along. This strategy (called reciprocal teaching) is described in detail later in this chapter.
- Have the teacher read aloud. For those teachers who can read Shakespeare with the proper effect, it is very helpful for the students to hear how the language sounds, where the emphasis falls, and how the names and words are pronounced.

Read it on the screen.   To improve your ability to read, watch and discuss how different actors and directors interpret the play your students are reading. This activity emphasizes one of the unique aspects of plays: they are meant to be interpreted differently as actors and directors bring their particular slant to the story. I've seen *Julius Caesar* performed as a South American revolution complete with cigar-chomping, M-16-toting generals in combat fatigues. Surely the 1997 film *Romeo and Juliet*, which might be compared to an extended music video, invites serious and enthusiastic discussion about the choices the actors and the director made.

I have focused here on Shakespeare because the author remains the primary challenge for most teachers, especially those new to the profession. Obviously most of these strategies would also work with any other play. I use the same techniques when teaching Arthur Miller's *The Crucible*. I have not done so, but I can envision how a powerful class adaptation of Miller's play could be made about the McCarthy era, since Miller himself was using the Puritan past to comment on his Communist present.

I have required and always encourage students to dress up for their performances. Costumes create a dramatic space and get kids into character. I have photographs of girls putting lipstick and wigs on tough athletic boys decked out in dresses. As I said earlier, I also like to get outdoors if we can: the classroom is too familiar and too restrained for the volume and movement you hope students will bring to dramatic performance. I have seen otherwise shy and troubled readers bring a sense of fun and passion to the dramatic reading of Shakespeare which never fails to move me. As I said, the kids know Shakespeare is hard, and for that reason they consider it a formidable achievement if they are able to climb that mountain.

Teaching Poetic Texts: Courting the Elusive Muse

> A poem is anything said in such a way or put on the page in such a way as to invite from the hearer or reader a certain kind of attention.

—WILLIAM STAFFORD,
Writing the Australian Crawl

Poetry was my passport into the world of literature. Unfortunately, not everyone shares my love for it. Yet few other texts offer so much substance, such rich fare as poems; nor are there many other texts, Shakespeare included, that frustrate teachers and, of course, students as much as poetry does. A bad joke is defined as one that people don't "get"; this may be why some resist poetry. They just don't "get it." Who wants to teach something that they themselves sometimes find hard to grasp? Surely this just feeds those fires of insecurity in teachers, that our students will one day rise up en masse and shout "Admit it! *You* don't even know what it means!" But the elusive quality of poetry is exactly what intrigues us about it. The students that created the following poem from a selection of words supplied by the teacher, for example, were excited about what they created because they could *feel* something—some meaning—inside the poem that they could not quite name:

> What is love
> is it a blurring vision
> or a feeling of waiting
> a jealous man shifting a long
> night of love into a miserable mist.
>
> Can a kiss of the cheek or
> sudden words work incapable stubbornness
> into the eyes that once saw young light?
> —LEIMANNA, MELISSA, VINCE, and ANOUSH

The same is true of this one, created by a different group in the class:

> Somewhere waiting
> trying to work at your refusal
> failing to reason with your own feelings.
> Maybe waiting is the obvious knowledge.
> Forget your old lines
> see the flooding
> see the love ahead
> know what you're waiting for.
> —RHEA, LUCAS, JULIA, and ANTHONY

What these students "felt" was probably the "passion" that Irish writer Sean O'Casey refers to in his play, *The Shadow of a Gunman:* "If I was you I'd give that game up. It doesn't pay a working man to write poetry. I don't profess to know much about poetry—I don't profess to know much about poetry—about poetry—I don't know much about the pearly glint of the morning dew, or the damask sweetness of the rare wild rose, or the subtle greenness of the serpent's eye—but I think a poet's claim to greatness depends on his power to put passion in the common people."

　　Poetry offers the teacher one other benefit that is worth mentioning: the invitation to keep challenging ourselves as readers. Nothing complements a teacher's demanding schedule better than poetry, which can be read while waiting to use the Xerox machine, while waiting for the faculty meeting to start, while waiting for a parent to show up for a 3:15 meeting.

Poems can be read many ways. The following is one approach, each step of which provides choices depending on what you want to accomplish with the poems you're teaching.

First, look at the poem's title for some clue as to what it might tell you.   Sometimes a poem's title won't offer any insight until after you read the poem; nevertheless, treat the title *as part of* the poem, or its first line. If you get a title like Louise Glück's "The Garden," you should immediately ask yourself what place or idea this might allude to (e.g., Eden) as you begin reading.

Read the poem straight through without stopping to analyze it.   In *The Color Purple*, Alice Walker writes that it makes God angry when people pass by and don't notice the color purple; when reading a poem through the first time, I say don't be distracted by trying to find "meaning"—come back later to pick that flower. It is crucial to first read the poem for what it is: a performance, an event, an experience at once personal and musical, private and public.

Start with what you know.   I give my students any poem so long as there is even one phrase that can help them to climb into it. It might be the last line or some other phrase embedded within the poem. It doesn't matter, so long as there is some toehold within the poem for them to begin the climb toward their own understanding. Sometimes they grab onto an image, or to their own emotional reaction. If the poem makes the reader angry, that is the first question to be asked: Why does the poem make you angry?

Look for patterns.   Patterns in poems might be grammatical, sensory (e.g., a combination of sounds, colors, scents), or object-related, evolving and changing from the beginning to the end of the poem. Edward Hirsch, in his essay "How to Read a Poem," illustrates this notion best with Elizabeth Bishop's "One Art," in which the theme of loss changes in scale as the poem unfolds: the car keys lost in the early part of the poem grow into larger objects or abstractions until, in the end, the narrator complains of having lost entire continents and her lover. Other patterns reveal themselves in the architecture of the poem. William Carlos Williams took great pains to arrange his words just so on the page (in part because he wrote many of his poems on the backs of prescription pads!). The reader's charge is to understand the relationship between the different pieces of the pattern.

Identify the narrator.   Too often we assume that poems are narrated by the poet, unless an alternate voice or persona is clearly established, as in John Berryman's *The Dream Songs*. We mistake Charlie Chaplin for the Tramp and Woody Allen for the fool. Louise Glück's poem illustrates the idea well: in "The Garden" the narrator (the "I") could be anyone from God to a neighbor, or even a former spouse observing the couple in the garden planting peas. Test the different narrative voices out in a poem to see if the text supports your notion of multiple personae and be willing to concede that it does not.

Reflect in writing.   Periodically, stop and write in your journal to help you digest your thoughts. Reflective writing helps you make greater sense of disparate insights while taking you deeper into the poems (and other texts) you have read so many times. This is also an ideal time to model for students how to think through the reading process of a complicated text. The teacher can read aloud to the class from her own reflective writing, explaining her thought process to the class. Students do not know what thinking looks like sometimes, and so teachers must show them.

Read the poem again.   If you haven't read the poem aloud yet, be sure to do that now. It is important to maintain a sense of the poem as a whole, as a complete performance. Too much analysis will cause the poem to otherwise fall apart in your hands. If a student reads the text aloud but offers no dramatic emphasis, now is a good time to talk about where the moments of emphasis are and how it is possible to find them. Try giving them the poem's entire text, retyped without line breaks. Have the students reconstruct the poem, putting the breaks where they think they should go; then ask them why they broke the lines where they did. (This obviously works a little better with free verse). A variation: give them the poem without the title at first; then have them brainstorm possible titles and explain why they fit the poem.

Find the crucial moments.   Often a poem, like a story, has moments when the action shifts, the direction changes, the meaning alters. Here is a "found" poem—i.e., a group of words lifted from another medium—I wrote using words from an article in *Harper's Magazine*. It is titled "Sarajevo":

> She apologized for the burnt skins
> on the peppers she made for
> lunch,
> but,
> she said,
> "that's what happens when you fry
> peppers on a fire
> made from an encyclopedia."

The poem has, arguably, two crucial moments—"but" in the third line and "made from an encyclopedia" in the last line. Both moments change the course of the poem, the final line providing the dramatic shift from the normal, expected, and common to the strange. I sometimes ask students to find the "moments of heat" or "tension" within the poem, then we write about what makes these aspects of the work so important.

Consider form and function.   At certain points, some features of the poem become more apparent and seem more important than they at first did. There are, after all, no accidents in poems: every word is carefully chosen, each line is broken just where the poet decided it must be, all words are arranged in an order that struck the poet as perfect.

This is the point at which a knowledge of poetic elements is helpful and when the teacher should be prepared to introduce or review such terms. In this context, the terms will help to explain the poem and, secondarily, illustrate the meaning of the terms themselves. Form and function shape meaning in most poems and their discussion must not be avoided. Consider the following passage from *Romeo and Juliet* and how the sonnet form of the verse functions to underlie the passage's meaning.

> ROMEO: (*to Juliet, touching her hand*)
> If I profane with my unworthiest hand
>   This holy shrine, the gentler sin is this:
> My lips, two blushing pilgrims, ready stand
> To smooth that rough touch with a tender kiss.
> JULIET: Good pilgrim, you do wrong your hand too much,
>   Which mannerly devotion shows in this.
> For saints have hands that pilgrims' hands do touch,
>   And palm to palm is holy palmers' kiss.

ROMEO: Have not saints lips, and holy palmers, too?
JULIET: Ay, pilgrim, lips that they must use in prayer.
ROMEO: O then, dear saint, let lips do what hands do:
    They pray; grant thou, lest faith turn to despair.
JULIET: Saints do not move, though grant for prayers' sake.
ROMEO: Then move not while my prayer's effect I take.
(*He kisses her*)

The student reading this poem must know the sonnet form if they are to appreciate the ballet going on between the two lovers. The alternating lines suggest the back-and-forth play of the young couple, the teasing. All of this culminates when they physically and literally couple in the last two lines—the *couplet*—as they kiss. The poem warrants further discussion as a fine example of the poet's use of imagery and metaphor. If such elements are ignored, the reader cannot get much further with this or any other poem.

Two other elements that often contribute to the meaning of a poem are repetition and compression. Both are common to most poetry and sometimes play a significant role in shaping the poem's message. *Compression* refers to the way words and images are juxtaposed against or woven into each other, often through the economical use of language (e.g., see how Shakespeare combines images of hands, pilgrims, lips, and prayer in the previous example). *Repetition* implies both rhythm and emphasis, each of which needs to be discussed for a full understanding of any poem.

One last comment about the poem's form. Poet and biographer Paul Mariani, when discussing the work of William Carlos Williams, spoke of the white space surrounding the poem—what I had, until then, considered just the blank, unused part of the page—as part of the text, in the same sense that the empty space of an artist's canvas is an element of a painting. Sometimes extra space between words is used, as in some of the poems of Muriel Rukeyser, for example, or John Berryman's dream songs, to convey meaning. The space between stanzas suggests presence—of time passing, scenes changing, and so on—more than absence. So, too, does the space that follows the last word on a line: sometimes that space is like the space between notes in a Miles Davis song—silence or, in this case, white space, a kind of negative moment or sound that may contribute to the poem's meaning. Poets must make great use of their resources, some of which are not immediately apparent to us.

Look at the language of the poem.   Language is everything in a poem. Words are the poet's medium, their paint, and what they do with them merits serious scrutiny if you are going to understand a poem. It is interesting to note that, despite their resistance to immediate comprehension, poems do not tend to use difficult words; they use words with deep possibilities for meaning.

Many modern poems, written in free verse as they tend to be, depend on grammar and syntax to provide their structure. Here's a poem that illustrates the point well enough—my five-year-old son Evan dictated it to my wife:

> Midnight Rider (*noun*)
> ride, ride, ride (*verbs*)
> through the forest (*prepositional phrase*)
> over the mountains (*prepositional phrase*)
> across the river (*prepositional phrase*)
> Midnight Rider (*noun*)
> ride, ride, ride. (*verbs*)

Some poems use verbs to do all the work; they begin each line with a verbal phrase that places the emphasis on what the subject is *doing*. Others might use adjectives to surround the main subject of the poem and provide perspective to it. Such structures also provide a rhythmic pattern to the poem, a pattern that sometimes conveys meaning, especially if the poet takes liberties with punctuation.

Punctuation and typography both demand consideration in the reading of a poem. Typographical considerations are rather straightforward: You might ask, for example, "Why did the poet capitalize or italicize that word or phrase?" Punctuation, on the other hand, often remains a nagging source of confusion in a poem: Why doesn't the poet just put a period where there obviously should be one? Guided by the question "How does it change the meaning of the poem?" try looking, for example, at how the poet runs words together, separating them only by a line break. What you often find, in such instances, is that the blending of the different lines offers an opportunity for not just different meanings but deeper ones as well. The words begin to rub up against each other, creating semantic possibilities the poet recognizes and chooses to use to convey a full range of meaning. As I said, there are no accidents in poems; therefore we must, upon encountering patterns we do not immediately understand, consider them from other perspectives. This is another point at which pulling back and rereading a poem through, perhaps aloud, can help you to *hear* what the eyes may not be able to see.

Go deeper or call it quits?   By this time you have achieved a functional—if not solid—understanding of the poem. Depending on the poet and the particular poem, there may not be much more to learn from it, or you may just not have the time for an extensive inquiry. Some poems, especially those we use to supplement discussions of other literature, may not warrant further scrutiny. Other poems may lack emotional depth or thematic complexity.

Some poems, however, do invite further study. Consider, for example, Phyllis Wheatley's "On Being Brought from Africa to America" (1773):

> 'Twas mercy brought me from my pagan land,
> Taught my benighted soul to understand
> That there's a God, that there's a Savior too:
> Once I redemption neither sought nor knew.
> Some view our sable race with scornful eye.
> "Their color is a diabolic dye."
> Remember, Christians, Negroes, black as Cain,
> May be refined, and join the angelic train.

This poem will only begin to reveal its full intelligence to the reader who recognizes Wheatley's use of irony, who senses the wry grin on her poem's face as the poet capitalized on the different meanings of *benighted soul* (e.g., in the sense of *knight* as in "regal," "superior," and *night*, as in "darkness" and "confusion"). Eva Heidemann, a German exchange student in my American Lit class, wrote:

Phyllis Wheatley was a slave and sure experienced a lot of bad things in her life. In this poem she is talking about the fact that white people tried to force slaves to their religion, Christianity, and to adopt the white culture. They tried to assimilate them. Wheatley is talking about this whole process in the view of whites so it might sound ironic to black people. Whites taught her "benighted soul" to understand what it means that they tried to force her into their religion and culture. The black or "sable" race was for the whites something that had to do with the devil. She expresses this by using the words "diabolic dye." She always talks about redemption, meaning that she would be released and refined from her religion if she would join the whites' religion. The angelic train in her poem is a symbol for the Anglican Church. Wheatley clearly understood that by using the word *mercy* that whites at her time thought the best thing that could happen to an African was to come to America where they could be cultivated and given the opportunity to "escape" from their "pagan land."

Though discussion and examination of this poem may have yielded an understanding of its surface structure, the poem contains a whole range of other, more subtle meanings if you look at its deep structure, as Eva obviously did. This is the point at which it is helpful to turn to other sources to better grasp the source of such a poem's complexity:

- a good dictionary (e.g., *The Oxford English Dictionary*)
- the Bible (usually the King James Version, the favored translation by poets and writers)
- other works (literary or artistic) to which the poem may allude

Return to the title before going on.   Just as we tell students not to finish an essay without revisiting the initial writing prompt, so the reader should go back to the title of the poem at this point to see what additional information it might offer. This is especially helpful and important if a poem's title did not make sense to the students before they began reading the poem—as with a title, for example, like Robert Frost's "Birches." In such instances, the poet expects the reader to return to the title and consider it as a commentary on or complement to the poem's meaning.

Remind yourself why you are having students read this poem in the first place.   Sometimes we get so involved in the reading of a poem that we forget why we read it in the first place. I use lots of poems, for example, while reading William Golding's *Lord of the Flies*; at this juncture it is essential that I not get lost in the labyrinth of analysis and forget about the links I wanted to make to Golding's book. I would typically have students do some focused writing in which they build a bridge between the two works and, through their writing, construct their own understanding of the relationship between the two (or more) texts.

Engage in other activities to help students move beyond particular poems.   Depending on your objectives and the time available, you might want to consider some of the following activities for further study of poetry in general:

- *Unmagnetic poetry.* Photocopy the poem (ideally enlarging it and using a heavier stock of paper) and cut it up into its lines or words. Students then use these pieces to construct other poems as a means of manipulating language to better understand what it can and cannot do. When they have finished a poem, have them write it down, and read it aloud or post it in class.
- *Revelation through revision.* In *Deep Revision*, Meredith Sue Willis (1993) shows how to understand a poem by revising it through additions, changes in point of view, or verb tense. Willis writes, "One theory of literature states that what is written is only fully realized when a reader fully receives it, that the reader is, in a way, the true creator of a text." She admits that she does not entirely agree with this theory, but finds it creates rich possibilities for teaching how texts work. Her chapter, titled "Revising as a Response to Literature," provides a wide range of activities and strategies for manipulating the text of a poem (or story) to better understand its content and structure.
- *Draw your own conclusions.* Fran Claggett and Joan Brown's *Drawing Your Own Conclusions* (1992) shows all the different ways you can render a poetic text (i.e., poetry and

fiction) into images that help the student understand the poem better, but also inspire them to create new visual and verbal texts to convey their ideas about the same subject or new ones.

- *Perform the poem.* I once watched Bill Clawson and Carol Jago, two master English teachers by anyone's standards, recast an ancient poem by the Mexican writer Sor Juana into a ten-minute play in which different parts of the poem were performed and, through these performances, interpreted. This led to a subsequent discussion of what went on in the performers' minds as they inhabited those different roles, and why they chose to interpret certain lines the way they did. This differs from choral reading, which focuses more on creative ways to read the poem but not, typically, on how to better understand what the poem is about.

Final Thoughts about Teaching and Reading Poetry

Students should read or hear at least a hundred poems a year. Obviously, not all of them should be studied; not all poems merit such close attention and we don't always have time for it. If used simply to teach literary devices and poetic terms, poetry will be something kids avoid. Such displeasure represents an acute failure given the extent to which kids' lives are filled with poetry already in the form of the music they listen to.

In *How Does a Poem Mean*? John Ciardi (1975) recommends that teachers follow a couple of simple principles:

- The minimum assignment is always at least two poems, never one alone.
- Discussion must be kept to specific likenesses and differences.

While I disagree with these as strict principles, they offer helpful guidance when you are learning how to use poetry in your English class. For instance, it's fine to use one poem, though the poem is better used if included as part of a larger discussion that involves other texts (which may or may not be poems). When teaching *Lord of the Flies*, I use somewhere in the neighborhood of twenty poems to supplement our discussion of human nature and the notion of evil. I bring in the story of Cain and Abel to help us understand the poems that refer to this story as well as to further complement the reading of Golding's text. These texts all start talking to each other in ways that help students learn to read better and to comprehend the immediate text at hand. They also inspire a conversation of substance that matters much more to them than a conversation about poetic terms or literary genre.

The Myth of the Hidden Meaning

Sometimes we feel overwhelmed by all we want to accomplish when studying a text. What we demand of students depends on the purpose at hand. In this chapter I have considered two primary objectives of reading—appreciation and comprehension. Students are frustrated by what they sometimes experience as a third objective: finding the hidden meaning. My colleague Elaine Caret wrote a memo to her AP class one year that addresses this issue nicely:

To: My Students
From: Ms. Caret
Re: "The Myth of the Hidden Meaning"

Most of you, at one time or another, have expressed frustration with a piece of literature because its "Hidden Meaning" has eluded you completely. In fact, much of school-based literacy study for students has been a search for this elusive Meaning. Teachers probably aided and abetted you in this search because, after all, we have the map and know where to find the treasure!

I believe that hidden meaning is a myth, an old myth. There was, in the Middle Ages, a doctrine of poetry that likened it to a nut with a tough husk protecting a sweet kernel. The function of the poem is not to disclose but rather to conceal the kernel from the many, the unworthy, and to disclose it only to the few who are worthy (an idea that comes from Peter Elbow's book *Embracing Contraries*). I have wrestled with this belief many times, both as a reader and a teacher. As a teacher I know that I have waited through many a class period of discussion for the chance to tell what I think a text means. Students have assumed that my meaning is *the* meaning, and I used to believe that somehow I was closer to it than my students because of my vast experience with reading and, of course, graduate courses in literature. (Read a sardonic tone here, please.)

However, my reading and teaching has evolved over the years in such a way that I understand that meaning is a transaction between the reader and text. We construct meaning as we read, as we think and talk about what we read, and as we reread. How could a novel have only one meaning when, if I read it again ten years after the first reading, the text seems so different? It is because I have changed—my experiences have changed me. Perhaps the novel even changes me because the transaction I am having with it is, at that time, a totally new one.

So what I am recommending in this memo to you today is that you

- *Abandon the myth.* Set yourself free from your frustration over not "finding" hidden meanings. Set me free from the inevitable class where you will not risk talking about a piece of literature but safely choose to wait for someone else to tell you what the text means.

- *Begin to read as a writer.* The words, ideas, concepts, themes, etc. are in the text not to confuse high school students but are there because the writer chose them as his or her form of expression. Ask lots of questions—why? what if?

- *Understand that some texts will be inaccessible at first and will require hard work.* By being in the messy process called learning, you will be transformed, but I do acknowledge that the process is not easy and that an answer is not the real purpose for reading.

- *Recognize that I can help you become a critical reader.* And this is the tricky bit. Sometimes a reading of a text may be impoverished because the text is too difficult, the language is challenging in the extreme, or the reader latches onto one detail, ignores many of the others, and draws a superficial reading.

Your teacher,
Ms. Caret

How We Read: A Brief Explanation

What goes on when we read, anyway? Let me illustrate with a few examples from my own experience or my classroom's. First, we try to make sense of the textual information as it comes in through our eyes or, if we are listening, our ears. We try to impose order on this stream of words and images by predicting what it means, then checking all subsequent information against this theory. Only when we encounter information in the text that does not agree with our assumptions do we stop to reevaluate our understanding. For instance, I was listening to an audio recording of South African writer Nadine Gordimer's novel *None to Accompany Me* while driving to work. I grabbed the wrong tape from the box without realizing it and popped it in. I had been distracted while much of the book was being read to me, so it did not surprise me much when the new tape made no sense. But the more I listened to what I thought was chapter 3 (it was actually chapter 9!), the more confused I got: here were characters I had not met talking about events I had not heard of with people I clearly did know. When, a day later, I changed the tape again—not having caught my sixty-mile-per-hour mistake—it turned out to be the tape I originally needed. Suddenly the text made sense!

The reading process requires that we use our own experiences and knowledge about the world to help us further understand the book. However, everything changes over time. We cannot read the same book twice, to adapt Heraclitus's famous maxim. These personal biases or experiences tend to profoundly shape our interpretation of the text, blinding us sometimes to other, equally valid readings or important details. Perhaps my most personal reading experience came while teaching *Hamlet* to a class of seniors the year after my father died. During the time I taught the play, my mother began to date other men for the first time since my father's death. This confused me and allowed me to identify closely with Hamlet throughout the reading of the play. My own feelings were so raw at the time that they interfered with other readings I might otherwise have come up with.

We so often have students with personal problems in our classes these days. Others are simply going through phases of personal evolution that can either confuse or inspire them when they encounter the text. Tracy, a young woman in my junior class, had some trouble at home with her parents and, after reading the chapter of *Huckleberry Finn* in which Huck decides to run away from his dad, got in her car and took off for Santa Cruz for a weekend without telling her parents. She stayed at a friend's house to talk things through. She was back at school Monday, thankfully. Laurel, another student of mine, had a hard time focusing on any other aspect of the novel than Huck's father's cruelty, since the following week her mother had thrown her out of the house for reasons that were not at all clear to Laurel.

Finally, while reading we often encounter passages that we simply cannot understand. My students often have trouble reading *Cry, the Beloved Country* because it assumes a familiarity not only with South African customs and apartheid, but certain stories from the Bible. In addition, the book's writing is idiosyncratic, offering typographic as well as stylistic variations they have not previously encountered. As for myself, I've tried to read Faulkner's *Absalom! Absalom!* maybe three times and failed each time despite my best efforts. I encounter portions that confuse me as well as those that bore me. One of Faulkner's novels, *The Sound and the Fury*, was such a complicated story that Faulkner asked his publisher to print it in three different-colored inks to indicate both the speaker and the time (i.e., remote past, recent past, and present). His publisher, of course, refused, telling Faulkner that if the book was that confusing he should rewrite it. This final point characterizes the trouble many of my students have with texts we read, some of which can be chalked up to the inability to "see" what is happening, and some of which is related to the cognitive disorientation they feel due to lack of knowledge or information.

Profiles of Readers

Having considered, however briefly, the reading process, let me offer a more concrete profile of three different types of readers before looking at specific strategies to help all our students read better. Returning to the Continuum of Complexity (Figure 4.3), I find it helpful to measure students' reading performance by their capacity to juggle simultaneously the various demands of reading. This idea of a continuum also suggests that the student who is a confident reader of even difficult nonfiction texts—perhaps because he just loves history—may not naturally transfer those strengths to the task of reading a novel like Ralph Ellison's *Invisible Man*. Certainly many strong readers of all ages react to poetry as if it asked things of them as a reader that they just can not provide. So as teachers we must keep in mind that our students may be, at any particular time, each one of the proceeding types of readers depending on the text at hand.

Powerful Readers

Powerful readers have a variety of habits when they read, all of which make them confident navigators of texts. By "habits" I mean they have skills they use reflexively, such as asking questions of the text, its author, or its characters; looking outside the text to consider the events in the larger context of the author's other works, the historical period, or other books on the same subject; and reading using all their senses. For example, when I read Arundhati Roy's novel *The God of Small Things*, I taste the spicy foods she describes (because our Indian neighbor has fed us similar dishes), hear the sound of the river beside which the characters in the book work on their boat, and smell the different vats of pickles brewing in the factory that is one of the book's settings. Powerful readers also bring a fierce and sustained attention to their reading, drawing on their previous experiences and knowledge to help them understand what they read. In short, they make *connections*. The powerful reader's associative capacity will enable him or her to read Sandra Cisneros's *The House on Mango Street* and wonder if the author had Cinderella in mind when she wrote a particular chapter of the book, since the stories contain parallels. Powerful readers are also able to read for subtle aspects of a text such as style and nuance, since their ability affords them the extra attention needed to attend to these minutiae. Chances are that powerful readers enjoy reading on their own and would do so whether you asked them to or not, though this does not mean that they necessarily like to read required texts. Powerful readers are a picky lot and even quarrelsome, as you yourself probably know.

Proficient Readers

"Proficient" describes most of our students. They have mastered the requisite skills, but these readers have stumbling points that the powerful readers do not. For example, vocabulary or contextual information (e.g., about history) may be lacking, and so a solid understanding evades them. If they drift from comprehending a text, however, most of them can be easily brought back into the fold by the teacher's questions or guidance. This attention spent elsewhere keeps them from being able to easily focus on such smaller details as style and voice, however. In this respect, thinking again of the Continuum of Complexity, they have the skills and attention to handle several competing demands for their cognitive attention but not all. Thus a proficient reader might be able to read Rudolfo Anaya's *Bless Me, Ultima* with reasonable success but gets distracted by the use of folktales and Spanish in the novel. The most important help we can offer this kind of reader is a challenging book about something they really love: this will push them past their current status and, using what is already familiar to them, allow them to read a more demanding text.

Reluctant Readers

The reluctant reader is typified, in my mind, by my friend's wife, who is a college graduate but has a reading disability. When an English teacher casually remarked at dinner that he couldn't understand how anyone could not like reading, she asked, "How would you feel if every time you picked up something to read it made you feel stupid?" People fall into the reluctant reader camp for different reasons, and thus need different strategies to help them improve. English as a Second Language (ESL) students, for instance, are still learning the language and the American culture, so they have considerable trouble with some of the books we ask them to read. For students in this last category, such devices as summaries, Cliffs Notes, and even films can help to ground them in the general plot of the story. For this is the primary challenge at this stage of reading: most kids in this category don't have a basic understanding of what is happening in the story. They are overcome by the complexity of the text: too many things are going on within the writing and the story itself. Some reluctant readers encounter difficulties here because of genuine reading disorders that affect how they process information. The expanded availability of books on tape offers real help for these kids. Finally, some have not learned to read well because they haven't given reading the attention it requires. What unifies all these readers is the anxiety that their reading limitations will make them appear dumb or otherwise embarrass them in front of their peers.

Strategies to Improve Reading Skills

There are three types of reading that all students do regardless of their level of proficiency. First, there is the required reading of school, exemplified by Shakespeare, an author hardly any kid would voluntarily pick up and read. This is "have to read" reading. Second, assuming that you provide opportunities for students to read books of their own choice as part of your class curriculum, there is personal reading, which I think of as "get to read" reading—it is anchored in students' own interests, but it is still "school reading." The last kind of reading is everyone's favorite, and kids won't let the other types keep them from it: "need to read" reading. This is reading that students are compelled to do because it is integral to who they are. I immediately think of the boys in my classes who carry a seemingly endless supply of car magazines which, no matter how hard I try, I cannot keep them from reading in class. Also included in this category of "need to read" would be the Internet, sports pages, teen magazines, and computer manuals. Students may not like to read what we ask them to, but just about everyone needs to read something. That is the place to begin with your reluctant reader.

The following strategies to improve reading skills will help, but none of them will work with all students and none will work all the time, if for no other reason than they begin to feel redundant to the students who use them. In addition to all these specific methods, there are three contributing factors in creating a literate environment that helps students develop as readers. I discuss them more fully elsewhere, but I want to emphasize them here. First, the teacher is the model. If our students don't see us reading, don't hear us talking about what we are reading, then we run the risk of losing our credibility. Second, the classroom library is crucial to any literate environment: kids must walk into their English class and see books. These books should inspire their interest through their diversity of topics and range of difficulty. Finally, the class must become a community of readers, creating among themselves a culture that gives everyone permission to read, that says it's "cool" to read. Now let's look at the nitty-gritty: What can you do tomorrow?

Students as teachers. We always learn things better if we have to teach them to others. Throughout the course of a novel you can call on individuals or groups to lead discussions of previously assigned portions of the text. This can be done in different ways, varying from focused (e.g., be prepared to lead a discussion about why Holden Caulfield is obsessed with ducks) to open-ended (e.g., read a chapter in *Catcher in the Rye* and be prepared to lead a discussion about whatever you think is most important or interesting). At year's end, students often remember these student-led classes as some of the most powerful. Students see that their peers—and thus they themselves—are capable of thinking effectively and publicly about important ideas. Under such circumstances, students can start the honest, essential conversations that we might not know quite how to address. The most compelling example of this was a class' period-long spontaneous discussion of Twain's use of the word *nigger* in *Huckleberry Finn*, during which I did little but ask occasional questions to push students' thinking deeper on particular issues (e.g., "Okay, why might some black people think it's okay if they use that word but entirely wrong for anyone else to?")

Reciprocal teaching.   Working in pairs, students can be asked to read an assigned portion of text during a specific period of time. The two students alternate reading, switching off every few minutes or so, but pushing each other to work efficiently within the allotted time. The listener can interrupt the reader at any time to ask questions; in fact, that is one of the listener's responsibilities: to challenge both himself and his partner to think closely about those aspects of the text that raise questions about style, usage, authorial intent, character, or vocabulary. When one reader concludes their portion of the text, the other summarizes what was just read as a way of transitioning into the next section of the story and orienting the previous reader (since we don't always follow stories as well when we read them aloud to others). Students ask two kinds of questions: "surface" and "deep." Surface questions address literal aspects of the story—e.g., "Where are they now?"—and basic details such as vocabulary. Deep questions help to establish and reveal the depths of essential events. Such questions would examine not just that it is important that, in the *Odyssey*, Penelope remains loyal to Odysseus for so many years, but why she does. During such readings, it is absolutely necessary that both students give their full attention to the story and the discussion; they should not take notes or partake in any other activities that might distract from their talking, listening, and reading. It is possible to have the students read to answer some previously established question (e.g., "How might we compare the people in Arthur Miller's *The Crucible* to Senator Joseph McCarthy and the 'Red Scare' of the 1950s?"). They might begin such discussions by predicting what they will find; this helps to orient their reading and thinking. To bring the converstion to a close, ask the participants to come to some final conclusions, perhaps in writing, concerning what they have learned about the story during their conversation.

Reading aloud.   Although reading aloud can help us to appreciate and enjoy a good story, I include it here because it helps many students learn to read better. This is particularly the case for ESL, special education, and reluctant readers who often don't know what a text is supposed

Beau teaching the class about racism and Huck Finn *in one of the more memorable classes that year*

Lucas and Chris find a quiet hall for some reciprocal teaching with a difficult article.

to sound like. Sometimes students just grow tired of not "getting it," especially with poetry or Shakespeare. When someone who can read very well "performs" the text, giving careful attention to the need for emphasis and mood, students literally understand it better because they hear what the author wanted them to hear. This is another reason why dramatic activities that grow out of reading fiction can be so effective. I have to admit that I did not read very well when I began teaching; however, early on I realized the value of reading aloud and I worked on my technique, so that now students often say that they enjoy it when I read to them. No doubt reading all those bedtime stories to my sons helped me in this area. For more detailed suggestions about how to read aloud, see Jim Trelease's *The Read-Aloud Handbook* (1995).

Reading for patterns.   Almost any English teacher convention will include a workshop on the "Hero's Journey." This concept is based on the work of Joseph Campbell (see Campbell's *The Hero with a Thousand Faces*) and, sometimes, Carol Pearson's *The Hero Within: Six Archetypes We Live by*. Using Campbell's idea of the journey as both a metaphor and an archetypal pattern that exists in nearly any story, I created the diagram shown in Figure 4.5 to help my students better understand narrative action.

   After introducing the heroic cycle and explaining that, for instance, "the call" refers to the invitation to do something, go somewhere, or become something, I ask students to use the diagram to describe a story. *Catcher in the Rye* conforms to this diagram very nicely, as do most of the stories we teach. The pattern allows them to create a holistic picture of the story and, since I often have them do this exercise at the book's end, provides an ideal opportunity for them to write about their own journey or certain stages of it. The greatest benefit of this approach is that they begin to think about stories in terms of their shape or pattern, something that helps them better understand the architecture or "story grammar" of subsequent works they read.

Using study questions.   Quality and sequencing are the crucial elements of good study questions. You can ask all the questions you want, but if they are not the right ones, asked with a clear and useful purpose in mind, they will not help the students, who will dismiss them as busywork, something they resent. Quality is, in important ways, linked to sequencing, since

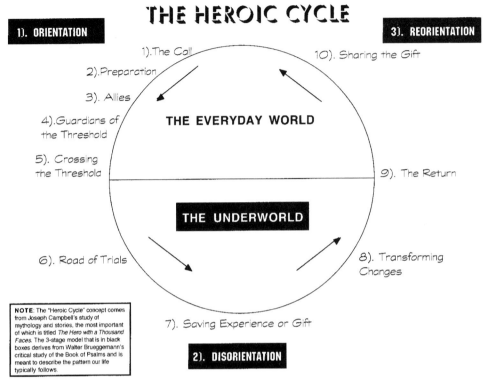

Figure 4.5

part of what makes a question good is that it builds on previous knowledge and inquiry. I use study questions when we are reading a particularly difficult text and I want to be sure my students know the "what"—i.e., the plot—of the story. Thus I might ask initial questions about the *Odyssey* that focus on who Odysseus is, why he is absent, why the characters are so frustrated with Telemachus and Penelope. Once I have established that students understand the basics of the story—as evidenced by their answers to these initial questions—I know I can go deeper with such questions as "Why does it matter that the suitors keep referring to Telemachus as 'Odysseus's son' instead of by his own name?" and "What does it mean to 'make a name for yourself?' " If the questions are carefully sequenced ahead of time, students will be prepared to write an effective literary analysis later on, since they can draw from their study questions those quotes and responses that support their ideas.

Reader response.   Students should be required to respond to texts in writing. Some aspects of this technique are addressed in Chapter 9. Briefly, students improve their reading ability by looking closely at specific portions of the text to improve their interpretive or analytical skills. One method allows the teacher to take specific quotes they feel are essential to a full understanding of the story or a character—the obvious example from *Hamlet* would be the "to be or not to be" soliloquy—and have students explain them. Such analyses can be written out in a journal to be collected at the end of the unit or on separate sheets of paper for more ongoing accountability and assessment of students' understanding of the text. Another option is the "notes and quotes" method, which typically asks students to divide a page in half and, while reading, jot down on the left side of the paper quotes or events that seem essential to the story. Later on, the student reflects on the meaning and importance of these quotes on the right side of the page. My own experience with this exercise is that students have a tendency to concentrate more on the left side of the page than on the right; they think they have completed the assignment because half of the page is full. The teacher should, therefore, stress the importance of the reflection aspect of the assignment. Students should also be asked to note the page number of the quote or, if it is a play, the appropriate act, scene, and line numbers. While I choose the quotes when it seems appropriate to the task, I prefer that students choose their own. This allows them to select those textual moments that mean the most to them and about which they will have the most to say.

Annotating texts.   While annotating a text is similar to responding to it, in this case I treat it as a specific strategy and skill. I teach students how to annotate or "mark up" a text by giving them a photocopied version with an extra-wide margin; sometimes I copy the text onto an overhead transparency so that we can all see a student's work. I do this, for example, with the prose poem that opens Steinbeck's *Cannery Row*, telling my students to make notes in the margins, writing down any of the following:

- questions
- quotes
- ideas
- statements
- patterns
- essential information
- textual connections to other books or poems we have read

When students come in the next day with their annotations, we use them as the basis for comparison. I ask them to explain what they underlined and commented on and why. It is the *why* that helps me to assess their understanding of both the text and the skill, and determines where we go next. It is also the why that makes them go beyond the obvious.

Dramatic interpretation.   Students should be encouraged to go inside the text and manipulate it. The title of Jeffrey Wilhelm's book says it all: *"You Gotta BE the Book"* (1995). The first year I taught American Lit I had my students read Hawthorne's *The Scarlet Letter*. We found it predictably difficult, especially those with reading difficulties and those who were in the ESL transition program. We managed to have some fun with the book and increase our understanding of it through discussion and dramatic interpretation. Working in teams of two, students were assigned one chapter of the book and, using the actual dialogue in the chapter, asked to type up (to integrate computer skills) a script, adding an introduction and stage directions. Here is an example:

Chapter 2 ("The Market Place")

Setting: The grass-plot before the jail, in Prison Lane, on a certain summer morning, not less than two centuries ago, was occupied by a pretty large number of the inhabitants of Boston; all with their eyes intently fastened on the iron-clamped oaken door.

DAME: *(She addresses them in a fierce voice, charged with vengeance, her eyes wide.)* Goodwives, I'll tell ye a piece of my mind. It would be greatly for the public behoof, if we women, being of mature age and church-members in good repute, should have the handling of such malefactresses as this Hester Prynne. What think ye, gossips? If the hussy stood up for judgment before us five, that are now here in a knot together, would she come off with such a sentence as the worshipful magistrates have awarded? Marry, I trow not!

WOMAN #1: *(She speaks softly, apologetically to the others, looking about nervously.)* People say that the Reverend Master Dimmesdale, her godly pastor, takes it very grievously to heart that such a scandal should have come upon his congregation.

AUTUMNAL MATRON: *(She addresses the group with a wise tone, her arms crossed on her chest, her head tilted back in a smug attitude. She has the air of a judge.)* The magistrates are God-fearing gentlemen, but merciful overmuch—that is a truth. At the very least, they should have put the brand of a hot iron on Hester Prynne's forehead. Madam Hester would have winced at that, I warrant me. But she—the naughty baggage—little will she care what they put upon the bodice of her gown! Why, look you, she may cover it with a brooch, or such like heathenish adornment, and so walk the streets as brave as ever!

YOUNG WIFE: *(She seems scared, as though she were speaking to herself to warn herself.)* Ah, but let her cover the mark as she will, the pang of it will be always in her heart.

These dramatic renditions take students inside the character they are trying to learn "to read" and, through occupying them, understand them and the text better.

Reading workshop.   In my class "reading workshop" means that students can choose from a variety of strategies, some of which I have already discussed here and others of which I will consider elsewhere in the book (see Chapter 9). On workshop days students might choose to use one of these strategies to help them improve their reading:

- translating a scene or passage into pictures or modern-day English (if they are reading Shakespeare, for example)
- holding student-teacher conversations about the story each particular student is reading or that the class is reading together
- creating book groups that meet to talk about what they are reading
- listening on such days to audio recordings of the books they are reading

The English Teacher's Dilemma: How to Reinvent Reading for Yourself

After reading the same books again and again and again, boredom threatens the joy we initially felt when we first taught them. It would be nice if we could all mix things up whenever we felt like it: I get dangerously envious of private school teachers I meet during the summer. They might be reading a book like Charles Frazier's *Cold Mountain*, and will say something like, "I just love it. I think I'll have my kids read it this year." The harsh reality for most of us is that we are stuck with the books we have. For one reason or another I have taught *Lord of the Flies* every year since I was a student teacher. How do I keep from reverting to automatic teaching?

Zen master Shunryu Suzuki (1988) describes the "beginner's mind" as one of "many possibilities"; he goes on to say that "in the expert's mind there are few." According to Suzuki, "The goal of practice is always to keep our beginner's mind. Suppose you recite the Prajna Paramita Sutra only once. It might be a very good recitation. But what would happen to you if you recited it twice, three times, four times, or more? You might easily lose your original attitude toward it. . . . [If] you continue to practice one, two, three years or more, although you may improve some, you are liable to lose the limitless meaning of original mind." Aside from the endless flow of papers, nothing seems to threaten the English teacher's lively practice like repetition. It was largely for this reason—the danger of falling asleep at the wheel of our own reading, and thus our teaching—that Ron Padgett wrote *Creative Reading*. While I don't agree with all his ideas, Padgett's premise is important: we must each reinvent the reading experience for ourselves if we are to continue to find in it the satisfaction we did when we began. Poet Rainer Maria Rilke's admonition that we are always a beginner each time we sit down to the task of writing is true, but it's an ideal and requires a discipline we can't always muster in the course of the daily grind.

Reading literary criticism has not satisfied my need to plumb the depths of the books I teach. For one, such reading only helps if you teach AP classes, since few American high school students are interested in such things as the literary and philosophical influences on J. D. Salinger's writings. I like books such as David Denby's *Great Books* or even Harold Bloom's *The Western Canon* because they invite you to participate in a serious conversation about a book's worth and meaning. This kind of literary writing leads you back into the books you have taught so many times, in part demanding that you challenge them as to why they should be taught all these years. My colleague Elaine Caret exemplifies for me this habit of reflecting on books she has taught again and again. Elaine keeps a journal in which she writes about the different stories or poems she teaches, dating each entry. She can go back and check what she thought the previous year about *Hamlet* after writing this year from her new perspective. A more social variation is to have literary dinners, as my former department chair, Doug Rogers, did. Doug thought we should engage in regular conversations about the books we taught to appreciate why we taught them. Each month we agreed on a different book and met for a delicious dinner at his house.

Whether through conversations over gourmet meals or reflections in a journal, we realize that we cannot step into the same text twice from the very same vantage point. We are always reading a book as if for the first time. As Suzuki writes, "The most difficult thing is always to keep your beginner's mind. There is no need to have a deep understanding of Zen. Even though you read much Zen literature, you must read each sentence with a fresh mind. You should not say, 'I know what Zen is,' or 'I have attained enlightenment.' This is also the real secret of the arts: always be a beginner."

Endnote: Evolution of the Story

When I began this book, I felt far removed from the "reading wars"—the professional discourse about how kids learn and thus should be taught to read. Most of us have been taught that in the earliest grades our students learn to read and when they come to us in high school they read to learn. Certainly we are always learning to read *and* reading to learn. However, we must be better prepared to "teach reading" if we are to meet the needs of all our students. We can learn what we need to know about reading from a book like Margaret Moustafa's wonderfully concise (ninety-five pages!) *Beyond Traditional Phonics: Research Discoveries and Reading Instruction* (1997) which taught me what my own credential program did not about reading. I share Jeff McQuillan's (1998) position that even though we have real reading problems that must be addressed, today's students are not reading worse than they did in the past. As I have said throughout this chapter, however, I believe we must adapt our practice to the wider range of documents that exists today. For the diverse texts they will encounter, students need greater skills.

As I write this chapter, the first "e-books" are appearing. Some of these computerized books, such as the RocketBook, are the size of conventionally bound books. They display an entire text, complete with graphics, in a traditional booklike format. It is hard not to wonder where this technology will lead us. Might subsequent issues of these books have the option of voice-overs that can read the text aloud to you with the click of a button? Perhaps others will have video options, allowing us to cut out of the book and view, for example, a film version of the story—the scene we just read in *Hamlet* could be accompanied by Kenneth Branagh's film version of the play. Maybe these books will someday be all our students carry, each little one-pound machine containing the text of all the books they need for the year—which might allow schools to use a wider range of books than their budgets currently allow. The future seems like a pretty wild story to me: I can't wait to see how it turns out. Whatever happens, we can count on being able to read about it in one form or another, for we love no story so much as our own, which we never seem to tire of telling—or reading.

REFLECTION

Write your own reading autobiography. Describe your early childhood, if you can: Did your parents read to you? Do you remember a crucial moment when you suddenly became a reader? What book(s) most influenced you?

ACTIVITY

Conduct an informal survey of people, asking them what they read during the course of a week. Another way to do this, if you take public transportation, is to see what people read on the bus or train; this is often people's "need to read" time and will give you some interesting insights into personal reading habits. One other possible activity might be to have your students write down the books they liked and hated the most in their school careers, following this up with their own reader's autobiography. Such autobiographies can be revealing to both them and you, for they inevitably uncover a time when reading was fun.

RECOMMENDATIONS

The nature of this chapter calls for several different recommendations.

Reading Theory

There are a couple of books I especially like in this area:

Literature as Exploration, Louise Rosenblatt (Modern Language Association of America, 1995).

The Protocols of Reading, Robert Scholes (Yale University Press, 1989).

Envisioning Literature: Literary Understanding and Literature Instruction, Judith Langer (Teachers College Press, 1995).

Reading Lessons: The Debate over Literacy, Gerald Coles (Hill and Wang, 1998).

How to Teach Reading

Mosaic of Thought: Teaching Comprehension in a Reader's Workshop, Ellin Oliver Keene and Susan Zimmerman (Heinemann, 1997).

"You Gotta BE the Book": Teaching Engaged and Reflective Reading with Adolescents, Jeffrey D. Wilhelm (Teachers College Press, 1997).

Questioning the Author: An Approach for Enhancing Student Engagement with Text, Isabel L. Beck, Margaret G. McKeown, Rebecca L. Hamilton, and Linda Kucan (International Reading Association, 1997).

It's Never Too Late: Leading Adolescents to Lifelong Literacy, Janet Allen (Heinemann, 1995).

Reading, Thinking, and Writing About Multicultural Literature, Carol Booth Olson (Scott Foresman, 1997).

General (but very interesting)

A History of Reading, Alberto Manguel (Penguin, 1996).

The Guttenburg Elegies: The Fate of Reading in the Electronic Age, Sven Birkerts (Fawcett, 1994).

The Struggle to Continue: Progressive Reading Instruction in the United States, Patrick Shannon (Heinemann, 1990).

CHAPTER 5

THE PLACE AND PURPOSE OF VOCABULARY INSTRUCTION

Language is very difficult to put into words.

Voltaire

"Define courage."
"This is."

—An alleged college essay prompt and the essay written in response to it

---

We know that words matter. Sometimes the inability to understand the implications of a word, even one we may "know," can get us into trouble. When I was in the Peace Corps some years ago, I learned Arabic in order to teach retarded children. Walking home from work one day, Hedi, a rather seedy man who ran a film-developing shop, called me in and introduced me to a young woman. Given that it was an Arab country, she did not seem very traditional. He asked me, "Tahib ha?" Now this could have meant any one of several things: Do you like her? Do you want her? Do you love her? Do you desire her? Thus to discuss vocabulary is to discuss language, meaning, and culture.

Scanning those professional books most commonly used by English teachers, you find, with rare exception, few references to teaching vocabulary. Similarly, the curriculum courses of most teacher education programs offer little or no actual instruction in how to incorporate it into the English curriculum. The absence of such instruction and guidance undermines what most high school teachers are expected to do once they begin teaching; it also ignores what a growing number of states, through standards and frameworks, are demanding of secondary teachers. In my own credential program, which was typical of most, we were never told that we should include vocabulary in our curriculum. Even in my reading class, the only time this subject came up was when the professor, a woman whose intelligence and work I respected, passed out an article she had recently written. In this article she argued that students did not need direct vocabulary instruction because they learned their words through reading and so, she concluded, we should ask our students to read as much as possible.

Rationale for Teaching Vocabulary

While much of the research I surveyed for this chapter supported that professor's second argument—read, read, read—some teachers question the validity of her first assertion—that providing instruction in the area of vocabulary does not benefit students. Moreover, while many teachers struggle with what to do when it comes to vocabulary, they all teach students whose parents expect their kids to have strong lexicons since this is one of the most significant predictors of success on the SAT test. Last, and perhaps most significantly, high school teachers now find themselves teaching students who, for various reasons, need a stronger vocabulary to read the texts required of them.

Knowing a wide range of words and how to use them effectively helps students in several important ways, by:

- providing a helpful foundation that allows them to read and understand difficult texts
- expanding their ability to communicate through writing by using more precise words
- raising their scores on such standardized tests as the SAT
- empowering them socially by giving them the language of the dominant culture of power
- improving quality of subject matter discussion by creating a common vocabulary between all teachers and students in that area (e.g., literary terms)

What to Teach: Expressive versus Receptive Vocabulary

There are two domains of vocabulary: expressive and receptive. Expressive vocabulary is exemplified by speaking and writing; another description might be "productive" because we are producing language—with our mouths or pens—and thus must have a more direct mastery of it than when we read or listen and can use the context to decipher meanings. Receptive words are those we encounter while reading or listening. Both types are important and have instructional components which are, in ways, complicated by our definition of what it means "to know" something. How we determine what it means to know affects how we assess that someone does, in fact, know. For example, just because a student defines an unfamiliar word and uses it in a sentence does not mean they know—i.e., own—that word; similarly, because they cannot define a word encountered while reading does not mean they don't understand it.

This leads us back to the inevitable question: Which words and why? When and how to determine mastery of these words? And which words are the domain of English and which ones fall into the realm of Social Studies or the sciences? According to some researchers (Baumann and Kameenui 1991), students in grades three to twelve acquire an average of three thousand new words each year through osmosis or the context that their studies provides. We might begin then by asking several focus questions to clarify our objectives in this area:

- What do you want your students to accomplish in the area of vocabulary?
- What is the best way to accomplish that?
- What do you need that you do not currently have to accomplish it?
- How will you know when you accomplished it?
- How important is vocabulary in light of all your other curricular obligations?

Content Standards for Vocabulary

Another source that guides our thinking in this area are the standards documents by which more and more of us must learn to teach and to which we are increasingly held accountable. Here are the content standards for California:

> *Word Analysis and Systematic Vocabulary Development*: Students determine the meaning of, and use accurately, new words encountered in reading materials by applying their knowledge of word sources in British and ancient literature.
>
> *GRADES 9/10: Vocabulary and Concept Development*:
>
> **1.1** Identify and use idioms, cognates, and the literal and figurative meanings of words in speaking and writing
>
> **1.2** Distinguish between the denotative and connotative meanings of words and interpret the connotative power of words
>
> **1.3** Identify and use knowledge of the origins of commonly used words and phrases derived from Greek, Roman, and Norse mythology to understand the meaning of new words (e.g., the word "narcissistic" drawn from the myth of Narcissus and Echo)
>
> **1.4** Apply such context clues as definition, restatement, example, comparison, contrast, cause and effect to discern word meanings
>
> *GRADES 11/12: Vocabulary and Concept Development*:
>
> **1.1** Trace the etymology of significant terms used in political science and history
>
> **1.2** Apply knowledge of Anglo-Saxon, Greek and Latin roots and affixes to draw inferences concerning the meaning of scientific and mathematical terminology
>
> **1.3** Discern the relationship of word meanings between pairs of words encountered in analogical statements (e.g., synonyms/antonyms, connotation/denotation) (California Academic Standards Commission 1998)

Performance Standards for Vocabulary

These performance standards, which I developed, offer one approach to teaching vocabulary.

- Students acquire and use at least one thousand new words each year.
- Students read a wide range of increasingly difficult texts.
- Students choose more precise, appropriate words when revising their documents in order to enhance style and rhetorical effectiveness in their writing.
- Students use the dictionary to define words they do not know.

- Students participate in literary discussions during which they use literary terms (see Appendix M) to describe the elements of literature being considered.

Strategies for Vocabulary Development

Since we use words in different ways, it makes sense to learn more words through a variety of approaches. None of these is the cure-all that guarantees perfect SAT scores and soaring reading performance. Like all aspects of the curriculum, vocabulary is integrated with other areas—speaking, reading, and writing. Thus we learn to use new words in these different domains as we become more proficient in those same areas. Vocabulary cannot be developed without the student's help; some of the strategies listed below are for students to implement on their own.

- Read, read, read: There is no better way to pick up words than by reading good books by authors who use language with precision and imagination.
- Keep a good pocket dictionary with you at all times. If you have extra minutes, pull it out and read from it. As someone once said, all the books that have ever been written are in there if you just read the words in the right order.
- Have a good college-level dictionary at home. I like the *American Heritage Dictionary of the English Language* (third edition). Use this to look up words and their roots when you find a word you do not understand.
- Keep a supply of three-by-five-inch index cards with you at all times. When you find a word you do not understand, copy it down on one side, along with the sentence it appears in; on the other side, later on, write down the definition. Carry these cards around with you, and quiz yourself periodically until you feel you know the words.
- Use an interactive computer program that will give you immediate feedback on your learning while making it interesting. Various SAT programs are ideal for this. Some of these programs do an excellent job of entertaining while instructing.
- Create mnemonic devices to help you remember certain words, particularly new words that have no prior association in your mind (e.g., scientific or technical terms). In Tunisian Arabic you say "mghrir mziyya" when you want to say "you're welcome." A woman I studied Arabic with created the mnemonic device "men's rears in museums," so each time someone thanked her, she thought about men's rears in museums, then said "mghrir mziyya!"

Activities for Building a Better Vocabulary

The previous section offered strategies; this portion offers activities, things your students can do for homework or in class. My one concern with vocabulary activities is that some teachers end up allotting an inordinate weight to vocabulary when it comes to grading (see Chapter 11).

Draw the words.   Fran Claggett and Joan Brown (1992) found that students who drew the words—i.e., translated them into symbols and pictures—remembered the words longer and better than those who used various other methods. One way of doing this is to write the word on one side of an index card and draw the symbol or image on the other.

Use poetry to improve vocabulary.   Irish poet Seamus Heaney says he was introduced to poetry through a text published to teach kids "comprehension lessons." He spoke of reading, for example, Blake's "The Tyger" and Andrew Marvell's "Bermudas," and said such lessons taught him to love not only poetry but language itself (Heaney 1990). A poem was read "not for its art life or its pleasure-giving qualities" but its "difficulty quotient," the idea being that so long as you were going to do the work of learning to read better, you might as well read things worth your attention. Poetry teaches us, among other things, about the elasticity of language and thereby helps improve our "language sense." Here is a sample of this vocabulary assignment:

> *Overview*. After reading the following poem by Phyllis Wheatley, please make notes about the italicized words or phrases; where necessary, please write down the definition from the dictionary; if you have a clear sense of the word's meaning, then write that in the space instead. At the bottom, please write your response to the poem, linking it to your studies in English and/or History.
>
> *Poet note*. Phyllis Wheatley is considered the first African American writer of importance in America. Her owner—she was a slave—set out to prove that blacks were as intelligent and able as whites if provided the same education. When she submitted her first poems as proof of her education, the most prominent men refused to believe she had written them until she wrote them again in their presence. American scholar Henry Louis Gates, Jr., credits Wheatley with launching not only the black American literary tradition but the black women's literary tradition.

On Being Brought from Africa to America (1773)

'Twas *mercy* brought me from my *pagan* land,
Taught my *benighted* soul to understand
That there's a God, that there's a Savior too:
Once I *redemption* neither sought nor knew.
Some view our *sable* race with *scornful* eye.
"Their color is a *diabolic dye*."
Remember, Christians, Negroes, black as Cain,
May be *refined*, and join the angelic train.

—PHYLLIS WHEATLEY

mercy

pagan

benighted

redemption

sable

scornful

diabolic

dye

refined

> *Part two*. Written analysis: Please explain what you think the poet is talking about in a paragraph of thoughtful, errorless prose. Be sure to support what you are saying with examples from the poem. Two questions might help get you going: what is she writing about (and why do you think that?) and what kind of a woman does she seem to be, based on what she says here (and why do you think that?)

Here is an example—from a different poem—of the kind of thoughtful analysis you can get from this assignment. In addition to having defined fifteen words in Langston Hughes' poem "Weary Blues," Fannie Chou paid close attention to word choice and usage:

> This poem is saying how the narrator rocking on his chair remembers what he heard the other night. It was down on Lenox Avenue by an old gas light that a black man was playing the weary blues. This poem basically talks about the melody that the black man is playing. You know that the melody was being played by a black man because of the lines in the poem, "With his ebony hands." The whole poem expresses a sad mood and this can be detected by the words such as *moan, melancholy, raggy, weary, blues*. The man was singing how there isn't anybody but yourself, and that he got the weary blues and he isn't happy, and wishes that he had died. After the singer finished the song he went to bed. The author said that "he slept like a rock or a man that's dead" which I think means that the man would wake the next morning and continue with life or that he died and would never wake. I think the poem itself is like a song of blues.

Challenge students in the context of the class.   When appropriate, e.g., on handouts, in discussion, when giving directions, use words that best describe your ideas but also challenge students. Make sure students understand the words, by questioning them about the terms' meanings. Example: The statement "I will now segue into the next method for developing vocabulary" presents the class with an opportunity to incorporate the word *segue* into their own vocabularies. Similarly, while reading or discussing a text in class, stop when it seems necessary to inquire about the use or meaning of a word. For example, while reading portions of Nathan McCall's memoir *Makes Me Want to Holler*, we encountered the word *surrogate* three times in one paragraph. I stopped and asked the class if they could understand what the author was talking about if they did not know what that word meant. "No," they said. We talked about the word in the context of a surrogate mother, an issue that was being discussed in the news at that time, then returned to reading the book. This was effective and natural, as it grew out of the class context. Don't go overboard, however, and define and discuss every other word in a book—this fragments the narrative and bores your students.

Make word clusters.   Give students a vocabulary cluster (also called word web, semantic mapping, and vocabulary mapping) similar to the one shown in Figure 5.1. The teacher provides root words or prefixes (e.g., *auto*) in the central boxes. Such words, by the way, are easily found in lists provided in books like *Writer's Inc*. Students are asked to provide the definitions of these words in the cloud-shaped space (e.g., self). Students next come up with words that use the root word or prefix (e.g., *autobiography*) and define them (e.g., the biography of a person written by that person). My students like these exercises: they create an awareness of the language around them while expanding their vocabulary. As freshman Chuck Schulz said, "I like this style of learning vocabulary for a lot of reasons. By doing it this way, I feel I learn not only the meaning of the new words but new prefixes. Also I find myself more interested in learning the words."

Create a dead word list.   Have students get out a paper they wrote. Write up all variations of the verb *to be* on the board: *am, is, are*, etc; then all contractions: *isn't, weren't, aren't, it's*, etc. They must then find all of these in their paper and rewrite the sentences as much as necessary to change them to strong, active verbs. As the year goes on, we add to the dead list: *to get, to have, to go, a lot, very*. On other occasions we hunt down and exorcise adjectives or adverbs, too, though the point is not to imply that students should never use these words. I tell them it is okay to use them, but to do so knowingly, sparingly, so as to make sure that each word adds something to the sentence. Keep the dead list up on the front wall as a reminder. I've heard of

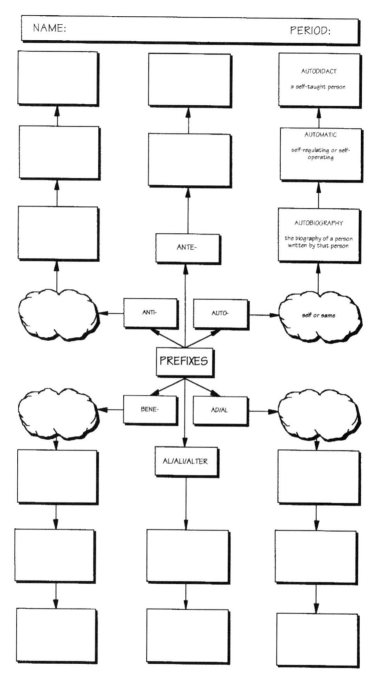

Figure 5.1 *Sample vocabulary word map*

teachers who draw a giant tombstone and write the words on this. Students find it frustrating but also fun: it challenges them to use more precise words and a wider range of words as well.

Play the dictionary game.   If you visit the ERIC Web site, you will find explicit directions for how to play this game as a class; it may also be enjoyed in small groups. A student looks up a word, then tells the group. Each group member writes down what they think it means in dictionary-like language. They pass their cards to the keeper of the dictionary for that round; this person shuffles the cards, then reads them all. Each student must vote for a definition. Points go to those who choose the right definition as well as to the one whose false definition was chosen. This is a great rainy-day activity. A commercial version of the game is also available by the name of Balderdash, though it has more "adult" words than you would want kids defining in your classroom.

Teach students how to read a dictionary entry.   Point out, for example, the word-history information. Good dictionaries, such as the *American Heritage* (third edition), also contain "usage notes" which examine the different meanings of words we commonly misuse.

Teach and use the vocabulary of particular disciplines.   Specific to each discipline—e.g., English, Biology, History, Health—is a vocabulary that allows everyone to use the same words to describe the same ideas. In English, for example, you need to instill in students a clear understanding of certain literary terms (see Appendix M for a list of essential literary terms) and grammatical terms to allow for effective discussion of stories and their writing.

Generate words for writing.   This works best with verbs, adjectives, or nouns. The focus is on descriptive writing. It is sometimes helpful to put up a picture on the overhead or show a clip from a video. Have students brainstorm—as a class—verbs to describe what they see; for example, I show them the opening five minutes of *Last of the Mohicans* in which the three men hunt a buck. We fill the board with words that describe what the buck did, what the hunters did, what happened; then I tell them to write descriptively using as many of these words as they can. We then read them aloud, discuss why a word works well, how it does or does not affect the reader's sense of what happened.

Keep a vocabulary log.   Students write down a specified number of words each week or grading period, and provide for each word the following: part of speech, sentence in which the word was used, dictionary definition, and a sentence you create, using the word correctly. The jury is still out on this method's effectiveness. One advantage of it is that each student is working with those words that seem important and unfamiliar to them; thus vocabulary work is individualized. On the other hand, there is little follow-up or accountability, since everyone has different words. It is, in the end, another option, one that can be used when it seems to fit the current assignment.

Construct words from parts.   Have students use the chart shown in Figure 5.2 to build words using one "piece" from each column. They then look up the word in the dictionary to check the accuracy and define the word. After some practice, more advanced students can create their own lists and offer these to the class.

Endnote: Reflecting on Vocabulary

The *Handbook of Research on Teaching the English Arts* (1991) suggests we need to do more research on vocabulary. Few things seem clear, though what researchers do know has instructional implications. As the strategies and activities listed above demonstrate, we use words to

PREFIXES	ROOTS	SUFFIXES	YOUR WORD
• in- • im- • con- • com- • pro- • per- • de- • pre- • re- • ex- • trans- • poly- • mono-	• dic • dict • voc • duc • duct • vert • vers • trac • tract • junc • junct • cep • cept • spec • spect • cred • jec • ject • scrib • script	• -ion • -ive • -ator • -ible • -able • -er • -or • -ation • -ment • -fy • -ed • -ing	• inscription

Figure 5.2

accomplish many tasks. Research done on short-term memory shows that such methods as mnemonic devices (e.g., "men's rears in museums") help students remember terms for such specific tests as they encounter in the classroom and during such examinations as the SAT. (Whether it is the English teacher's responsibility to prepare students for this test is a separate issue, one this chapter will not attempt to resolve.) Research further reveals that semantic mapping or analysis of words—which many of the activities listed above exemplify—yields the greatest improvement in the area of vocabulary development. Furthermore, these studies show that the direct inclusion of such vocabulary in the curriculum results in students learning more words than those who do not receive such instruction at all and in learning and understanding more words than those who simply receive a list of words they must memorize and recognize on a test. Only meaningful discussion and examination of words, which can include the construction or deconstruction of words, helps students to integrate these words into their existing knowledge structures (Mayher 1990).

Such knowledge about words and language grants students access to the larger world of ideas and power. We cannot really understand things for which we have no words. In a short essay titled "Language and Hope," Leon Botstein (1997) discussed this idea of language and culture, focusing on the commonly misused term *hopefully*. Botstein invites us to look at not only how the word is misused but why our culture consistently uses it as we do. He concludes that the evolving usage reflects the larger trend in our society to believe that we are not in control of our world. He recollects a time when people saw themselves in greater control of their destiny, when they would say "I hope," because they saw themselves as the ones who would make things happen; instead, today we say "hopefully," feeling somehow like outcomes are not our responsibility. Such ideas as Botstein raises would allow for meaningful discussion in any high school class and would (hopefully!) help students realize that language does, for many reasons and in many ways, matter.

REFLECTION

Are you supposed to prepare your students to take the SAT in your English class? In this instance, I am referring specifically to the development of vocabulary and analogies, both of which are key parts of the verbal portion of the SAT test. Explain why you should or should not prepare students for these portions in a letter addressed to a parent or a colleague; include both sides of the argument to better understand why people think as they do about this issue.

ACTIVITY

Find an SAT vocabulary computer program and test yourself on the vocabulary section. If that seems too boring to you, read any Cormac McCarthy novel and relish the sheer power of what language can do in the hands of a master.

RECOMMENDATION

I don't have a specific text to recommend. I have surveyed many different workbooks. Though many have some merit, I imagine schools use them so they can say what they do in the area of vocabulary, as opposed to what students know and can do. It is worth your time to go to a big book store, however, and survey the shelves of different vocabulary books. I have a copy of the Princeton Review's *Word Smart: Building an Educated Vocabulary*, which I use primarily to see what Princeton Review thinks kids should know, and to find word roots, suffixes, and prefixes for the clusters discussed above.

CHAPTER 6

PUTTING GRAMMAR IN ITS PLACE

When a thought takes one's breath away, a lesson on grammar seems an impertinence.

Thomas Wentworth Higginson, Preface to Emily Dickinson's *Poems*

It is grammar, first of all, that makes language possible, that allows us to articulate our thoughts, our selves, in utterances.

Oliver Sacks, *Seeing Voices: A Journey into the World of the Deaf*

Grammar stalks us all, teachers and students alike. Grammar—the ways words are used to shape meaning, voice, style—strikes a chord in everyone: some judge others by the measure of their correctness, while others judge people by the extent to which they judge others' correctness. When I told some people I was writing a book for English teachers, several suddenly exclaimed that if only I could get "those teachers" to teach kids how to use "proper English," I would be doing the country a great service. I certainly care about the country; I am also interested in students succeeding in life and being recognized as the intelligent, thoughtful individuals I know they are. I want their language to be appropriate to whatever situation they are in and something over which they can assert the necessary control, to be an instrument of their success, to be a source of pride.

Too many of us don't receive any training at all in the area of language prior to teaching. In her article "The Invisible Discrepancies in Teaching Language," professor Kyoko Sato (1998) found new teachers' lack of such knowledge compromised their ability to teach reading and writing effectively. My grammar and linguistics classes were some of the hardest I took in graduate school and I can't tell you I enjoyed them at the time; few lessons have left me better prepared to confront the complexity inherent in reading and writing. Some teachers question whether they need to know much about grammar if they are going to teach high school. We don't need to become obsessed with words and grammar, but language is our medium, it is the structural foundation of what we teach.

States throughout the country are drafting legislation for curriculum standards and frameworks that calls for a renewed emphasis on the teaching of grammar (or what is sometimes called "conventions") at all grade levels. This demand stems from a frustration in the workplace and college writing programs with students' lack of grammatical correctness, a problem that some believe derives from those teachers who say "grammar doesn't matter" when kids are writing, a remark we should never make. What we can tell our students, however, is that at the preliminary stage of their writing they need to concentrate on developing their ideas and that we can look at their grammar and conventions later when they revise and edit. Even this is not enough, however: if students aren't regularly held accountable for their correctness, it just won't seem important to them. Imagine a math class where it "doesn't matter if you get it right." (See Chapter 11 for an example of how to make conventions count without undermining students' confidence.)

Content Standards for Grammar

As in other chapters, I'd like to use an example here from the content standards from California to illustrate what the public expects of us in this area:

> *Grammar and Mechanics:*
> **1.1** Identify and correctly use clauses (e.g., main and subordinate); phrases (e.g., gerunds, infinitives, and participles); mechanics (e.g., semi-colons, ellipses, and hyphens); usage (e.g., tense consistency); and sentence structure (parallel structure, properly placed modifiers).
>
> *GRADES 11/12: Manuscript Form:*
> **1.1** Demonstrate control of grammar, paragraph and sentence structure, diction, and usage
> **1.2** Produce legible work that shows accurate spelling and correct use of the conventions of punctuation and capitalization
> **1.3** Reflect appropriate manuscript requirements in writing (California Academic Standards Commission 1998)

Vignette: Teaching Appositives

The argument has always been that knowing grammar does not improve your writing and thus its study serves no purpose. If, however, students learn elements of grammar in the context of expanding their options as writers, it has its place. It also has its place in the curriculum as a tool for thinking about relationships, patterns, and logic (e.g., predication and parallelism). What I offer here is a brief vignette of one approach—among the many that exist—that has proven successful in my own class. For this example, I will focus on appositives.

When my students come in, I tell them we will focus on how to make their writing more descriptive and their sentences stronger. After they sit down, I distribute the handout, turn off the lights, and flip on the overhead projector. Before reading the "Sunglasses/Altered" paragraph on the handout, I tell them to write down any questions they have or make notes (on the handout) about parts where, as a reader, they need more information.

Appositives: Sunglasses (Altered)

Back in the 1920s, John Macready should have been famous. He flew nonstop across the Atlantic Ocean (in a blimp) six years before Charles Lindbergh; and he approached Bausch & Lomb about developing lenses to block the sun. Bausch & Lomb responded by making Ray-Ban aviator sunglasses. But it took the stars of Hollywood to make sunglasses into an item of fashion. Hollywood stars wore them for one reason. A few years back the popular Ray-Bans lost out to Wayfarers. There remains one thing I cannot understand about people who wear sunglasses.

When everyone seems ready, I ask them what questions they have. Habib asks who John Macready is. Maria wants to know what the "one reason" is that the stars wore these sunglasses. Roushig inquires about the "one thing I cannot understand about people who wear sunglasses," wanting to know what this thing is, and why the writer left it out. Having established what the writing lacks, I tell them to turn the paper over and read the unaltered version. I tell them to underline or highlight any additions that have been made to the paragraph and to be prepared to explain what effect these have.

Appositives: Sunglasses (Unaltered)

Back in the 1920s, John Macready, an Army Air Corps lieutenant, should have been famous. He flew nonstop across the Atlantic Ocean (in a blimp) six years before Charles Lindbergh; and he approached Bausch & Lomb, the leading manufacturer of sunglasses, about developing lenses to block the sun. Bausch & Lomb responded by making Ray-Ban aviator sunglasses, the glasses made famous by General Douglas MacArthur. But it took the stars of Hollywood—Greta Garbo, Katharine Hepburn, Gary Cooper—to make sunglasses into an item of fashion. Hollywood stars wore them for one reason: to avoid having to look into the eyes of pestering fans. A few years back the popular Ray-Bans lost out to Wayfarers, the sunglasses made popular by Tom Cruise in the movie *Risky Business*. There remains one thing I cannot understand about people—mostly rock stars and actors—who wear sunglasses: why they wear them at night.

Within a few minutes we have established, through their own observations, that the "additions," as we are calling them for now, add more information about the things the text refers to, that they make the writing more specific, and that they all have some kind of similar pattern that the students can't quite describe yet. I then stand in front of Karina and announce that I am standing "opposite" Karina. When I move to her side—the class wondering what I am doing and Karina wishing I had picked on someone else—I say I am standing "in apposition to" her. Thus I help them to understand the concept of these "additions" by defining their function and, subsequently, their effect.

We end here, then move into the other work for the day. I send them home with the following short exercise for homework. When they return the next day, we will begin with this exercise as a way to assess their understanding of appositives. This information will also help me gauge where we need to go next in the sequence.

Homework: Appositives (1)

Directions: Using each example provided, write your own sentence in which you mirror the structure and appositive.

1. Stephane Gripelli, *a world famous jazz violinist*, began his music career as a piano player for silent movies in the 1920s.

2. Throughout college I considered trading in my bike, *a rusted old bomb with half a handlebar, no seat, and no breaks.*

3. As children, future drummers beat out sketchy rhythms on just about anything— *their mother's head, the cat, the coffee table, large pieces of fruit.*

4. The typical digital watch, _____ , is always being improved upon by engineers, _____ . They are invariably made of black rubber or plastic and perform a con-

stantly growing number of strange and interesting functions—_____ . The problem with digital watches is that they are usually worn by certain types of people—_____ [give at least three different kinds of people].

I start with a short fill-in exercise as a way to measure their ability to mimic what is already before them as a model. If they cannot do this, which requires little more than rewriting a reasonably easy pattern of words, I get a clear idea of what to do next (i.e., return to the previous day's lesson, and review and revise their understanding). This is the most concrete level of practice. We walk through their sentences, stopping to examine each volunteer's sentence with the simple questions "What is the appositive?" "What is it modifying?" and "How does that change the sentence?" Such small steps allow them to gain confidence and help them to see a sentence as a pattern to which they can add details in logical, beneficial ways.

If my teaching is really in the groove, this unit ties in with other work we are doing—an essay we are writing or a book we are reading—so as to make it that much more integrated. I don't have any specific week when I trot out our work on, for example, appositives; instead I look for the most effective time to do so and wait until then. If, for example, we are studying *Huckleberry Finn*, I borrow my examples for the punctuation discussion from Brent Staples's brilliant essay, "Just Walk on by: How Black Men Alter Public Space," which I found in *Harper's Magazine* some years ago and kept as a model of excellent writing. If we are reading Amy Tan's *Joy Luck Club*, we might use an essay Tan wrote about how bank tellers treat her Chinese-speaking mother.

We end that day's lesson on appositives and punctuation by going over the following sheet on the overhead. I do so because punctuation taught in context makes much more sense to students; they see how the comma functions and, if they don't, I can easily explain it to them.

Punctuating Appositives

1. The most common punctuation for appositives is the comma.

   Example: I came upon her late one evening on a deserted street in Hyde Park, *a relatively affluent neighborhood in an otherwise mean, impoverished section of Chicago.*

2. To set off appositives when the appositives have commas inside them, use a pair of dashes to *enclose* the appositive.

   Example: To her, the young black man—*a broad six feet two inches with a beard and billowing hair, both hands shoved into the pockets of a bulky military jacket*—seemed menacingly close.

3. You can also use the dash to give the information special emphasis by separating it from the rest of the sentence.

   Example: It was in the echo of that terrified woman's footfalls that I first began to know the unwieldy inheritance I'd come into—*the ability to alter public space in ugly ways.*

4. Although less frequently used—partly because it is so formal—the colon can also punctuate appositives.

   Example: And on late-evening constitutionals along streets less traveled by others, I employ what has proved to be an excellent tension-reducing measure: *I whistle melodies from Beethoven and Vivaldi and the more popular classical composers.*

When my students leave class that day, they take along what I call the "Popcorn" handout, which asks them to combine sentences to make appositives. This next step, construction, involves a deeper understanding of the appositive and makes things more complicated by involving a secondary task—sentence combining—which is difficult for some to grasp. We go over the examples and the first actual sentence to clear up any confusion.

Homework: Popcorn (Sentence Combining)

DIRECTIONS: Combine the following sentences using noun phrase appositives whenever you can, as in the following examples:

    a.   *Popcorn* was the result of an accident.

    b.   Popcorn is *a favorite snack for many Americans.*

Solution: Popcorn, *a favorite snack for many Americans*, was the result of an accident.

    a.   Compared to *other snacks*, popcorn gives you the most for your money.

    b.   *Cookies* are another snack.

    c.   *Ice cream* is another snack.

    d.   *Candy* is another snack.

Solution: Compared to other snacks—*cookies, ice cream, candy*—popcorn gives you the most for your money.

1.   **a.**   Orville Redenbacher started the vogue for gourmet popcorn back in the 1970s.
     b.   Orville is a real person.
     c.   The 1970s were a time during which many food fads began to appear.

2.   **a.**   Gourmet popcorn comes in a variety of flavors.
     b.   It comes in root beer.
     c.   It comes in nacho cheese.
     d.   It comes in watermelon.
     e.   It comes in piña colada.

3.   **a.**   Popcorn companies have strange terms for unpopped kernels.
     b.   They call them "old maids."
     c.   They call them "widows."
     d.   They call them "duds."

When students walk in the next day, the overhead displays the following examples taken from a range of books in other disciplines. I ask them to read these quotes and, while doing so, identify the appositives. This helps me to immediately assess my students' understanding of the subject. It also addresses the attitude that appositives and grammar are just "an English thing" and have nothing to do with anything else.

Anthropology. "In the Northeast corner of the Belgian Congo, almost exactly in the middle of the map of Africa . . . lies the Ituri Forest, a vast expanse of dense, damp, inhospitable darkness" (from Colin Turnbull's *The Forest People: A Study of the Pygmies of the Congo*).

Astronomy. "Welcome to the planet Earth—a place of blue nitrogen skies, oceans of liquid water, cool forests and soft meadows, a world positively rippling with life" (from Carl Sagan's *Cosmos*).

History. "On the same day, August 22, General de Langle was experiencing a commander's most agonizing moments—waiting for news from the front" (from Barbara Tuchman's *The Guns of August*).

Business. "Safeway Stores, the Oakland-based supermarket chain that has been stripping its assets like a latter-day Gypsy Rose Lee, may put on another performance by selling stock to the public within 18 months" (from the *San Francisco Chronicle* business section, September 29, 1988).

We take the first half of the class period to discuss each sentence on the "Popcorn" handout. I make this and other handouts myself in order to engage students' interest. I look for articles about strange or important subjects in the newspaper or magazines and use these as the basis for the assignment. One of my favorites was about people who eat bugs ("Edible Insects: Bugs Are a Good Source of Protein for Chicken Feed—or a Between-Meal Snack," *Christian Science Monitor*, October 18, 1986.) Another popular article was about people who eat dirt. Let's face it: American papers are filled with articles about how weird we are; you might as well use this stuff for your class. If the kids don't like appositives they will still pay attention to the strange story line of the boy who is half alligator and half human (according to the latest tabloid). There is a conjugation anyone would find interesting!

They have moved from the concrete, hand-held phase of imitation to the independent phase of recognizing most appositives when they see them. In the coming weeks I will have them search their writing for places where they could add such information. Or, when conferencing, we now have a shared vocabulary that allows me to say, when I see two or three sentences all chopped up but complete, "Why don't you turn that into an appositive and put it all together?" They know what I mean and know how to do it.

How to Improve Students' Grammar

When we are not doing such focused mini-units on modifiers—adjective clauses, absolutes, verbal phrases—we work with sentences and grammar in other ways.

Intuitive knowledge. I like to take time early on to have students play around with Lewis Carroll's poem "Jabberwocky" because its nonsense language reveals to my students that they do already have a profound understanding about grammar. You can ask them what "brillig" and "wabe" means (" 'Twas brillig, and the slithy toves/Did gyre and gimble in the wabe;/All mimsy were the borogoves,/And the mome raths outgrabe.") They might not know what it means, but they almost certainly understand how it works. This activity, along with unmagnetic poetry (see Chapter 4 for an example), awakens their natural understanding and quickly calms them of their fear that they know "nothing" about grammar.

Use student examples in context. When you are reading through a set of papers, keep a pad of paper nearby to jot down any choice examples of error or excellent use of verbs, for example, that you can use for further discussion in class. You might put these examples up on the overhead or make up a handout of "real" errors and excellent moments; however, it is also crucial that you not embarrass anyone by using their work in a way that could humiliate them. I know which students can withstand public scrutiny and who can't; if I'm not sure, I ask a student's permission ahead of time. Some teachers also mark up grammatical errors in the context of work, and then require students to return to the site of the error and make the correction right there. Some go so far as to require students to write down the rule there also. Having made these changes, the students can then resubmit their papers for re-evaluation.

Daily language workouts. There are several different publishers who put out books with sentences that need repair or revision. I prefer Don Killgallon's *Sentence Composing for High School*

(Boynton/Cook) and *Daily Language Workouts* (Write Source/Houghton-Mifflin) because I can copy a week's worth of sentences onto a transparency. My restless juniors settle right into this activity; I also find it fascinating to see who in my classes really wakes up to this activity. Let's face it: kids like to solve puzzles and problems so long as they feel the solution is within their reach. These exercises allow us to talk about how language works, sometimes giving us the chance to review what we've already learned or examine what we have yet to study. "What does a semicolon do anyway, Mr. Burke?" Vince asks, and I have a chance to quickly explain before we move on to the day's main course, though I promise him we will return to it in greater detail later. There are critics of this approach, and I certainly don't see it as the cornerstone to any effective study of grammar; however, most state tests will give students such sentences, and this is yet another way to prepare them without surrendering your entire curriculum.

Students' favorite songs.   Nothing means more to students than their music. One way to individualize grammar study is to allow them to bring in the lyrics of their favorite songs to examine them for such structures as parallelism and verbs. This activity has the added benefit of honoring their culture, something students appreciate.

Grammar and reading.   You can't discuss poetry without examining its use of language. That would be like examining someone's back without feeling their spine. And poems are so small they invite rereading for better understanding and close discussion of what the poet is trying to achieve and how they are achieving it. I will start class, for example, with a poem like Jimmy Santiago Baca's "Fall," a poem kids love and which can, by the way, inspire them to write wonderful poems from their own perspective or that of a literary character. Here is Baca's poem:

> Somber hue diffused on everything.
> Each creature, each emptied stalk,
> is richly bundled in mellow light.
> In that open unharvested field of my own life,
> I have fathered small joys and memories.
> My heart was once a lover's swing that creaked in wind
> of these calm fall days.
> Autumn chants my vision to sleep,
> and travels me back into a night
> when I could touch stars and believed in myself. . . .
>
> Along the way, grief broke me,
> my faith became hardened dirt
> walked over by too many people.
> My heart now, as I walk down this dirt road,
> on this calm fall day,
> is a dented
> tin bucket
> filled with fruits
> picked long ago.
> It's getting harder
> to lug the heavy bucket.
> I spill a memory on the ground,
> it gleams,
> rain on hot embers
> of yellow grass.

I ask my students, after they write their initial response to the poem, to find all the adjectives. Then I ask them to explain what these words do in the poem, what they have in common. This allows them to learn and reinforce what they know for some purpose which, if they like the poem, makes sense to them. They are not ripping the poem apart, an activity they generally resent (though which has its place), but looking at it more closely in order to appreciate how Baca affected them so deeply.

Sentence additions.   Some days I put up a simple sentence on the board (e.g., The car was on the street) and have them add information (e.g., The *red* car *sat* on the *busy* street) as they go. We will then define what that addition is by examining its function. "*Red* refers to the car and so it must be an adjective," someone will say. This is good to play with and can help you make use of those spare few minutes at the end of class. Build grotesquely ornate sentences as a means of having intelligent, productive fun.

Prewriting grammatical brainstorms.   If students are going to write about an excerpt from a film or a piece of art with which they are already familiar, have them first brainstorm parts of speech that they could use to do so. Organize words into columns: nouns, verbs, adjectives. Or, if you are focusing on some aspect of the language or their writing at that time, brainstorm instances of, for example, active verbs which, if used, would make for particularly powerful description.

Stylistics: Any close reading of a literary text or the style of a particularly well-written essay (like Brent Staples's example referred to above) demands careful analysis of how language is used to shape meaning and create voice. Sometimes I will have students go through and find all the verbs in a section; then they look for some kind of pattern of usage and speculate on how this pattern affects the text and reader. An example might be all the words that have anything to do with the color gray or stone in Gina Berriault's incredible story "The Stone Boy." The other example might be to read the prologue to *Romeo and Juliet* to find all the words that somehow relate to the idea of two, thus providing through the grammar and usage a structural coupling that mirrors that in the story. Other activities might include: rewriting certain sentences into or out of the passive voice to contrast the effect and examine the purpose of each; rewriting the same sentence several different ways using a range of informal to informal structures (e.g., *that* versus *which* or, in other circumstances, *whom*) to study how usage shapes tone.

Endnote: Reflecting on Grammar

The above lessons and exercises are intended to show you how you might teach grammatical concepts. They must be reinforced throughout the year, whenever it seems appropriate. As I said earlier, though there are many times when students should write without immediate concern for correctness, you should avoid such statements as "grammar doesn't matter for now," or "don't worry about your grammar," as these comments, while developmentally appropriate, undermine the truth that grammar—when we speak, when we read, when we write—does, in fact, matter. My primary hope is that my students develop a sound grammatical sense, an awareness through our different kinds of "word work," that will enable them to create the perfect text that is required of the final essay, the job application, or the condolence letter.

REFLECTION

The obvious topic here is your own attitude toward the subject. Discuss your own knowledge and experience with grammar and why you think or feel that.

ACTIVITY

Go on-line and visit the Grammar Lady (www.grammarlady.com) and see what her site offers, taking time to submit your own question (e.g., "Do you *always* have to put a comma before you use *also* or *too*?) if you have a question you can't find the answer to. When I visited it, the site had received nearly forty thousand hits. This is actually a slick little site that is carefully maintained and professionally designed.

RECOMMENDATIONS

I have several books to recommend for the different areas discussed in this chapter.

Practical

Sentence Composing for High School, Don Killgallon (Boynton/Cook 1998).

Reference

There are dozens of different books to choose from. I have settled on two for regular reference:

A Writer's Reference, Diane Hacker (Bedford 1997).

The Right Handbook: Grammar and Usage in Context, Pat Belanoff, Betsy Rorschach, and Mia Oberlink (Boynton/Cook 1993).

Hacker's book is as close to an industry standard as any book is likely to get; her indexing and clear examples make it consistently useful and easy to check for the quick answer. *The Right Handbook* offers a more reflective approach and gives teachers helpful ways to think about how to work with and understand grammar and usage in context. If you feel insecure about your understanding of the basics, check out *Woe Is I: The Grammarphobe's Guide to Better English in Plain English*, by Patricia T. O'Conner (Grossett/Putnam 1996) or Karen Elizabeth Gordon's mischievous *The Deluxe Transitive Vampire* (Pantheon Books 1993). Both books will help you learn while you laugh.

Theory

Teaching Grammar in Context, Constance Weaver (Heinemann 1996). *Lessons to Share*, Constance Weaver (Heinemann 1998).

Both of Weaver's books offer a wider perspective on grammar and practical suggestions to improve instruction in your class.

CHAPTER 7

TEACHING WRITING
FROM PRACTICE
TO PERFORMANCE

Writing gives you a discipline and that in itself is lifesaving. It is character-saving, which for me is the same thing. Very active writing creates character and a sense of will and orders your day. It forces you to find meaning, not only in your own life, but in your life among others. It gives you consciousness, basically. Other people find other ways of doing this, but for me, for one reason or another, it was writing.

—Tobias Wolff

I hate writing. I will do anything to avoid it. The only way I could write less was if I was dead.

—Fran Lebowitz

We are all apprentices in a craft where no one ever becomes a master.

—Ernest Hemingway

The Components of an Effective Writing Program

Writing is the heart of the English class. In one form or another it is constant: we are reading it, doing it, or preparing to do it. Writing invests students with an authority that challenges them to ask themselves, and express in language, what they know. Few things give me greater satisfaction than watching a student's voice and style grow and improve over the course of a year. This close attention to students' writing is what makes writing so important in my class: it is through our conversations about their writing, their ideas, even their lives that I come to know my students. These talks, which might take place in my class or in the margins of their papers, form a private space where my students and I meet to discuss their development as writers— and as individuals. It is here, in the drafts, notes, and clusters, that we watch our students compose their lives and try on different voices, as they cast off one draft after another of themselves, in search of the voice they will recognize as their own.

*Writing creates a personal space where students and teachers can talk about
what matters. Here Tony and Sevag share their writing with each other.*

Vanessa Veneziano, who was a freshman in my class the year she wrote the following letter, had this to say about what she wants from a writing teacher:

> I believe that there are two things that make a great teacher. One is teaching a person the technical
> aspects of writing, which most teachers almost always can accomplish. That is what they are
> trained to do at college. The second thing that makes certain teachers great is something that isn't
> taught. It is sending out a feeling of their own aspiration and love for writing in a way that their
> students pick up on. That is what you did for me. I am grateful for knowing that I had a teacher
> who cared and whose critiques I really even bothered to read. You can always tell when a student
> respects their teacher. You always commented and thanked me for sharing my "real" views on
> things in my writing and I was glad to do it. The reason I did it was because I had the self-
> assurance that you would be able to grasp what I felt. It wasn't so much that I thought you would
> understand it more than anyone else, I just felt that I could unburden myself in any particular as-
> signment without having to think twice about what I wrote. I was aware that you had a heavy load
> this year and that is what made it even better. I have had so many teachers in the past with not
> even half the load that you carried and they still only seemed to write down their comments in
> point value. Every time I got comments back from you (good or bad) I was glad to even get them.
> I also noticed when you would verbally give feedback, I listened and really appreciated it. That is
> why I hold you in such high esteem as a person and as a teacher. I am grateful for having had you,
> and I want to thank you for your time and passing on your dedication in helping me become a bet-
> ter writer. Many thanks.
>
> Sincerely,
> Vanessa Veneziano

Writing is exciting because it's productive and creative; it's where "the rubber hits the
road." You can't write and not think. There are no Cliffs Notes for writing. Written expression is
one of our primary means of reflecting on what we think and what we know. We use it to get
the class started or bring it to a close. We use it to assess and to explore. As Vanessa's comments
show, though, it is a very personal medium, one that causes in some kids profound stress and in
others sheer disappointment when, despite their long hours, their paper earns a C+ or they sim-

ply feel misunderstood (see Chapter 25 and subsequent strategies in this chapter for more help on these issues).

Which brings us quickly to the catch-22 of teaching writing: the paperwork. Once we begin talking about writing, we start thinking about what students should write, how much paper students should fill with writing, how often we should read their work, and what we should do when we read it. We wonder how best to work with student papers given the number of students we have and our inevitable time constraints. I certainly have those days, like everyone, when I wonder how I will get through all the papers on my desk. Somehow I find the personal aspect of the work, my relationship with the student writer, transcends any feelings of drudgery, especially if I am able to work through their papers in conference, in person. Perhaps it calls to mind childhood memories of my father holding the nail while I learned to use the hammer, that close, familiar space in which he taught me to do things I eventually learned to do on my own.

My purpose in this chapter is to provide an overview of what we should include in our writing curriculum and then look at how we can do that. I made the decision to include writing in response to literature in this chapter, as opposed to working it into the reading chapter, because I wanted to emphasize the connection between these two—and the other—aspects of the curriculum. I cannot possibly address all the different aspects of writing here, so I will look at those most common to our classes, providing where I can those strategies I have found most effective.

A brief survey of the research on writing suggests that any successful writing program includes the following:

- opportunities to write and the time necessary to work through the process of thinking and, ultimately, writing
- focus on syntax (including sentence combining, examination of common errors, and Francis Christensen's rhetoric)
- focus on the developmental sequence (moving from personal to analytical writing, from thesis to logical arguments)
- use of small-group techniques (peer criticism, writing for real audiences within the classroom, reading aloud in small groups)
- ongoing use of assessment (holistic evaluation, systematic school-wide assessment) to improve student performance
- an active role for students, minimal teacher dominance, and natural emergence of writing out of other activities
- delayed or "as needed" instruction in grammar
- modeling (e.g., teachers write with students) to provide subsequent examples of the assignment if they are needed to help students see what was expected
- nonthreatening evaluation of student writing that focuses on first establishing fluency before correctness (Holbrook 1984)

Performance Standards for Writing

In addition to these components, the following performance standards describe what some consider an effective writing curriculum. Once again, the sample performance standards come from the New Standards document. I prefer to use these standards because they were developed with a national audience in mind and have also been used to shape numerous states' standards. Thus, whether you agree with them or not, they are representative of what some people think a writing program should include.

a) The student produces a report that:
- engages the reader by establishing a context, creating a persona, and otherwise developing reader interest;
- develops a controlling idea that conveys a perspective on the subject;
- creates an organizing structure appropriate to purpose, audience, and context;
- includes appropriate facts and details;
- excludes extraneous and inappropriate information;
- uses a range of appropriate strategies, such as providing facts and details, describing or analyzing the subject, narrating a relevant anecdote, comparing and contrasting, naming, explaining benefits or limitations, demonstrating claims or assertions, and providing a scenario to illustrate;
- provides a sense of closure to the writing.

b) The student produces a response to literature that:
- engages the reader through establishing a context, creating a persona, and otherwise developing reader interest;
- advances a judgment that is interpretive, analytic, evaluative, or reflective;
- supports a judgment through references to the text, references to other works, authors, or nonprint media, or references to personal knowledge;
- demonstrates understanding of the literary work through suggesting an interpretation;
- anticipates and answers a reader's questions;
- recognizes possible ambiguities, nuances, and complexities;
- provides a sense of closure to the writing.

c) The student produces a narrative account (fictional or autobiographical) that:
- engages the reader by establishing a context, creating a point of view, and otherwise developing reader interest;
- establishes a situation, plot, point of view, setting, and conflict (and for autobiography, the significance of events and of conclusions that can be drawn from those events);
- creates an organized structure;
- includes sensory details and concrete language to develop plot and character;
- excludes extraneous details and inconsistencies;
- develops complex characters;
- uses a range of appropriate strategies, such as dialogue, tension or suspense, naming, pacing, and specific narrative action, e.g., movement, gestures, expressions;
- provides a sense of closure to the writing.

d) The student produces a narrative procedure (e.g., a set of instructions or rules) that:
- engages the reader by establishing a context, creating a persona, and otherwise developing reader interest;

- provides a guide to action for a complicated procedure in order to anticipate a reader's needs; creates expectations through predictable structures, e.g., headings; and provides smooth transitions between steps;
- makes use of appropriate writing strategies, such as creating a visual hierarchy and using white space and graphics as appropriate;
- includes relevant information;
- excludes extraneous information;
- anticipates problems, mistakes, and misunderstandings that night arise for the reader;
- provides a sense of closure to the writing.

e) The student produces a persuasive essay that:
- engages the reader by establishing a context, creating a persona, and otherwise developing reader interest;
- develops a controlling idea that makes a clear and knowledgeable judgment;
- creates an organizing structure that is appropriate to the needs, values, and interests of a specified audience, and arranges details, reasons, examples, and anecdotes effectively and persuasively;
- includes appropriate information and arguments;
- excludes information and arguments that are irrelevant;
- anticipates and addresses reader concerns and counter-arguments;
- supports arguments with detailed evidence, citing sources of information as appropriate;
- uses a range of strategies to elaborate and persuade, such as definitions, descriptions, illustrations, examples of evidence, and anecdotes;
- provides a sense of closure to the writing.

f) The student produces a reflective essay that:
- engages the reader by establishing a context, cresting a persona, and otherwise developing reader interest;
- analyzes a condition of situation or significance;
- develops a commonplace, concrete occasion as the basis for the reflection, e.g., personal observation or experience;
- creates an organizing structure appropriate to purpose and audience;
- uses a variety of writing strategies, such as concrete details, comparing and contrasting, naming, describing, creating a scenario;
- provides a sense of closure to the writing.

The Writing Product: The Process of Working with Words

Figure 7.1 illustrates one of the central aspects of the writing process: the choices we face as teachers and writers at every stage of writing. It also emphasizes what some have a hard time accepting: *process is a product*. However, another point not so easily conceded by some process practitioners is that product is the result and the final measure of the quality of any process. Though the arrows in the diagram suggest a somewhat linear progression through the different

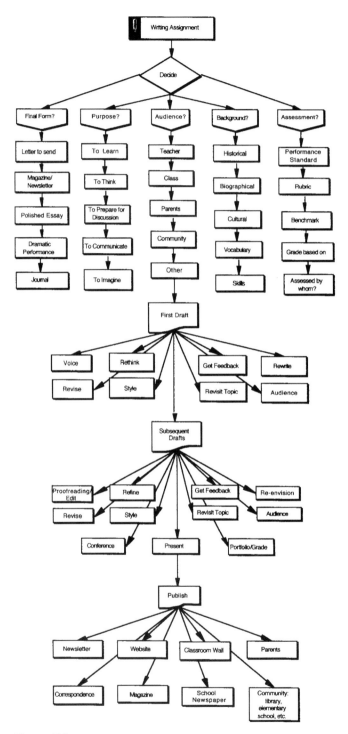

Figure 7.1

stages of composing, I experience (and teach) writing as a wave that is constantly falling back on itself to gather greater force; this process of recursion takes into consideration both the surface structure (i.e., grammar, predication, tense) and deep structure (i.e., ideas, guiding metaphors, meaning) that are both essential to coherent writing.

If this diagram of the writing process captures the dynamic nature of that process, there exists at its core a set of common elements. Good writing is built word by word, sentence by sentence, each comma thunked down as sure as the bent nail it resembles. Here, then, is a more concise approach to the process of writing, which I adapted from the principles of sound construction in *The Carpenter's Manifesto* (Ehrlich and Mannheimer 1990). This text outlines six stages for any building project, each of which directly relates to any writing assignment:

- beginning
- visualizing
- gathering
- constructing
- finishing
- presenting

Beginning

The beginning phase includes recognizing or creating the need to write about some subject that the writer may or may not have chosen to write about. The writer begins to make crucial initial decisions, such as what form the writing will take (essay, poem, dramatic monologue) and which voice or style best suits their purpose. They determine the scale of the project: Is it just a short exercise to get them thinking or is it the beginning of a much larger effort? As with all written work, these decisions can be changed at any time in response to the evolving nature of a particular piece of writing.

Visualizing

When I build furniture, I first establish the needs and the parameters of my project; once having done this, however, I must begin to visualize what I want the piece to look like. Writers need to do the same: as a writer, instead of going to furniture stores or looking through catalogs for ideas about cabinet design, I get out books and see how other writers solved the problems I now face. This is where exemplars, ideally created by other students, make all the difference. For example, the exemplars of children's books based on myths (see Figure 7.2) allow students to visualize what I am asking them to do when I assign them such a project. These samples help students see not only *what* I want them to do, but *how* they can solve the problems presented by the assignment. Exemplars often inspire students to take the assignment to the next level now that they have a starting point. They demystify the act of writing by helping students see not only that it *can* be done, but *how*. Otherwise many students will believe, as they do with math, that writing is something you either can or cannot do.

You will find many ways to get kids thinking independently in Chapter 9, but here are several strategies you can use to help your students "visualize" the subject:

- "quick writes" or other journal techniques (see Ralph Fletcher's *Breathing in, Breathing Out*)
- clustering (see Gabriele Lusser Rico's *Writing the Natural Way*)

Figure 7.2

- listing or outlining
- talking (see Douglas Barnes's *From Communication to Curriculum*)
- questioning (see the chapter "Metaphors for Priming the Pump" in Peter Elbow's *Writing with Power*)
- imagining

Gathering

During this stage you gather ideas and evidence to help give shape to and provide support for your writing. When building, I start this part of the process by gathering and organizing all the wood and other materials I will need prior to actually picking up the hammer and nails so as to be ready once I begin building. The only difference between building and writing here is that I never hit my thumb or lose fingernails when I write. A few examples of what gathering might include in the writing process are:

- reading a range of books
- interviewing different people
- surveying the Internet for relevant information

Constructing

Obviously there comes a point when you've done your thinking and it's time to start writing. This phase of the process can go on as long as it needs to. It may involve false starts or failed attempts, though each failure inevitably helps you find your way toward the version that works. For me, such failures typically involve writing an entire draft of an essay, then realizing that my conclusion should be my introduction. This requires that I throw everything else out and start over, but this time with a much clearer idea of what I want to say. This last idea—revision as creation—is crucial to improving writing (Hillocks 1995; Lane 1993; Willis 1993), if for no other reason than that it expands the writer's options. Such revelations about their writing, however, can only come to students through recursive writing—circling back around to reflect on what they already wrote and thought—and the opportunity for sustained thinking about what they are writing. Four quick steps for your students to consider here are:

- reread the opening
- read the conclusion
- narrow or reaffirm the focus and revise/rewrite as necessary
- have others—peers or teachers—read the work or a piece of it

Finishing

Just as the table or cabinet I make needs to get sanded down, oiled or lacquered, and polished to perfection, we have to "finish" each piece of writing. Not all writing, however, needs all the aesthetic touches; much of the writing students do is a means of thinking in order to better understand what they are studying. This is the stage when, through conferences and peer-response groups, writers work to satisfy the particular requirements of the assignment. If the assignment calls for perfect prose with no errors, students do what they must to achieve this end. If, on the other hand, the assignment calls merely for personal reflection, then the process is brought to a close. It is this stage that obsesses so many people in the writing profession and society at large. Tom Romano (1987) writes, "Our profession has become synonymous with fastidiousness. And I don't like it. Spelling, usage, grammar, punctuation—editing skills—are part of a piece of writing, along with organization, diction, clarity, voice, style, and quality of information." Romano continues, arguing that, "Mastery of editing skills will not ensure the production of high-quality writing. I've read too many samples of writing from government officials, lawyers, and school and hospital administrators that were wordy, pompous, vague, mealy-mouthed, and perfectly edited." Several helpful questions at this stage of the process include:

- What does "finished" mean for this specific piece of writing?
- What do you (i.e., student or teacher) need to do to accomplish that?
- How will you (i.e., student or teacher) know when you have accomplished this (i.e., it is finished)?

Presenting

This final stage of the writing process involves the debut of the work to its intended audience. This might mean presenting it to the class by means of an overhead projector, or displaying it on the wall of the classroom. Our writing takes on many forms and serves many different functions, all of them "real" and, we hope, meaningful to the writer in that context. Many different avenues exist for publishing and celebrating students' writing these days—more than ever before, in fact. I've put my kids' work onto our classroom Web site, on the walls of the city's and our school's library, and in the class newsletter that goes home to all parents. We've also published books and pamphlets that went out into the wider world. Those children's books my freshmen made (Figure 7.2), adaptations of folktales and myths, were circulated among different elementary schools. The principal of the first school they went to liked them so much, she took them home to read to her own children; she later wrote my students a letter telling them how much she admired their work. A community resource directory my remedial senior class made was distributed throughout the community. A grant my students wrote earned several thousand dollars from local organizations. And students' letters to authors, experts, and the United Nations have received wonderful responses over the years. I almost forgot to mention that sometimes I just collect those papers when they are done, read them, and return them to my students.

Henry and Chuck performing their finished script for the class as part of the "presentation" phase of the writing process

Error as an Invitation to Improve

When I first taught seniors, I was amazed by the sudden fervor for precision and excellence in the writing of those applying to universities. Their college application essays underwent merciless scrutiny; they knew that perfection mattered. I watched students revise their essays six or seven times, coming back the next day, their eyes shining with the hope that I would say, "It's done. Send it off now." Often I found yet more flaws that I felt they should have detected and fixed without coming to me for guidance (see Appendix B for more about college essays). At some point it occurred to me that these students were, for the first time, working as real writers.

Some teachers resist focusing on errors for fear that such criticism will diminish students' self-esteem. Some teachers have even been taught not to use the word *error*, to talk only about what the student did well. Taken to the extreme, however, such "teaching" is no longer a "process," since a process involves stages and changes throughout. When I set out to master tennis as a thirteen-year-old, I played for as many hours as the day was long. I got better, but I did not get good until my parents hired a coach, a thin, humble man named Dave Harris. Only then did I improve my ability to play and to think, developing what we then referred to as "court sense." This progress was the result of demonstration sessions during which Dave pointed out to me my errors. Later on, when subsequent coaches began using video technology to provide me with immediate feedback, I knew what it meant to work toward mastery. For those who would argue against the idea of mastery, who say that "students cannot achieve it and so it sets them up for failure," I would ask them how we achieve esteem and maintain it if not by attaining elusive goals through hard work. When I ripped a winning backhand down the line to win my first tournament, I knew it was the result of hard work and good teaching. Such experiences also taught me that I could learn anything, a lesson that became very important years later when, after nearly failing to graduate from high school, I enrolled in college and eventually became an English teacher.

The writing process, when used without clearly defined purposes, has sometimes been translated to mean "The only thing that matters is that students write all the time." Unfortunately, most teachers are not trained to teach writing; many therefore just have their kids write with minimal purpose, often reverting to such models as the five-paragraph essay. It was certainly never the intention of those early advocates of the writing process that students be turned loose like this. This laissez-faire approach—and meaningless writing assignments—has, in some classes, resulted in lazy thinking and a shortage of students who can effectively support their thinking. It is precisely this lack of structure in students' thinking and subsequent writing that leads me to see expository writing—which includes but is not limited to the essay—as the centerpiece of the writing curriculum. Expository writing provides the best opportunity to directly teach the most important foundations of good writing: the development of coherence, logic, and ideas within the structural confines of the paragraph and the essay while supporting with evidence those claims that writers wish to make.

　　Don't misunderstand me: I do not see the essay as some orthodox, proper noun, as a tradition I am sworn to uphold. Instead, I prefer Paul Heilker's (1996) conception of the essay as a verb, the activity of moving around in and through (among other actions) a subject that we want to better understand in all its complexity.

Teachable Moments During a Writer's Development

In the course of the writing process, moments arise when we should stop and teach our student writers what they next need to know. What this may be is impossible to say, since it depends entirely on the stage of the writers' development and the particular assignment. There are also different ways to deliver any particular instruction, one of which is the minilesson, a short informative talk designed to get the kids focused on the task at hand. Another option is a more sustained focus on the particular writing lesson, a lesson that might take a day or two before the class returns to the primary assignment (e.g., story, essay, research paper).

　　Some of these crucial moments are structured within my class. This is possible, for example, in my freshman class because my students' study of India in their History class provides me a ripe opportunity to teach them how to compare and contrast ideas within the context of their study of the caste system. Such lessons provide another way to integrate your class with others. Some opportunities to teach arise spontaneously, deriving from a sudden sense that nearly everyone in the class is just not getting the idea of transitions, for example, as evidenced by their last paper. So I call for a pit stop and we focus for a day or so on this idea before returning to their writing.

　　I provide examples of these types of writing lessons in the following section. The paragraph unit is very structured; I tend to get to it early in the year because I see the paragraph as the primary unit of thought. By this I mean that the paragraph is a distinct unit, with one idea, and everything within that paragraph ideally works to develop this main idea. Thus I try very hard not to toss the word *paragraph* around loosely, as in "just write about a paragraph on that," since this gives the idea that a paragraph is more about length than focus and structure. Nor do I railroad them into one narrowly conceived idea of the paragraph. I try instead to establish and build upon the idea of a paragraph as an idea that needs cohesion but also needs to support the larger idea of which it is a part (i.e., the thesis, the main idea in the essay). My objective with the paragraph then is less focused on the paragraph itself; the goal is to develop disciplined, logical minds that use certain guiding, habitual questions to drive their writing: What is the main idea? What are the different aspects of this idea? What examples can I use to clarify this idea? Why are these good examples? Who? What? Why? And my favorite: So what?

Sample Unit: Teaching the Paragraph

First, whenever I talk about the paragraph, I query the class for fun: How many sentences are in a paragraph? Five! Seven! Eight! I ask them what other teachers taught them and listen to a range of explanations about what a paragraph is and what it does. I don't speak against their former teachers; my goal here is to get us talking about the subject and establish what they do and don't know about it. Also, I point out to them that we are talking about paragraphs in general, not specific types like conclusions or introductions. The following three exercises build on each other in carefully planned ways. The first, "The Interior Logic of the Paragraph," is always done in a group so that students can talk about and, ultimately, complete the assignment successfully. Successful completion is essential because it demystifies the subject, by tapping into their intuitive or natural knowledge. In other words, the lesson begins by establishing that they do know something about this topic already.

The Interior Logic of the Paragraph

Directions: Paragraphs A, B, and C have been scrambled, but each set of sentences makes up a complete paragraph. Your group must reach agreement about how the sentences should be ordered. You must also be able to explain why you think each sentence goes in the order that it does. This can best be done by asking yourself, "What is the relationship of this sentence to the one before it?" Put the number 1 next to what you think should be the first sentence; then number the rest sequentially after that. (If you have time, there is some benefit to having students write out each paragraph in full.)

A) _____ Their songs typically open up with elegant sacred voices chanting in what sound like medieval cathedrals.

_____ Then a steady hip-hop beat begins to weave into the choral sounds, creating a haunting music that makes you want to pray and dance at the same time.

_____ Some music just cannot be categorized.

_____ The band Enigma is a classic example of this dilemma.

_____ Finally, just when you expect some lush American voice to rise up through the chorus, a man's voice soars above all others, singing in French, or Arabic, or even English.

B) _____ My roommate's opera music was turned up so loud I could hear it in the elevator on the way up to meet him.

_____ By far the strangest of them all, however, was a girl named Lana who dyed her hair a different color every day until it fell out.

_____ Olaf, the Swiss exchange student, seemed only to live on chocolate and Coke, and owned only the clothes he wore.

_____ I also noticed at least five pizza boxes stacked on *my* bed, two of which had been there so long mold had begun to grow inside them.

_____ The next wake-up call came when I went to the dining hall for the first time.

_____ Despite the fact that it was September, they were serving something called "Spring Stew."

_____ While I waited for them to serve me, I noticed a box against the wall that said "low-grade beef—edible" on it.

_____ The last surprise of the day was the realization that everyone on my floor was strange in one way or another.

_____ Nothing prepared me for the strange and unpleasant discoveries I made when I first moved into my college dorm.

_____ Lance, a brawny surfer, earned extra money by betting people he could rip their phone books in half.

_____ By the end of the first week, no one on the whole floor had a phone book.

_____ First, I knew I would have roommate trouble before even walking into the room.

_____Then she began to ask her roommate, who was an artist, to draw faces on the back of her bald head so it looked like she was always walking backwards.

C) _____ They have a particular fondness for dirt found near the coast of Florida, which has a very bitter, salty flavor to it.

_____ They relish the dark clay-like variety that some compare to a rich fudge.

_____ They look long and far for soil found only in remote parts of Georgia, and which has a reddish color to it and smells of raspberries.

_____ People who eat dirt appreciate a wide variety of different characteristics of this unique food.

_____ They like dirt taken from the lower Sierras where the pine nuts fall and settle into the earth to give the earth an added treat of nuts, which some compare to a Snickers bar.

Paragraph Development: Lunchtime!

This exercise builds on what students now know about paragraphing, but allows them to begin working individually. We study a "malnourished" paragraph; I ask students to reflect on what information it lacks. We do this first on the overhead. After brainstorming different ideas about how to develop the paragraph, we look at the fleshed-out version. Both are provided in the following handout.

Directions. Write a paragraph, modeled on the second one in this exercise, in which you argue either for or against eating at the school cafeteria or a particular restaurant. Have fun with it!

I.   Eating at the Castro Valley cafeteria appeals to me much more than dining at any of the nearby establishments. I can eat with friends and do not have to drive to get there. I also hate waiting in line at restaurants. Castro Valley High's cafeteria is much quicker. Also, I used to work in restaurants and know what they do to their food.

II. Eating at the Castro Valley cafeteria appeals to me much more than dining at any of the nearby establishments. At Castro Valley I can eat with friends, enjoying a nice conversation because I do not have to drive to Zeke's or Taco Bell. The meals are more expensive at those restaurants, also. Another reason I detest going to those restaurants is that I always spend the first thirty minutes of my forty-five-minute lunch hour standing in line for my food. Invariably I end up shoveling the stuff into my mouth while I quickly drive back to campus. Castro Valley High's cafeteria is much quicker and I don't have to worry about running any students over while I eat. When I was in college, I worked at Sammy's Garden Cafe and saw what they did to their food. One time I accidentally poured a large bucket of coffee grounds into the plastic garbage can in which they made salads. When I told him, the manager said, "Oh, just stir it in. No one will notice." At school, I can see everything they do back there and be sure that if I have coffee grounds with my meal they will be in my cup, not in my salad.

Paragraph Exercise: I'm Organized—What Are You?

After giving the students a sample essay in which I describe in exaggerated terms how organized I am (so that they can laugh at me), I have them write their own paragraph that begins "I am _____." They must fill in the blank with an adjective (which inevitably returns us for a moment to a refresher of what these are) that describes some aspect of themselves. They can certainly fictionalize, and can also begin, "I am not _____" if they prefer. We concentrate here on those aspects of paragraphing that will become our mantra for the year: focus, organization, and development. This also allows me to create a vocabulary of practice, so that if I have only a minute when reading or talking with them about a paper, I can write "Focus" next to a paragraph and they will know what to do.

Instead of including the example I wrote for them—do you really want to know how organized I am?—I will include two examples of student paragraphs I copied and used the next day in class as exemplars. Typically, I copy such examples to transparencies and put them up on the overhead as a way to focus our discussion and to recognize students' success.

Sergio Franco, who was repeating junior English in my class, wrote:

> I am unique. I am the last one out of my friends who is holding a paper and pencil, learning and getting my education. I am the only one of my friends putting money in the bank, knowing I will receive it later in life. Some of my friends are probably holding a cell bar which is what they have been doing for years and they probably have many more to go. Others are probably working full time for a low salary, waiting to get off work so they can feed their children or satisfy their needs for drugs and alcohol. Then they sit at home and bitch about society putting them down. They're the ones who chose the path in life. I always tried to help them out. I tried to tell them to do good. But they would just laugh. Now with the help of God, I will get to be somebody. I'm unique because I believe in me.

Angela Brosche, a student in the same class, wrote about her world, which is pretty different from Sergio's:

> I am traditional. I'm the kind of person who doesn't like change. Every Christmas the trees must go in the same place. I will spend my whole night hanging ornaments while listening to Christmas music and a fire in the fireplace. For Halloween we must have lots of pumpkins, but they must come from the Half Moon Bay pumpkin farm—not anywhere else. When mom and I decorate for holidays, we must have hot coffee and cocoa to sip on and a fireplace going. Grandma's on Thanksgiving must have her *homemade* pumpkin pie, not bought. It makes Thanksgiving most special! Lake Tahoe trips are definitely not the same without John Denver playing "Rocky Mountain High" in the car, or you don't get the feeling of Tahoe's fresh air and beautiful mountains the way Johnny sings it. Most of all, Grandma's house on Christmas Eve. Baking cookies and window watching for Santa while the soft tunes of "White Christmas" and more play on the old stereo. There is nothing better than a great tradition.

Both of these paragraphs have certain surface errors that warrant attention, but not in this context: this is a lesson about paragraphing, a concept that both students have shown they understand very well. If, later on, they were to further develop these paragraphs into essays, then we could work out those grammatical kinks. When we teach new material, we must remember that people can only juggle so many new concepts at any one time without dropping them all. Sergio's and Angela's paragraphs invite two very different worlds and voices into the classroom, honoring them both while allowing paragraphs to teach much more than just paragraphing. No one in class can miss the invitation to reflect on how different our worlds often are from each other. Thus even the writing lesson can, at its best, be about life.

Sample Activities

The paragraph sequence addresses one aspect of the writing curriculum. Other assignments sometimes require specific skills if students are to do them well. I offer the following examples, which are models of how to meet certain needs of your student writers; using these examples, I hope you will create your own.

Getting Specific: Activities That Lead to Precise Writing

A famous writer I know said once that adjectives are evidence that you did not choose your noun carefully enough. Without precision in writing, the reader is lost. More importantly, writing that is not specific fails to accomplish what it was invented for: to communicate. You and your students can use the following activities to help you both think and write more specifically. Your readers will thank you and, more importantly, understand you.

Find and replace.   Take any piece of your writing—a poem, dramatic monologue, essay—and read through it, highlighting or circling every noun you used. Now go back through and revise general nouns into specific nouns—as many as you can manage. Find all instances where you use *thing* or *something*, for example, and replace with specific word(s). After you finish, consider trading papers with another student, who will then further revise or recommend specific words for you to replace.

Sensory details.   Read your paper through one more time and add one more detail (color, size, shape, number, type) to bring the image into better focus in the reader's mind.

Description.   In *The Writer's Workout Book: 113 Stretches Toward Better Prose*, Art Peterson (1996, 106) writes, "Writers with style never just eat breakfast. They munch on granola, wolf down hotcakes, savor Frosted Flakes, or gorge on jelly doughnuts." Take any one of the following subjects and bring all of your descriptive abilities to bear on it, focusing on using specific words, especially nouns, to capture the subject.

- cafeteria food
- the school locker room
- your bedroom
- a scene from a favorite movie
- your last class on the last day before winter break or summer vacation
- a _____ store (e.g., a pet store)

Dictionary.   Often we use words without thinking about what they actually mean; we let their meaning drift from the specific definition of the word. Take the following words or types of people and, using specific words, describe them in vivid detail, focusing on concrete nouns to evoke their essence.

slacker	skeptic	techie
sibling	sycophant	dangerous
bully	diligent	arrogant
leader	mellow	lunatic
boring	indifferent	shy

Police report.   Often police ask witnesses of a crime to re-create in exact detail what they saw. Look for opportunities in class or around school to have students write about. Examples: when the substitute lost control; your first-period class; gym class on a rainy day; a fight that many saw; what happened in class that day.

This last activity was invaluable one year in helping to establish the "truth" about what happened in an unusually difficult sixth-period class. Returning from a conference, I found several pages of comments from the sub narrating what had taken place in my absence. The kids, however, emphatically disputed the sub's analysis. I immediately turned it into an observational (a.k.a. "police report") assignment that yielded some of the best writing of the entire year. Here is part of Lynette's report:

> Yesterday the sub came in and everyone was talking as usual. Before I went to my desk, I drew a little face on the board, then I proceeded to my desk. A couple of minutes passed by and I guess Mr. D—— noticed the picture on the board. He was then "stressed" because the eraser wasn't working and there had been a previous erase made above the face. So Mikey volunteered to go get some toilet paper like Mr. D—— had suggested. Personally I thought the situation was becoming bigger than it should have been so I went up and erased the face with the sleeve of my sweatshirt. So in my head I'm thinking "See! It's not that big of a deal" but I still ended up staining my sweatshirt. Mr. D—— then came over and said, "Oh you're so sweet. You didn't have to do that." Mikey then came back with the toilet paper which he used to clean the spot where the face had been plus the smudge above it which the faulty eraser had caused. A lot of people started talking after he had given us the directions so he then asked how many had finished reading the packet. After we raised our hands, Mr. D—— asked us if we would rather take a nap for fifteen minutes. We then had a vote for who wanted to nap, read, or stand at attention (yes, like the army does). Obviously the nap won.

Observational Writing: One Approach

Lynette's "police report" offers a compelling example of one writing skill that always has room for improvement: observation. Whether students are writing an "observational" essay or doing a lab report for their biology class, they need to be able to see the world around them and translate that world into words that are both accurate and interesting. The following assignment, which involves students viewing a scene, preferably from a film, was used to improve freshman students' observational skills in preparation for an essay, but also as part of a larger unit that included reading William Golding's *Lord of the Flies*.

Overview

The ability to observe is essential in our lives for so many reasons. As parents, we need to be able to look carefully at our own kids to see that they are learning and doing what they should as they grow up. As workers, we need to watch those around us to better learn our job or to help others do their work better. As students, you must learn to observe how the world around you works so as to succeed in it and better understand it. This assignment is designed to help you not only make observations but draw insight from them into your subject.

Step One

Watch the film, taking notes about specific actions that seem important to the story and that also reveal significant aspects of the peoples' character. Take these notes on a separate sheet of paper, dividing them into different categories such as "Actions," "Events," "Gestures/Voice," and "Other Notes." These distinctions will help you better organize and analyze your thoughts when you write later. Remember also that observations are, by definition, based on what you see; you are not to speculate about what characters are thinking but only report what they do. *NOTE.* If you are not watching a film, but are instead observing something else—a class, a school event, a person at work, your friends—adapt these ideas as it seems appropriate.

Step Two

After watching the film, go back through your list and highlight or somehow mark those observations you feel are particularly important to discuss.

Step Three

Having identified those events or actions you feel are essential, begin making notes about why they are important. Your writing here should answer such questions as: What does it mean that _____ did _____? Why do I think it means that? Why did _____ do this? Why do I think that?

Step Four

Look over your notes and observations and come up with some conclusion about this person or situation (e.g., if writing about *Lord of the Flies*, you could say "People act differently in groups than they do when alone"). Now that you have begun to analyze your observations and provide some support for these analyses, it is time to give them a shape. Look for those observations that cluster around a person, and could be used as a character analysis of that person, for example. Another example of a main idea might be, "Things are not always as they seem."

Step Five

Return to your notes in step three and, using these as the basis for your paper, write your observations into a rough draft. During the writing of this draft, pay extra attention to the importance of description, doing your best to use active verbs and specific nouns that help the reader to see what it is you observed.

Step Six

Conference with me for suggestions on further revision.

Step Seven

Revise as directed and turn in.

Forms and Functions: Writing in Our Lives, at School, and in the Workplace

In the course of a day, we write for a range of purposes, some of them more consequential than others. In Chapter 4 we examined the different types of reading we do (what I called "have to, get to, need to"). The following list (Figure 7.3) includes as many forms of writing as I could think of; while I don't think we are supposed to directly teach all of these forms, students need to know about them, to learn them when appropriate, and to practice them when possible.

The Essay

I like essays, I'll admit it. Not the old dusty formal ones, but the modern, lively ones that have made them worthy of books like Robert Atwan's annual *The Best American Essays*. The essay has enjoyed a popular renaissance. We see personal and reflective essays, often not too long, in most magazines and newspapers. They have voice and style. And because they are written for the general public and often in response to current events, they serve as excellent examples for our students.

The essay remains central to our writing curriculum for other, more practical reasons. Colleges weigh student essays heavily when evaluating their applications. (See Appendix B for further information about writing college essays.) Many districts use essays to determine

Advertisements	Letters/E-mail	Scientific reports
Affidavits	Memos	Scripts
Applications	Observations	Speeches
Captions	Plays	Stories
Commentaries	Poems	Summaries
Complaints	Proposals	Tables/Charts
Directions	Requests	Technical reports
Editorials	Responses	Websites
Essays	Responses to literature	Grants
Evaluations	Résumés	Brochures
Interviews	Reviews	Minutes
Journals	Rules	Newsletters

Figure 7.3   *The different types of writing we do and read*

whether students have satisfied the district's writing competency test, a requirement for graduating. Exams such as the AP test demand that students write a range of different essays, most of them focusing on argument and analysis. An increasing number of states are administering performance-based assessments that require students to write essays. And finally, some jobs require their applicants to write an essay as part of the interview process. I learned about this only after a former student of mine applied to be a firefighter; the first step in the application process, he later told me, was to write an essay about how to solve a certain set of problems that existed among the fire station personnel.

The five-paragraph essay is *not* what I have in mind when I refer to essays here. Such essays have a pattern we are all familiar with: an introduction delineating the three main points the essay will explore, followed by one paragraph about each idea, and a typically very weak conclusion restating the introduction. Some teachers find that this model provides an entrée into teaching the more complicated aspects of writing essays; if it works for them, that's fine. Such formulaic writing otherwise suffocates real thought, reducing the essay to an exercise instead of raising it to a thoughtful examination of a substantial idea. Students prepared only to write a five-paragraph essay often suffer for it. For instance, incoming freshmen at San Francisco State University who, on their writing placement test, write a five-paragraph essay just barely qualified for entry into the required freshman composition class—but only if the quality of their content compensated for their essay's form.

Rhetorical Modes

The different rhetorical modes of the essay (see Figure 7.4) don't interest me as much as the different ways they teach students to think. My district divides these up across the four years, linking our district writing competency to them. So freshmen, for example, are expected to be able to write either an autobiographical incident or observational essay by April, when the test is delivered. While each of these rhetorical modes requires specific traits in the essay, the writer in me says I use most of these different modes in the course of any good essay. I might be making observations about characters which I must then analyze; this analysis might spark in me some personal connection which I then narrate in my essay to emphasize the point and make it more interesting. So I tend not to teach the modes as discrete units except when I know my students will be assessed according to their ability to write a reflective essay, for example, with precision and based on a rubric with which I am already familiar.

Teaching the Literary Analysis Essay

One type of essay that is specific to our curriculum and can prove difficult for both students and teachers is the literary analysis essay. I've found the following approach helpful, and students

California Assessment Program Categories

AUTOBIOGRAPHIC
- Focus on a single incident--a moment, a few hours, no more than a day; also give reader a sense of what this meant to you personally
- Recreate the experience by using vivid sensory details, scene description, dialogue, action, internal thoughts, personal commentary, explanations
- Use essay format--beginning, middle, end.

OBSERVATION
- Focus on the topic: a specific place to describe
- Imagine that you are a reporter and a camera person all in one
- Recreate the scene by using vivid sensory details, names of people and places, action, dialogue, personal observations
- Give the reader a sense of movement and perspective--in and out of the scene, move around, a sense of the writer's attitude toward the observation as expressed through the choice of language and detail
- Have an organization--beginning, middle, end

INTERPRETATION
- Take a stand (i.e., have a clear thesis) and support it
- Give good reasons, examples, "for instance," factual information, experiences that support
- Organize into clear paragraphs; topic sentences
- Provide logical supports--don't stray from the topic
- Conclude with both summary and an extension of your ideas

EVALUATION
- Take a clear stand--for or against the issue to evaluate
- Establish criteria for evaluating--these are the points by which you judge something to be good or bad, right or wrong, pleasant or unpleasant. They may be stated directly at the beginning and then used throughout, or they may be scattered throughout the essay as you argue your points
- Use specific examples and details to support your arguments. These may be taken from your own or others' experiences or from what you have read or seen or heard.
- Begin essay with your position--**thesis**--statement in the introduction. Organize all subsequent paragraphs logically into main points to develop your thesis.
- Conclude with summary and a good recommendation that fits your thesis.

REFLECTION
- See the instructions for the AUTOBIOGRAPHICAL ESSAY. This essay is similar but more sophisticated.
- Use the technique of recreating an incident but raise your commentary and observation to a philosophical, universal level. How does this incident reflect a truth about life in general or about something universal to human experience? As you develop your paragraphs, you will want to include commentary that is more reflective about the meaning of events.

CONTROVERSIAL ISSUE
- Take a side on the issue given. Argue either for or against.
- Write an introduction that does what you have been taught: hook the reader, give background material, present a clear arguable thesis.
- Organize your main arguments into logical paragraphs with clear topic sentences.
- Support your arguments with specific examples and details drawn from your own or friends' or family's experiences. Don't worry about having to use precise statistics, but do not use logical well known "facts."
- Use counter arguments: these are points that someone on the other side would use and that you "demolish" with your own arguments.
- Write a conclusion that pulls together your main ideas and provides perspective and a recommendation.

Source: California Department of Education (California Assessment Program)

Traditional College Rhetorical Modes

NARRATIVE
- answers the question "What happened and when?"
- emphasis on chronological order of events; use of transitional words helps such events to flow smoothly from one to the next.
- point of view is important as it shapes the voice, tone, and purpose of the story.
- mood is of fundamental importance as it directs the reader's response: is this a fond memory of a loved one or an angry account of an event that left a lasting scar?

DEFINITION
- answers the question "What is it?"
- attempts to explain an important word or concept to the reader
- uses negation to also clarify what the word does *not* mean
- might focus on the origins of the word as a means of establishing its meaning

DIVISION/CLASSIFICATION
- answers the question "What kind is it?" or "What are its parts?"
- arranges information into categories in order to establish and articulate the relationships between items in each category
- categories should be distinct to avoid confusion
- exemplary essay, "Friends, Good Friends--and Such Good Friends," by Judith Viorst

PROCESS ANALYSIS
- answers the question "How did it happen?"
- two choices: how *to do* something or how something *was done*
- establish who your audience is so you know what must be carefully explained
- uses other modes such as narration to explain the process

CAUSE AND EFFECT
- answers the question "Why did it happen?
- carefully examines what happened and why
- clear, logical writing is crucial in order to be effective
- descriptive writing helps illustrate the relationship between the cause and the effect

ARGUMENTATION/PERSUASION
- answers the question "Why should I want to do or think that?"
- the thesis is especially important as this is what your essay will convince the reader to think or do
- logic is crucial so as to make argument effective
- you must anticipate the counterarguments and address them in your essay
- *Argument* focuses on the logical appeal
- *Persuasion* focuses on the emotional appeal

COMPARISON/CONTRAST
- answers the question "What is it (not) like?
- in *comparison* the similarities are carefully established and developed
- in *contrast*, the differences between the two elements or sides are emphasized
- you must clearly establish early on the basis of the comparison so as to provide a context for all that follows it

EXAMPLE/ILLUSTRATION
- answers the question "For example?"
- clarity depends on concrete, vivid examples that reveal the concept being discussed or the position advocated
- active verbs will help the reader by showing them exactly what this subject does
- exemplary essay: Nikki Giovanni's "My Own Style," in which she illustrates her way of living by describing specific objects and explaining how they exemplify her lifestyle

Figure 7.4 *The different types of essays students write, otherwise known as rhetorical modes*

generally appreciate the structure it provides. As with the other exercises I've included (e.g., paragraphing, using appositives), this one is based on the idea of developmental stages. Simply put, I create the sentences that students will begin each paragraph with. I admit to and apologize for the artificiality of the exercise right up front. The following example, which includes three paragraphs with the required sentences underlined, compares *Nectar in a Sieve* by Kamala

Markandaya and the movie *City of Joy*. I should point out that I tend to use this approach only with freshmen or those in later grades who have no idea how to approach such a paper.

The structured nature of the assignment allows me to teach the essay's component parts to my class of literary novitiates. It allows them to go home and find examples from Markandaya's book that illustrate the "need for change" that their assigned topic sentence introduces. Such assignments also allow for further work on writing paragraphs that are well-developed, focused, and organized to support their main ideas. The example provided below is my own—i.e., I did the assignment along with them to use in our subsequent discussions.

> The modern world is defined by its need for change. We want to change who we are, where we live, what we do. Nothing satisfies us, for as the poet Rainer Maria Rilke wrote, "staying is nowhere." Ours is a restless generation no matter where we live. This is largely because we all live in an increasingly small world where everyone knows everyone's business. The poor man in India sees through television what the rich man in Texas has, and as a result he is changed. Having seen the other side, where the grass promises to be always greener, he cannot go back to what he had and be content. Now he must devote his life and change his values to get what he suddenly feels he needs. Thus we become an increasingly impatient world where we want it better, faster, cheaper; never mind that in the wake of these changes one finds a terrible trail of broken traditions, abandoned people, suffering countries. We ask if it is worth it but have no time to hear the answer. We are committed to the necessity, the value of change. Our one true faith has become: change is good.
>
> Certainly some changes are for the better. Medical technology has brought with it innumerable advances that not only save lives but improve the quality of those lives. In the movie *City of Joy*, for instance, the American doctor changes the lives of those poor people he meets through his medical clinic. The clinic itself is a symbol of that change: the will, the organization, the love that went into creating that dream helped to change the way people saw themselves and their world. And such clinics offer new opportunities to those with ambitions to serve their communities. In the novel *Nectar in the Sieve*, Kenny, an English doctor, recruits a young man from the village to serve as his assistant in the new clinic; this opens up an opportunity for the young man to change his whole life, to lift himself above the constraints that caste would otherwise place upon him.
>
> Yet it is precisely such changes as these that undermine and threaten the structure of the society. The initiative and responsibility for such change comes from outside of the community. Such change is thus sown in shallow soil, and is unlikely to survive the harsh winter of adversity and reality. If change is to succeed it must come from within, be internalized by the people who would then implement it. The people in the *City of Joy* fear change because they can only understand it as long as "Doctor Max" is there to explain it to them and to help them carry it out. Once he is gone, as many of them point out, the Indian people will be left to fend for themselves. We return then to the familiar truth that change is dangerous and inspires at least as much fear as it does progress.

The Group Essay

The group paper does not fall into any specific type of writing assignment, but can be done as an essay. Obviously students need to develop their own ability as writers; there are occasions, however, when people work together to create a single paper. This realization occurred to me when I was hired by a school to write a grant for them and, on a later occasion, when our own school had to write its accreditation report. The format is quite simple: a group is assigned a topic to work with, to have a conversation about; the final product of that conversation—or at least one option—is a paper composed by the group. The format of such papers also exemplifies what I discuss elsewhere as the ideal assignment: creating the Declaration of Independence or the Constitution. How groups solve this particular writing problem is up to them: the group can do the thinking, while one takes notes to be used by yet another student who is "the writer" (as was the case with the Declaration). That is how it works when people ask me to write grants for them: I sit and listen, knowing my part of the process is to take their ideas and the requirements

Scott, Taylor, and DJ during the "gathering" phase of their group essay for Huckleberry Finn

of the grant, and translate them into effective prose. Another option allows for the group to break up the assignment into parts. Each person, after and while the group talks, writes their piece, which the group then assembles and together revises for correctness.

Sample group topic: The *Huckleberry Finn* rationale. Near the end of our study of *Huckleberry Finn*, I sometimes give students the following assignment, which they must do as a group. Groups, in this case, provide further opportunity to discuss complicated issues in different contexts (i.e., not just as a class). As I link the assignment to real-world events, it also provides a clear lesson in the politics of literacy by showing them that words (e.g., Mark Twain's) do matter and that theirs can too (to the extent that they are able to articulate their argument).

Assignment: *Huckleberry Finn* Rationale

Overview

This week a group of parents formally demanded that Mark Twain's *Adventures of Huckleberry Finn* be barred from the classroom at Burlingame High School. This group, comprised of parents and community members of different races—among whom are included both whites and blacks—based their argument on several assertions:

- The book perpetuates outdated and unjust stereotypes of African Americans through its depiction of Jim and the use of the word *nigger* upwards of two hundred times.
- There are other books that can be read to understand the nature of that period of our history, which are written from a more balanced cultural-historical perspective.
- The last portion of the book is considered by such respected, award-winning authors as Jane Smiley to be flawed writing, which ultimately undermines the novel's literary merit.
- The book, due to many of the reasons listed above, and the fact that some classes at Burlingame have no African American students to lend their voice to the discussion, harms those who read it because of its "racist aspects" and thereby harms the society as a whole.

Assignment

Your group must write a one-page defense of the book *Huckleberry Finn* in which you explain why it should be read and kept as part of the curriculum. It is appropriate to include in your writing why the book and our discussion of it was personally meaningful to you. You should, in the end, explain what you got out of our reading and discussions in class over the course of the last six weeks. You may not agree with the position that it should be read; I respect your right to that opinion, and you will have ample opportunity to share your views in class tomorrow when we present these papers. My rationale for insisting that everyone argue in defense of the book is based on the belief that it is always helpful to try to understand people who think differently than you do. Please remember our previous study of persuasive writing and how important it is, for example, to acknowledge the arguments of those who disagree with you as a way of respecting their views while emphasizing yours by contrast. Your paper, by the way, is due at the end of the period tomorrow and should include all notes and drafts.

"The Five Principles of an Essay"

Fed up with the different conceptions of the essay—what it is and is not—a group of respected English teachers in my district (John Christgau, Norm Smith, Bob Chambers, John Field, Art Fisher, and Dick Fleming of Crestmore High School near San Francisco) began a conversation over lunch in the early 1970s. Their dialogue led to the development of the following principles. While the "five principles" are themselves valuable, at least as important is the example they present of professional conversations about what, why, and how we teach what we do. Such dialogues achieve what "canned" or "off-the-shelf" materials cannot: a sense of pride, local buy-in, greater cohesion within the department or school, and enhanced professional credibility. I include "The Five Principles of an Essay" here as a model of brevity and coherence, but also as an invitation to begin your own local conversations in your department about writing, poetry, grammar. I have also created a one-page worksheet for students to use to evaluate their own or other students' essays according to these five principles (see Appendix C).

1. Thesis

An essay should have a thesis. What is a thesis? It is the main idea of the essay. It should be an idea you believe in. The point of writing the essay is to explain your thesis and then prove it. In doing so, you will be offering the reader your own opinions and values. Your essay will have a thesis if you prove something, argue something, or present a personal opinion. This is the key: you should be *personally committed* to your subject.

The subject should be something you are willing to stand up for. Repeating a few stale clichés or obvious truths such as, "Life is rough" or "Skiing is fun" will not pass for personal commitment of any depth. Without commitment your essay will not have a strong thesis. Also, your essay will not have personal commitment if you merely repeat an opinion you heard somebody else give. That is no more than rumor or gossip.

An essay which has only description in it will lack a thesis. It is possible to describe the colors and shapes of the room you are in without ever giving much of an opinion about it. Of course, the ability to describe something clearly is important, but in high school you will be expected to go beyond that. For instance, an essay describing the color and accessories of a new Buick would lack a thesis because it would not reflect a personal commitment. Furthermore, essays entitled "The Trip I Took to Yosemite," or "My Vacation," or

"The Plot in Steinbeck's *Of Mice and Men*" are all forms of describing a Buick. Essays written on these subjects will probably lack judgment, personal commitment, and finally, a thesis. On the other hand, if in your essay you set out to prove that the Buick is the finest American-made automobile, you will be delivering an opinion and your essay will have a thesis.

We encourage you to tackle essay subjects far more complicated than simply judging Buicks. You will be asked to give your opinion about such things as political and social issues, characters in books and movies, philosophies, historical events, and controversial ideas.

2. Focus

The second principle of a good essay is focus. Before you start writing, ask yourself, "What is my *specific* thesis? What exactly do I want to prove?" The opinion you deliver must be on a specific subject, and once you choose it, then stick to that subject. You are encouraged to title your essays, using restrictive titles rather than vague and general phrases which lack focus.

In order to keep "in focus" it might help to think of your essay as if you were writing it with a movie camera lens which zooms in on a subject, enlarging whatever is in the center of a scene so that details and features can be seen sharply and clearly. Likewise, think of an essay which lacks focus as being written with a wide-angle lens, where things in the background or on the outer edge of an argument appear to be just as important as ideas in the center of your theme. For example, you should avoid broad titles like "Death" or simply "*Of Mice and Men.*" These titles are too wide and too general and they do not demand that you concentrate on a narrow, central, specific subject.

However, titles such as "Mercy Killing Is Wrong" or "Why George Was Justified in Killing Lennie" (if you were writing about characters in Steinbeck's novel *Of Mice and Men*) would be both narrow and in focus.

3. Concreteness

If you support your thesis with facts and examples, your essay will have concreteness. However, without concreteness your essay will be just pie in the sky—opinions dreamt up on the spur of the moment. For instance, if you state in your essay that two characters in a book have a lot in common, and then you fail to explain *what in specific* they have in common, your essay will lack concreteness.

A good essay needs facts and information to provide concreteness. When a teacher writes "Prove it!" in the margin of your essay, he's asking you to support your generalization with details. Any opinion delivered without the force of evidence is not likely to be very persuasive. Evidence can be in the form of quotes from some other source, or personal incidents from your life. Whether the information takes the form of cold statistics or personal anecdotes, your teacher will want to know where your opinions come from.

If you are having trouble with concreteness, it might help you to imagine that the reader of your essay is a juror. This juror has to make a decision about the case being presented in your essay. Vague statements won't do much to persuade the juror. He'll want facts, information, and evidence. He'll also want to know that the thesis being presented has been thoughtfully and carefully arrived at. It has to be much more than just a vague idea which crossed your mind immediately before you sat down to write, or, worse still, *while* you were writing. An opinion arrived at on the spur of the moment will usually lack supporting evidence and facts.

Again, one warning: you should be careful you don't provide only concreteness in your essay. Facts, with no conclusions drawn from them, are not enough. That is an essay without a thesis. Book reports and research papers are not essays, because they are *all* information, with no thesis. The teacher will want to see that the facts and specifics in your essay work toward some conclusion.

4. Organization

We have now explained three of the necessary ingredients of an essay. Putting these ingredients together successfully is called "organization."

Making an outline before you begin writing can be an indispensable tool for organizing your material. How do you outline? Begin by putting your thesis into a simple sentence such as, "The American government should ban nuclear power." Then under this sentence list three reasons why your thesis is correct. Beneath each reason give at least two concrete examples, facts, statistics, or true life experiences to support your reasons.

Once you have completed your outline you may begin writing the introductory paragraph of your essay. The introduction should contain your thesis statement and briefly mention each of the reasons which support it. In addition to supplying this basic information, your teacher will explain additional information which may be included in your introductory paragraph.

In organizing the body of your essay, keep this in mind: present your information in a clear sequence. If you get out of sequence, you will confuse the reader. For example, if someone were to count out loud, "One, two, three, five, four . . ." we would immediately recognize the illogical sequence.

Clearly organized paragraphs will go from one fact and example to another, explaining how they are related. Each sentence will clearly lead to the next, and transitional words and phrases such as *also, however, therefore,* and *in contrast* are helpful devices to use.

Just as transitional devices are used to connect facts and examples within each paragraph, they should also be used to link paragraphs. In this way you will develop an orderly progression through the essay from your introduction, to your facts and examples in the body paragraphs, and finally to your conclusion.

5 . Mechanics

An essay must have correct grammar, spelling, and punctuation. Once you have mastered correct mechanics, you will be expected to concentrate on developing a mature vocabulary and varied, smooth sentence structures.

Our goal as English teachers is to help you develop your skills as an essayist in each of the five categories we previously explained. We do not expect to make you a professional writer or a journalist. Rather, by working hard to master the five principles of good essay writing, you will develop personal and intellectual characteristics which will serve you well no matter what you choose to do in life. You will develop the ability to state clearly and logically those things you believe in and are personally committed to, and consequently you will learn to have *confidence* in your ideas. In taking the time to write with concreteness, you will learn qualities of *patience* and *perseverance*, because no lazy or hasty argument will hold water. Focusing on a specific issue will help you learn how to *concentrate*, because a mind that can't concentrate is no better than a muscle that can't flex. And finally, you will learn how to be *logical* and *organized* in your thoughts.

The Journal: Practice Makes Writers

The journal is an essential tool for my students. It is the petri dish of the mind. Journals allow students to write more, on a daily basis, because I do not have to worry about collecting the papers and responding to them. They also provide my students with a space where they can take risks, think differently and, at times, write more honestly than they could if their thinking was public. The journal also allows a record of their thinking, a sort of road map that charts where they've been and where they are as thinkers, students, and writers. In his foreword to Toby Fulwiler's *The Journal Book*, Ken Macrorie (1987) writes: "The conclusion of most of the teachers and students using them is that [journals] get people thinking, they help them test their own experience against the ideas of many others—the authorities they're studying, their teachers, their fellow students. As they become more and more engaged, they often write more clearly, and their journal entries display fewer mistakes in spelling, punctuation, and grammar, although the teachers have taken pains to let them know that they will not be graded on these mechanics of writing. For the majority of these students, journals are *yes* places."

Several traits distinguish effective journals in the English class:

- They promote fluency of thinking and writing, and thus are *never* graded based on conventions.
- They are used for a variety of purposes but most commonly as a place to think about a subject to be discussed, a text you are studying, or aspects of your own life.
- They promote, indeed even require, experimentation as a means of learning to write or think in new ways without the fear of judgment.

High school kids often lack room and opportunity to think about all that their lives are asking them to consider. Such questions as who they are, where they are going, and what they think about the world around them demand time and space. People call these journals different names—daybooks, think pads, notebooks; Anne Frank actually named her diary ("Kitty") so that she could feel like she was talking to someone. I've had students who addressed their entries to me, each one beginning, "Dear Mr. Burke." I did not ask them to do this, nor did I mind it, so long as it helped them. As it happened, I tended to develop very close relationships with these students, who, through addressing me personally, formed a more intimate connection to me by drawing me into conversation with them. When I asked students what benefit writing in the journal offered, they replied:

> I think writing every day in our journal gives us a better understanding of what we are listening to. If we hear somebody reading a book to us and we have to write after it, it will make us think about what we are writing about. Being able to listen to something then write it out in our own words is helpful.
>
> —Aaron Grossman

> I enjoy writing in a journal because it helps me pour out my feelings or mood swings or whatever and clears out my brain for new things. It makes my self-esteem higher because I see that I can write stories and there are never any red marks or wrong issues in a journal. Everything is up to you and no one can put you down. You can put your ideas down in your journal . . . well you know where I'm coming from. Writing in journals frees your mind.
>
> —Andrea Wong

Writing in a journal helps me a lot. Well, there are some things that I want to say but sometimes I feel that if I say them I'll get in trouble with students or they will look at me with a weird look in their face so in that way the journal helps me. It also helps me with things we do in class, like in class I don't talk that much about class work but when it gets to be time to write in our journals about class work, I do it with no problem at all.

—WERNER RAMIREZ

Student Journals and Liability

The personal nature of student journals raises what is a real concern for some teachers: fear of liability or accusations of violating students' privacy. (See Chapter 21 for more information about English teachers and the law.) You must be very clear about the purposes of the journal in your class and about the parameters of the writing. I write the following advisory on my journal introduction sheet and go over it in class:

> *A Note About Confidentiality:* I encourage you to take risks in your journal writing: write in ways you have not before, and do not worry about spelling and punctuation and grammar in here. Be willing to be honest in your thinking or emotions when you write. I am not saying you should tell me all your deepest darkest secrets. Nor am I telling you to refrain from writing about personal subjects (if you feel the need to do that). But you must realize that the law requires me (and I would want to anyway) to report anyone who tells me that someone is hurting them, they are hurting themselves, or they are harming others.

I tell students that if they write about hurting themselves or others, if they write about doing things that are against the law, I am required to report this and that I will assume they are asking me for help by including it. In ten years I have had incidents that required attention, and I wonder what would have happened if these students lacked the opportunity to communicate that information. Students themselves seem grateful for the journal.

When to Write

My students come into class every day knowing they will have to write. Some days they find a transparency of a painting or photograph on the overhead and know they will be asked to focus on descriptive writing. We might use the journal to brainstorm words they could use to write about the picture before them. On other days they sit down to a poem (which might be on an overhead and which is always read aloud, sometimes by me, sometimes by a student, sometimes by the author, if I have a recording). I ask students to respond to or use the text as a springboard to their own thinking. Still other days we begin class with me reading from a book that serves as a complement to our required curriculum. *The House on Mango Street* by Sandra Cisneros or *Makes Me Want to Holler* by Nathan McCall are ideal for this, as they are broken up into small sections. Also, because a book like McCall's has controversial sections that would prevent it from being a part of the school curriculum, I can read selectively. Ultimately, however, students write everything in their journal in the course of a year: letters, clusters, poems, essays, stories, and so on.

Students don't just write in their journals at the beginning of class; they use them regularly for homework, including in them their responses to reading, early drafts of ideas or papers, clusters, and so on. As Ralph Fletcher writes in his excellent book *Breathing In, Breathing Out: Keeping a Writer's Notebook* (1996), "the notebook serves as a container for selected insights, lines, images, ideas, dreams, and fragments of talk gathered from the world around you. In this way it gets you into the habit of paying closer attention to your world." *Breathing In* suggests that the notebook is a fine place from which to take what you have collected and use it to spark your original writing. It is Fletcher's reference to "paying closer attention" that intrigues me

A group of freshmen using their journals to settle into English and prepare for the day's work

when it comes to the journal. Psychologist Mihaly Csikszentmihalyi (1996) describes attention as a "limited resource" of which we must learn to make the most. Poetry is defined by William Stafford as a way of paying attention to things in a certain way.

What to Write

I feel like I am getting my students into the deep terrain of important ideas when I get them to pay attention to ideas, words, events. Over the summer, for example, the newspaper carried an article about the crisis a high school junior caused her school when she refused to say the Pledge of Allegiance. If school was in session, I would have brought that article in the next day and had students first read the article then write about it. In a related example, we took time one year to define what the word *freedom* means if looked at from different perspectives; thus we used the journal to define not just a word, but to reflect on a very complicated concept central to our culture. Here is what Charlotte Perry, then a junior, wrote in her journal:

> Freedom to me is the right to do what you want. It's to be the way you choose, the way no one else can tell you to be. Freedom is to have choices and the right to choose. I'm glad for my freedom, though I think everyone needs to be told things now and then. For instance, my mom gives me a lot of freedom, but reasonably. She has some limits. Without limits we'd be in a lot of trouble with money, life, relationships, etc. I think everyone needs freedom, but never too much.

Charlotte then spontaneously shifted into a different mode of thinking in her journal entry, using a cluster to continue to make distinctions about the different aspects of freedom (see Figure 7.5).

What else can we have students do in their journals? I will address using journals to respond to reading later in this chapter. Following is a list of some other ways for students to use their journals (see Chapter 9 for more), both in the class and at home:

- make lists (of words, ideas, characters)
- draw (images, scenes, clusters)

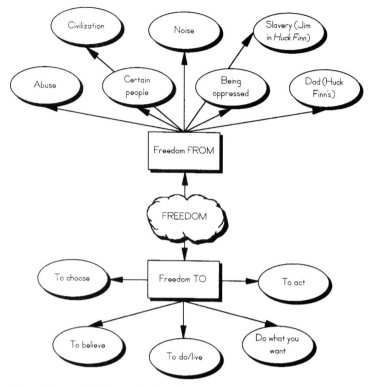

Figure 7.5   *Charlotte's "freedom" brainstorm*

- include quotes (from the radio, books, friends)
- write poems
- write early drafts
- write sketches (from life, art, books)
- incorporate lyrics (their own or others)
- ask questions (of themselves, the teacher, characters)
- make observations (about life, people, books)

Modeling: Keeping a Teacher's Journal

It is not always appropriate to turn students loose on the white open plains of their journal pages; sometimes they need guidance in how to think so that they can learn how to do it better. When we say, "Get out your journal and think about this poem a bit and see what you have to say about it," we are casting students out onto the waters without an oar unless we have, at some point, shown them how to begin such thinking.

I encourage and allow a wide range of responses to images, ideas, and texts in the journal. I keep my own in-class journal handy so that I can write whenever possible. This modeling helps establish a routine and the thinking space we need within the class as the year progresses. Here is an example of one of my entries about Rudolfo Anaya's novel *Bless Me, Ultima*:

What is a book like *Bless Me, Ultima* about? Is it about witchcraft and black magic? Native spiritualism and mystical practices that use indigenous herbs to both heal and hurt? Is it about being a Latino in the Southwest? A Chicano in the United States? A boy who sees what adults cannot? What it means to fight wars for a country that is reluctant to claim you as one of its native sons no matter how long you pay your taxes, how many of the enemy you kill, how hard you work with your hands under the sun? Is it about what it means to be old and what you deserve in your old age? Or is it about growing up, becoming a man, becoming what you are—whatever that is? Maybe it is about the relationship between a six-year-old boy and an ancient *curandera* to whom many are indebted. Think about the relationship between the people—especially between Antonio, his father, and Ultima—and the earth, the soil, the *llano*: is the book about how the land we come from and live in shapes who we are, what we want, why we want it? What if someone said this book was about such things as tradition, secrets, power, identity, or change: Would they be wrong? What would they mean, for instance, if they said this book was about power? Whose? What kind? From where? Toward what end? Some think the book is about the way the world divides itself within us: he is of the *llano* and yet he is a Luna, too; he is a boy, yet sees the world with adult, wise eyes; he is Catholic ("Bless me, father") and thus believes in God, yet is also an apprentice to a *curandera* (Ultima) who convenes with pagan spirits and darker forces to do what for many, religion or modern medicine cannot: heal them, help them, hurt them.

Through such examples, I try to show my students how to roam the wider spaces of their minds, by giving them permission to speculate, to wonder, to essay (i.e., travel around in and develop) an understanding of the subject before them through writing. In academic settings, the journal is primarily a conversational space where they can think about the essential ideas raised in class. Some entries might be more imaginative than others, but their common link is that the writing serves the purpose of getting the kids to think.

Journal Writing About Reading

How then can we use journal writing to think about and improve students' ability to understand what they read? My students use the journal frequently as a way into class discussions and other assignments. Thus they write about quotes, scenes, or related ideas from the text we are reading at that time. These writings tend to be opportunities for students to think in any direction, to let them explore the perimeters of their thinking in hopes of stumbling onto personal insights. Again, when I can, I write with them, a practice that is sometimes difficult to maintain, but always yields exciting new understandings for myself, as in this response to the epigram of Bharati Mukherjee's novel *Jasmine*, which my freshmen read as part of an integrated English–World Studies program:

> "The new geometry mirrors a universe that is rough, not rounded, scabrous, not smooth. It is a geometry of the pitted, pocked, and broken up, the twisted, tangled, and intertwined."
>
> —JAMES GLEICK, *Chaos*

When I think of geometry I think mostly in terms of shapes and differences and the relationship between these shapes and the way these differences affect the relationship between shapes. For instance, if you think of a building like the new San Francisco Museum of Modern Art, what you see is an arrangement of shapes all within a common space, each one working with the other to create what they hope we will think of as a coherent whole. But throw the word *new* into that and I wonder what it means. Does it mean the relationship between the shapes means something different? Does the perception—i.e., what once seemed beautiful, aesthetically pleasing—change and am I now supposed to see it as less than it was, or just different, or just another competing arrangement that is neither better nor worse—just is? What if my conception of geometry was initially limited to squares, circles and triangles, because that is all I knew of in my culture; in the new geometry do they offer me new shapes—quarfas, timboras, saqquiras—for which I lack any name and therefore have no idea of them, no word to call them and thus no way to see or understand them? If you think of "chaos" you think of randomness, the only pattern being that there is no pattern, or at least no way of predicting a pattern. What happens if you lost the ability to predict, to expect things from your world? If you woke up one day and someone came to you and said "What you thought was right or real yesterday is not today"? Einstein said that God does not play dice with the universe, that it is not random, that there is no such thing as chaos, only patterns we are unable to see because of our human limitations. As Mukherjee says, the world is evolving, changing; evolution is a messy process, especially when it is creating a new type of person, a new type of country, a new kind of world where an Indian man educated at Berkeley, who still carries with him a preference for Blondie's pizza, can sit at his PowerPC in a posh villa in the hills above Calcutta, chatting via e-mail with a woman he once dated in grad school at MIT, who makes her living by transmitting documents to women in rural Ireland, who earn their living typing up American documents for companies owned by Dutch firms, which provide Mexico with its latest movie about a family of orphans, who dream of finding their way home to a country they no longer know the name of. Is this Babylon—or Eden? Is this the Promised Land or the Land of Broken Promises?

Journal Jumpstarts: How to Write

Students don't always have a great idea to grab onto and write about. In these situations they can lose valuable class time, which can render the journal useless. Here then are some introductory phrases that can serve as ways into their writing about their reading:

> I wonder . . .
>
> I began to think of . . .
>
> I suppose . . .
>
> I don't see/I see . . .
>
> I like the idea . . .
>
> I know the feeling . . .
>
> I noticed . . .
>
> I love the way . . .
>
> I was surprised . . .
>
> I can't really . . .
>
> What if . . .
>
> I thought . . .
>
> I can't believe . . .
>
> If I had been . . .
>
> I was reminded of . . .
>
> Why did . . .
>
> Maybe . . .
>
> I wish . . .
>
> I don't like . . .
>
> It really bothered me when . . .
>
> My first thought was . . .
>
> One that thing that grabbed my attention was . . .

Examples of Using the Journal to Help Students Read

Such openers, like keys, unlock the mind of students who just don't know where to begin, sometimes because they are not used to being asked what they think. Writing helped my students read a very difficult article in *Time* about teens' attitudes about race. I presented them with the magazine's statistical table, which students immediately found confusing. I had them use writing to break it down and provide a narrative of what they saw in the table. Reading *Adventures of Huckleberry Finn* later on that week, we discussed Jim's feelings of abandonment in the wake of what he imagines to be Huck's death; then we read Shakespeare's Sonnet 29 ("When, in disgrace with fortune and men's eyes"), again, using writing to understand it the poem. We write our way into an understanding by looking at specific words. Here's what Erika Lum contributed as an introduction into our discussion of the poem and its relationship to the novel:

> This poem is very confusing. I don't know for sure what Shakespeare is feeling and what is making him feel that way. He is feeling some kind of regret for love, fate, or wealth. Shakespeare seems to want to describe something of a misfit. This, to me, relates to Huck Finn and Jim and all the other examples of a misfit and an outcast to everyone. They despise Huck for his unmannered ways; Jim, because of his born color; a homeless person, for his lost wealth; Hester Prynne, because of her letter "A." "In disgrace with fortune and men's eyes" and "outcast state" gives a deep impression of being shunned out. Shakespeare wants to change his fate, "deaf heaven," even God won't listen. Shakespeare is feeling hatred for himself, but at the end he says "For thy sweet love remember'd" shows that his love for someone makes the "sullen earth" bring happiness.

Erika not only assesses her own understanding, which she does not initially trust, but arrives at remarkable insights, using close reading of the text to support her thinking. She makes significant connections between other works we have read (e.g., *The Scarlet Letter*) and the modern world (e.g., the homeless).

When, later in the week, we begin class with a discussion of prejudice, the students are asked to write a personal narrative in their journals to get ready to examine aspects of Jim's role in *Huckleberry Finn*. Here is what Edwin writes:

> Last Saturday night I was sitting on the corner garbage can hanging out with my two white friends. It was about eleven o'clock or so, I guess, and these cops pull over and start hassling me to get moving. I look to my two white buddies and wait for the cops to tell them to get off the newspaper racks they're sitting on and get moving, too, but they don't even look at them. So what can I do? I get down and start walking away, but I'm thinking to myself, This ain't right, this ain't right. My friends catch up and want to know what's bugging me and I just shake my head and say "nothing, man, it's cool."

When they watch the film *The Gods Must Be Crazy*, I ask students to compare the visual text of the movie and the written text of *Huckleberry Finn* by comparing the journey metaphors in each and the connection between white South African civilization in the film and Huck's encounters with "sivilization" each time he leaves the river. Taylor Vogt, a junior, wrote:

> In [*The Gods Must Be Crazy*] it seems civilization is a bad thing. It makes the people of civilization look like savages. Even though they take the extremes of the two cultures, Bushmen (nicest of the nice) and compare them to Terrorists (meanest of the mean) the comparison still has a great impact and shows how vicious civilization can be. I think Huck Finn is in a way like the Bushman. Both go on a journey, the main difference is one runs away from civilization and one runs into civilization. Huck hated civilization and is trying to escape. The Bushman is not trying to get into civilization, but he gets trapped in civilization.

Collaborative Interpretation Through Writing

Another effective use of journal writing to improve reading involves having two students read and write about the same text. Here is an example of two students writing about the same paragraph in Emerson's essay "Self-Reliance."

> Explanation of paragraph 4: To be a man means to be an individual. Nothing but the respect of your own mind is more sacred than anything. One time he asked a question about what he would have to do with the respect of tradition if he lives fully from within himself. Then a friend of his suggested that maybe those impulses were from the Devil not from God. Then he replied that if that is so then he is the devil's child and he will live then for the devil. He explained how no law can be more respectful to him than his nature. Good and bad can change. Different people see them differently. Then [Emerson] concludes saying that he is embarrassed of how easily we give in to badges and names, to large societies and dead institutions.
>
> —KENIA VILCHEZ

> Explanation of paragraph 4: You cannot say an immoral man is good unless you live it and find out. Nothing is better than your own mind. Find your own self. Why live by the churches' rules when the feelings from inside are moral. If you're evil you will live from the evil. Nothing is more important than yourself. People and things are tagged and easily changed by society. You have the right to live by your own set of rules. "What have I to do with the sacredness of traditions, if I live wholly from within?"
>
> —KIMBERLEE MORRIS

When they finished, students traded journals and responded to each other in writing, following this "written conversation" up with a face-to-face one in which they compared their different interpretations, using their journal notes to facilitate the discussion.

Reader Response

Call them "dialectical journals" or "reader response logs," they all amount to a variety of strategies designed to force student readers to enter into and engage meaningfully with the text. Unfortunately, many kids burn out on this method when it is the habitual practice of their teacher; teachers need to find ways to mix the exercise up a bit. I find it helpful to allow students a range of options to choose from, all of which accomplish the desired textual interaction while allowing students the freedom to work in whichever genre they prefer. Also, the opportunity for choices allows me to individualize instruction by saying to the kid with reading difficulties, for example, "You should try the reading response option, because that will help you stay more focused throughout and better understand what is happening and what it means as you go along."

Sample Assignment: Writing Options for The Kitchen God's Wife

Here is a sample assignment for Amy Tan's *The Kitchen God's Wife* that provides a range of writing options. I generally tend to allow students to come up with their own options so long as they can persuade me that their idea will yield as much serious thinking and understanding as mine; this invitation to argue their case typically gives them the chance they need to develop their persuasive abilities and verbal skills.

The Kitchen God's Wife **Response Options**

Overview

Your response journals to Amy Tan's *The Kitchen God's Wife* must amount to at least ten pages. You can respond as you wish to the novel so long as it shows a consistent attempt to both understand and "talk back" to the story. I include here several possibilities. You can also vary your response: try a few notes, a poem or two, a couple of "notes and quotes," and a short essay on a particular theme. You may not do poems only but must balance these with examples of other prose options.

Reader Response Logs

Reader response logs are like a ship captain's log: they chart your course as you navigate your way through a text—a novel, story, movie—by describing the things you find along the way and how you react to them. They demonstrate your interaction with the text, showing the process you went through to make sense of the text. Thus they might include notes on things you found interesting, bizarre, upsetting, or confusing. Here's an example:

> In Robert Olen Butler's *A Good Scent from a Strange Mountain* I find myself constantly amazed by the way the Vietnamese use language. Their common speech is studded with a poetry that comes so natural to them. And they seem to see in everything symbols of a larger, more magical world. For instance, the guy at the table is not just a soldier—he is a ghost to the narrator; the parrot is not just a parrot, but is the reincarnation of the girl's grandfather. This seems all the more possible when the parrot starts saying things her grandfather used to say before he died such as "What now?"

The above example is meant to give you an idea of how to respond to texts; it is NOT an example of a complete entry. You must take responsibility for seeing that your responses are thorough. Bring in an example of your early responses to the text, so that I can make sure that you are confident in the quality of your initial responses to the reading.

Written Dialogue

You may pair up with another person and do your responses together. This involves writing each other letters about what you read. Your responses could even take the form of notes written on the fly—e.g., a note you write in class and pass along later to someone out in the hall. The letters should show you participating in a thoughtful discussion of such things as what the book is about, why it is good/boring/confusing, what the author is trying to accomplish, or why a particular character acted a certain way. You could also do this assignment with friends in other periods or even—if you wanted—with someone outside school (e.g., a parent or friend) who wanted to read the book. (This option grows increasingly popular with students' increased access to e-mail and has proven particularly engaging due to the conversation it allows them to have in a different medium than the classroom.) Here is an example from Colleen O'Neill:

> In your last letter, you talked about Winnie "controlling" her situations and I think that it was almost like she was allowing herself to be more free, sharing her thoughts and not covering up her real beliefs and actions. She also seems to be more confident in herself that she could stand up for herself and prove that in the long run she would win. She did not ever give up, either, which I think is a very strong attribute when you think about it because she went through so much abuse, yet she still managed to get through her life and be a successful mother to Pearl. I cannot believe either that Wen Fu could possibly treat her that bad and everyone else just stood back and watched it happen day after day.

Letter Poems

This idea stems from different ancient Chinese poems written in the form of letters, typically by wandering tax collectors who were writing to their wives, whom they had not seen in some time. The best example is Ezra Pound's translation of Rihaku's poem "Exile's Letter." Write a poem in the form of a letter, addressed to or written by one of the main characters in *The Kitchen God's Wife*.

Thirteen Ways of Looking at a Story/Character

Wallace Stevens's famous poem "Thirteen Ways of Looking at a Blackbird" offers an interesting way of responding to what you read. Consider, for example, writing a poem called

"Thirteen Ways of Looking at a Mother" (through Pearl's eyes, or your eyes). You would take your materials from the story and use all the different Winnies you see as she moves through her life. Other possibilities: use the poem's format to discuss daughters, fathers, families, moments. Another option is to use the poem "Autobiography in Five Chapters," by Portia Nelson, as an example for a similar poem.

Character Log
Choose one character at the beginning of the book and follow them throughout the novel, noting essential details and discussing in your log the complexity of their character. Questions to consider: Why did they act or think as they did in a certain situation? What do they believe in? What motivates them? What is important to them and why? How do they change and why? What is their relationship with others in the story and how does that relationship change? Primary options for *The Kitchen God's Wife* are:

- Helen
- Winnie
- Wen Fu
- Pearl

Creative Writing: Drama, Fiction, and Poetry

I agree with Tom Romano (1987) when he writes that *all* writing is, by its nature, creative; however, *creative writing* is the term commonly used for drama, fiction, and poetry, so I won't confuse you by introducing some new term. I do not have room to go into depth about teaching each of these, but I will offer a few approaches that can help you right away to get kids going.

Dramatic Writing

Drama offers an often overlooked opportunity to help students better understand personal issues as well as literary works. I am speaking specifically about students writing dramatic scripts, which they subsequently perform for an audience, usually the class. The following two approaches describe the main ideas involved in this exercise.

Write into.   First, find what appears to be an opening of time in the sequence of a story. For example, in *Bless Me, Ultima*, Antonio is depicted hiding in the bushes beside the river while Tenorio is hunted down. Have students write an internal monologue of what Antonio is thinking, in his voice, as the action unfolds around him. Other examples: Holden Caulfield (*The Catcher in the Rye*) as he waits for a phone call at the diner, or Esperanza (*The House on Mango Street*) as she sits in the window looking out on the world. This activity is very popular with students because it helps them understand characterization and author's style.

Dramatic interpretation.   When students were unable to continue successfully with *The Scarlet Letter*, we decided to divide the novel into chapters and transform it into a play. Each group had to take the dialogue from their chapter and adapt it into script format, supplying an accompanying narrative to help the audience make sense of the action. Students then performed their scripts.

Short Fiction

Not all students love writing short stories, but those who do resent not having the chance to work in this genre. Few activities teach them to read fiction better than writing it themselves.

Rana and Rebecca performing their adaptation of The Scarlet Letter *for the class*

We will not discuss here how to teach students to write short stories; there are, however, exciting new forms worth pointing out as possible avenues for exploration.

> *Sudden fiction.* Also known as "flash fiction," these stories must be no longer than three typed pages, but must have all the components of a story. There are several different anthologies (*Sudden Fiction* and *Flash Fiction*) that have begun to explore this form, some of which offer fun stories for the class that can be read in as little as five minutes.
>
> *Microfiction.* Developed by writer Jerome Stern, these stories were originally conceived as pieces for National Public Radio. NPR and America Online both began holding annual contests for these very short pieces (250 words maximum), which were required to have all the components of a working story. They are fun, particularly as they have a performatory quality to them, rather like a joke that wants to be told out loud.

To compensate for the lack of other guidance in this area, I want to emphasize two books which offer rare help for those who write or teach students to write short stories. One, *Steering the Craft*, was written by Ursula K. LeGuin as a follow-up to a series of workshops she offered on writing short fiction. The book, available in an affordable paperback, is subtitled *Exercises and Discussions on Story Writing for the Lone Navigator or the Mutinous Crew*. It is a deep but accessible reflection on how writers accomplish what they do on the page. The second book, *Making Shapely Fiction*, is written by Jerome Stern and is also available in an inexpensive paperback. Stern's book is organized, as he says in the book's introduction, "so that you can start writing serious fiction (or non-serious, if you like) from the first page." It is efficiently laid out and very funny. My favorite chapter is "Don't Do This: A Short Guide to What Not to Do," which includes advice about why, for instance, you should not end your story, "He realized he was alone, and slowly blinked his third eye."

Poetry

Poems visit my class all the time. I don't favor the big poetry unit myself, though there is nothing wrong with that approach. My colleague Jackie Estes, for example, does a large unit requiring each student to study in depth one American poet, and many students fondly remember the unit long after they leave her class. I prefer to sneak up on my students—especially the boys—with something that seems benign enough that they have no grounds to oppose it. Then, once I have them, I get some poetry out of them before they know what happened. Poems help us get inside texts and the characters inside those texts. They help us place ourselves in the world in relation to others. Mostly, however, they give us a different way of thinking about things. I didn't fully understand this until one of my students died: suddenly poetry was the only way for his classmates to express what they felt. Here is a quick list of some of the kinds of poems my students write:

> *List poem.* See "I Hear America Singing," by Walt Whitman. An accessible form that allows for a variety of uses in the class.

> *Found poem.* See Annie Dillard's *Mornings Like This* or Julius Lester, whose found poem, "Parents," about a young girl who shoots herself when her parents tried to force her to shoot her dog both devastates and inspires my students. You can have students create powerful found poems from the text of stories and novels they read.

> *"Thirteen Ways of Seeing."* Taken from Wallace Stevens's poem "Thirteen Ways of Looking at a Blackbird"; you could also use James Wright's poem "Three Sentences for a Dead Swan" as a similar model. Examples of poems students have written: "Thirteen Ways of Seeing Hamlet," or "Thirteen Ways of Looking at Winnie" (in response to *The Kitchen God's Wife*).

> *"Autobiography in Five Short Chapters."* Written by Portia Nelson, this poem's structure offers students an effective and powerful way into writing about their own life or that of some character in a story (e.g., what would Huck Finn write in such a poem when thinking back on the different stages of his life?)

> *Odes.* Kids love Pablo Neruda's *Elemental Odes*. They can adapt this form to their own lives ("Ode to My Telephone") or a character or object from a story.

> *The Irish Curse poem.* A poem in which the writer/narrator rains down a long and delicious curse of all they hope will happen to some offending party in brutal, powerful language. (For more on this poem, see Sandra MacPherson's poems, or her appearance in Bill Moyers's PBS series *The Language of Life*.)

> *Journal poem.* Inspired by Stanley Kunitz's poem "Journal for my Daughter," in which he writes nine entries in elegant verse, each entry made up of a different event or period in his daughter's life. The same idea could easily be adapted to a student's own life or the lives of different characters in a story.

> *Ancient Chinese and Japanese poems.* These beautiful poems, many of them translated by Kenneth Rexroth, offer models that can help students find their way into a good poem about their world or the story they are reading. (See Czeslaw Milosz's excellent anthology *A Book of Luminous Things*, Harcourt Brace, 1996). I wrote the following example as a model based on Winnie from *The Kitchen God's Wife*:

> > I have been alone for many years now.
> > Outback leaves fall from my plum
> > tree like children leaving home.
> > They will not return. They think
> > they are different, that life will be
> > different—even better.

My daughter visits according to the
rituals of birth and death and holidays.
At night, when she visits,
I offer her my slippers worn thin
by all the years of walking these halls
looking for her.
Outside the plum tree sleeps
while in the cold, wet earth the leaves
dream of the arms that once held them.

Magnetic poetry. I have a large "Wall of Words" in my classroom that consists of a piece of sheet metal with many magnetic word tiles stuck to it. Another variation on this idea is to cut up poems they have read and use the same words to make other poems as a means of discussing the elasticity of language.

Renga. In ancient Japan, contests would be held between poets, who battled against each others' lines in a sort of poetic guitar jam to see whose lines could take the prize. Pass around a piece of paper and have each student add a line, then see what you have at the period's end. A variation on this: fold the paper over after each line so that the current writer sees only the previous line while making his contribution. This is reminiscent of the game "telephone."

Spoon River Anthology poem. Based on Edgar Lee Masters's anthology of voices and characters, this poem consists of voices in poetic form all talking about some central theme or set of characters. See also Dylan Thomas's play for voices, *Under Milk Wood*, which follows a similar format and offers other ideas for students.

Dialogue poems. I got this idea from Louise Glück's brilliant book *Meadowlands*, which uses Homer's *Odyssey* as a metaphor for a failing marriage. Poems use alternating stanzas to indicate different voices discussing a topic often suggested by the title. Examples to consider: Hamlet and Ophelia, Holden and Phoebe, Huck and Jim, Winnie and Pearl, Lenny and George.

Letter poem. I use Ezra Pound's translation of Rihaku's "Exile's Letter" as an example of this form. The poem's structure is simple: I sit here thinking about you and these different memories while we are apart, and send this poem/letter off thinking of you. Examples to consider: Holden to Phoebe, Huck to Tom, Jim to his wife/kids, Celie in *Color Purple* to her sister or God (you could even take this last example and turn her letters from the book into found poems).

Arabic poems. A variation on the letter and dialogue poems, the Arabic poem is best exemplified by the Persian poet Rumi. Most often dealing with love and such ideas as beauty and what is sacred, these poems have a recognizable voice: "My love, you have been away so long/ the stars begin to fall from the sky./ I speak your name at night/watching the sky for word of your approach." Another poem in this tradition is the *Ruba'iyat* of Omar Khayyám.

Question poem. A very fun poem that allows for playful use of language and imagery as well as intelligent speculation. The best example that comes to mind is Pablo Neruda's poem "Enigma," in which he begins by asking what the lobster is spinning in his nets down in the ocean. Such poems often begin with questions the rest of the poem tries to answer: e.g., "What is the meaning of all this wandering?"

Journey poem. The journey poem asks the student to choose a metaphor that best describes the journey they or some character is on and explore it through the poem. Some students choose bridges (e.g., that help you cross from adolescence to adulthood), others pick roads; the most common choice, however, is a mountain, something which seems to embody all their different obstacles. I offer students an example of a poem I wrote to help them get the idea. It's somewhat difficult, but the exercise creates a context for their thinking in more metaphorical terms; this helps them to be able to understand it better than they might on other occasions.

> So dangerous to sleep
> on a tightrope: the umbilicus
> stretched between past
> and present, tied to the future
> while below you the promise
> of the net yawns like nighttime.
> Ahead: the sanctuary of honesty,
> mother's open arms
> holding me back
> like a kite she won't let take the wind
> or a word she won't let the tongue tell.
> On either side of the rope—certainty,
> my spine twisted into a question
> only the earth can answer
> and the future will ask.
> My arms tire beneath the yin of family
> and yang of self, the yang of past and
> yin of present, the Tao of always.
> All around me the audience expecting my fall,
> wanting it, wanting to save me so they will
> feel needed, tied to me, bound
> by a rope we walk together,
> forever falling into each others' lives
> where we meet in a future we feel
> but cannot reach.

Here is Melissa Mendoza's poem which she wrote while reading *Huckleberry Finn*. Huck's journey along the river was discussed by the class as both literal and metaphoric:

> Life is like a mountain.
> Sometimes scary to look at,
> but at the end of your journey
> you will have the whole world looking
> at you.
> I try to climb the best that I can.
> Sometimes the rocks slip.
> I fall.
> Sometimes the branches scratch me.
> It hurts

Sometimes I see a beautiful flower.
I smile
Sometimes I get scared of the height.
I cry
All of this can stop my journey but
not for long
I get up again.
The scar heals.
The flower blesses my soul
and the fear makes me wiser.
Then I'm at the top with the
whole world looking at me.

Writing in the Workplace

What the Standards Say

In recent years schools have been asked to address the needs of the workforce through their curriculums. The juxtaposition of this section against the poetry section only emphasizes the contrast between the literature we love and the world in which we must work. Not everyone agrees with this trend, obviously; and when you hear some of the ideas, it's no wonder. Some would have students read *King Lear* as an example of poor decision making when it comes to real estate. Several colleagues of mine have seen their English departments come under attack from superintendents or district administrators who try, under the banner of "reform," to create "Business English" courses that do little more than teach students to write memos and use the bullet function on their word processor.

Yet these reforms have a place and value: NCTE itself lists among its standards several that support such objectives:

NCTE Standard #5: Students employ a wide range of strategies as they write and use different writing process elements appropriately to communicate with different audiences for a variety of purposes.

NCTE Standard #12: Students use spoken, written, and visual language to accomplish their own purposes (e.g., for learning, enjoyment, persuasion, and the exchange of information). (NCTE/IRA 1996)

As with many reforms, "Workplace English" seems to contradict what we feel compelled to teach. On closer inspection, however, this criticism doesn't hold up. In fact, the practical, document-based curriculum of the business world offers us interesting ways to diversify our own curriculum. Consider the different types of writing common to the workplace (see Figure 7.3), many of which have a logical place in our existing curriculum if taught in the proper context.

Sample Assignments

I have used several of the activities that follow to complement my curriculum with freshmen and seniors, honors and remedial students alike. Here is a brief summary of examples, and descriptions of how I incorporated them into the curriculum without doing away with other, more "essential" components.

Newsletter. My freshman classes publish a newsletter each month that includes cartoons, book reviews, surveys, charts, interviews, articles, and pictures that capture what we did in the previous month; these are then distributed to their intended audience: parents and administrators.

Minutes. Each day a different student is responsible for taking the minutes of class that day. They focus on accurate reporting and voice, while providing important opportunities for continued public speaking practice. Each day begins with that student getting up before the class to read their minutes (which takes all of two to three minutes at the most); they then put them in the minutes binder so that students who missed class can find out what they missed. Minutes must have the following components: date, name of recorder, bullets at the bottom listing any homework assignments or announcements, and the name of the person responsible for the next day's minutes. (See Chapter 8 for an example.)

E-mail. I have students, when possible, use e-mail to correspond with experts for large projects that allow for Internet research. My favorite example involves freshman students communicating via e-mail with people from Ireland, South Africa, India, and China over the course of a semester as part of our United Nations project.

Brochures. When I teach seniors and we need to mix things up, I have them get into teams and design their own product or business, part of which requires that they develop a brochure that incorporates various aspects of effective commercial writing. (See Chapter 4 for a sample brochure.)

Résumés. In my senior classes, in preparation for the world of work and college applications, students write a résumé and cover letter which, when perfected, go either to the local Rotary Club for feedback or to their own employer for their feedback. Only if they are perfectly correct are they accepted for evaluation.

Letters. I've had freshmen write to the United Nations to propose solutions to the problems in Ireland and the Middle East; sophomores write to officials to propose solutions to social problems ranging from gangs to deforestation; juniors write legislators to protest new teen driving laws; and seniors write to local businesses requesting an opportunity to shadow an employee for a day and then follow up these outings with letters of thanks. All are written in proper business-letter format and are actually sent. I have also had students write to authors of books they read on their own; on my classroom wall are copies of personal letters from such authors as Sandra Cisneros, Gary Soto, Pam Houston, Sharon Olds, and Stephen King.

Interviews. Students have gone out into the community for a variety of reasons to interview people and then write these up. The most impressive of these endeavors involved sending my remedial freshmen out to interview centenarians (people over age one hundred); the interviews were collected, revised, and published in a booklet by Eden Hospital, which then threw a publication party where the students and their centenarians came together for lunch and dancing. (See Chapter 15 for more on this project.)

Proposals. When I require large projects of students, I try to always require an initial proposal that spells out what they will do, how they will do it, what they will need to do it, and the steps they will follow. This advance planning helps them succeed at the project, and it provides an efficient structure for quick conferences during which I can find out the status and direction of their project. Several years back my freshmen worked in teams to create very ambitious proposals. Our school's library improvement committee was to oversee the renovation of the library. My freshmen created multimedia proposals that included all aspects of the design, then presented their designs to the committee using a multimedia system to the committee, explaining the reasons for their design. The final multimedia presentations remain some of the most sophisticated, impressive productions my students have done. Here was the assignment:

> Burlingame High School's library improvement committee met for the first time last week. The school has had trouble turning the library into the center of learning and study it should be. This year we have a new librarian, Mrs. Jones, who is committed to reinventing the library so it will work better for both teachers and, more importantly, students. I volunteered you guys to think about the library and come up with some formal proposals for what it should look like, how it should work, what it should have—and why. My plan is simple: You have this entire week at school to complete this project. You will work in teams and will be graded on the following criterion:
> - participation during the period
> - quality of your presentation
> - use of technology in your presentation
> - whether your presentation is worthy of being forwarded to the Library Advisory Committee for consideration

Grants. One year, working with a group of remedial seniors, I started up a computer lab, which they helped me develop by writing grants (i.e., letters requesting funding and support) to the district superintendent, who was so impressed he couldn't help but send the few hundred dollars they requested. The letters were flawlessly written, properly formatted, and produced on a good word processor, which students had to first learn to use. The lab became "theirs" and has never been so well cared for since. (See Chapter 15 to see a winning grant written by students.)

Primary Objectives of Workplace English

The primary objectives of workplace English are mostly stylistic. Instead of thinking of *texts*, this curriculum thinks more in terms of *documents*. In particular, this curriculum concentrates on how documents work and how to create them to be read in different ways: bullets, short paragraphs, concise sentences combine for efficiency in such documents, allowing the reader to skim, scan, and search for information quickly. Typically, these documents must adhere to standardized formats such as the business letter. Finally, there is a strong emphasis on correctness as an individual's or business' credibility is often measured by their attention to details. If you question the truth of this, ask students what they think of "professional teachers" whose handouts are riddled with errors.

In her book *The Art of Workplace English: A Curriculum for All Students,* Carolyn Boiarsky (1997) illustrates the difference between writing in a literary style and what she calls a "technical" style:

> *Technical.* The brown wooden bookcase held over 300 books, approximately 200 small paperback books, 70 medium size hard-back books, and 50 tall coffee-table books. The five shelves, approximately three feet long, rested in a frame three feet wide by six feet high.

> *Literary.* The bookcase groaned under the burden of the heavy, hardbound books lining its shelves. Creaking like an old man arising from his rocker, the old shelves gave up centuries of knowledge as a borrower lightened its load by removing a volume of Tolstoy's *War and Peace.*

The definitive statement about the workplace is the Secretary's Commission on Achieving Necessary Skills (SCANS) report, titled *What Work Requires of Schools*. In that report, its authors provide the following examples of writing on the job:

- writing memoranda to justify resources or explain plans
- preparing instructions for operating simple machines
- developing a narrative to explain graphs or tables
- drafting suggested modifications in company procedures (United States Department of Labor 1991)

In addition to its "Five Competencies," the SCANS report identifies what it feels are the foundations for such competence: basic skills, thinking skills, and personal qualities. Under "Basic Skills," you find what you would expect: reading, writing, arithmetic and mathematics, speaking and listening. The report goes on to stress the important role technology plays in the workplace, listing as one of the five competencies that "effective workers can productively use . . . computers to process information . . . and select equipment and tools, applying technology to specific tasks."

Responding to Student Writers

I can remember all too well when, as a student teacher, I began talking to other teachers about writing. I would walk to the bus stop after each day and swell up with pride that I, in contrast to these experienced teachers whom I misjudged to be burnt out, would read everything my students wrote, that I would respond thoroughly and thoughtfully to every page my students wrote. How could I do anything less? Only a man newly married to a woman who was also a new teacher and thus equally busy, only a man without two children, only a man whose student teaching required that he teach two classes, could say or think such thoughts in the face of the daunting workload that any English teacher carries.

How to Handle the Paperload

With this in mind, let me identify the components of effective response to student writing:

- personal but productive
- specific (e.g., targets a pattern of error students can effectively address)
- immediate (throughout the composing process or directly after writing)
- no more than three items to focus on (e.g., read only for verbs)
- cumulative (i.e., builds on previous responses) so as to maintain continuity and accountability (e.g., "Let's see how you're coming along on that paragraph development this time around, Matt . . . ")

My first response is to balk at the scale of these demands on my time and life. And so we come to the challenge of how to cope with the paper load. Consider the math for a moment, just to put this in perspective: if you have 150 students and each one writes one page that warrants your response, you will spend over two hours responding to this assignment *if you take only one minute to read each page*. It is easy to see how out of control this can get when you start talking about essays and more formal writing instruction. And yet if there is not another way, many teachers will simply avoid having their students write. Luckily, there are some tricks of the trade, many of them outlined in *How to Handle the Paper Load* (Harris 1986).

- Ask yourself the following focus questions about your assignment:
  - What am I reading this paper to establish? (grade? mastery? next step in revision process?)
  - What purpose will my response serve? (to improve performance or explain grade?)
  - How much time should I spend responding to these papers? (prioritize your work to achieve the greatest effect on student performance)
- Have students seek response from various other sources that are able to read and say what did or didn't work for them as a reader.
- Use checks (✓/✓+/✓–) to indicate that it was read and evaluated for its quality; these marks allow you to satisfy your students' need for evaluative feedback and your need to get out from under the pile of paper.
- Have students read their writing aloud, enter a mark in your gradebook as they do so.
- Conference with students in class and assess them on the spot through conversational evaluation.
- Have groups responding to literature or other texts use the overhead projector to display their presentation notes instead of writing them on paper.
- Instead of having thirty-five kids write about the importance of "secrecy" in *The Kitchen God's Wife*, have them do a "quick write," then form groups and use their quick writes to get a conversation started and focused. At end of the period, collect the quick writes and staple them behind a front sheet with the group's names and notes on it. Give them a grade based on participation in the conversation.
- Use rubric scoring (discussed further in Chapter 11). This type of evaluation is based on a general impression and allows quick response. You read through a paper and assign a score—e.g., a score of 4—according to those attributes described in a particular rubric. The example shown in Figure 7.6 comes from the Six-Trait Rubric, a model that carefully integrates writing and assessment to improve performance.
- Circulate and check off work in class when possible so as to deliver personalized response and, at the same time, direct response to the problems or achievements you encounter in students' writing.
- Have students write a short essay every week but check only that they did it; after they have written four essays, have them pick one, then revise and perfect it.
- Create a rubber stamp based on a local or recognized rubric to use for quick but specific responses to writing. You can buy the Six Trait Rubric, for example, on a rubber stamp through the Northwest Regional Educational Lab.
- Respond "So what?" Based on the assumption that so long as students keep writing and working with the paper it stays separate from your workload, this method helps students write much deeper into their topic. Ask them to rewrite their entire paper using only this question to drive them deeper into the subject; I've used the response as many as three times (for the same paper) and found the resulting writing to be remarkable for its depth.

Ideas and Content	Organization	Voice
5 This paper is clear and focused. It holds the reader's attention. Relevant anecdotes and details enrich the central theme or storyline. 3 The writer is beginning to define the topic, even though development is still basic or general. 1 As yet, the paper has no clear sense of purpose or central theme. To extract meaning from the text, the reader must make inferences based on sketchy details. The writing reflects more than one of these problems....	5 The organization enhances and showcases the central idea or storyline. The order, structure or presentation of information is compelling and moves the reader through the text. 3 The organizational structure is strong enough to move the reader through the text without undue confusion. 1 The writing lacks a clear sense of direction. Ideas, details or events seem strung together in a loose or random fashion--or else there is no identifiable internal structure. The writing reflects more than one of these problems....	5 The writer speaks directly to the reader in a way that is individualistic, expressive and engaging. Clearly, the writer is involved in the text, is sensitive to the needs of an audience, and is writing to be read. 3 The writer seems sincere, but not fully engaged or involved. The result is pleasant or even personable, but not compelling. 1 The writer seems indifferent, uninvolved or distanced from the topic and/or the audience. As a result, the writing is lifeless or mechanical; depending on the topic, it may be overly technical or jargonistic. The paper reflects more than one of the following problems....

Word Choice	Sentence Fluency	Conventions
5 Words convey the intended message in a precise, interesting and natural way. 3 The language is functional, even if it lacks punch; it is easy to figure out the writer's meaning on a general level. 1 The writer struggles with a limited vocabulary, searching for words to convey meaning. The writing reflects more than one of these problems....	5 The writing has an easy flow and rhythm when read aloud. Sentences are well built, with strong and varied structure that invites expressive oral reading. 3 The text hums along with a steady beat, but tends to be more pleasant or businesslike than musical, more mechanical than fluid. 1 The reader has to practice quite a bit in order to give this paper a fair interpretive reading. The writing reflects more than one of the following problems....	5 The writer demonstrates a good grasp of standard writing conventions (e.g., grammar, capitalization, punctuation, usage, spelling, paragraphing) and uses conventions effectively to enhance readability. Errors tend to be so few and so minor that the reader can easily overlook them unless hunting for them specifically. 3 The writer shows reasonable control over a limited range of standard writing conventions. Conventions are sometimes handled well and enhance readability; at other times, errors are distracting and impair readability. 1 Errors in spelling, punctuation, usage and grammar, capitalization, and/or paragraphing repeatedly distract the reader and make the text difficult to read. The writing reflects more than one of these problems....

Source: "The Six-Trait Analytical Writing Assessment Model Scoring Guide (Rubric)" Northwest Regional Educational Laboratory, Portland, Oregon. 1997. See *Creating Writers: Linking Writing Assessment and Instruction*, by Vicki Spandel and Richard J. Stiggins (Longman 1997) for a more complete version of this rubric.

Figure 7.6   *The Six-Trait Rubric (abbreviated version)*

- Check any "patterned error" such as the tendency to misuse the semicolon or produce sentence fragments; then, upon returning the papers, have students go through and identify the error and make the corrections at that time. Once all corrections have been made, they turn their papers in again for reevaluation.
- Conference with students at their desk to quickly and orally respond to questions or specific aspects of their writing.

- Conference with students at your desk in one-on-one meetings in which you use one of the following methods:
    - read through their writing quickly and focus on whatever jumps out
    - read through for a specific aspect of the writing (e.g., paragraph organization) and provide appropriate feedback—what works and what does not and why—orally, making short notes ("paragraph focus," "verbs") at the top of the paper for quick reference when you meet to discuss subsequent drafts
    - have them, prior to the meeting, highlight/underline specific aspects of the paper they want you to attend to
- Ask students to have their parents read their papers and respond to them as they are willing and/or able.

Responding Through Conferences

Those strategies and activities listed above will help you, at times, reduce your paper load and thereby allow you to concentrate on teaching your kids better and enjoying your life a bit more. There remains, however, one method that accomplishes more than any other: individual teacher-student conferences. I have organized the following description around the writing process model described earlier in this chapter.

Beginning. Through such discussions, the teacher can assess the merits of the student's topic or help them develop one by inquiring into those ideas that have been most interesting to the student.

Gathering. During the idea and evidence gathering phase of the process, the writer may struggle with the parameters of their subject or, to quote Mark Twain, "the well may run dry," and so they might need help filling it back up. Sometimes students don't know where to look for ideas; this allows the teacher, through the conference, to help students make some connections that might not have been apparent to them because they were unable to see them. A freshman I once taught struggled to write a paper about the *Odyssey* that interested him; when, in the course of our conference, he mentioned that he was really enjoying Ken Kesey's *One Flew over the Cuckoo's Nest*, a book I was teaching in my senior class, I suggested he compare the two stories to see what happened if he put Odysseus and Telemachus along side of McMurphy and Chief. (The result was a remarkable paper; note that I had not told him what to write only pointed him in a direction I thought might help him).

Constructing. During this phase of the writing, the writer often gets lost in the labyrinth of ideas. You must be like the building inspector who came to check some stairs my friends and I built for a woman once: you use your superior knowledge to determine the student's progress toward the goal. (Hopefully your writing is better than our stair building, for the man took one look and made us tear them down right there in his presence lest anyone try to climb them.) The "construction conference" is particularly important to the writer, but also serves as an especially helpful assessment tool for the teacher who, through such conversations, gains insight into the student's effort, their thinking, their writing. This information then helps the teacher decide what they need to do next in class.

Finishing. Conferences at this stage of the process focus on editing and proofreading. If you have students keep track of their patterns of error, you might spend this conference going through the paper after they have scrutinized it themselves first, and marked those words or other elements they suspect might need attention.

The Characteristics of Effective Conferencing

There are different modes of conferencing. You can confer with students at their desk even as they shuffle into class by inquiring where they are on that paper or how they solved the writing problem they discussed in conference the day before. Or you can arrange for the more formal conference, where you and the student sit down side-by-side and work with their paper. Here are some helpful suggestions for such work:

- Narrate your reading and thinking about the writing as you go through, so that students get feedback on what they did well and why ("See, you make your main idea clear here and then go on to support it with these three examples, the first one of which is brilliant because it not only shows support but provides insight into the cause-effect relationship. . . .").
- Don't use grammatical terms that you will have to waste time defining and explaining.
- Arrange the furniture so that you are side by side with the student. According to Tom Romano (1987), the absence of eye contact helps the work by keeping it less confrontational.
- Get the students who are not in conference with you engaged in something that will help insure a reasonably quiet and productive class.
- Use nonthreatening language, stance, and environment.
- Come to the meeting with helpful focus questions to get you started:
  - What did you learn from this piece of writing?
  - What do you intend to do in the next draft?
  - What surprised you in the draft?
  - Where is the piece of writing taking you?
  - What do you like best in the piece of writing?
  - What questions do you have for me?

(Harris 1986)

Conferencing allows you to individualize instruction to better meet your students "where they are," and help them get where they need to be. In our increasingly heterogeneous classes of thirty to forty students, we struggle to meet our own standards. In a conference, I can help the student who wants to get into a major four-year university where precision and correctness will matter, without the pretense of protecting his self-esteem when his paper is riddled with errors. On the other hand, when I meet with a student like Anthony, who shows me half of a page of wrinkled paper for his "essay," I can honestly share my enthusiasm for this progress since his biggest problem is production, not, as it must be for Mr. Stanford, perfection. Once I have helped Anthony to achieve some measure of fluency, then we can move on to the next level in the hierarchy of his needs.

Such conferences clearly allow me to better address those students with special needs. Not only do they need specific strategies to triumph over their difficulties, but also a more focused, quiet environment than I can sometimes achieve in a classwide setting. Such students are not, generally speaking, equipped to help themselves or other students through peer editing; they can, however, benefit from the direct instruction you can provide them through conferences. It is through such direct instruction, in fact, that Lisa Delpit says we best address the problems so many struggling minority students face and don't know how to overcome. If Delpit

(1995) has any one criticism of the process model, it is that such a model does not serve the marginalized students who lack the "power" of the prevailing culture. Delpit would argue that peer-response groups containing such students are based on cultural assumptions about knowledge and ability that often do not apply, and therefore cannot serve such students; the conference, then, becomes the means by which to correct for such differences that keep students from getting "inside" the culture of power.

Computers and Writing: The Promise and the Problems

I include the use of computers within the writing chapter because it is here that computers seem to offer the most clearly established benefit to student performance. My students use computers to research different topics, communicate with others via e-mail, publish their poetry and papers, make presentations (with HyperStudio), and create interactive books (with 3-D Movie Maker). However, it is only in the area of writing that computers allow for effective direct instruction (especially if the teacher can conference with the writer on-screen and take advantage of the opportunity to highlight and discuss specific elements of the student's papers).

Based on observation in my own classes and discussion with other high school English teachers, I see several advantages to the use of computers which are worth pointing out. These include:

- Students write more because they can (sometimes) write faster; also, when they write and see so little on the screen (as compared to a handwritten page), they realize that they need to write more. I can, through quick conferences, point the cursor to places in the text and simply say, "Why don't you tell me more about that?" or "This would be a good place to insert an example and explanation of the relevance of this."
- Students are willing to revise more since there is less effort involved in doing so (i.e., in the precomputer era, revising would have meant retyping the entire paper).
- Boys, who tend to be drawn to computers but not drawn to English necessarily, work with a diligence and interest that is otherwise absent at other times.
- Students with serious academic difficulties seem to benefit from the lack of distraction and more individualized mode of working, and can succeed in such an environment as opposed to a full class of thirty-five students.

Computers at school often make me feel like I am in the ocean on a small raft as a tidal wave comes my way. I see it and, imagining what will happen if I do not paddle like mad, begin to do so until I am atop the wave, which I must then slave to keep up with lest I be sucked under and destroyed. Yet even as I ride this wave, I see where it would take me, and resent the lack of control I too often feel. So here are some other aspects of computers in the writing class that have caused me to sometimes resist or resent what I felt I was supposed to do:

Loss of instructional time. Given the time to get to the lab (which we can only use for three consecutive days max), get the computers up, programs running, disks distributed, notes and drafts out, type at ten to twenty words per minute, and stand in line while drafts print up on shared printers, we end up with maybe twenty-five minutes of actual writing time. When you factor in the thinking time so necessary to the composing process, you end up with still less instruction.

Malfunctions. Between printer failure, computer crashes, and server errors, the period I imagined to be full of productivity and learning is sometimes lost to down time.

Style over Substance. Sometimes kids spend inordinate amounts of time on such details as color cover pages and fonts, forgetting that none of that matters (or should) if the paper itself is not well written. The same distinction between style and substance is particularly clear when students create multimedia projects which are overly dependent on images and downplay the importance of good, correct writing in an otherwise impressive product.

Overdependence on machine at the expense of skills. I love my spell checker and firmly believe in knowing how to use tools to help you. Yet students sometimes turn in papers with a flippant note across the top saying, "Sorry Mr. B. the spell checker wasn't working," and assume that this absolves them of all responsibility. These students would seem to lack the skill and, more importantly, the sense of pride in the quality of their work.

Endnote: The Last Word

My own passion for writing drives my classes. The most consistent complaint I hear from students who get all groany on me is that we "write too much." My biggest challenge is to get students invested in the process. If there is no heart to the writing, what the men who wrote "The Five Principles of an Essay" called "personal commitment," there is no hope of engagement. Then writing is a mere exercise. One day, realizing the stunning spring weather would win my students' attention, I dragged them out to the huge baseball stadium next to our school. I told them they could not sit within fifteen feet of each other and had to write about whatever they could see, and what these sightings made them think about.

In June, asking them what assignments of the previous year stood out, this opportunity to reflect, to just get quiet and think, ranked near the top with most students. Time and again they said they just had no time to do such thinking. Perhaps most memorable from that day was Rhea Coulter's writing. I had Rhea as a freshman a few years before and was impressed with how she had grown as a thinker in the intervening years. She was at a crucial period of her life right around that time. She called me over and asked if she could write a poem instead of prose. I told her that that was fine. She consciously sat on the border of the grass and dirt near second base, the position she had played for years before quitting softball. Her poem and how it made her feel captures all that I hope will happen when my students write.

Rhea's poem reminds me of Joyce Carol Oates's comment that "writing changes everything." Through her words, Rhea transforms her world. Through the act of reflecting on such a morning, she changes herself. Through her writing and the sharing of that writing with the rest of us, Rhea changes others. When the curtains come down and the house lights come on in June, it should be voices like Rhea's that remain in our heads, not our own.

> Each pebble, each stone
> With a different story to tell
> Some mud red, others as pale as bone
> Large ones, small ones, even too small to see
> Are mounded together in this field
> Broken twigs, dried out needles from nearby trees
> Litter the soil
> Unconscious blades of grass try to sprout

Each blade trying to survive
While most are brown and drying out
The sunlight hits so bright
The entire ground glows
Showing the significance of each object
Underneath the soil gets darker and moist
Like cutting into an unripe orange
Dig deeper and still you find stones
Some even shine and sparkle
Fooling someone to believe they're gold
Precious enough each one is different

A footstep?
Ruins the wholeness of the soil
It's nature
The birds chirping
The bugs clicking
A lonely ant strolls by
In reality you would see it
As where second base belongs
On a baseball field.

REFLECTION

Write your own writer's autobiography, beginning with whatever seems to you the most appropriate moment in your history as a writer.

ACTIVITY

Watch Bill Moyers's *The Language of Life* (or listen to it on audio tape while driving to work, like I did!). Consider writing in your journal about the poems or writers you encounter. Do you see room in your class for these poets, these videos? Why or why not?

RECOMMENDATIONS

The subject of writing is so vast, it is impossible to recommend one book, though if I had to, it would be Donald Murray's *A Writer Teaches Writing*, a book that has taught me more and better than any other book. Other books to consider follow, listed by category.

Writing Assessment

Creating Writers: Linking Writing Assessment and Instruction, by Vicki Spandel and Richard J. Stiggins (Longman 1997). This book offers wonderful strategies to improve student writing at all grade levels by using the Six Trait Rubric, an approach the book discusses at length. Highly recommended.

Exercises

The Writer's Workout Book: 113 Stretches Toward Better Prose, by Art Peterson (National Writing Project 1996). Peterson's book offers fun and effective techniques for improving all aspects of writing, many of them designed to be done in class and often in short stretches of time. Based on methods he honed in the classroom, these strategies work.

Revision

After the End: Teaching and Learning Creative Revision, by Barry Lane (Heinemann 1993). Barry Lane's book turns the notion of revision upside down and makes it an act of creation. Full of proven activities that improve writing. The other book to check out, as I have already mentioned, is Meredith Sue Willis's *Deep Revision: A Guide for Teachers, Students, and Other Writers* (Teachers and Writers Collaborative 1993).

General

Community of Writers: Teaching Writing in the Junior and Senior High School, by Steven Zemelman and Harvey Daniels (Heinemann 1988). One of the best books I've come across when it comes to the different aspects of teaching writing at the high school level. This book deals with how to teach writing, conduct conferences, create a writing community, evaluate writing, and much more.

Theory

Teaching Writing as Reflective Practice, by George Hillocks, Jr. (Teachers College Press 1995), is the culmination of years of thinking and teaching about writing. What I like about this book, aside from its smooth writing, is its approach to the different uses of writing. Hillocks, who teaches at the University of Chicago, has collaborated with a middle school near the university for years, each year having his college students develop a writing program for the school. This book includes, in part, the insights Hillocks gained from that ongoing collaboration, which has consistently resulted in improved student writing.

Fluency

Writing with Power, by Peter Elbow (Oxford University Press 1981) is a wonderful book that gives you many different ways to think about and get students writing. Highly recommended.

Journals

Breathing In, Breathing Out: Keeping a Writer's Notebook, by Ralph Fletcher (Heinemann 1996) is one of those slender gems (ninety-seven pages!) that teaches while offering a pleasant read.

Integrating Reading/Writing

For the daily work of improving students' ability to both read and write, using each to complement and improve the other, I strongly recommend:

The Daybook of Critical Reading and Writing, by Fran Claggett, Louann Reid, and Ruth Vinz (Great Source 1998). This is a series of four different books meant to be purchased and used as a journal by students. The book is worth getting for yourself as both an anthology and a practical guide to using reading and writing to improve each other. Wonderful selections and very affordable.

Creative

What a Writer Needs, by Ralph Fletcher (Heinemann 1993). Described by Donald Murray as one of the best, most "unique" books about writing he has come across, this book offers very focused and proven methods to teach students how to write just about everything, with specific activities to teach voice, style, beginnings and endings, character, and so on.

CHAPTER 8

TEACHING SPEAKING AND LISTENING
THE VERBAL CURRICULUM

Speak the speech, I pray you, as I pronounced it to you, trippingly on the tongue; but if you mouth it as many of your players do, I had as lief the towncrier spoke my lines. Nor do not saw the air too much with your hand, thus, but use all gently: for in the very torrent, tempest, and—as I may say—whirlwind of passion, you must acquire and beget a temperance, that may give it a smoothness.

Hamlet, Act 3, scene 2

He who listens, understands.

—West African proverb

When I was a high school senior, we were each assigned a different aspect of grammar or usage to teach to the class. I was to teach how to divide a word by its syllables. I strolled up to the podium, hands in pockets, no papers, and turned to address my fellow students. I had thought about my presentation for nearly ten minutes, and never even opened the grammar text. I began to improvise—with predictable results. With all the cool I could muster, I said, "Let's take the word *participation*, for example," and I wrote the word on the board. "A very easy word to divide, really." I turned to the board to divide it for the class—and immediately I stalled, hand raised, stuttering as I began to waffle audibly between *par-ti* and *part-i*. The class reeled with hysterics at my failure. I turned around and said very calmly, "Well, let's look at a different word, shall we?" and wrote *responsibility* on the board. Needless to say, the same embarrassing failure ensued. I soon gave up and took my seat, having earned a B for making the class laugh so hard. (This B brought my grade up to a D–, which allowed me to pass the class and, ultimately, to graduate on time!) So ended the first presentation I can remember, and one which those in attendance have never allowed me to forget.

Types of Speeches

Since my own high school experiences, I have come to understand that speaking well, whether to an individual or a group, is essential to our social and professional success. After all, we speak much more than we will ever write. Among other reasons, students must learn how to speak successfully for job interviews, to communicate effectively in the workplace as well as within their relationships. And, if for no other reason than the sense of achievement it affords them, students need to learn and practice how to speak—and listen—in public. In *The Elements of Speechwriting and Public Speaking*, Jeff Cook (1989) identifies the five primary types of speeches most commonly given:

- to stimulate (When this kind of a speech concludes, what do you want your listener *to feel*?)
- to inform (When this kind of a speech concludes, what do you want your listener *to know*?)
- to persuade (When this kind of a speech concludes, what do you want your listener *to think or believe*?)
- to activate (When this kind of a speech concludes, what do you want your listener *to do*?)
- to entertain (When this kind of a speech concludes, what do you want your listener *to have experienced*?)

In a high school English class, students can and should be asked to do a wide range of different kinds of speaking, some of which are formal and involve the whole class, and other types of which are informal and involve a small group or an individual. While these and other reasons challenge us to prepare students to speak effectively, another compelling reason is more self-serving but no less important: speeches can help to decrease teachers' paper load by providing students a paperless means of communicating information.

Some of the most common types of speaking and performing done in an English class include:

- book talks
- book clubs
- debates
- dramatic interpretation/adaptation of literary text
- dramatic monologues
- exhibitions
- formal speeches (e.g., graduation)
- genre speeches (e.g., how-to, impromptu, informational, persuasive)
- interviews
- presentations
- reader's theater
- reading aloud
- simulations (e.g., newscasts, talk shows, court trials)
- storytelling (personal narrative)
- teaching the class

Standards for Speaking and Listening

Various standards documents agree that there are several contexts for speaking:

- One-on-one: These might also be called conferences or interviews. Whatever you call them, they ask students to talk with a specific purpose about a particular topic with one other person.

- Small groups: Such groups range from three to ten people and are charged with specific tasks to complete within the context of the group.

- Full class or large groups: These occasions might involve a class presentation or a formal (e.g., graduation) speech to be delivered to hundreds of people.

Content standards for speaking and listening provide specific objectives for us to consider when planning our classes:

1. *Listening and Speaking Strategies*: Students formulate adroit judgments about oral communications and deliver focused and coherent presentations that convey a clear and distinctive perspective and crisp reasoning, using gestures, tone, and vocabulary tailored to the audience and purpose.

2. *Speaking Applications* (Genres and Their Characteristics): Students deliver polished formal and extemporaneous presentations that combine traditional rhetorical strategies of narration, exposition, persuasion, and description, demonstrating a command of standard English and the organizational and delivery strategies outlined in Listening and Speaking Standard 1.0. (California Academic Standards Commission 1998).

Focus Questions: How to Get Started

As with so many other assignments, speeches benefit from focus questions that can help the student speaker get off to a good start. At this stage the student is thinking and writing—but writing to speak. This is an important difference that students must understand, one that allows for productive conversation about diction and tone in general. The following are intended to help students establish who they are speaking to, what they want to say to their audience, and how best to say it.

- Who is your audience?
- What is the purpose of your presentation or speech?
- What does your audience know about this subject already?
- What will they need to know in order to understand your presentation?
- What resources—visual aids, props, machines—will you need to make this presentation?
- What does your audience care about that you can link to your speech to draw them in?
- How can you best establish your credibility as a speaker in this situation?

Parts of a Speech

Speeches are often much more complicated than they used to be. We live in an era of "presentations" using multimedia devices that were impossible to imagine when I was in high school twenty years ago. Like essays, speeches demand a certain form to achieve their ends. This shape also helps the reader by establishing in their mind a clear set of expectations about what to listen for and how long it will go. Presentations have an opening or introduction that establishes what will be discussed. Next is the substance (i.e., body) of what the student has to say, carefully organized into distinct points for emphasis that are linked by transitional words or phrases. All this concludes with some closing remarks that help bring home their main ideas in a way that makes the listener remember them. Or as one colleague said, a speech has three parts:

- Tell me what you will say.
- Say it.
- Tell me what you said.

Tricks of the Trade for Student Speakers

Good speakers have several methods to engage the audience right away. They:

- tell stories they know will draw in the audience
- use humor to help themselves relax and to entertain the audience
- connect with the audience to establish their sincerity
- incorporate, when appropriate, compelling visuals—video, cartoons, art, presentation graphics—that immediately help to capture the audience's attention

Once they begin speaking, students need to use different strategies to help them better engage and inform their audience. Examples of such strategies include tone and gestures, but also metaphors and analogies that are sure to connect the subject with the audience's interests, to assure that they will "get it." This is where students should incorporate visual aids—handouts, overheads, videos—to help their listeners keep track of ideas or better understand what the student speaker is saying. These visual aids come in all different media and shapes, some of which are included in Appendix F.

Activities for Speakers

The following are some activities that I have used in my classes to strengthen students' verbal expression.

Be the teacher. Often my large projects allow students the option to teach the class as a way to demonstrate their knowledge (and improve their speaking skills). They prepare the lesson, run the class, facilitate all conversations, keep the class moving.

Roundtable discussions. Regular classwide discussions require students to talk about a story or idea we are studying.

Chad presenting his final project using video to complement the Web site he created for the presentation

Read the bulletin. At my school we get a daily bulletin, which we read at the beginning of second period. I pass it to a different student each day and ask them to read it to the class.

Formal presentation. As a culminating activity for our integrated Social Studies–English class, students are required to make a fifteen-minute presentation on a thoroughly researched subject. They must use handouts and other visual aids. A variation on this is the United Nations project, which culminates in the formal presentation of a solution to a lasting political conflict within one or between two countries.

Storytelling. This strategy is especially helpful early on, when students can get up and speak without notes or script because they are telling the class a story they already know. (I will sometimes use storytelling as a follow-up to the Neighborhood or Life Graph assignments; Chapter 9.)

Newspaper article. Each day one or two students get up and read or summarize an article from the day's news to supplement the curriculum and practice their speaking.

Various read-aloud activities. Choral reading, Quaker reading, communal reading, interrupted reading all have their place on a regular basis in the high school English class. These approaches are further discussed later in this chapter.

Book clubs. After organizing your classroom into different groups that follow the "book club" model, each group chooses the book they want to read and checks it out or buys it; then, when they get together during book club time, they talk about the book and the ideas or issues the book raises for them (Raphael and McMahon 1997).

Minutes. A different student each day gets up in front of the class to read the minutes they wrote about the previous day's class as a means of reorienting the class at the beginning of the period and getting daily speaking practice. (The idea comes from English teacher Flossie Lewis.) Here is a particularly amusing example from Yvonne Wu, a junior in my composition class:

Once upon a time there were many dungeons near the Lowell Castle. I, one of the unlucky ones, was sent out to one of them to do a task—the minutes. When I arrived at this dungeon there were only a few other prisoners. One prisoner commented that she saw our torturer, Mr. Burke, earlier that morning and said he didn't look healthy. Soon everyone arrived. And Mr. Burke began class with a Beethoven joke. He announced that we would now begin class each day with a different Beethoven joke. The joke for February 23 was about Beethoven decomposing in his grave to stay busy. Then Natalie got up to read the minutes from the previous day. Mr. Burke then handed out our paragraphs from yesterday. He had some of the prisoners read their paragraphs about what being in high school meant to them. At that point we got into our writing groups and began working on what Mr. Burke called "specificity," which he demanded we all try to say three times fast. Mr. Burke finally assigned our homework. The class was to write a paragraph in which we filled in the blank ("I am _____") with an adjective that describes us. He gave us an example. Mr. Burke's example was "I am messy." The class burst into laughter again. He then gave us all sort of disgusting examples of just how messy he is, getting very specific. Finally, I escaped the dungeon, laughing all the way to my next class as I thought about Beethoven decomposing.

The Golding Trial

Students studying *Lord of the Flies* as part of an integrated Social Studies and English program choose or are assigned a role as either a lawyer, a character from the book, or an expert witness who must testify at the trial. (I have done a variation using Orwell's *Animal Farm* of "The Trial," which was originally conceived by teachers Greg Jouriles and Sue Bedford.) Students must research what they (as witnesses) will say on the stand, in their (lawyers) opening statements, or as they (judges) reconvene the trial each day. (See the photograph of a classroom Golding Trial in Chapter 2, p. 7.)

On the opening day of the trial, all participants arrive in appropriate costume with props befitting their role. The judge, having rehearsed her remarks, starts things off by establishing the parameters of the case and giving instructions to the jury. The lawyers each make their opening statements, which can go no longer than ten minutes. The witnesses, upon stepping into the witness box, make their prepared statements before then taking questions from the lawyers.

Several components of this activity make it a complicated and demanding—but ultimately satisfying—assignment. Students must first master a range of difficult ideas in order to, for example, play Sigmund Freud, who has come to testify regarding our natural instincts toward aggression and the role civilization plays in regulating these instincts. They must then, having mastered the information, work out gestures, style, costume, accent, in order to evoke a particular character when they are "on." Once they are up on the stand, they cannot read from notes, but must be in character and able to speak to a larger audience.

Rules of the Game: Applause, Applause!

No matter what you do, public speaking remains intimidating to many students. Josh, one of my juniors, said his stomach did flip-flops and he couldn't sleep for two days prior to his culminating speech at year's end. Other kids are conveniently absent on the day they are scheduled to speak; somehow they think I will conveniently forget. I never do. But we can help students feel more at ease in front of an audience if we establish with absolute certainty two fundamental rules of conduct:

- Everyone who speaks gets a round of applause when they get up to speak and when they finish.
- Absolutely no heckling or other comments that might unnerve or distract the speaker are allowed.

It is up to the teacher to check each student's topic before a presentation (so as to avoid embarrassing situations for both yourself and the students). One other thing you can do as the teacher to help create and maintain a supportive atmosphere is to sit in the audience with all the other kids. This allows you to model how to behave, listen, and respond when students are speaking.

All of these, and any other methods you might develop yourself, help to create a safe environment that allows students to risk the embarrassment that can come with such activities. If students know they are safe, they will take greater risks to do innovative speeches or presentations, knowing that if they fall flat on their face, the class will be there to pick them up. Some of the most memorable presentations made to my class have come from adolescent boys who wanted to share their obsession with guitars in speeches; the fact that they could hardly play at times, that they were still learning the basics, didn't stop them from plunking out what could have been greeted with giggles and groans. A respectful audience is crucial, as it creates an important opportunity to celebrate and validate students' interests, which at that age are linked to their very identity.

Dealing with Anxiety

First, remind students that the single most helpful technique for alleviating the anxiety that comes with speaking is to be prepared. Students' biggest fear is that they will "blow it." Students worry that they will forget their lines, that they will stutter, that classmates will leave, start doing math homework, or worse, start talking and simply ignore them. In *The Elements of Speechwriting and Public Speaking*, Jeff Cook (1989) suggests several strategies for reducing stress before or during a speech, some of which I have included here:

- Do your homework on the audience: anticipate how they will respond to your ideas and be ready to undercut their resistance, for example, with humor.
- Memorize the opening of your speech so you can start off powerfully, looking at the audience, drawing them in, concentrating on *how* you speak instead of *what* to say.
- Realize that bodily reactions to stress—sweating, increased heart rate, clammy hands—are normal.
- Move around while you speak: hands, body, arms, whatever works to keep you limber and relaxed; gestures are especially helpful, as they can be used to emphasize an idea or direct the audience's attention to the visual aid.
- Be rested, so that you will not have that edgy feeling and your mind will be clear.
- Don't read from a script; even though it seems easier to do so, relying on note cards with key words and phrases written down will allow you to talk to the audience instead of reading to them.

Returning to the Continuum of Performance (Figure 2.1), it is helpful to realize that some kids are not going to overcome their anxieties immediately, and maybe not even while they are in your class. Our teaching is a long-term investment, one we don't always get to see pay off. One year I gave a colleague the chance to see her work rewarded nicely. My seniors that year each had to write graduation speeches—what else can you do with seniors a week before school is out, when the school requires you give them a "demanding final exam"? Several of these students entered our school as ESL students, and some of them had really struggled to achieve that diploma. Sandy Briggs, our ESL teacher, came in for the final exam period for which the kids had prepared a nice feast to add a celebratory atmosphere. The principal, too, came in for the period to listen as one kid after another stood up to talk about what they had done and what they would do. The principal took many notes from their speeches, and that night, at the real graduation, he quoted many of these students in his opening remarks. Meanwhile, Sandy applauded enthusiastically as each of her former students spoke, telling them later how proud she was that they could speak so well. The speeches ended with what was perhaps the most powerful one: Robin Hastings, a wonderful young woman, got up to speak to us about shyness, going on to say that she had spent the last two years participating in the Stanford University Shyness Clinic workshops. Her speech was, in many ways, the culmination of several years worth of work. She was a model of confidence and poise, and received an amazing ovation from her peers, who seemed to take pride in one of their own overcoming such an obstacle.

Rehearsal Tactics to Help Students Prepare

In most cases, students don't need to rehearse to read aloud in class, but for real speeches or major presentations in your class they must if they are going to avoid the failure I encountered during my previously mentioned speech. Also, many English teachers end up helping the school's graduation speakers, and so must have some strategies available to insure success under such high pressure. One year the girl I coached burst into tears five words into her speech! We had talked about this possibility, however, and she was able to compose herself as everyone looked on, applauding her courage. Here are several possible tactics; have students try whichever ones work best for them:

- Speak your entire text aloud. Just get through it, rather like a golfer walking through the course to know where the hazards lie so he can watch for them. Make notes on your text if it helps.
- Lay on your bed, mind cleared of all other distractions, and recite the speech again and again. Without distractions, the words can better lodge themselves in your memory.
- Block the speech off into segments of emphasis, and work on each segment separately. I've found this particularly helpful when working with students giving graduation speeches. It allows them to experience success faster and feel more confident if they can master their opening paragraphs. This technique also helps them break it into units of emphasis for a more effective speech.
- Envision success. When I played tennis as a kid, the big book at the time was *Inner Tennis*, a book that encouraged players to play a match in their head before playing it in reality so they could *see* what to do and anticipate the obstacles to winning. The argument was that you could not play a great match if you could not *imagine* yourself doing so.
- Practice in the place where you will speak. If it is a serious speech and you have access to the room or auditorium in which it will be held, try to get in a few rehearsals there, ideally with a microphone, if you will be using one.

• Edit out any troublesome words or phrases that you repeatedly trip over during your rehearsals. Whether it is a combination of words or a long word is irrelevant: cut it out!

Reading Aloud: How, Why, and When

Perhaps the most common form of speaking students will do in your class is reading aloud. Whether it's their own work in a small group or a student reading a Lucille Clifton poem to the whole class, a good English class does lots of oral reading.

Choral reading. This involves having one portion of the class read certain assigned sections while students in other parts of the room read others. (Instead of "Row Row Row Your Boat" sung in rounds, think of Gwendolyn Brooks's "We Real Cool" read this way.)

Quaker reading. Based on the reading practices at Quaker meetings, this strategy calls for whomever feels like reading to stand and read for as long as they want from the chosen text. A variation on this allows students to read for as long as they want, then to call on someone else who must then pick up where the previous reader left off (a method that clearly encourages close listening, also).

Interrupted reading. Students pair up and read aloud to each other, interrupting whomever is reading to talk about some aspect of the text. The text in this case is used as a means to facilitate thoughtful dialogue about the book and the ideas it contains. The privacy of such reading makes it ideal for ESL students and those with reading difficulties.

Freshmen performing a scene from Romeo and Juliet *using Reader's Theatre techniques*

Dramatic reading. Another name for this could be reader's theater, depending on how you approach it. Students perform the text, investing dramatic interpretation and force into their reading.

Listening for Participation and Assessment

By making students responsible for much of the assessment, you can increase the emphasis on *listening*, another important component of the curriculum that is often overlooked. I create a variety of different evaluation sheets for students to make comments on; these typically have some kind of rubric that allows students to quickly check off a box, and room for comments if they have them. In a class of thirty-five, there is not a lot of time for me to make lengthy comments before the next speaker is up. Another way that I encourage listening is to make a hatch-mark on my seating chart for every question a student asks of a speaker (when they should ask questions) or response to a speaker's questions. Using the seating chart allows me to keep track quickly; in fact, sometimes I give the chart to a student and ask them to keep track. If students are making major presentations, such as teaching the class, I will ask students to fill out a three-by-five card in response to the student's speech, commenting on what that person did that stood out most.

Here is an example of one student's evaluation of Anthony, another student speaker:

> I feel he [Anthony] conducted the class well because he showed courage when he told his story, and he had good ideas. He kept the class on subject and under control. It was a good experience personally because it expanded my views of the idea of growing up. It also gave me a chance to look at my own situation and how my life compares. Anthony did an excellent job in teaching the class and was very open minded.

Some teachers will go so far as to assign students the task of listening for a purpose. For example, in the Golding Trial discussed earlier, twelve kids are jurors; thus their *assignment* is to

Anthony taking over the class to lead a discussion about growing up as part of his project

listen carefully to what the witnesses and lawyers say. Other students in the class act as judges and lawyers; they, too, must listen with great care to gather information for arguments or objections. In other situations, a teacher might appoint a panel which, like a graduate "orals" panel, will follow up the student's speech with questions that the momentarily relieved student must then answer extemporaneously.

Endnote: Last Words

The year during which I wrote this book ended with two speeches which I will never forget. Michael Kostanian, a talented but troubled student of mine, did his final project in the form of an autobiography. We talked about this choice together; I encouraged him to do it as a means of making some sense of his life which, in his own words, seemed so out of control at times. Monday, June 1, he stood before the class and talked with a rare calm about the process of reflecting on his own life which, he told us, he was getting together. His autobiography was titled "The Unfinished Symphony of Michael Kostanian," and it deeply affected all of us. When, thirty-six hours later, Michael died in a terrible car accident on his way to school, everyone of us in that sixth-period class was overcome by a sense of loss, for Michael had, through his speech, invited us into the story of his life, a story we all thought had many more chapters to go.

The second speech came only days after Michael's death when Alex, who was a childhood friend of Michael's and a student of mine, was asked to speak at the funeral. In the midst of his pain and confusion, Alex sat down with me and just talked about what he remembered of Michael during their years growing up. We talked often during the next few days as he wrote, revised, rehearsed his speech in my classroom and over the phone with me at home. Speaking was not easy for Alex under the best of circumstances. However, when he stood before the hundreds of people who came to Michael's funeral, Alex read his speech with a power and elegance I had not seen in him before; the speech itself was a rite of passage that changed him even as he delivered it. Standing in the church, I could not resist my own pride as a teacher to see one of my own students speak so well at such a moment when people needed his words so much.

REFLECTION

Think about the first time you taught a full class, or your early days of teaching. How did it feel to be in that class, your students' eyes watching your every move, as you learned how to teach? Can you recall one specific incident when you felt you made a terrible mistake when you were speaking? What happened?

ACTIVITY

Next time you assign any kind of oral presentation or speech, do the assignment yourself and model for your students how to give such a speech. Take some risks with it, so that they can see that you, too, are reaching to learn something new. It is always helpful for kids to see us challenging ourselves, so that they know it is okay to stumble on their way toward mastery. A second activity for those who can find it: check out the four-cassette collection *The 20th Century's Greatest Speeches*.

RECOMMENDATIONS

The Elements of Speechwriting and Public Speaking. Jeff Scott Cook (Macmillan 1989). Helps kids give different kinds of speeches.

Douglas Barnes' *From Communication to Curriculum* (Boynton/Cook 1992) and *Communication and Learning Revisited: Making Meaning Through Talk* (written with Frankie Todd, Heinemann/Boynton/Cook 1995). These books offer excellent guidance in the use of talk in the classroom, particularly in groups.

CHAPTER 9

TEACHING THINKING IN THE ENGLISH CLASS

I know a good many fiction writers who paint, not because they're any good at painting, but because it helps their writing. It forces them to look at things.

—Flannery O'Connor

The little girl had the making of a poet in her who, being told to be sure of her meaning before she spoke, said, 'How can I know what I think till I see what I say?'"

—Graham Wallas, *The Art of Thought*

Ways of Thinking

I want my students to walk out of class each day able to say they had to think. Whether it is about the structure of a poem or the function of language, the amazing complexity of American society or the complicated nature of the human mind, I want them thinking, making connections, building knowledge. The building blocks of such thinking are words, language; and this work is often done best in groups, where people can, through "exploratory talking" (Barnes 1992), not just add new information to old, but use the new to transform and revise the older ideas they have about the world. If students settle for surface or horizontal knowledge, which is the precursor to deep or vertical knowledge, they are not meeting my standards, nor am I. I know we've done some good "thinking work" when students, quickly assessing their performance at period's end, say things like "I never thought about it that way before!" or "Now I see what you were talking about yesterday," or, "Jeez, Mr. Burke, this poem is hella sick [i.e., cool, deep, good] when you really think about it."

Three key aspects of thinking demand our constant attention in the classroom. First, kids need time to think and encouragement to use different strategies. Second, students need to be taught to "embrace the contradictions" and the complexity we find everywhere in our world; there is no room for either/or thinking. Finally, we must always model how to think in the classroom; whether it is a poem, an idea, or a classroom situation, it is essential that we demonstrate for students how to arrive at some thoughtful solution or new understanding.

Kids need time to think and different ways to be able to think. As Frank Smith writes in *To Think* (1990), "Books are a traditional, obvious, and easy way to bring students into contact with creative and critical people. Writing is a traditional, obvious, and easy way to encourage students to become creative and critical themselves. Talk of all kinds (monologues, dialogues, discussions, debates, interviews, and arguments) and art of all kinds promote creative and critical thinking." Howard Gardner's theories of multiple intelligence (1992) have taught me the most about using a variety of strategies and methods to develop in students the skills necessary to think better on their own, using all their different senses.

Like everyone else, kids, if hit between the eyes with a sudden or random question, will get that deer-in-the-headlights look; this is especially true for those students with special needs in your class who require extra time to process information. Such "wait time" is essential when having discussions: wait a bit after you ask a question of the class or a person. Let the question sink in, percolate. This is how deeper thoughts come. In discussions, when kids say "I don't know" to your question, say "I will come back to you," or ask, "Well, what would you say if you *did* know?" This is my personal favorite; it gives students permission to speculate without having to worry they will be wrong, since they have already established for the dense teacher that they do not know. "But okay, Mr. Burke, for you, I will take a guess. . . ."

Embracing Complexity

This freedom to speculate is essential, for we must, whenever possible, teach to complexity or, to put it differently, avoid the simplicity of dichotomies. Professor of anthropology Mary Catherine Bateson always requires her students to study *three* cultures at a time, to keep them from reducing differences down to "us" and "them." Physicist Richard Feynman lectured specifically about the value of doubt and uncertainty as defenses against oversimplified thinking that strives to reduce complexity down to a simple equation (Feynman 1998). Frank Smith (1990) wrote, "Certainty stunts thought, in ourselves and others. The fruits of understanding grow from the seeds of doubt. . . . Critical thinking begins with the readiness to challenge received wisdom. . . . Thought flourishes as questions are asked, not as answers are found." Bruce Pirie, in his book *Reshaping High School English* (1997), warns us about the dangers of limiting thinking to its relevance to the self when the greater needs of the society as a whole are so urgent. To think about racism, for example, in relation to the society at large addresses its inherent complexity, whereas to focus on its effect on the individual is to limit it to a personal problem. In the end, "what counts is the extent to which instruction requires students to think, not just report someone else's thinking" (Nystrand et al. 1997).

Domains of Thinking

I have divided different strategies for helping kids think—about ideas, texts, cultures, structures, their lives—into those domains common to our work. Each domain offers different "tools" for thinking, some lending themselves to one student or task more than another. And none of them tends to work in isolation: we talk to prepare to write; we draw to understand what we think about what we read; we read to prepare for the discussion that will lead to the essay. Thus the approach of multimodality in the area of thinking implies that there is a method which can be effective with any student; we just need to be ready to draw from this repertoire as needed to find it. We also need to decide which mode of thinking is best for the task at hand: rapid brainstorming to create mess, formal planning to create structured arguments, or transactional interactions that involve different texts and conversations to help construct knowledge. I offer the following domains of thinking, realizing that there are others or different ways of conceptualizing the notion of thinking:

- talking
- writing
- drawing
- questioning
- reading
- integrating

Before I examine these different strategies in depth, let me quickly discuss the importance of modeling. While Frank Smith (1990) correctly points out that we are born thinking, we are not born with an innate sense of, for example, how different texts function or how our own mind works as it tries to make sense of these texts. When we ask students to do "thinking work," we need to model how to do this, especially if we are introducing a new type of thinking into the class or a new context for established thinking. Simply show them briefly how you make sense of a short passage of a poem, or how you think through a particular scene in a film to arrive at your conclusion that the character has just undergone some important change. To borrow from Vygotsky's concept of "zones of Proximal development" (1994), you as the teacher serve as a sort of ferryman who, at such moments, helps students cross the river from one place to another. You do this by using your knowledge and capacities to show them how to do it so they can then complete the task themselves. Such instruction, often referred to as *scaffolding*, "allows students to develop a sense of ownership in their work because they are able to 'develop their own meaning rather than simply following the dictates of the teacher or text' " (Nystrand et al. 1997).

Conversation as Curriculum: Using Talk to Help Students Think

Imagine an elegant boardroom in one of the nation's top corporations: some of the most powerful men and women in the world gather here monthly to talk seriously about the meaning of different stories in Genesis. They are there at the invitation of Burton Visotsky, author of *The Genesis of Ethics: How the Tormented Family of Genesis Leads Us to Moral Development* (1996). Visotsky's Genesis Seminar, which he has also conducted with artists and psychologists, among others, exemplifies what Douglas Barnes, in *From Communication to Curriculum* (1992), calls "exploratory talk." Barnes defines such talk as "marked by frequent hesitations, rephrasings, false starts and changes of direction. [It is] very important whenever we want a learner to take an active part in learning and to bring what he learns into interaction with that view of the world on which his actions are based." Jerome Bruner (1986, 28) sums up what I mean nicely: "We have a need to share the objects of our attention with others."

This need is exemplified by research conducted in my junior class. When a doctoral candidate surveyed my students about different strategies that helped them learn and allowed for "meaningful moments," he found students overwhelmingly favored discussions (85 percent ranked it first), particularly full-class discussions about issues of substantial importance (e.g., race, identity, morality). While full-class discussions can be effective and exciting, talking can improve thinking through a range of activities. Here are some different ways to use talk in the classroom, some of which I will go into greater detail about later on:

Interrupted reading. The listener can interrupt the reader to talk or ask questions about anything in the text at any time; the text is essentially used as a conversation starter. A variation on this would be a student-teacher conference in which the teacher used questions to measure and increase the depth of a student's understanding of a text or an idea.

Paired conversations. Huddle up and talk for a set time about a specific subject (often as prelude to a larger class discussion).

Small-group discussions. Get into previously arranged or impromptu groups to talk about a particular text or idea (often as prelude to writing or class discussion).

Class discussions. Known as "roundtables" in my class, these classwide discussions are especially engaging and helpful at certain times (e.g., a crucial moment in the novel or a poem, like Marge Piercy's "Barbie Doll," that sparks heated discussion about "beauty" or human nature).

Debates. I suggest organizing debates so as to avoid either/or thinking, something Jim Moffett once said debate promoted. Surely there are more than two sides to any debatable topic. Consider organizing a three-way or five-way debate and see what happens.

Interviews. Have kids go out into the community, home, or the workplace to participate in thoughtful conversations with others about certain topics; let their thoughts interact with and challenge your own.

Arguments. I like to get kids involved and thinking by creating argumentative occasions; this might mean creating a set of moral dilemmas and asking them to reach unanimous consent about which of the following are, for example, evil. Here is an abbreviated version of one such assignment:

> *Directions*: Decide which actions you feel are evil and why you feel that way. Your entire group must agree on each one (i.e., your decision must be unanimous). First, your group must define *evil* and establish criteria before you begin; or, if you prefer, you can come up with a definition and criteria after you pass judgment on the actions, but make sure that it accords with your decisions about the dilemmas.

1. The pilot dropped the atomic bomb on Hiroshima.
2. The scientist designed the atomic bomb.
3. The president ordered the man to design the bomb and told the man to drop it.
4. A major league pitcher in a World Series game throws a wild pitch at the other team's best hitter, hitting him intentionally in order to take him out of the game.
5. A professional boxer hits his opponent, killing him.
6. A person with AIDS has sex with many different people.
7. One person confides in another that they are HIV-positive; the confidante tells another person who tells another; eventually the infected person's boss hears of it and fires the HIV-infected individual because they are HIV-positive.
8. A pro-life activist murders a doctor who performs abortions.

Dramatic performances. Students speak and act as a character from story or history then follow up performance with discussion about what they/their character thought—and why—during the scene. It might also mean simulations or role playing; during our study of India (when we read *Jasmine*), my freshmen take part in a *panchayat*, which is a village court before the elders. Individuals must argue their case about the proposed shoe factory and its effects on the village.

Puzzle game. Take all of the names and other important themes or objects or places in a text and write them down with plenty of space around each word. (It is easier and quicker to do this on the computer and then you have it all saved for the future.) Cut these words up into inch-wide strips, ideally on heavy-stock paper. Students should be in groups of five to six so that many minds can work from many angles. Have them arrange the cards to represent the relationships between pieces of the text; then ask them to explain the relationship to the class, supporting their reasoning by showing the connections in their diagrams. I have had students work in this way to organize the different names of characters in Homer's *The Odyssey*, in order for them to better understand the complex network of relationships between people in the story and such ideas (written down on the strips) as place, piety, and strength. Thus different names might be arranged for a time around *strength* to reflect the different types of strength each character represents.

Conversational roundtable. Using a graphic organizer (Figure 9.1), talk about what each section contains—characters, themes, events—and why. Then, still using the organizer, expand the discussion to include the whole class. Figure 9.1 is an example from my freshman class, in which students made connections among several different books they read in preparation for their final essay.

Magnetic poem. Take a text—at random or one that the students have studied—and cut it up into just the words. Have the students build poems from the words. They immediately begin talking about how language works, what certain arrangements mean—and how they mean that (see example in Chapter 2).

Transparent texts. Photocopy specific passages from texts or poems onto transparencies, then ask groups to explicate the text using the overhead to lead the discussion. They will

Freshmen collaborating to use the puzzle game to better understand the relationships in The Odyssey

The Conversational Roundtable: What Characters Might Talk About

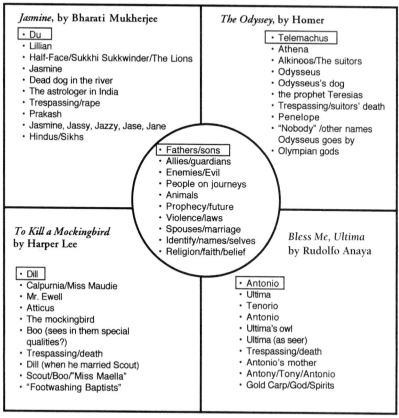

DIRECTIONS: The general idea is to look for "foursomes" between stories students read: i.e., what could a particular character or group from each story talk about if you brought them together? I have put boxes around one such foursome: Antonio, Dill, Telemachus, and Du, all of whom have in common that they are sons and have complicated relationships with their fathers. You could even add yourself, or modern teens in general to the mix, to see what they would have to say in such a discussion; in that scenario you might end up with a foursome like Holden, Esperanza, Hamlet, and a high school senior at BHS or some variation on that theme. Then take any foursome and actually write the conversation they would have: e.g., what would Holden, Esperanza, Hamlet, and a high school senior at BHS say, for example, about identity or their place in the world and how they feel about it? Write it up as a dialogue to be performed/read to the class or to smaller groups.

Figure 9.1   *A sample conversational roundtable*

think about how the text works, what to mark, how to mark it—all while talking about the text at hand.

The Power of Collaborative Talk

The United States Constitution is a document that exemplifies powerful thinking inspired by conversation. The minds of the founders were like pieces of flint that sparked off of each other. My previous example of Visotsky's Genesis Seminar embodies the power and excitement we all find in good conversations about ideas of importance. Indeed, after the business leaders finished their seminar with Visotsky, they agreed to continue on their own, so important had the discussions become to them. Finally, as Csikszentmihalyi reports in *Creativity* (1996), the American business world needs people who can sit around and dream up new products and approaches so as to help us remain competitive; he suggests that our country's economic future may well depend on such capacities for creative thinking through collaboration with others.

Using Writing to Help Students Think

Writing is an activity that forces thought: you cannot write without thinking, for to arrange language into meaningful units—sentences, phrases, poems, narratives—is to use the mind. True, we might not be conscious of our thinking, especially if we are doing "automatic writing"; however, one reason for using writing to think is precisely to bring the unconscious more to the surface, where we can "see what we have to say." In *How Writing Shapes Thinking*, Judith Langer and Arthur Applebee (1987, 3) argue that "to improve the teaching of writing, particularly in the context of academic tasks, is also to improve the quality of thinking required of school children. [Historians] attribute [the development of "rational" or "scientific" thinking] to the fact that writing facilitates a logical, linear presentation of ideas. . . . Written language not only makes ideas more widely and easily available, it changes the development and shape of ideas themselves."

If used well, the steps discussed in the following section will accomplish what Langer and Applebee found in their research, helping students to better know and understand what they think not only about a character in a novel or some literary construct such as conflict, but also about principles in science, historical events, or psychological trends. In many ways, this process reminds me of my two sons' Lego constructions: like writers, they pull everything out of the box and fasten it to everything else in order to see what meaning or form can be found within the pieces from which they make something new. What they come up with is not always apparent to me but often leads them to create, by day's end, remarkable castles, vehicles, or bridges.

Sample Activity

While the following model contains those components common to any thoughtful writing task, I do not wish to imply that there is only one way to use writing to think. Others abound: brainstorming, automatic writing, clustering, dialogue journals. It is worth reiterating that few if any of this chapter's strategies operate independently: We write to help us think about what we will say; we draw or "brainstorm" in order to spur the mind to new levels of insight; we talk about what something means, thinking that the combined mental power of four people can surely solve the problem one mind alone cannot. For now, we focus on a sequence of steps that lead the writer deeper into the subject at hand.

I usually start class by asking my students to get out their journals, telling them they will write for about ten minutes so they know what to expect and can settle down into the task. These steps can be adapted to any class and will serve to get students ready to discuss, read, or write (a larger paper).

Next, I write on the board or overhead a focus question which all students will be able to write something about because it will be of interest to all students (e.g., "Why is America so fascinated by violence?").

The rationale for this writing activity might be any one or all of the following: To establish a baseline that shows what they know now; to create the "frame" for the subsequent discussion or assignment; to prepare them to write a larger, more formal paper; to open the possibilities or establish their stance in relation to the subject.

The students then write for ten minutes. Ideally, I write with my students both to model and create a possibly helpful example of "what thinking looks like" for students who might have trouble with the assignment. Another option, if I don't have time or feel able to write with the students, is to have several exemplars of the assignment from former students which I can put up on the overhead or pass out to examine. This allows me to integrate assessment into the activity by giving students a benchmark against which to compare their work.

At this point I have several options, all of which are sound, each one of which does something slightly different. Note that all of these are particularly effective for reluctant students or those, such as ESL students, who are uncomfortable speaking up in class.

Examine their own text. Students take their own writing and go through the text with a highlighter or pen, and identify—by underlining or highlighting—those items they wish to share in a group or class discussion. Then, in their journal (for a few minutes) or when they introduce their idea, they explain why they selected those particular ideas to share.

The class responds to student's ideas. Again, this option allows for either oral or written response to an idea the student has presented to the class. In this instance I might use the student's ideas to get into the discussion or larger activity that is the main course for the day. This option requires students to listen, a skill they all need to work on, and which the new standards place emphasis on developing.

Students participate in a written conversation. Students buddy up and trade journals with each other. Sean and Naoki read each other's journal entry; then Sean responds in writing

Sevag and Jeff following up their written conversation with a spoken one to help understand a story

to the entry in Naoki's journal, perhaps comparing it to his own or writing about the new ideas Naoki's entry may have inspired in him. Then, Sean gives Naoki's journal to Elena who reads and responds to both Naoki's entry and Sean's subsequent response to it. The journal finally returns to Naoki who then brings closure to this stage by writing his own response to what the others have written. Class discussion, using these responses, can then proceed.

Get into groups and talk. Using those different strategies outlined earlier in this chapter, have students talk—about what they think, why they think that, the implications of what they think, and so on.

Assessment. It is now possible to assess their understanding of the task at hand (i.e., learning how to use writing to think) or the subject (e.g., how character reveals itself in this story) and thereby determine the level at which they are currently thinking. You can determine this informally by looking at their journals or listening to the discussions they have. If they are just learning to use writing to think, you do not want to create a judgmental environment that will stifle their learning; yet learning happens by revising one idea into a new one until you arrive at the pleasure we call understanding or mastery.

Provide or gather exemplars. As I mentioned above, it is extremely helpful to show students examples of what this work looks like, especially if it is new to them. If you do not have any exemplars, now is an ideal time to gather some for future reference. You can also stop to brainstorm characteristics of good thinking by breaking down the exemplars or students' responses. This would be particularly helpful, for example, in a class where writing to think was the actual subject of the lesson.

Wrap it up. These steps have led your students down into the subject and readied them for any number of demands. At this point you could push further into the subject by having them write a poem in which they synthesize their ideas (e.g., about change), act out their ideas in a dramatization, start debating about the subject, or simply get down to the larger assignment (e.g., the essay, experiment, project) for which all this was a preparation.

Such steps, if they become habits, serve the students remarkably well in subsequent years as they move out of the domain of academic writing and into the larger world of personal experience and work. Furthermore, such activities help me all the time; after teaching *The Catcher in the Rye* for ten years, I find it rewarding and helpful to sit down and rouse my own thinking and make the familiar once again interesting by seeing it anew.

Graphic English: Using Drawing to Help Students Think

We often pay our respects to Howard Gardner's theories in conversations with other teachers, but often we wonder just how to integrate such ideas as multiple intelligences in the English classroom. Seventeen-year-olds sprawled all over the floor in the hall with crayons spilled out on large butcher paper doesn't always look so serious; if such work is not approached intelligently, it is unlikely to be worth the time spent.

The guiding principle in graphic English is that we think differently when we transform our ideas into images and patterns than when we use words to express our thoughts. We are using the metaphorical mind that seeks to make connections between the initial idea being examined—e.g., freedom, family, gangs—and its associations. Such thinking is typically more fluid as, at least in its informal stages, it is more messy: just throw around whatever ideas visit you without questioning their connection. Consider, for instance, how much better students can grasp a play like *Hamlet* if they see the symmetry of its characters as they construct a map on the board to reveal that each character has its antithesis on the other side; this strategy will also work with *Romeo and Juliet* or novels like *My Antonia* and *Lord of the Flies*.

Much of the work described in this section is best done on butcher paper or transparencies so that students can present their work to the class for further discussion. Such discussions should emphasize how they arrived at their understanding or how, for example, their thinking changes the meaning of the idea being considered. The nature of the task is also engaging, social, collaborative; thus I tend to have them do such work in groups, though I will sometimes allow them to work individually if they prefer. It is also ideal if they can spread out during such work. Sometimes I take them down to the library for the large tables; other times we divide ourselves between the classroom and the hallway. While "visual thinking" is instrumental in my class as a tool for thoughtful engagement of all students, I often feel compelled to make them go deeper and to do so individually and in writing. In this respect, visual thinking often serves as an intermediary step, becoming a means to help students on subsequent assignments. The visual thinking has prepared them to know what they think; thus the writing is often some of their best. The writing, meanwhile, offers more individual accountability and assessment of each person's understanding of what the group accomplished. Finally, though I love doing all the activities listed below, there is a fine line between keeping such work grounded in "English" and drifting into what feels like an arts and crafts class; such activities can be drawn out, often to great success, but students should not be taking days to make a mask. The process of making a complicated, multi-textual production, however, can demand days of serious collaboration as students try to incorporate text, symbols, connections, images.

Strategies for the Classroom

I have used all of these strategies, adapting the ideas of some and implementing the ideas of others without change. Each one is briefly described and a few others are thoroughly discussed.

> *Personal roundtable*. Have students draw a circle to indicate a table, and then at each of the table's "seats," have them identify those people who have had the most influence on them. Then, using each seat as a node on a cluster, brainstorm more specifically in what way, why, and how that person had an influence on them.
>
> *Graphic organizers*. One example of such an organizer would be the Conversational Roundtable (see Figure 9.1). Others might be spreadsheets, outlines, Venn diagrams, or any other page designed to organize information—about characters, ideas, words—for a purpose. Such organizers invite examination of structure and relationships; the activity should be created with that objective in mind.
>
> *Masks*. Masks offer powerful avenues into themes and stories (Figure 9.2). Also, there are ways of making these masks look very nice regardless of one's artistic talent. Have students make masks to illustrate themes (e.g., evil, confusion, family), ideas (e.g., the many sides of human nature, the stages of life), characters (e.g., Jack in *The Lord of the Flies* is an obvious example), and themselves (or some aspect of themselves). Be sure to have them write an explanation of their mask, as this is a rich cognitive encounter.
>
> Charissa, who created the mask with the stitched lips shown in Figure 9.2, offered the following explanation of her mask:
>
>> My mask was created to represent my self-image in my own eyes. I have stitched lips or mouth, which represents the fact that I feel I am never heard. I seem to be loud, and can speak to

Figure 9.2   *Three masks created by freshmen as part of our study of* The Lord of the Flies

everyone, but no one actually seems to hear or understand what I say or the point I am trying to get across. I feel that no one takes me seriously or really cares about my opinion. Through the mask, I wanted to emphasize the fact that people need to listen. I feel I am a good listener and that is why many vent their anger in my presence. I don't interrupt or criticize what they say, and feel I just listen to others and am not heard. I just wish sometimes that I had someone to listen to me, and that is what I am trying to deliver through my mask.

Clusters/brainstorms/idea mapping. Have students do this messy thinking work as a way to get them started; or use it yourself on the board to narrate the class' thinking as you discuss a story or idea.

Renderings of ideas or texts. Translate ideas or texts into symbolic or visual representations to better understand them. Consider, for example, how much better a student who "draws" Robert Frost's "The Road Not Taken" will understand its different aspects (see Figure 9.3).

Mandalas. I use these in many different ways, but always to get students to think about the relationships between parts; about structures and patterns; and about distinctions that can be made (e.g., stages, phases, eras). Anthony's three-layer mandala in response to *The Kitchen God's Wife*, shown in Figure 9.4, still amazes me every time I look at it. The students were to create a mandala with three rings to it: one that charted the stages of life for human beings; a second that related *The Kitchen God's Wife* to these stages; and a third that used the stages to describe and anticipate their own life.

Anthony provided the following explanation of his work:

> I tried to have my mandala represent a target shape with a small circle in the middle and then two larger circles around it. Then I thought that since the circles were just circles, I could make them different shapes. Since life was a circle, I kept it that way. Winnie's life could be made a shape of China, since that was her homeland. After that idea, I thought that my life could be represented by the United States, my country.

Life Graph. This idea comes straight from Linda Rief's *Seeking Diversity* and continues to be one of the most productive prewriting activities I use. Within a day, my students have done some serious personal reflection in the course of graphing their life and, most important to

Figure 9.3   *Sergio's artistic interpretation of the "The Road Not Taken"*

me, now have many topics to write about. I will just say, from time to time, "Take one of the moments from your Life Graph and write that story." (See Figure 9.5.)

Timelines. As visual narratives, timelines are particularly helpful when dealing with a book that has a long or sometimes confusing plot (e.g., *The Grapes of Wrath*, *The Invisible Man*, or *Joy Luck Club*). It helps to impose a sort of schematic order to the story that keeps kids oriented; it is like those maps that have a big arrow that says "You are here." Such maps also give students a schematic overview of the book, thus allowing them to think about patterns, stages, or motifs in the story.

Metaphor project. Students take a book or idea and to better understand its complexity, develop a metaphor for it. The metaphor itself is a means of symbolic thinking; however, the important work comes when they take their metaphor (e.g., "War is a nightmare" is an example from *All Quiet on the Western Front*) and create a collage or piece of art that illustrates that idea.

Graphic novel. In the wake of *Maus*, the "graphic novel" by Art Speigelman about his father's experiences in the Nazi concentration camps, this form has enjoyed a renaissance. The serious artists in your class will exceed all expectations for the assignment if given the room and freedom to work. I've seen it done for *The Odyssey*, *Huck Finn*, and short stories (see Figure 9.6).

Vocabulary pictures. In *Drawing Your Own Conclusions*, Fran Claggett (1992) recalls having her students "draw their vocabulary words" in hopes that they would better retain them; she found their retention of these words dramatically higher when they made an illustration to accompany the terms.

Multimedia projects. Students think in visual terms more than ever thanks to computers. The integration of words, images, and sounds is a skill many already have and others need the opportunity to develop. This category is too broad for any one strategy. I will, however, offer the exemplar I created for my students one year: an interactive timeline of the history of poetry which combines images (of the poets and related art) with sound (music

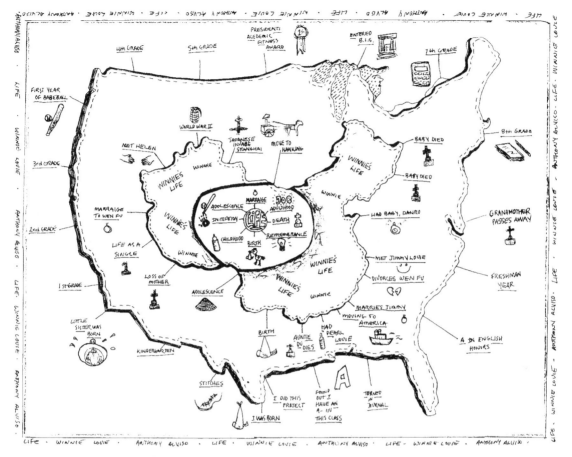

Figure 9.4 *Anthony's multilayered mandala incorporating the stages of life and how they apply to Winnie from*
The Kitchen God's Wife *and his own life*

and readings) and design components (layout and related features) that become an increasingly important part of graphic thinking.

The Neighborhood. Some books or stories (and students' lives) really lend themselves well to this assignment. Briefly, have them draw a map of their own neighborhood or the neighborhood of the story they are reading (e.g., *The House on Mango Street, Bless Me, Ultima*, or *To Kill a Mockingbird*) and use that map as a tool for describing and thinking about the different aspects that make up a neighborhood. This activity lit up my class the first time I tried it; once they started sharing their maps in groups, they thought of other stories or said, "Oh, yeah, I forgot all about that time the cloud of butterflies swarmed us at the park!" Remember, however, that not all kids live in houses (apartments are just a different version: a vertical neighborhood) and many kids (myself included) moved many times during their early years. You can solve this problem by having them draw a composite of all their different neighborhoods. Figure 9.7 shows the neighborhood conceived by junior Charlotte Perry.

The open mind. Ben Martinez's open-mind drawing of Richard Wright in *Black Boy* (see Chapter 11 for an example) exemplifies the kind of thinking that can be achieved with

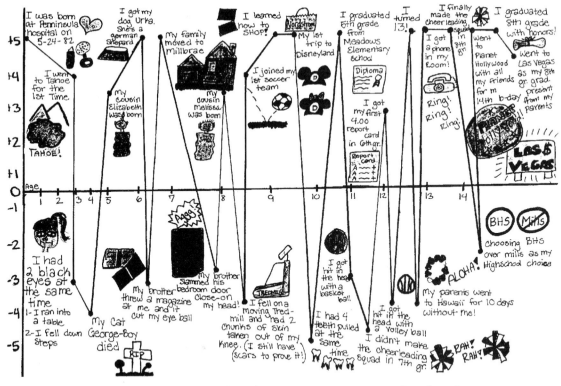

Figure 9.5 *Lisa's Life Graph served as her basis for many writing assignments throughout the year.*

this strategy. Because the "open mind" concept struck some as controversial—i.e., going inside students' minds—some teachers have resorted to alternative designs, the most amusing of which is "the bathtub," which requires you to fill a tub with images and events instead of bubbles and duckies. Again, as Ben's written explication demonstrates, having students follow up such drawing with writing is ideal.

Visual text. A "visual text" in this case means anything from a video to a painting, a political cartoon to a photographic essay. Such visual texts provide excellent opportunities to begin thinking about a subject from a different perspective. For example, students reading *The Grapes of Wrath* or *The Scarlet Letter* look at Dorothea Lange's photograph of a poor migrant woman with three children hanging on her, what I have come to call the "Dustbowl Madonna." They can talk or write about her—or *as* her, or any of her children. This, or other works of art, invoke the imagination to occupy the reality of the painting or photograph; such imaginative thinking or interpretive responses often break new ground in the students' perception of characters in literature. The magazine *Doubletake* provides rich visual texts, mostly in the form of photographic essays on a theme, that invite powerful writing and elicit students' interest. Also, poet Edward Hirsch's wonderful *Transforming Vision: Writers on Art* (1994) offers a rich sampling of art coupled with responses to the artwork in poetry and prose by many great writers, some of which provide helpful examples of how to write or think about art. In Chapter 13 I offer other strategies for using video in the classroom to get students thinking. Cartoons, which invite laughter and insight into the classroom, often deal with important and current issues and events. Put

Figure 9.6 *A sample from Nikola's remarkable "Illustrated* Huck Finn*"*

these onto overheads to use for quickwrites; such exercises allow students to sharpen their minds by looking critically at visual information. Here is a good example of art eliciting critical thinking; it comes from Lynette, who was a junior in my class when she wrote this:

When I look at Edward Hopper's paintings, two words come to my mind: dulled and somber. I guess it's because the scenes he chooses to illustrate/portray are scenes where the people in-

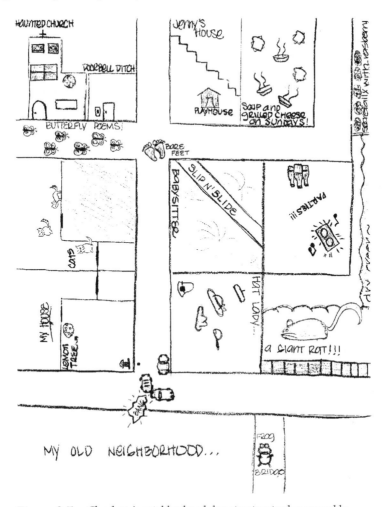

Figure 9.7 *Charlotte's neighborhood drawing inspired memorable conversations that lead to improved understanding of John Steinbeck's* Cannery Row.

volved look like something is on their mind or something is troubling them. That's why the tone is not very alive. Hopper's colors are also dulled, which reflects his portraits of people whose expressions, if they have any, look like they are down.

We were looking at a series of Hopper paintings as part of our study of John Steinbeck's *Cannery Row*; thus we used Hopper's paintings to help us get thinking about people's lives as depicted in art and, ultimately, the novel by Steinbeck. The visual themes of alienation so prevalent in Hopper's work allow them to "see" what Steinbeck is working with in words.

Such visuals, particularly with difficult stories that reluctant readers struggle to understand, give some students a doorway into the book: they understand what they can see. Consider, for example, the simplicity—coupled with the insight into the central dilemma of the text—of the drawing by another junior who was trying to make sense of *The Scarlet Letter* shown in Figure 9.8. The picture, which I copied, along with others, onto an overhead transparency, allowed the class to focus on this one aspect of the text. Her drawing captured the essence of the character's crisis in a way that everyone in the class found helpful.

This last point merits discussion. Some of the best artists in my classes are some of the most disengaged boys in the class. When given an assignment that taps their artistic skills, the student everyone thought was lost suddenly shines and becomes, for a moment, the master. Students see that this student has real talents and realize he is a human being like they are; the dynamics change and everyone learns something about the complexity of human beings (Rief 1998). Such success is all the more important, for often such students as I just described are troubled by some reading difficulties. In today's high school English classes, where as many as half of your class might be reading significantly below grade level, students like these need different tools to learn what they need to know but also to demonstrate their knowledge of what they know in a medium that is familiar to them. On the other hand, students in honors or AP classes often resist such activities describing them as a waste of time, saying they are "not in kindergarten anymore." Fran Claggett (1992) addresses this situation nicely, referring to it as an imbalance in their academic learning: "the drive to academic excellence tragically prevents them from the very activities that would tap the essence of being an educated person." She goes on to say that once these students see what conclusions can be drawn from these activities, they are quickly won over and use them to great effect; my experiences with such students further confirm this.

In the end, when I consider such art-based or graphic strategies and whether they help kids think, I remember what Shawna Fraher, one of my juniors, wrote after we did The Neighborhood assignment. Her note was unsolicited and thus, to me, all the more poignant. Shawna wrote: "I would like to say that I really did like you making us draw the neighborhood maps.

Figure 9.8 *Lynette's drawing captures Dimsdale's dilemma in* The Scarlet Letter.

That project seemed to open up my mind and fill it with a whole bunch of childhood memories. I felt that by doing more visual types of activities or doing more drawing, our work became better. By saying better I mean that our writing would be more descriptive."

Using Questions to Help Students Think

Questions include; they invite. By their definition they demand a dialogue: someone is asking another to respond. After five years of studying high school English classes, Arthur Applebee (1996) found that the most engaging—and, one might argue, effective—courses developed their curriculum so as to answer a question that the course asked. Just as Grant Wiggins, the assessment guru, says that what gets tested is what gets taught, so, too, might we say that what gets asked it what gets considered. Notice the difference between the following two questions and imagine how differently they would shape discourse in the classroom:

1.   Why do Jim and Huck run away?
2.   What does it mean to be "free"? If we are a free society as we claim, why are there so many alarms, fences, and bars on people's houses? Do today's teenagers feel more free than teenagers a hundred years ago? Compare your own life to Huck's and think carefully before you answer: which of you is more free?

Obviously I stacked the deck a bit by embellishing the second question, but this serves to illustrate my point. The first question is important: it establishes that kids understand the plot (i.e., what is happening). The second question invites a series of related inquiries that force them to think in more directions simultaneously, for the truth is that there is always more than one reason why someone does something. Thus the questions we ask define what—and how and why—we teach. Is your American Literature class about the evolution of independence in American culture or is it about *Huckleberry Finn*? Is it a survey of American writers or an investigation into the question of what it means to be an American? Is it based on a question that wakes your students up or puts them—and you—to sleep? Is your course allowing your students to engage intellectually and emotionally or is it forcing you to test them every day to insure that they are doing the reading (in order to pass the quiz)?

To push this line of inquiry a bit further, you could say that a class is not only defined by the questions we ask, but the extent to which our students themselves help to shape or ask these questions. It is not that the questions must be internalized, but that this habit of questioning must be adopted, the questions becoming the students' questions, which they ask of the world when confronted by the inevitable complexity.

What follows are some of the most common types of thinking I try to achieve through questions. "Dense" thinking is characterized by its effort to make connections within and outside of the text you are teaching; these questions truly exemplify the complexity I mentioned earlier in the chapter. "Revealing questions" here refer to those moments when students' comments reveal an opportunity for further inquiry or an invitation to challenge their assumptions. Reflective thinking is what some have called a "habit of mind," the kind of thinking we hope to see all our students practicing both as students and citizens.

Dense Questions

To develop in students the capacity to question, I use a specific strategy from Leila Christenbury's book *Making the Journey: Being and Becoming a Teacher of English Language Arts* (1994). I use this strategy throughout the year (see Figure 9.9), asking students to develop specific questions in class sometimes, or to create their own "dense question" for their semester's final exam. Christenbury's strategy provides a very clear process for developing good questions; the process of developing the questions themselves is worth hours of direct instruction. But there is something else that questions achieve: they create a space and opportunity for a meaningful conversation that involves everyone. While it would be wonderful if everyone came to class having done their work, this is too often not the case; thus some days we find ourselves with one quarter to one half of students who, for whatever reasons, did not do the work. Students do not have to have read the text to do this work; however, they do better if they have since any essential conversation is, by definition, of interest to all participants. Consider these questions which my

Type of Question	Description	Example
TEXT	info found in text	Who is the narrator of the story?
READER	reader's experience, values, ideas	Have you ever felt fed up with everything and just wanted to take off, get away on your own?
WORLD or OTHER LIT.	knowledge of history, other cultures, other literature	What other character--in a book or a movie--would you compare the main character to?
SHADED: TEXT/READER	Combines knowledge of text with reader's own experiences, values, ideas	What characteristics do you share with the main character?
TEXT/WORLD	Combines knowledge of text with knowledge of history and cultures	In what ways is Holden similar to teenagers today? In what ways are today's teenagers different?
TEXT/OTHER LITERATURE	Combines knowledge of text with knowledge of other pieces of literature.	How does Holden's relationship with his sister compare with Esperanza's?
READER/WORLD	Combines knowledge of reader's own experiences with knowledge of other cultures, people.	In what ways are teenagers in other countries similar to American teens? In what ways are they different?
READER/OTHER LITERATURE	Combines knowledge of reader's own experiences with other pieces of literature.	In what ways are you similar and/or different from Holden and Esperanza?
DENSE QUESTION TEXT/READER/WORLD or TEXT/READER/OTHER LIT.	Combines knowledge of all three areas into one DENSE question.	Why does Holden feel alienated and how is that related to what many of today's teens feel? Include in your answer a discussion of the extent to which you do or don't share these same feelings and why.

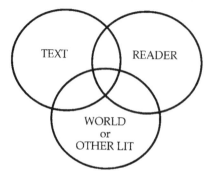

Figure 9.9   *The Dense Question Strategy (developed by L. Christenbury, used with permission)*

freshman honors students created for their final exam as part of a course that integrated the history and literature of, in this case, South Africa:

- What connections can you make between *Romeo and Juliet*, *Cry, the Beloved Country*, and our study of Apartheid in South Africa regarding the notion of conflict?
- In what way are *Romeo and Juliet*, *Cry, the Beloved Country*, and South Africa like Newton's Third Law (for every action there is an equal and opposite reaction)?
- Explore the types of and reasons for violence in an essay in which you compare *Romeo and Juliet*, *Cry, the Beloved Country*, your own life and society, and South African society at large.
- Is it really what you want? Explain how desire affects decisions in *Romeo and Juliet*, *Old Man and the Sea*, *Cry, the Beloved Country*, and South Africa.

Such questions, aside from being better than some of my own earlier attempts at dense questions, allow students to engage with those aspects of the curriculum that interest them the most while linking them to those parts of the curriculum that do not grab them. Students feel the power of their own inquiry and the responsibility for making the most of it. On the day students wrote about these final questions, they were prepared, absorbed, and proud of what they had accomplished.

Revealing Questions

Some questions, however, assess not only students' understanding, but your teaching as they put your assumptions to the test as in this scenario which is all too common for those of us in the classroom:

TEACHER: In what way could you compare Huck Finn to Holden Caulfield or Taylor in *The Bean Trees*, two books you all read in sophomore English last year?

STUDENTS: (*Silence. Evasive eyes. A few snickers and chuckles.*)

TEACHER: You know, those books you read last year, the ones about the kid who runs away from private school and that woman who finds the Indian baby she calls Turtle?

STUDENTS: Oh yeah. Those. (*Snicker. Silence.*)

TEACHER: Okay, so no one read them. I get it. How about that Gary Soto poem "Saturday at the Canal" that I gave you yesterday to read last night. How could we compare the teenagers in that poem to Huck and Jim?

STUDENTS: Oh, did we have to read that? (*Crowd mumbling.*) I wasn't sure, so I didn't read it. You just passed it out at the last minute, then the bell rang. I thought you said we'd read it tomorrow in class.

TEACHER: Did you read it, Roberta?

ROBERTA: I did. [This from the one girl who always seems to hear what I say, who always has her work done, who always comes to class on time.]

TEACHER: Can you get out the poem then please, everyone?

STUDENTS: I can't find mine. Do you have another copy, Mr. Burke?

Reflective Questions

Such encounters leave me feeling confused and disillusioned, an experience common to all teachers who love their subject and want their students to feel the same way. At such moments it becomes essential to regroup, to get away as soon as possible and ask myself the following focus questions:

- Why were they doing this assignment in the first place?
- What was my expected outcome?
- What was the pedagogical foundation on which the instructional strategy or assignment was based?
- How is this linked to what came before it; and was this clearly linked in the minds of the students?
- Did I explain the assignment to them clearly?
- Did I give them enough time?
- Did they know everything they needed to know to do this assignment successfully?
- What should I do next to address today's failure?
- Why is that the right thing to do?
- Again: what is the goal I am trying to achieve here?

On such days, I find a café after school and sit down with my journal and a cup of good coffee and think a while, letting these questions guide my thinking. It is what I have always done, for to write is to think and to think is, ultimately, to ask questions of ourselves, to enter into the private conversation with ourselves, we who are, in the end, our one truly devoted, most patient listener.

Once we put these texts into their hands and the discussion begins, certain problems can arise. Good stories, by their nature, raise difficult questions and stir up emotions which sometimes hit close to home. *Huckleberry Finn* is one obvious example: given its use of the word *nigger*, the book inspires heated debate about whether it should even be read. *The Kitchen God's Wife* offers a different set of dilemmas: rape, spousal abuse, racial themes, stereotypes, all of which must be discussed in the context of the story and all of which can be explosive. That is why it is important to teach students how to ask the right kinds of questions to achieve an atmosphere of respect and tolerance that allows for all reasonable views to be heard and inspires serious thinking about important questions. (See Chapter 25 for more information.)

Using Reading to Help Students Think

As I have already said in this chapter, students think better and deeper if they have texts to respond to, to argue with, to check against their thinking. Obviously, most of our reading in the class takes place via the content of our class, the *what* of the curriculum; sometimes reading a different text, written from an entirely different perspective, can give us new insight into the familiar or, as important, make the familiar seem newly strange to us. Anthropologist Mary Catherine Bateson (1990) writes of reading to think, using books as tools to get the mind going. My own process of writing this book validates this strategy in the extreme: I would pile up books about thinking, for example, and read across them, jumping from one to the other to get my own thinking about the subject going. When I had written a draft, and received some feedback, I would then go back to the books and read to revitalize my thinking and challenge the truth of what I had already written. In Chapter 4, we looked at other approaches—e.g., Question the Author and reciprocal reading—that lead to improved thinking in response to what students read.

Making Connections: Integrating Thinking Across Disciplines

The ultimate goal of the thinking curriculum is obvious: to get them to think. But, as we have seen, questions arise immediately: think about what? how best to think about it? why think about that? My own ambition, both for myself and my students, is to think about the different structures, patterns, and ideas that govern our lives, stories, and cultures, and see what they have in common. The question above—In what way are *Romeo and Juliet*, *Cry, the Beloved Country*, and South Africa like Newton's Third Law (for every action there is an equal and opposite reaction)?—exemplifies what I mean by thinking across disciplines. When my students start thinking about narratives or poems in musical or biological terms, I know they are getting into the rich thinking that is at the heart of our enterprise. Here lies the metaphorical, analogical thinking that takes the student—and the class—into new terrain. Think of how you might integrate into your curriculum such ideas or stories as these: the Second Law of Thermodynamics, the myth of Sisyphus, Maslow's Hierarchy of Human Needs, Freud's tripartite theory, Clifford Geertz's ideas about human cultures, or Kohlberg's theory about moral reasoning.

Endnote: Asking Questions

The moment we stop asking them to wonder, to ask, to think, is the moment we cease to be their teacher. The moment we no longer ask ourselves questions, the moment we stop reflecting on what we are doing, is the moment we should sit down and ask ourselves: Why do I teach? Should I still teach? So long as we get the following kind of responses from students, the answer should always be an affirming yes. David Muzio, a student in my senior class, wrote the following for the in-class graduation ceremony we held one year:

> By the time we graduate from high school, we have spent some 14,500 hours in the classroom. But in all that time, what did we learn? We learned how to determine the sides of an isosceles triangle (invaluable in daily life), but did we learn how to determine the direction of our lives? We may know what pi is, 3.14 or 22/7, but we're not sure who we are. Did we learn about worthiness, the power of thoughts or the value of mistakes? We can tell who is the best at taking tests, but can we tell who the best people are? In school, we learn how to do everything . . . except how to live. We know who wrote, "To be or not to be? That is the question," but we don't know the answer yet. There is still so much for us to learn. Commencement does not just mean graduation; it means a new beginning. The real teacher in life—is experience. We are the ones who must decide what is true for us and what is not, what applies to us and what does not. We learn simply by the exposure of living. The fact is that we are being educated the most when we are least aware of it.

This is what we do and why we build education on questions; *educe* means "to draw out," and so we do with each question, draw ourselves further out into the world of uncertainty and amazed understanding in which our skills and abilities allow us to live our lives as stories we hope we will recount with pride and satisfaction when, at the end of them, people ask us: did you leave the world a better place for your time here?

REFLECTION

Write an autobiography of yourself as a thinker, charting your progress, looking at specific events or people who challenged you by teaching you to think better or differently. Include in your autobiography an examination of how your thinking has changed since you were a high school student.

ACTIVITY

Read some poems by Li Young Lee, Elizabeth Bishop, or Mary Oliver. Try to use some of the different strategies described in this chapter to help you think more deeply about the poems. Consider drawing them, for example, or creating a graphic organizer with different columns in which you place the colors, verbs, and images in these poems in order to see if any pattern of meaning appears.

RECOMMENDATIONS

Because this chapter addresses different realms of thinking, I would like to recommend texts for each of the following:

Talking

From Communication to Curriculum. Douglas Barnes (Boynton/Cook).

Visual Texts

Drawing Your Own Conclusions. Fran Claggett with Joan Brown (Boynton/Cook).

Writing

Writing the Natural Way. Gabrielle Rico (Tarcher).

Questioning

Bridging: A Teacher's Guide to Metaphorical Thinking (NCTE/ERIC).

Integrating

Consilience: The Unity of Knowledge. Edward O. Wilson (Knopf).

Overall

Cultivating Thinking in English and the Language Arts. Robert Marzano (NCTE).

CHAPTER 10

COMPOSING A CURRICULUM
HOW TO PLAN A UNIT

A good meal, like a poem or a life, has a certain balance and diversity, a certain coherence and fit. As one learns to cope in the kitchen, one no longer duplicates whole meals but rather manipulates components and the way they are put together.

—Mary Catherine Bateson, *Composing a Life*

There are three rules to good teaching of the novel. Unfortunately no one knows what they are.

—Adapted from W. Somerset Maugham's quote about the rules for writing a novel

Planning: Getting from Here to There

You wouldn't get in your car and just start driving without any idea of where you wanted to go. Nor, having decided on a destination, would you start out without considering the best route to take. The same principles apply to teaching a story, a book, or a course. This chapter does not offer a specific set of steps, but rather a way of seeing, a philosophy of looking at a subject. The basic scenario, however, is one we all know: You sit at your desk with a book or story you intend to teach. You wonder why it should be read, what students—and you—should get out of it. You think of what you were studying before and what you will study after, and wonder how this book will relate to what follows. You also ask yourself—or should—how your unit will meet those content and performance standards that your state or district have created. These standards are, in some ways, like the studs in a wall: they maintain the structural integrity of your curriculum and help to make sure the curriculum you create is "up to code" as defined by your profession, your district, or your state.

Though there are certainly other examples, a "unit" might consist of any of the following:

- "essential questions" the course is structured to answer (Sizer 1996)
- "conversations" the course is organized around (Applebee 1996)
- themes or "envisionments" the class will explore (Langer 1995)

- "Great Books" the students are required to read (Adler 1982)
- "final tasks" the students must master (Wiggins 1998)
- skills or capacities the students will acquire
- genre the students study

The following questions, and those that come to mind while reading them, should help you to plan a successful assignment or unit.

Initial Steps: Guiding Questions

Begin with the end first. What do you want students to have learned or done by the end of this unit? What is the guiding or essential question you want them to be able to answer by the end of the unit? What are the relevant content and performance standards that this assignment/unit help students to master? "What task should we design in light of the evidence we need?" (Wiggins 1998). Example: I want my juniors to be able to give a five-minute presentation using visual aids and incorporating information from at least three sources, none of which is an encyclopedia.

Establish a clear rationale. Why is this an important, valid objective? (For example, what relationship does it have to what came before, or to what they need to learn to prosper later in their life?). This rationale should be clear to both you and your students; part of this rationale should be that it helps students meet certain standards successfully. Example: This five minute speech satisfies a socially recognized need—to be able to communicate effectively—while also meeting the state standard for public speaking. Also, the no-encyclopedia requirement is not because I dislike them, but rather because in this era of CD-ROMs, students are becoming overdependent on the encyclopedia instead of doing more focused and extensive research.

Make a road map. Having decided where you want to go (e.g., study early American literature in order to understand the evolution of the American ideal of independence as well as the relationship between the individual and the group), how should you get there: Project? Essay? Dramatic performance? Speeches? Character journal? Graphic? Creative writing response? Interviews? All of the above? Example: In the case of the speech, I will show them examples of other speeches I might have videotaped; the students will also write and talk as much as time allows to help prepare for and write the best presentation they can.

Create a mental timeline. How much time should you allot for this unit? How much work can you reasonably assume they will do each night? How does this affect your use of class time? What are the large and small pieces of this unit, and how can you achieve the appropriate balance between them for maximum learning? Example: Because I have thirty-five students in my junior class, I need to spread these presentations out so that I don't lose all my class time for two weeks. I say two weeks because five-minute presentations almost inevitably take twice that long if kids do them right. So we take a week to prepare and get the presentation ready; then we set up a schedule and do two or three presentations a day so that we can keep up in the other areas of the curriculum.

Determine your needs. What equipment or other resources do you need to teach this unit? Who must you see to get them? If you cannot get them, what is your backup plan? Are there other support materials such as poems or articles you need copied? When do you need those by? What do students need to know in order to do or understand this? (e.g., how to use HyperStudio, the history of the Puritans, certain concepts, or vocabulary words). Example: Students will need an overhead transparency and pens; some might need a TV/VCR combo; still others, with increasing regularity, ask for LCD projection devices or monitors connected to the computer so that they can integrate images found on the Internet. In the last example, I must then coordinate with the librarian.

Decide ahead of time about assessment. Without assessment, there is no way to determine whether you achieved your original goal or answered the guiding question the unit tried to answer. There are several questions you must ask and answer *before* beginning your unit:

- *What* am I assessing in the end? (e.g., their ability to take tests, or their understanding of the characters or ideas discussed during the unit)
- *How* can I best assess this?
- *Why* am I assessing this?

Example: Since I have identified it as a "speaking" assignment, I emphasize the importance of this component. I write up the evaluation form I will use, clearly indicating each aspect of the assessment so that students will know what is expected of them.

Anticipate obstacles. What obstacles might you reasonably expect to encounter during this unit of study? (e.g., attitudes, limitations, resources, time). How will you solve those problems, and why do you think this is an effective solution? (e.g., If you have students with identified learning difficulties, will simply writing down the directions for them to read again later-help them succeed on this assignment?) Example: I conference with all students whose anxieties or abilities make this a difficult assignment. In addition, I use the "Components of an Effective Presentation or Speech" (see Appendix F) to help them develop their ideas for their visual aids.

The above model presents an amazing complex of strands, all of which must somehow be woven together into one coherent fabric we call learning. I think of the brain as a loom that must be worked with precision to shuttle the information back and forth to get the best weave within students' minds and the curriculum itself. There are certain elements—time, balance, flexibility, and the seasons of learning—that are essential if the curriculum is to achieve all we need it to. Such complexity cannot be managed by accident; so we need conceptual models to help us understand the relationship between the curriculum—what we teach versus what they learn—and our pedagogy—how we should teach versus how they will best learn.

A Way of Seeing: Designing a Unit of Study

The diagram (Figure 10.1) offers one way of looking at time and learning within the larger context of your class. After all, once you answer the big questions listed above, you need to get down to the reality of the daily classroom, where the guiding question is "What the heck am I doing today?" Today, however, if approached as a discrete unit, soon becomes a source of anxiety, a bridge you find swinging in the wind because it is not attached to the other side.

Time. A brief explication of Figure 10.1 focuses first on each of the days of the week. You have these separate days, each one asking what you will do with it. Yet what you do on Monday should have some coherent link to what you did the previous Friday and the proceeding Tuesday. Think of the week as a paragraph: The guiding question for any writer is, What is the relationship of this element to the idea that I am trying to develop?

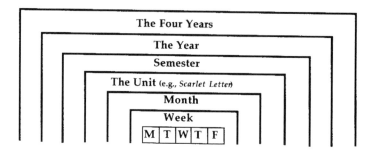

Diagram: Schema for planning your curriculum

Figure 10.1   *Conceptions of time as they relate to units of study*

You wouldn't write a paragraph filled with sentences that had no connection with each other: it wouldn't make any sense and your reader would turn away within minutes. The same goes with your days: they are like sentences in the larger paragraph of the week, and each of them must expand on and advance the discussion of the essay's—or in this case, the unit's—subject.

Balance. It is a real challenge to achieve a balance between the formal or structured curriculum and the one that emerges as our course unfolds daily. All teachers approach planning differently. Eventually an organic structure or set of expectations emerges that creates a certain rhythm to the days, one that has harmony. Think of it as a balanced meal with all the food groups included. There is the opening of each day, a time during which the teacher can take care of business or get the students thinking with reading or writing to help their minds settle down into "English" for the hour. The class then moves on to the main course; this might be a continuation of previous days' work or some new activity. When it comes to linking the days, I refer you to Hemingway's advice to writers: Always stop when you know what to write next, so you come back to the work able to regain your momentum.

Overview of a Period: How Time Works

Many teach within a confusing array of schedules. My school has two different weekly schedules, with several others it implements for rallies and special events. Some schools have block schedules that afford them as many as two hours for their English class. Still others, such as the one where I student taught, have only forty-minute classes. My own (usually) fifty-minute class period runs something like this:

Opening five to ten minutes. We begin with one or more of the following activities: daily writing about an idea, piece of art on the overhead, or text I read aloud; examination and correction/revision of a passage of flawed writing followed by discussion of different solutions; minilesson on some aspect of grammar followed by opportunity to learn and practice it; or time to take care of other business that sometimes comes our way (e.g., administrative demands such as surveys or announcements).

Middle thirty to forty minutes. We proceed to the daily unit work and discuss how it links to what we may have done in previous days. The introduction may simply remind them of what we are doing and tell them to get on with it. For example, with an assignment like the Dictionary of the American Mind (introduced later in this chapter), they know where they are and should just be told to pick up where they left off. If, on the other hand, we are working with a novel or a writing assignment, I will tell them what to expect and then transition into that discussion, activity, or assignment. This is the main course and takes up the bulk of the class. I periodically interrupt this thirty to forty-minute segment to remind students what we are trying to accomplish; some call this recursive teaching, by which they mean that the instructor circles back around to make sure students understand and are achieving the objectives.

Final five to ten minutes. This is where I determine where the students are and where they need to go next. Sometimes they are not ready for the homework I prepared for them; other times they were hot, and finished within the period what I thought they would need that night to complete. Sometimes I use these final minutes to have them fill out three-by-five-inch cards to reflect on what they did or learned; other times I have them debrief and use the cards to let them communicate with me about concerns they have about the assignment and their progress on it (especially if it is a large project). Obviously, these final minutes also allow me to explain the homework and take any last-minute questions that students might have. Sometimes I will pass back papers at this point, but this is my Achilles' heel: I usually am too carried away with what's going on to remember to return papers, though they are always in the out boxes for kids to retrieve themselves.

Flexibility.   Sometimes it seems like every minute of every day should be accounted for and penciled in; how else to explain the fact that a school year is measured in minutes? In fact, I like structure primarily because it ensures that I will find time for certain activities, the most overlooked of which is time to wonder or think. In his book on creativity, psychologist Mihaly Csikszentmihalyi (1996) refers to "attention as a limited resource," which is essential for creative thinking. This reminds me of a cartoon I saw years ago: A little grass hut on the beach has a sign, WRITER AT WORK, stuck to the door; inside we see a man lying down with his hands behind his head, looking out the window. Thus when we plan, we must include time to dream and time to master, time to study and time to learn.

Seasons of learning.   Finally, when we consider the structure of time in our classes, we cannot forget to consider the seasons of the school year. You must, while planning a unit, think about the particular time frame and ask yourself if you will have the time and your students will have the mental energy to do what you ask. My first few years, for example, I kept introducing *Julius Caesar* just before Thanksgiving. Not only were my students distracted and frequently absent at that time, but the play was rudely interrupted by the Thanksgiving vacation and the proximity of the winter holidays. I like to take advantage of students' early good will and initiative in September and October so that in late November we experience a natural slowing down. This pace allows me to ask as much as I can from them when we return in January. By viewing such inherent complexity as natural to the seasons of learning, we can use seasonal rhythm to create or anticipate culminating moments that, at their best, add a dramatic aspect or ritualistic component to the curriculum. A course, after all, is like a story: it depends on tension and release or conflict and resolution to keep the reader—or in this case, the student—engaged.

Sample Unit: The Dictionary of the American Mind

I begin each year, each unit, by asking myself—and sometimes my students—what conversation we should have and what readings would help us most to plumb the depths of that topic. Put another way, What is the essential question my class or this particular unit is trying to answer? The Dictionary of the American Mind assignment was intended to create a context for the entire junior year that would culminate in an intellectually stimulating final exam.

The Dictionary of the American Mind

Overview

This assignment asks you to think about our country and how, as a society, we think and act. The work you do on this assignment will culminate in the semester's final exam. You will be ideally prepared for this essay so long as you follow these steps.

Step One. In a group of four, do the following:

- Get copies of *The American Studies Album.* Use this book as a reference text, something to bounce ideas off of or pull ideas out of as you work.

- Brainstorm as long a list as you can of single words (e.g., *independence*) that capture the essence of the American mind.

- Pick ten words for your final list; none should overlap (e.g., *independence* and *freedom*). If yours do, decide which of the two words works best and make sure your ideas are reflected in your definitions for each word.

- Write down two distinct definitions for each word:
  - *"Our definition":* This should be in your own words, and should capture the essence of the word as you think of it; for example if you have *justice* on your list, what do *you* mean when you use this word?
  - *Dictionary definition:* You should include as many of the dictionary's definitions as are relevant; certainly this will include more than one of the many different definitions.

- Each person must then choose the one word from your list that seems the most important or crucial attribute of the American mind (or that most interests you).

- Next, everyone writes a one-page quick write about this idea based on their own experiences or historical knowledge, bringing to their writing any examples that illustrate what they say about it. For example, if you write about *independence* as the crucial characteristic of the American mind, what examples from *Huckleberry Finn* can you use to show what you mean? *Each member of the group must do their own one-pager.*

Step Two. Research the idea and come up with the following, all of it written down in your notes, which will be collected later; you will be able to use them on the final exam:

- Use *The American Studies Album* to find those articles you will read as part of this assignment.

- Read a total of eight articles—two per person—for your research.

- Summarize each article by making a list of its three most important points or listing those specific examples that will illustrate your paper's main idea. Be sure to include in your notes the title of the article, the author, and the page numbers on which you found your information.

- Organize your group's information as follows:
  - Get a folder (from me) and write each group member's name on it.
  - Put your eight summaries in the folder, with each person's name on the summaries they wrote.
  - Put your list of words and definitions (Step One) in the folder, along with all other associated notes.
  - Designate the most responsible, consistently present person in your group to keep this for now (or put it in the portfolio cabinet).

- List those examples that best illustrate the idea you chose from the different books you read this year.

Step Three. Dig deeper on your idea before proceeding.
- *Evolution of the idea:* How did we think about this idea in the past; how do we think about it in the present; how will we think about it in the future?
- *Origins of the idea:* Where does this trait in our character come from? Why do you think this? If you must speculate, that is fine; just be sure to support why you think this *might* be where the idea comes from.
- *Aspects of the idea:* Take the idea and try to divide it into as many different categories or aspects as seem reasonable and meaningful to you. For example, if you say *freedom*, you could talk about two kinds of freedom right off: freedom *from* and freedom *to*. There are, of course, other types or categories of freedom.

Step Four. Working together or individually, use your notes to write a rough draft or outline of the essay you will each write on the day of the final exam. Be sure your essay has the following:
- Examples from the past and present, and scenario from the future
- Examples from the literature we've read and *The American Studies Album*
- Examples from *The Crucible* and any other film we watched
- Examples of irony, contradiction, or the opposite of what you discuss; for example, Walt Whitman, white poet of the 1860s, writes, "I hear America singing . . ." and Langston Hughes, African American poet from the mid-1900s, writes "I, too, hear America singing . . . I am the darker brother. They send me to the kitchen." *My point here is that I don't want you to simplify your thinking into either/or but to recognize and examine the complexity of an idea like* justice *or* independence *as it applies to all Americans these last 222 years.*

Step Five. Take the final exam and on that day use your notes, drafts, outlines to help you write the best essay you are capable of writing at the end of your junior year.

Example of the beginning of a final essay (written by Mr. Burke).
  Revolution is a complicated word, coming as it does from the idea of rolling something over violently. Its origins go back to the word *voluble*, from which a series of other, related words derive: *evolution, devolution, involve,* and, of course, *revolt.* As I think about the evolution of the American mind, I see a long series of struggles and revolts, most of them based on some sense of injustice. Through such opposition we find out who we are and understand that we have a clear purpose: to defeat this enemy or get past this obstacle. Thus we look back with a sort of envy to those who participated in the civil rights movement, for they were able to confront a social issue larger than themselves. They took a stand that helped them understand what they stood for, what they wanted from the world. Too often it seems our lives now, so many years after, lack this sense of something to revolt against, and so we turn against ourselves, our parents, our culture's traditions.
  The tradition of resistance culminated in the birth of our country and continues to define those who seek admission to the country even today. (First example here . . .)

Though this assignment draws heavily from themes my students study in their American History class, it is an English assignment foremost. The emphasis is on writing, reading, thinking, and speaking. The assignment creates a dynamic context within which we can discuss how, for example, characters from Mark Twain's, Amy Tan's, or Victor Martinez's novels embody the traits we have decided are common to all Americans. The unit allows me and the students to feel we are shaping the curriculum and defining the conversations our class is having.

A group of juniors collaborating on "The Dictionary of the American Mind" unit

This structure of the unit allows me the freedom to follow it where it wants to go: If students get excited by it, we can run with it for as long as their enthusiasm sustains itself; if they don't engage with it, it offers a sound, worthy course of study for a period of time during which I can plan what we should do next. In this way, mine is an evolving or emerging curriculum, but never a random one. It is structured to keep things moving forward while also circling back around at each step to check on students' progress so that no one gets left behind. Also, the assignment sheet itself is designed as a sort of road map: they have check-off boxes next to each task to keep track of what they have finished and what remains to be done, a device I find particularly helpful given the problems sometimes caused by absences.

What Music Does Your Curriculum Make?

If we are to think creatively (Csikszentmihalyi 1996; Greene 1998), critically (Wink 1997), or differently (Applebee 1996; Mayher 1990) about our curriculum, we must have a vocabulary of images and metaphors to help us conceive of these methods. Consider, for example, the following questions and ask them of yourself or your teaching:

- If someone connected your class to a machine that translated its action—physical, emotional, intellectual—into music, what would be the sound or rhythm of your class?
- If Mihaly Csikszentmihalyi, author of *Creativity: Flow and the Psychology of Discovery and Invention*, had your students quickly note down how engaged they were at random moments in your class, what would be the likely average (on a scale of 1 to 10) for a month?
- If it were possible to graph the movement of your curriculum, what would this diagram look like at the end of a "unit": straight lines, an EKG of someone with arrhythmia, or perhaps some combination that looks like a symphony's score?

- If your course or unit were a spider web, what would it look like and what would each filament represent?
- If your course were a story, what is the source of its tension, what are its themes, plot, style? How do you want it to end? And who is writing this story?
- If your course is an intellectual rite of passage, what is the experience within the course that will help your students achieve that transition from one stage to the next?

If I were to translate this image into the language of music, I would compare it to the improvisational pianist Keith Jarrett who, with one hand, would establish a sound, regular melody while with the other hand he began to introduce layers of complexity over that melody. Such a model allows for the organic, evolving nature of a curriculum, which should be seen or at least treated as a living organism that responds to the world around it. Yet another analogy might help: Mary Catherine Bateson, in *Composing a Life* (1990, 62), compares a life to the creation of a crazy quilt: "Most quilts . . . involve the imposition of a new pattern. But even crazy quilts are sewn against a backing; the basic sense of continuity allows the improvisation. Composing a life [read: unit or assignment] involves an openness to possibilities and the capacity to put them together in a way that is structurally sound."

Such flexibility in the planning of a unit or individual lesson is necessary for many reasons. What flies and triumphs in third period too often flops and fails in fourth period—and usually for different reasons each time. Thus the composition metaphor recognizes the "rough draft" nature of all teaching: We must revise and rewrite as we go along, paying attention to what "works" and what does not. Such notions of "what works" also help to keep the reflective teacher attentive to those questions they initially asked themselves: What am I trying to accomplish? Why do I want to accomplish this? Is this the best way to accomplish it?

Taking Stock: Did the Curriculum Work?

Once you have picked and used one or a number of these different modes, you will need to determine the progress the student has made; in other words, you must figure out how effective your curriculum was. You can use study questions, teacher-student conferences, exams, or some other means of measurement, but the assessment tools must fit the curriculum or skills being examined. Here are some helpful questions to get you thinking:

- How long did you think it would take to teach this particular unit/lesson?
- How long did it actually take?
- If there is a significant discrepancy, what happened?
- At what point, if any, did the students seem to be most confused by the lesson?
- How might I better approach that particular part of the lesson if I were doing it again?
- What did I want them to get out of this lesson?
- To what extent did they achieve this?
- How do I know this?
- What is next?
- Why is that next?
- How did this unit relate to the previous unit/lesson?
- To what extent did I make that connection clear to them?

- What did they like most? Why?
- What did I do best that I want to be sure to do again?
- Why did that work so well?

See Chapter 11 for more ideas about how to follow up such units or assess student performance.

Endnote: The Dream of a Unified Curriculum

I would like to close with what might seem, for an "English book," an odd example of my ideal when it comes to work, thought, and structure in the classroom. Consider, if you will, the creation of the United States Constitution as an assignment. The "assignment" responds to a common set of questions Americans were asking themselves about the world and their place in it. These essential questions, despite their obvious complexity, engaged people's imaginations, for they immediately realized the issues had personal, social, and existential meaning, that all the work they did on this subject served a real purpose. Structured as it was, this group project required that the nation's founders bring their divergent views to the table, and collaborate to create a common product that would demand discussion (about complex and compelling ideas), listening (to divergent views and sophisticated notions), writing (for many reasons, in many genres, to many audiences), reading (from a variety of sources), and thinking (about issues of great personal and social import). So integrated was this task that while they fought through the deeper philosophical questions of purpose and audience, they also had to address such essential subjects as rhetoric, grammar, and vocabulary in order to achieve their desired outcome. Finally, while the assignment helped to develop skills and capacities, it also taught the "class" (of 1776) about power, values, cultures, systems, and ideas, all of which strengthened their ability to negotiate the differences within their changing world.

Ours is a society and this a generation that faces serious existential crises. Writer N. Scott Momaday says the fundamental crisis facing the current generation is the absence of the sacred (Kauffman 1995). Social philosopher Cornell West says the crisis is the "nihilism" and sense of meaninglessness that faces so many children growing up in the inner cities (West 1994). Neil Postman might say that the crisis consists of the indifference today's kids suffer from after "seeing it all" on television (Postman 1985). Echoing and adding an edge to Postman's ideas, Albert Camus would certainly argue that absurdity has become epidemic within our adolescent population (Camus 1955). Psychologist Mihaly Csikszentmihalyi might say the danger is that too many kids lack opportunities to enter into the optimal state he calls "flow," a state of mind where we feel entirely happy, alive, engaged (Csikszentmihalyi 1996). Returning to Mary Catherine Bateson's notion of composing a life, I wonder if kids today aren't worried their life won't be a story worth telling.

We must, however, find a way to meet these many personal and societal needs through the units we create, the lessons we develop, the story our class tells through its curriculum. Students who go into their communities to interview people, to read to and work with little kids, find learning dynamic and satisfying. So, too, are students engaged when they are asked to enter into sustained conversations about issues about which they themselves are beginning to really wonder. Curriculum, the units we design, the questions our classes strive to answer—these are like tickets to places we want to go. If we are lucky, our class reveals to kids and prepares them for their possible lives, the kind of lives they can compose using the skills and knowledge they learn in our class.

REFLECTION

In your journal, write about what you are trying to accomplish with a specific set of assignments and how these fit into the larger curriculum. The word *curriculum* derives from the Latin *currere* which means "to run the course." It is also related to the word *current*. Thinking about your own class, what are your goals or hopes for the course that you ask your students to "run"? And what are the "currents"—strands, themes, threads—that run through this course?

ACTIVITY

Using the list of words provided here under "curricular modes," make time at the end of each day to analyze what you did and which word best describes it. Explain why, for example, *inquiry* best captures what your students did that day. Then write about why you had them do a particular activity and how it turned out.

RECOMMENDATIONS

Curriculum as Conversation. Arthur Applebee (Chicago 1996). An essential text based on the study of high school English classes for five years.

Standards for Our Schools: How to Set Them, Measure Them, and Reach Them. Marc S. Tucker and Judy B. Codding (Jossey-Bass 1998). Grew out of Tucker's work as director of the New Standards Project.

Reshaping High School English. Bruce Pirie (NCTE 1997). A brief but thoughtful meditation on what English should accomplish, written by a classroom teacher.

CHAPTER 11

MEASURING STUDENT PROGRESS

Here use and pleasure, practice and performance, are joined at last and for all time.

—Allan Gurganus, "The Practical Heart"

Those students get the highest grades who teach me the most.

—attributed to the poet Theodore Roethke

Defining the Terms: Assessment, Evaluation, and Grading

The terms *assessment*, *evaluation*, and *grading* get used so interchangeably, their specific meaning can easily get lost. Let me distinguish between them with an analogy. Throughout my teenage years I competed on the junior tennis circuit. My coach, Depaul Wannaquwatte, carefully monitored my tennis game and constantly *assessed* my progress in specific areas (e.g., the cross-court-sliced backhand, the hard, flat serve up the middle, etc.) using a variety of measurements: his trained eye, a video camera, my own description of what I was doing, why, how it felt, how it worked. His assessments were intended to improve my performance at upcoming tournaments. At these tournaments I played others my age, enough of whom I beat to secure respectable rankings in the state. The state officials would, at the end of each year *evaluate* my performance; my coach and I would, at the end of each match, do the same, determining what it was I needed to improve next time. Officials, like teachers, however, were the only ones able to *grade* my performance; this came in the form of annual rankings based on my performance that year.

If this analogy didn't help you better understand the differences, consider the following characteristics of each (all italics are mine):

> *Assessment.* "*Assessment* refers to a collection of data, information that enlightens the teacher and the learner, information that drives instruction" (Strickland and Strickland 1998). It is recursive and ongoing. Its purpose depends on the audience and the occasion. Its etymology derives from the Old French *assesser*, which means "to sit next to as an assistant judge." Or, as Grant Wiggins (1998, 192) says, "in assessment I *describe*. . . . I place students' performance on a continuum."

Evaluation. "[It] is the next step in a recursive process. *Evaluation* is the product of assessment, a step further toward understanding and drawing conclusions. After gathering data—information and evidence—teachers, like researchers, must put the pieces together, evaluating the products of their efforts and the progress of their students" (Strickland and Strickland 1998). Its etymology stems from the Old French *valoir*, which means to be strong or worth something; thus the act of evaluating determines a thing's value or quality. Wiggins adds that "in evaluation I made a *value judgment.*"

Grading. Of course, we all know what *grading* means: the reduction of different information on student performance down to a letter or score which is, usually, entered onto a report card. Returning to the etymology of *evaluation* for a moment, we can say that a grade is the chosen or agreed-upon symbol used to communicate that quality or value to the learner, other teachers, and the community at large (which, in this case, includes universities).

Guiding Principles for Measuring Performance

Come May, nearly all my time is devoted to thoughts of assessment, evaluation, and grading. The California state tests must be given in early May. Whether I like the test or not is irrelevant. My students will be measured by it and the newspapers will report their scores; so I want my kids to be ready and able to perform well on the exam. At the same time, their culminating projects—which assess their ability to read, write, speak, research, and think—and portfolios draw near and demand my attention. I provide them the draft criterion for their portfolios and projects, showing them a few exemplars to illustrate what "distinguished" or "competent" looks like. Meanwhile, I am also trying to determine their progress toward those standards I established at the beginning of the semester. They, too, have begun to evaluate their own progress toward those goals by assembling their portfolios. In short, I want to measure their growth in specific areas, and I need different measurements to help me—and them—accomplish this fairly and accurately.

Every discussion, each writing assignment becomes a means of assessing what they can and cannot do after a year with me; these assessments of their work thus become an assessment of my work. Meanwhile I am trying to figure out how to reduce all this rich complexity down to a single grade for the report card. To this end, I have them evaluate themselves and write a persuasive paper in which they must provide evidence from within their portfolio to support their claim for whatever grade they feel they deserve.

Assessment Strategies

Several principals guide my thinking when it comes to measuring students' performance:

"Begin with the end in mind" (Covey 1989). Whether this means a list of skills, a specific idea, or a concrete product, be clear about your intended outcome. Then, working backwards, figure out the necessary steps to get there and how these can best be assessed. I say, for example, I want them to be able to analyze and support an idea using a variety of sources then begin to craft the assignment that will both develop and assess their ability to do this. Marc Tucker and Judy Codding (1998), looking at the use of performance standards, suggest that we begin a description of the performance we expect from our students. These "performance descriptions" should be "confined to things that can actually be assessed."

Give students as much information as possible. Students should understand the requirements, the standards, and the criterion. For me, this typically means providing an introductory handout formatted with check boxes so that they can use the assignment itself as a to-do list. I provide, whenever possible, a rubric that clarifies what and how they will be evaluated. I also speak to students often about different types of standards—mine, those in the workplace, my profession's, society's, their own, and those specific to an assignment. Tucker and Codding, in an attempt to better integrate standards and assessment, also suggest that "performance descriptions" be supported by samples of student work. The information such exemplars provide keeps both student and teacher focused on the goal.

Ensure that the means of assessment, grading, and evaluation are fair and appropriate to all. This can be accomplished by providing students, whenever possible, a variety of ways to demonstrate their knowledge or skills. It also implies that students should be involved as much as possible in the evaluation and assessment of their own work.

Keep in mind the purpose of assessment, which is meant to improve and measure student performance while also clarifying for students what is expected of them (e.g., standards). This means that assessment involves an ongoing conversation—between the student and the teacher, their peers, parents, and, of course, themselves—about the work while it is in progress, and includes opportunities to improve that work in response to this information. The third recommendation from Tucker and Codding to help teachers use standards better calls for commentaries on student work. Such commentaries highlight those moments when the student achieves the standard and helps them to better understand their performance, thereby increasing the likelihood they will be able to repeat it or transfer this knowledge to a different task.

Develop the habit of critical reflection in both the student and the teacher. Any time we evaluate student performance we are evaluating our own. This "art of practice" (Schön 1983), also referred to as "reflection-in-action," is central to effective teaching or improved performance. When, for example, students use an index card to tell me where they are on a certain project, these self-assessments demand that I, in turn, think about what I wanted them to get from the assignment and whether they are getting it.

Whenever possible, assessments should also be:

- meaningful
- challenging
- engaging
- integrated into the larger context of the course
- one of several measures by which a teacher is determining the student's progress or performance
- specific in its focus (e.g., anchored to a specific standard with which the student is familiar)

What Assessment Demands of Teachers

Good, honest assessment necessarily involves risk. It demands patience and faith. It also demands hard work. Such assessments sometimes even require courage: to try, to ask, to fail. Innovative methods of measuring students' learning often invite criticism—from parents, other teachers, administrators, and, of course, students. Sometimes we even turn against ourselves when a method fails, seeing in it some confirmation of our insecurities when we should see it as an opportunity, a piece of information we can use in the future. Fair, accurate assessment involves all these elements because whenever we measure others we are also measuring ourselves.

A few years ago, for example, my department began a dialogue about portfolios and how we determined students' progress. I suggested that we all commit to having students keep "writing folders" beginning the next September and that we use these as a basis for a practical, ongoing discussion about portfolios—what they were, how they work, why they work. My department chair's reluctance grew into resistance, something that confused me. Eventually she explained that were she to require such a folder in her classes her students would have next to nothing to put in it. So extreme was her commitment to vocabulary that she devoted nearly 60 percent of her class time to drilling, reviewing, acting out, writing about words, that they essentially had no time nor cause to write. The potential instrument (portfolios, in this case) measured not the student so much as the teacher, the department, and, in certain ways, the school itself.

Testing

People get passionate about the subject of testing. Some subscribe to it with the zeal of the true believer, finding in the precision of the AP and SAT an order that keeps the chaos of the world at bay. Others, who often oppose these zealots, wave their own flags, often opposing testing, period. One thing stands out: Everyone knows what they believe, and steers by these beliefs with a sailor's calm faith. This is how it appears to younger teachers, those new to the profession; and it is primarily to them that I address my thoughts.

To assess is to question—constantly, honestly—where you are going and why you are going there. This is particularly difficult and trying when you are a novice teacher or trying something new. People so often want to tell you why you are wrong, how you could do it better, how you should test, and how often. Such scrutiny can undermine all your confidence in your ability and the ideologies that inform that teaching. Teaching, however, allows little time for reflection and so too often we do what our instincts told us was right, and sometimes is. So much easier, though, to just give the multiple-choice, "bubble" test: it's objective, safe, traditional—and often meaningless. Yet it comes with the validation of history: We've always done it this way.

At its best, good teaching, which necessarily includes effective assessing, is about paying attention. This is what we should all strive for in our teaching and testing: to invite particular attention to worthy subjects, and to use tests to measure the depth and accuracy of that attention. But let's not stop there: let every test be an invitation for us to pay specific attention to our own teaching, let students' portfolios be *our* portfolios and reflect not only what they accomplished but what we, their teachers, accomplished as evidenced by their progress, their pleasure, and their pride in their work.

The Role and Uses of Assessment

I once worked with a colleague whose "assessment" of her students' understanding of *The Scarlet Letter* required each student to knit a scarlet A, presumably, to demonstrate their understanding of the novel. She has since moved on to become a principal, I believe. Other teachers use different means of assessing students—posterboards, videos, scrapbooks—whose validity and quality depends on what they require of the students. A posterboard with hastily taped-on magazine cut-outs and scribbled names of characters underneath each picture offers more information about the teacher than the student's knowledge. However, a graphic response like Ben Martinez's (Figure 11.1) shows what can be achieved through alternative means of assessing a student's understanding:

Ben's "open mind" offers a range of insights into Richard Wright's *Black Boy* and Ben's reading of it. His teacher, Jeff Dowd, pushed him further, however; the writing requirement ensures

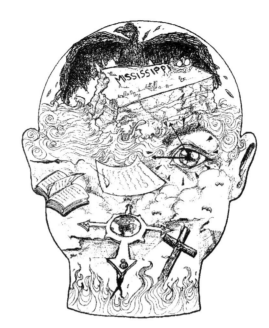

Figure 11.1 *Ben's illustration of the "Open Mind" of Richard Wright*

that more than Ben's artistic ability is measured. Any teacher would be pleased to read the following analysis of Wright's book:

> From the top of the picture to the bottom there are several items which symbolize many different components that Richard's life consist of. At the top of Richard's head is a massive crow spreading her wings over Mississippi where her eggs lay. The crow symbolizes the Jim Crow laws and the eggs reinforce the Crow law's presence in Mississippi. As if Mississippi drawn as an island just shows how separated it is from the rest of the U.S. Next is the aged eyeball with hands of time showing. That symbolizes how Richard gained as much experience as an old man at a very young age. To the left is a sheet of paper with a pen writing on it. This symbolizes Richard's love and addiction for reading and writing literature. . . . Flying in the clouds are books. The books symbolize the key by which Richard shall first attain his freedom from the South.

Ben's drawing is a good example of a structured assessment. The assignment has structure, a specific purpose, and takes some time to complete. More common is the daily assessment, the ongoing gathering of information about students' progress. There are several ways to conduct these informal assessments in order to obtain this information, most of which require the teacher to work up-close with students in a variety of settings:

- talking to your students as they work in groups, as class is beginning, in scheduled or impromptu conferences, and in full-class discussions
- watching how they work, what they struggle with, what they get engaged by, and what confuses them
- writing in a variety of quick, informal ways: index cards, journal writes, "one-pagers," on overheads they present to the class

A.J., Meagan, and Melissa evaluating their adaptation of The Odyssey *(a board game called "Odd-at-Sea") by playing it*

- quizzing them—in writing or verbally—about those details you have established are important and for which they should look while reading or studying
- using those objects (e.g., games) or programs you created (e.g., a Hypertext document you made) to see if they work as planned and to determine the extent to which they reveal students' understanding of the information.

How you assess determines what you assess. Do you just want to determine if students read the story or poem last night? Or is your purpose to see if they really understood the text and how it relates to the larger unit of study? A remarkable amount of information on a student's reading performance can be gathered from a quick write on a three-by-five-inch card. Consider the following explication from junior Daniel Weishar after he read Marge Piercy's brutal poem, "Barbie Doll," in which a young girl commits suicide after being constantly rejected by her peers.

> The poem writes how society can make people act strange or stupidly. The girl felt so convinced by people that she had these evil and vile things on her body [a large nose and heavy thighs] that she felt she had to remove them from her person. Obviously though, in removing these vital body parts, she died. When, for her funeral, she was "made up," everyone commented on how beautiful she was. So, in conclusion, in American society, natural is ugly and fake is beautiful.

Daniel's response, which took only about five minutes, immediately establishes that he understood both the surface and deep meaning of the poem. In addition, it provides an example of insight and analysis to the others in class and a means of entering into a serious discussion about the subject by building on his remarks and those of his classmates.

If, as his teacher, I wanted to look closer at what Daniel accomplished in this short but intelligent response, I could point out several other important points. One, the means of assessment (writing) is appropriate to and integrated into the course curriculum. Two, there is no single, narrowly conceived answer but instead an opportunity to evidence his thinking and understanding, to demonstrate not only what he thinks the poem means but why he thinks that. Three, this information helps me to assess the situation and determine my next action as the teacher. And, finally, I could, if I needed, easily identify the specific content or performance standard that such an assignment and response satisfy.

Assessment Tools: Rubrics, Checklists, Portfolios, and Exams

An informal survey of my 150 students showed a strong preference for rubrics. Their comments all said essentially the same thing: We like rubrics because they explain what we need to do, what we will be graded on, and how we will be evaluated. I use rubrics constantly for large projects and daily homework. They allow me to be specific, efficient, and thorough. This last point is important: while assessment is fundamentally important, it takes time, sometimes too much time given all the other demands on us as teachers. Rubrics, while not the answer to all problems, offer the most effective means for me to assess students the way I want by sometimes forcing me to look more closely; the categories I have established and the criterion impose greater discipline on both the student and me.

Rubrics

Homework Rubric. I grew tired of slapping "8/10" on homework assignments. This grade (based on a scale of 1 to 10) meant that students did good but not excellent work; there was sometimes a clear explanation for what cost them points, but not always. Then I created a homework rubric (Figure 11.2) that I can adapt quickly on the computer to meet the needs of any particular assignment. If I have the time, I ask students to fill it in first, then use it myself and evaluate the extent to which they have internalized the rubric's standards. This method allows me to communicate clearly what matters most, since "what gets graded is what gets done."

Exam Rubric. Students read widely outside of class, but there is no way for me to maintain a knowledge of these books. There is, however, a need for accountability when it comes to out-

1   □ Completion: Your work satisfies all requirements of the assignment.

2   □ Idea Development:
       □ you use effective examples to illustrate and support what you mean

3   □ Writing Quality:
       □ your sentences are coherent
       □ they are grammatically correct
       □ they do not have spelling or punctuation errors

4   □ Neatness/Aesthetics
       □ your handwriting is legible and neat
       □ your paper is in good condition

/4 **Score**

Figure 11.2 *Sample homework rubric*

side reading. I developed the following open-ended series of essay topics as a means of assessing that students did read the books and how well they understood them. The sheet comes to them as you see it here with the scoring rubric right on it (Figure 11.3). Saved on the computer as a template, it is easily adaptable for any other class or assignment and is very efficient to use.

Checklists

When assigning a large project or complicated assignment, I use lots of check boxes or bullets to clearly organize what it is I want students to do. The assignment sheet itself then serves as the to-do list. I then use this list, when it seems appropriate, as the basis for an assessment sheet. While it is a close cousin to the rubric, the checklist as I use it allows me a different range of responses. Instead of numbers (e.g., 0–6 scale), I use descriptive categories linked to specific criteria or requirements. Figure 11.4 is an example of such a checklist for my junior History Project, which comes due at year's end when I must be able to evaluate the assignments effectively but quickly.

Portfolios

Across America, thousands, maybe even millions, of portfolios lie dormant in darkened drawers like the child that no one wants to talk about in Sam Shepherd's play *Buried Child*. The reason for this is simple: the audience and purpose of these portfolios was not fully considered. In *Educative Assessment*, Grant Wiggins (1998) offers the following possible uses of portfolios:

- as a showcase for the student's best work, as chosen by the student or the teacher
- as a showcase for the student's interests
- as a showcase for the student's growth
- as evidence of self-assessment and self-adjustment
- as evidence enabling professional assessment of student performance, based on a technically sound sample of work
- as a complete collection of student work for documentation and archiving
- as a constantly changing sample of work chosen by the student, reflecting different job applications and exhibitions over time

Wiggins sees several different implications in these examples. "Portfolios can primarily serve instruction or assessment; they can be focused primarily on documentation or evaluation; their contents can be defined by the student or by the teacher; they can be seen as a résumé, as a representative sample of overall performance (good and bad) or as a constantly changing exhibit" (Wiggins 1998, 190).

My own use of portfolios mirrors, in spirit, what Wiggins calls an "anthology." Students keep their work throughout the year, weeding it at the semester and returning to certain pieces at different times for different purposes. In June, I require that they create a final portfolio, which accomplishes several important ends:

- It provides students an important opportunity to reflect on what they have done during the year. This can be especially important for students who forget that they did some distinguished work during the course of the year. In short, it allows them to see the "pieces" of their education as forming a more coherent and, I hope, meaningful whole.
- It requires them to evaluate the value of their work and assign to it a final meaning (i.e., important enough to go in my portfolio, meaningless, transitional, etc.).

JUNIOR OUTSIDE READING/SPRING SEMESTER
BURKE/1998

Overview   The following topics are general and should allow you to adapt your outside reading to one of them. There are several purposes to this essay: to give you an opportunity to make a range of personal and intellectual connections between the books you read, to determine that you read them, and to assess how well you actually understood what you read by having you communicate that understanding to me. Please see the rubric at the bottom of the page and refer to this throughout your essay to make sure you are doing your best to satisfy the requirements. You may write about any ONE of the following topics.

NOTE: Before writing about your chosen topic, please write the author, title and, if you have it, number of pages, in the book(s) you read.

1. You cannot open a book without learning something. (Irish proverb)
    □ Essay Topic: Using the Irish proverb, write an essay about what you learned---about yourself, about others, about the world, or about something else---in the course of reading your books. You should be able to discuss both books within one essay, even if you discuss them separately. (See the rubric provided below)
2. "There are three rules for writing a good book. Unfortunately no one knows what they are." (W. Somerset Maugham)
    □ Essay Topic: Using your two books as the basis for an essay, come up with the "rules for a good book." In your essay you should use examples from the books you read to illustrate your points; thus if you say that "a good book must be exciting," you should draw examples from the books you read to show what you mean---and HOW it makes it a good book. You should be able to discuss both books within one essay, even if you discuss them separately. (See the rubric provided below)
3. "We read to know we're not alone." (C. S. Lewis)
    □ Essay Topic: Explain what you think Lewis means, taking examples from your two outside books to illustrate what you mean and why you think that. Consider this: the man in solitary confinement for murder finds, reads, and relishes Shakespeare's 29th sonnet ("When in disgrace with man's eyes, I trouble deaf heaven...") because the jilted lover feels the same way as the man in prison. As the Roman slave Terrance said a couple thousand years ago, "Because I am a man nothing is alien to me." (See the rubric provided below)
4. "East is East and West is San Francisco, according to Californians. Californians are a race of people; they are not merely inhabitants of a State." (O. Henry, 1910)
    □ Essay Topic: Given that your books were supposed to have some connection to the idea, theme, place, or history of California, write about how your books relate to or what your books say about California. The O. Henry quote above suggests that our state has always had a unique place in the American culture. What did your books say about its culture, its people, its landscape? Be sure to draw examples from your reading to illustrate. (See the rubric provided below)

RUBRIC

READING	WRITING	ASSIGNMENT REQUIREMENTS
□ 4. Show a deep understanding of what you read as evidenced by your remarks about it in the essay. □ 3. Show a sound understanding of what you read but lack insight. □ 2. Show a limited understanding of what you read but have a basic understanding. □ 1. Didn't read it.	□ 4. Thoroughly address prompt and include strong, appropriate examples; no intrusive mechanical errors. □ 3. Competently address prompt; includes some examples; minor interference from mechanical errors. □ 2. Do not address the topic; have no examples or they are inappropriate. Intrusive mechanical errors. □ 1. Writing suggests you did not read the book(s).	□ 4. You satisfied all requirements of the assignment □ 3. You satisfied half of the requirement--i.e., you read one book. □ 2. You satisfied part of the assignment--i.e., you read part of a book. □ 1. You did not read as assigned.

Figure 11.3   *Sample reading assessment for outside reading requirement*

Project Rubric
Burke/English

NAME:				PERIOD
Distinguished	Competent	Unsatisfactory	Incomplete/Undone	**COMMENTS** □ check here if comments are continued on back
				Formal Proposal: write a formal proposal to me in which you outline the following in some detail: what you will investigate; why you want to do this; how you will do it; what you expect to find; what obstacles you foresee and how you might solve them.
				Oral History/Interview: interview someone or some people in depth about your particular subject. You can satisfy this requirement in person, over the phone, or via the Internet so long as the content of the interview is substantial. Remember that you will need evidence (e.g., notes, printed E-mail, etc.) of this.
				Movie or Documentary/Movie Review: after watching a film, write a review of the film/documentary in which you discuss what they tried to show about the subject and how well you felt they succeeded. Good work here will answer the question *why* you thought it was a good or bad film.
				Write Your Paper/Website: this paper must be *at least* five typed pages and written on the computer. It must also be: double-spaced; 12-point font; no more than 1.25 inch margins on any side. It should have a cover page with your name, title, etc.; and a bibliography at your paper's end.
				Presentation: each student will give a 10 minute presentation of their work during the final two weeks of class. It must include a visual component: charts, images, family tree, art, video. These presentations can be in any of the following forms: dramatic performance, multimedia presentation, video documentary, formal presentation, or some other form you might invent.
				Bibliography: all outside reading, films watched, and sources quoted must be documented and included in a properly formatted bibliography (please use the attached style and usage guide).
				□ Read five outside sources (only one of which can be an encyclopedia □ Use the Internet □ Find a poem about your subject □ Include all notes, drafts, outlines
				OVERALL GRADE

Figure 11.4 *Sample checklist rubric used to evaluate American Literature "History Project"*

• It creates an opportunity to involve parents in an important way in the process of their child's education. This presentation of work to parents provides an important chance for the student to show them what they accomplished. Such exercises have the secondary benefit of showing the parents what is going on in the schools so when they talk to others they can say, "Well, you know, the schools aren't all bad. Just last week her teacher had us read her portfolio and I thought. . . ."

Here is the handout I provide students in June as they begin to create their portfolios:

Overview
It's time to create your final portfolio of your junior year. First, sift through it and prepare to write a letter evaluating your work. Your reflective writing should refer to specific pieces of your work as examples of whatever you are saying (e.g., "I learned how to better support and develop my ideas when writing about literature. In my *Huckleberry Finn* journal, for example . . ."). Your portfolios provide me with the most insightful evaluation of my teaching and this course; I always look forward to reading through these at the end of each year as they are (I hope) a validation of your progress and my efforts. They also provide you a final chance to argue your case by presenting evidence of your progress and accomplishments in this class.

Contents
In your portfolio on the day of the final you should have the following:

- samples from your journals that show your "daily writing"
- your outside reading record (i.e., the titles and authors of the books read)
- evidence of at least one project you've done this year)
- your annotated bibliographies
- your portfolio cover letter (placed in front of all your work, so that it serves as an introduction to and commentary on all that follows)
- anything else that you feel completes the picture of your development this year as a reader, thinker, writer, and speaker.

Cover Letter
Write a letter to a prospective reader of your portfolio in which you provide a careful analysis of your progress since September. This reflective letter should address most of the following questions at some point:

- In which area have you progressed the most this year? How would you contrast your work in this area now with September? What helped you improve in this area?
- Which piece of work this semester means the most to you? Why?
- Which piece of work this semester challenged you the most? Why? In what ways did it challenge you?
- How would you characterize your experiences as a reader this year? What did you read and how does that compare with what you read in the past? In what ways have you improved as a reader?
- What was your most memorable book this semester? What made it so memorable?
- What book did you like least this semester? Why was that?

In your conclusion or introduction come up with a topic sentence in which you use an adjective or analogy to describe this semester as it relates to your work as a thinker, reader, and writer. Go on to explain what you mean and always use specific examples to support and clarify.

What I love most about the portfolios is what they tell me about my own teaching, for truly my students' portfolios are *my* portfolio. Here I see, when all is said and done, what they thought was their best work, which assignments they liked the most or felt challenged them the most. Here I see if the reading paid off: Did they read more than they did before taking my class? Do they actually *like* to read now? Do they feel they read better? Here, for example, is junior Chris Giuliacci's cover letter:

Dear Mr. Burke,

Where do I start. This year has been a breakthrough year for me in so many ways. From writing, reading, vocabulary, my report and most of all this class made me a better person all around. Even though you thought our class was a unique group of kids, it was you who united us to work as a group but to continue to be individuals. For example, working together on the grant. Eight of us wrote that grant, but at the end you were able to bring everyone together and have us do our own thing to contribute. Then at the end everyone is rewarded with the satisfaction of fulfilling the needs of little kids (and the ice cream too).

In writing, I never knew how much I could write and how powerful words could be. Now when I sit down to write an essay I figure it should be at least two or three pages long. Before then, I would write just one page if I was lucky. It seems like writing essays are so much easier than they use to be. I hated the fact that you always assigned essays as homework, I always said to myself why couldn't he make us read a chapter and answer questions about it. Now I know that you don't learn anything from that. From writing essays I have learned so much more than I thought I would. When I write my essays I always catch myself taking a peak in the thesaurus to discover a better word for the meaning. My vocabulary is twice as good as it use to be (my dad is happy about that). Now when I write essays or term papers it feels like second nature.

My report on my grandfather really surprised me because I never thought I could accomplish all the requirements needed. Gathering my information took a lot of time, from talking to my uncles and aunts, researching for any holocaust data, to getting into a really deep and intellectual conversation with my grandma that ended up with tears from both sides. I never would have known that an English class could have this much effect on your life. When I did this project it wasn't because it was assigned, it was for me to find out more about my grandfather. When I started to write on my project it came so easy for me to complete six pages.

Having all my data at my fingertips, the essays that you assigned over the year helped me in a great deal on this project. This project brought everything together from the whole year into one sum and just showed you how much you can learn in one year in an English class.

Individually this year I have learned so much from other students in our class and from you. Every person in fourth period is different and you learn to accept everybody. It didn't really seem that we were a class but more like a group of teenagers that have known each other for eternity. I feel that I have matured in many aspects this year, not just in writing and reading but as an all-around person.

Christopher Guiliacci

Exams

Exams are good to the extent that they invite powerful and appropriate intellectual performances linked to standards the profession and community considers valid. The foremost question is: What purpose does this test serve? The subsequent question is: What exactly is this test testing? The answers to these two questions are crucial. One type of test will only measure a student's ability to take tests, while another type of test—or the same question asked a different way—will determine the depth and breadth of a student's understanding and ability in a particular area.

We tend to have several occasions for testing: the end of a unit of study, the end of a grading period or course, and after the presentation of information the teacher feels must be kept in the student's memory. Other moments are common: the pop vocabulary or reading quiz at the beginning of the period; state tests; the SAT; the ACT; and the AP test. These national exams fall outside the scope of this book, though I will take time enough to say that they are inevitable and a measure of our own performance. Thus it is politically savvy and professionally responsible to make sure students are prepared for those tests they must all take (e.g., district competency or state exams given to all students). I foresee, based on the growing support for standards, end-of-course exams in different subjects, which are designed to determine mastery of a specific standards-based curriculum. In this respect, the AP test remains the most compelling example of effective testing: students know the scoring system beforehand, they know the kind of tasks they will be asked to complete; moreover, the course itself is designed to prepare them for the AP test by giving them the skills and knowledge that educators and the College Board have determined to be important.

Student-created exams.   The College Board believes the purpose of assessment is to determine mastery of specific information; Grant Wiggins (1998), however, constantly reminds us that, "the aim of assessment is primarily to educate and improve student performance, not merely to audit it." With this idea in mind, I often try to involve students in the development of their own exams; this process, which I have used for end-of-unit exams as well as final exams, forces students deeper into the material while it simultaneously helps them to prepare for the exam they are making. I have students use a variation of the "Dense Question Strategy" (Christenbury and Kelly 1983) to create the test. Simply put, they develop a series of questions that begin with obvious questions about the text ("Text Question"); then create a question that asks them to relate the reading to their own lives ("Reader Question"); they then come up with a question that relates this text to some other texts they have studied ("World or Other Literature Question"); finally, they develop a "Dense Question" which combines all three. Here is an example for *The Catcher in the Rye*:

- *Text Question*: Who is the narrator of the story?
- *Reader Question*: Have you ever felt fed up with everything and just wanted to take off, get away on your own?
- *World/Other Literature Question*: What other character—in a book or a movie—would you compare the main character to?
- *Dense Question*: Why does Holden feel alienated and how is that related to what many of today's teens feel? Include in your answer a discussion of the extent to which you do or don't share these same feelings and why.

The advantages of such a process are obvious. Students demonstrate their understanding of a book through the process of developing questions about it. The final or "Dense" question always requires my approval to be sure they aren't setting themselves up for failure by developing a question they can't write about. Mostly I ask if they know what they'll write about or give them a few ideas to expand it. Students write about those aspects of the novel that are most meaningful to them; thus they are motivated to do better work on the exam. And, finally, the process itself is intellectually demanding and a part of their learning; in this way the assessment enriches the curriculum by being integrated into it.

Here is another kind of student-created exam, one that could be adapted to any other unit; in this case it was for a biblical literature unit in a freshman honors class I taught:

We have studied the Bible as literature the last four weeks, reading a number of stories and poems from or inspired by the Bible. At the same time, we have continued to focus on effective paragraph organization and development.

Day One: On an individual basis, develop FIVE exam questions, each one about a different piece we read, none of which can elicit a yes/no response and all of which should challenge you and your peers to show a deeper understanding of the texts we've read and discussed. You must also formulate one essay question that relates to the readings.

Day Two: In groups, read and discuss each question your group members developed, then decide which ones meet the previously established criterion; be able to explain how they do this. Each group must then type up these questions on the computer and submit a disk to me [the teacher] by the end of the period.

Day Three: Review questions as a class, and determine which of them are the most valid, coherent questions; we will then discuss why these are good questions.

Day Four: Take the exam composed of the questions that have been developed and discussed.

Day Five: Evaluate your own performance on the test according to the criterion provided in the rubric.

Day Six: The exams are evaluated by me [the teacher] according to the same criterion and I then assign the final grade.

Teacher-created exams.　　When I create the exams, my students can count on the following:

- There will be options (usually three or four different prompts; students are allowed to come up with their own if they can convince me it is a good topic).
- Students will know ahead of time the general ideas for the test; sometimes even the topics themselves (though in such cases I might only use one topic on the day of the final).
- They will often be able to use notes, books, and dictionaries—sometimes even the Internet—during the exam.
- They will know the criterion by which their exams are scored before they take them, though I may slightly revise these criterion once I have looked at the tests.

Here is a sample exam I created for a freshman honors course (which was integrated with the Social Studies class):

Final Exam: *Cry, the Beloved Country*

Option I

The following five themes stitch their way through the fabric of Alan Paton's novel *Cry, the Beloved Country*. Write an essay in which you discuss, for example, the conflicts between the new and the old throughout the story. Your essay should thoroughly explore this theme from all possible angles in order to fully develop your ideas about the theme.

- forgiveness
- desire
- tradition
- religion
- new vs. old
- other _____

Option II

After reading the following quote by Antonio Gramsci, analyze the conflicts between the blacks and whites in South Africa using Gramsci's quote as the basis for your analysis. Write an essay in which you examine the conflict between the whites and blacks or between the "new South Africa" and the "old South Africa" and to include in your essay these same themes as they pertain to the novel.

The crisis consists precisely in that the old is dying and the new cannot be born; in the interregnum a great variety of morbid symptoms appears.

—Antonio Gramsci,
The Prison Notebooks

Option III
After picking one of the main characters in the novel *Cry, the Beloved Country*, write about their journey throughout the novel using the guidelines from the class discussion and your understanding of the Heroic Cycle. Be sure to provide examples whenever possible in order to illustrate your point. While you are not expected to develop each stage into its own paragraph(s), you are expected to develop your ideas as fully and effectively as you can in the time you have. Please remember that you are to write about only ONE of these characters! You can choose from any of the following characters for the exam:

- Stephen Kumalo
- Absalom Kumalo
- James Jarvis
- Arthur Jarvis
- Msimangu
- other _____

Option IV
Consider South Africa's journey toward independence and justice. Describe this journey using the Heroic Cycle ideas, carefully illustrating your ideas with examples from History class, your readings in my class, and the movies we watched. You are not required to refer to all of them; I am just trying to point out that you can take your examples from anywhere to support your assertions, though they should include references to *Cry, the Beloved Country*. You might, for example, make some comparisons to the United States' civil rights era.

Too many teachers use tests to punish students, to "catch them." I hear this all the time: "I hate to do it, but I just have to quiz them to death or they won't read the book." Is it any wonder why some students hate to read, when the point of their reading is reduced to passing a quiz? Quizzes and exams serve many different purposes—to measure, to "weed," to "audit," to determine if students read the book or not. (Just imagine if administrators could require such periodic "quizzes" of us to determine what we taught and how we taught it!) Their purpose should be overt, clear to both the teacher and the student. Whenever possible, they should be anchored in the curriculum, linked to standards, and viewed as moments of intellectual engagement that allow them to demonstrate what they know about the material.

Measuring Progress: The Role of Evaluation

Evaluation comes from many sources these days, depending on the purpose and the audience. Senior Projects or "exhibitions" are increasingly evaluated by committees consisting not only of teachers but parents, peers, and community members. As students, through Internet-based projects and other such interactive and immediate experiences, find themselves learning on the run more and more, they must be able to evaluate themselves, and provide evidence to support such self-evaluations. And finally, as we move further into the "standards era," teachers will find themselves increasingly guided by state or national standards in our evaluations of student work.

Briefly, I consistently use the following types of evaluations and find them helpful for both me and the students:

Self-evaluation. When collecting any serious piece of work—an essay, a project, a research paper—I have students use the rubric or other assessment tool to evaluate their own performance. This helps them to pay closer attention to the standards and criterion; it also helps them to develop or internalize these habits of mind for themselves. Sure, I could do this for them; but then who's doing the work of learning? Consider the following self-evaluation from junior Ariel Dowgaluk:

> Most of my assignments show some effort; however, they could show more. I tend to screw around when I have to get things done. I have completed one of my outside reading books and plan on starting my second book soon. I do awesome work every once in a while but most of the time it's mediocre.

If they say critical things about their own work, they have to listen; if I say it, I am perceived like Charlie Brown's schoolteacher, droning on like all other authority figures about the need to work harder, do better.

Peer evaluation. Peer evaluation might come in response to poems, essays students write, or presentations they give. Students listen to each other if given the chance; they appreciate being taken seriously, having the teacher recognize that they have something to say. Here is Scott Cunningham, one of my juniors, evaluating another student's presentation:

> I thought Beau did a good job in teaching the class [about racism in *Huckleberry Finn*]. But I don't think we as students gave him the respect we would have given a regular teacher. I heard people cutting him off. I give Beau credit because he didn't seem at all nervous. If I was up there I would have been nervous. He should have only told one personal story to help us understand it and stopped there. I did like how he had everyone get into groups; that's what made me realize how much it was like a real class and that he was the teacher. I also liked his discussion topics and how well he organized it.

Adult evaluation. When I can and when it seems beneficial, I ask students to have one or two adults read and respond to their work. This adult evaluation is particularly important as part of the final portfolio in June. Parents want to know what their kids have done; kids need to feel accountable for the quality—or lack of it—in their work. I ask students to show their parents their final portfolio, and encourage the parents write a short response to their child in which they evaluate the work and their child's progress that year. This has the added benefit of giving parents and teenagers something (mostly) neutral to talk about during a period when communication between them is not always at its best. Here is an excerpt from Mrs. Cydzik's letter to her daughter Tina, who was a freshman: "I've taken time to read all of your work and it brought me a smile and tears. Thanks for sharing such an extraordinary portfolio. Looking through it reminds me of a beautiful oak tree—the trunk represents great growth and the branches represent your innermost thoughts, which enabled you to explore. I bet spending this time reading and writing has changed your perspective. I rejoice in your achievements!"

Teacher evaluation. Our own role in evaluation depends on the assignment and what any particular student needs at that time. Some students merit all the vigor I can bring to an assignment because they have invested an equal amount of time and energy into it; my role then is to help them make it the very best they can. Others need momentary evaluation to help them focus. This is exemplified by an anecdote I heard about Henry Kissinger. A man just graduated from Harvard came to work for Kissinger. As the man was a China expert, Kissinger asked him to write a report telling him everything there was to know about China. Fifteen minutes after he submitted this massive report, he found it back in his box with a question scribbled across the top: Is this the best you can do? Infuriated and unnerved at the same time, the man charged into the task, redoubling his efforts, only to meet with the same question two more times. Finally, he barged into Kissinger's office and demanded to know what Kissinger wanted from him. Kissinger only asked, "Is this the best you can do?" The man said, "Yes!" and Kissinger replied, "Good, then I'll be happy to read it." Evaluation is thus individually calibrated to determine where each student is in relation to their goals or the relevant standards, which it is our job to help them meet.

Grading: The Catch-22 of the Curriculum

Few teachers find joy in the grading of student work; some, in fact, find it the greatest potential threat to their longevity in the profession for there are those stretches when, no matter what your different strategies, you find yourself buried in papers, most if not all of which you must read, touch, judge.

When I was a student teacher a girl I enjoyed working with, who was a great student, stormed into the class. She charged right up to me and screamed as loud as she could, "Thanks a lot! Because of you I don't get my license!" Progress reports had arrived that weekend and she had a B+, a grade which, in her house, was apparently not good enough. I was a bit unnerved by her tirade: When you are a student teacher you just want them to love and accept you—or at least not scream at you. I calmly answered, "Well, Miss Goddard, I wasn't aware that I was supposed to take your license into consideration when giving you a grade for a writing class."

To the extent that it is possible, I would like to discuss grading as separate from assessment, for though they are related, they differ in their ultimate goals. What are we supposed to take into consideration when grading, anyway? After surveying various English teachers, I find the following "grading" options the most commonly practiced:

- letter grades (e.g., A, B, C)
- points (e.g., 23/25 points possible)
- rubric score (e.g., score of 4 on a scale of 6)
- checks (e.g., ✓−, ✓, ✓+)
- narrative evaluation (e.g., "your paragraph structure is dramatically improved from the last few essays, Jane. I was particularly impressed by your use of . . .")
- completion marks (e.g., a mark [✓] or word [yes] that means only that the assignment, typically one in process or of little weight, was completed)

This is where the divide between assessment and grading breaks down for me: No matter what your philosophy or your attitude about grades, there comes a time when you get those Scantron sheets, and must bubble in one of the magic letters. Moreover, the means whereby you arrive at this judgment must make sense to your students and to yourself so that the grade is meaningful—and valid. I don't mean that there should be a gold standard to which we must all adhere, but whether for admissions into future programs at your own school or colleges, or for another goal, the grade must add up to a logical and fair assessment of the students' work in the class.

Again, my survey of teachers found a wide range of perspectives when it comes to what is appropriate to consider for a grade. While some said effort mattered and should be reflected in the final score, others felt that they were not doing a student any favor to give them a higher grade than the "product" deserved. Most factor in participation, though they have many definitions for what that means: speaking in class, talking in small groups, helping the teacher, bringing their books and supplies, being in class on time, paying attention. Other teachers, naturally, don't agree and think such considerations are irrelevant and only contribute to inflation of grades. Many teachers are required to include in their grading systems some means of reflecting attendance and tardies; this means that a student loses a certain number of points each time they are late or cut class. Other teachers, for various reasons (class size, short periods, too much to do that day, classroom management) cannot afford or do not allot the time for this activity. Some engage in "private practice." I know a teacher whose classroom has lines of duct tape running down the rows, and students are docked points if their desks are out of alignment with the duct tape. Another docks you points if you are late or allows you to do twenty push-ups in front of the class instead. Obviously, everyone concentrates on the meat and potatoes of the course: those assignments involving reading, writing, and speaking.

With so many different pieces to consider, it is hard to figure out what the categories are and what the different weight of each one should be. Configured one way, the categories and their respective weights will ensure that those diligent students who do all their work well earn an A; configured another way, those with native abilities in these areas can excel, pleasing their teacher with powerful essays and the great outside books they read while ignoring many of the small assignments. Thus equity and a sense of fairness—i.e., some balance between effort and ability—should define your grading system. Also, it must be logical and thus balanced across time. Some teachers have 500 points one grading period; 1,500 another; and 739 during another grading period. Here, then, are the categories most commonly used by the teachers I surveyed. They may not use them all, so you should think about which ones best adapt to your curriculum.

- daily/homework assignments
- in-class work
- participation
- tests/quizzes
- final exam (most distinguish between the final exam and all other tests)
- projects/performances
- attendance/tardies
- group work
- extra credit (or its equivalent: "challenge assignments," "honors assignments." I don't offer it as a rule, but am willing to if there is something—a museum exhibit, a play, a place [e.g., the actual Cannery Row in Pacific Grove]—they need an incentive to do or visit.)

If only it were that neat, if those categories could cover all the bases. They pretend a simplicity and coherence that the English curriculum inherently lacks. So in the end you must decide how you will factor in improvement in their final grade. You ask yourself how you arrive at a grade you can both consider a fair and accurate description of what they accomplished. To this end, I suggest trying some of the following strategies:

Self-evaluation. I usually have the students write me a letter the week of report cards explaining what grade best describes their work in my class. I use it as a persuasive writing assignment and give it a grade as I would any other assignment, this particular grade being based on how effectively they support their argument with evidence and examples. Here is Nicole Guether's evaluation:

I believe the grade I earned would be a B–. In the grading rubric, most of the boxes I checked were in the B category with a few in the C category. I also think I deserve a B– because I try to do all the assignments, but sometimes I'm not sure what to do. My assignments usually have thought and effort, but sometimes I just try to get it out of the way because I have lots of other homework. I have totally satisfied the outside reading assignment . . . but don't really participate in class discussions, though I do a much better job in groups. So I deserve a B– because I do try to do my work but I don't go overboard like an A student. I'm definitely above a D student and I'd like to think above a C, also.

Keep your own account. Some teachers create an accounting sheet on which students are required to keep track of their own standing in the class. They make this an assignment, and believe it instills in students a sense of responsibility and demystifies the process of grading. Some swear by it.

Create a course rubric. Others, myself included, prefer to experiment with rubrics for the class itself. Thus you would have the different categories laid out with descriptors for each grade (e.g., "An A means you . . .")

Draw up a contract. Some teachers draw up a contract with the class that defines the grading process. In many respects this is like a rubric but functions a bit differently. A contract, for example, would say if you read five books, write twenty-five pages in your journal, have no absences, and regularly participate in class discussions you get a B. Such contracts are very helpful for students, but it can take some time to work out the kinks in such documents.

Endnote: Making the Grade

Whatever you do, you need a system that is efficient but offers students the information they need to understand why they got the grade and how they can improve their standing in the future. When I asked my students which of the different systems "made the most sense," their comments reflected the complexity inherent in grading English work. You cannot, for instance, give a poem a "C+" or any other grade because it is not an evaluative occasion; here, as with certain other writing assignments, you work through the process until you arrive at what you both recognize as a terminal moment (e.g., a poetry portfolio or booklet) that warrants a grade. And points, for all their apparent "objectivity," don't fit: what does it mean to say you got 26/30 on an essay? My students consistently said that a rubric made the most sense, so long as they received it ahead of time, and the descriptors were specific. They liked rubrics because the expectations and criterion are clearly laid out, providing a road map for them to follow. Also, the marks on the rubric provide specific and immediate feedback as to why they didn't do well in that area; if they have questions, I as the teacher can easily figure out what to address, since the rubric provides me clear information about what went wrong.

Few things are more productive and healthy than to get together with a group of teachers and have an anchoring session for grading. It's quite simple: Get a group of teachers from your department together at lunch and pass out a set of papers for an assignment. Everyone reads the assignment, then they score the papers according to whatever system you are using. This leads to discussion about the importance of correctness or support or voice in the essay. Other teachers get a sense of what they should be expecting and assigning. You talk some more—about what makes an A paper, why this is a C. The grades feel more anchored in professional standards, and the agreement of your colleagues provides a new validity to your grades. Meanwhile, you have had an exciting conversation about writing, reading, and teaching. I can't recommend such anchoring sessions strongly enough: not only do they improve your teaching but they improve your relationships with your colleagues and break down the walls of isolation within which we too often work. These sessions also keep teachers in touch with their colleagues' expectations and standards, an issue of crucial importance when it comes to the validity of one's grades.

Grades do matter to kids—more than they should. English teachers are sometimes guilty of playing terrible games with grades, leaving many to feel that the whole process is a power trip or a mind game. At their best, grades are an invitation to reflect for both teachers and students. If we create grading systems that are clear and fair, if we help students to assess their own work and thereby internalize high standards, the grades they receive will be mere confirmations of what they already know. Such a process further empowers the student, for if they do have these internalized standards of performance, they feel they can inquire about the discrepancy between their standards and yours in a reasonable and mature way. These moments become powerful teaching events if both the teacher and student handle themselves appropriately. Kristine Hartman, who was in my freshman class, exemplifies what I mean:

> Mr. Burke,
>
> After I was walking home yesterday from tearing your ear off, I realized that although I still felt, and still do feel, strongly in my beliefs upon the subject of my grade, I should have approached you with more tact. Maybe if I had thought about the situation for more than five minutes before I opened my large mouth and stuck my foot in it, then I might have been able to communicate better my opinions. I hope you'll accept my deepest apologies and not think any worse of me.
>
> I write this fully knowing that you will make no changes in my grade, but I feel I should explain why I felt so strongly about having you change my score. This is because I felt I went out of my way to make my proposal unique and different from anyone else's. I really tried to draw my peers into my proposal, so I felt I deserved a higher score. While I may have worked very hard and put much time and effort to achieving this goal, ultimately I fell short, for I was the performer and not the critic.
>
> So, in conclusion, the point I am trying to get across is if I question my grade, it is only because I think it's important to understand the reasons for that grade, so that I might, in the future, learn to approach it in a different manner.
>
> Thank you again.
>
> Your student,
> Kristine

The psychology of grading is extremely complicated for reasons we all understand. For the students who are motivated, the system works: the grades mean something to them, they are motivated to improve them, and they feel a sense of accomplishment when they achieve the higher mark. But these are more the exception than the rule for many of our students. In my senior year I got a D– (one of those "gift Ds" we sometimes give because we just can't handle the thought of failing a certain kid we know will, in the long run, turn out okay) from the teacher who is responsible for inspiring me to be an English teacher. When the disconnected students get past the point of possibly being able to pass, they have no other hope than to undermine your class and your teaching. It thus somehow behooves us to offer them a means of achieving some final success that we can recognize as meaningful to them and acceptable to us. I don't mean to imply passing kids on; I assign Fs when they earn them. But what remains in my head are the words Gigi, a Latina girl in my sophomore class, wrote in her journal:

> Of all the things my mother told me, there was only one I remember . . . and that was that you are not expected to succeed. This was said to me by my mother. She was talking to me about education. She had asked me what was going on with my grades. Then she went off about "how do you expect to get anywhere if you do not do your work?" Then she told me about an article that she had read.

It said that the Latin American race are the lowest race to accomplish their education, to go ahead and finish high school. That the Latina girls just get pregnant and guys drop out. That hit the spot.

A few months later I wrote this student a letter in which I tried to coax her toward the kind of work we both knew she could do. Gigi wrote back, saying:

Your letter had a lot of things in it that related to me. I'll admit that. And I do need to put extra effort into my work. But I really don't know why I don't. I'm not concentrated but I have the ability to be. It's like I have no interest. Why? I don't know. I try but it doesn't work. Like for *Catcher in the Rye!* Every time I read that book I fall asleep. It was so boring! So was that last book, *House on Mango Street.* I like books of mystery, romance, suspense, and the civil war interests me, too. But I am trying. . . . I liked those short stories you read to us. And I did all the work that you asked us to do with those. Another thing is the environment in the classroom. I have a lot of friends in that class and they tend to talk to me and I tend to talk to them! But I'm trying to stop. Well, that's it. Thanks for your letter, Mr. Burke.

Gigi's letter to me brings the different elements together in an important way. Based on my observations of her work and level of engagement, my assessment was that she needed direct intervention and more accountability. Her subsequent letter to me offers a compelling example of recursive self-assessment in the wake of her promise to do better. These evaluations provide meaningful data to me, when added to her other performance information, that allow me to determine her grade, one we can both agree is accurate and fair.

In the end, it is results that matter most. What are the results of our teaching? What are the results of our students' learning? Their efforts? Our efforts? How can we best measure and achieve these results? Obviously this chapter suggests you must do it through different means, choosing from a range of options those methods or assignments that best meet the needs of the students and the moment. I have also tried to demonstrate that results, if they are to be lasting and meaningful, must come from the pursuit of goals students create themselves. If, in the end, we "give" students grades based on criterion they have not internalized (i.e., adopted as their own), they will never achieve the sense of purpose or pleasure that comes from working toward goals they have set themselves. Such accomplishments become the final measure of our work: did they learn what they needed to live well and succeed in the world? Lindsay Rosenthal, while a freshman in my class, wrote in the following project evaluation what seems the embodiment of the ideas discussed here; I will close with her words and let you decide for yourself what her remarks mean when it comes to assessment, evaluation, and grading:

Directions
Please take some time to answer the following questions as thoughtfully and specifically as you can.

Standards
I told you this project would be used to evaluate what you are capable of doing at the end of your freshman year. Is this your best work? Please explain.

> *Yes, by far this is my best work. From the day the project was assigned I worked at least two hours every day on this project, but more importantly, I worked well and thoughtfully.*

Topic
Why did you originally choose your topic? How did what you learned compare with what you thought you would learn? I am glad/sorry I chose this topic because _____ (please explain).

> *I chose the topic of astrophysics because I've always been interested in space and time, and how it all works, and I thought this would be a great opportunity to find out more about it. I simply wanted to know how it all works, but I found more about how the great physicists discovered the hows. I'm glad I chose this project because I learned an unfathomable amount about astrophysics, myself, and how to go about a huge research project.*

Process
What was the hardest part about this project for you? (Explain.)

> *The hardest part was staying sane, and being able to have enough endurance to work well each night.*

Product
What is one thing you are really proud of or that means the most to you about this project? (Explain.)

> *I'm really proud of my presentation script. It is by far my best written work this year. I spent a lot of time and thought on this most important aspect of my project.*

Just Curious
If you talked with other people about your project, who did you talk to and what did you talk to them about? Is there a reason you wanted to tell this person/these people about your project?

> *I talked [via e-mail] with Harvard graduate student Eric Woods and Professor Ben Bromley from Harvard's Harvard-Smithsonian Astrophysics Center. I talked to them about their impressions of the different aspects of astrophysics. I also talked to my parents because I practiced my presentation in front of them to get ready.*

Suggested Changes
What is one thing I should change about this project to improve it for future students? (Please explain how that would improve it.)

> *Have all students show you the day the writing portion is due some evidence of their readiness to present their projects so some students don't get extra weekends or days to work on their projects.*

REFLECTION

Begin with an end in mind: What is it you want kids to be able to do specifically by the time the year/course ends? How can you assess that best? What are the implications for instruction of such an assessment system? How will this translate into a grade on the report card that you can both recognize as fair and meaningful?

ACTIVITY 1

Make a short list of memorable evaluation/assessment moments in your life: What made them difficult or challenging? What experiences do you have with failure?

ACTIVITY 2

Unfortunately, you have run into trouble with some parents and they have challenged your final grade for their daughter. The panel, consisting of parents, colleagues, administration, and students has asked you to submit your grade books and a written explanation of your grading system and philosophy as it relates to the grade book they are examining. Write a letter to this panel in which you articulate your ideas on these topics.

RECOMMENDATIONS

Reflections on Assessment. Kathleen and James Strickland (Boynton/Cook 1998). This offers the most concise and practical overview of both the philosophies and practices of assessment of all the books I read for this chapter.

Results: The Key to Continuous School Improvement. Mike Schmoker (ASCD 1996). One of those rare one-hundred-page gems that crystallizes years of thinking about assessment. Specifically, Schmoker ran a Title 1 reading program that he reconfigured so that it was entirely focused on results, which were, in turn, used to provide immediate feedback to students and teachers.

Educative Assessment. Grant Wiggins (Jossey-Bass 1998). Provides more in-depth analyses of the issues discussed in this chapter. Wiggins's ideas are brilliant and will inspire new thinking in any teacher, even if you disagree with him.

Grading in the Post-Process Classroom. Libby Allison, Lizbeth Bryant, and Maureen Hourigan (Boynton/Cook 1997). Though written for a college audience, this book is very helpful. It is a collection of essays written by different teachers, each one looking at some different aspect of grading student work, all of which offer practical and thoughtful solutions.

A Portfolio Primer: Teaching, Collecting, and Assessing Student Writing. Geof Hewitt (Heinemann 1995). Hewitt's book offers the high school teacher a wide range of perspectives and approaches. For the teacher looking to buy one book, this one will be useful, as it surveys all the different types of and purposes for portfolios.

Standards for Our Schools: How to Set Them, Measure Them, and Reach Them. Marc S. Tucker and Judy B. Codding (Jossey-Bass 1998). The best book to read on standards to date. This book offers readers a balanced examination on what standards are, how to use and create them, and why we need them.

A Measure of Success: From Assignment to Assessment in English Language Arts. Fran Claggett (Boynton/Cook 1996). Offers the most succinct description of developing and integrating assessment into the English class; a wonderful book that expands your notions of how to assess while improving your thinking about what to teach.

CHAPTER 12

DIGITAL LITERACY
TECHNOLOGY IN THE ENGLISH CLASS

The tools are intellectual and attainable, for digital literacy is about mastering ideas, not keystrokes.

—Paul Gilster, *Digital Literacy*

Those who acquire [writing] will cease to exercise their memory and become forgetful; they will rely on it to bring things to their remembrance of external by external signs, instead of their own internal resources.

—**Socrates, on the dangers of depending on writing instead of the memory (in Plato, *Phaedrus*)**

Brave New Classrooms

I was confused when Elissa, on the day my students' final portfolios were due, handed me a simple floppy disk with "Elissa's Portfolio" written on it. My raised eyebrows signaled my concern, no doubt; detecting this, she said that her entire portfolio was on the disk. I had not offered this format as an option. The next year things got only more strange: A freshman, on this day of final reckoning, handed me an index card with a Web site address on it, telling me that I could find his final portfolio at that address. I didn't know what to say and so responded only, "Oh. Thank you." When I got home, I opened Elissa's electronic portfolio to find a magnificent HyperCard (multimedia) stack that included all her work carefully organized. I had only to click the button saying *"Lord of the Flies* Project" to suddenly find myself at the assignment. As I checked out the last of her offerings, I found a button that said "Comments" which, when I pressed it, offered me my own scrollable space in which to write my assessment and enter her grade.

Computers have changed how we work and how we think. The symbol of the asterisk was replaced long ago by the "bullet," allowing me to speak to my students of "thinking in bullets" when I teach them how to format documents or presentations. The nature of "text" has also changed drastically, as "hypertext" and "hypermedia" have evolved to allow users to navigate through documents by any route they choose. Computers have also changed our conception of time: "real" time has been replaced by some other standard wherein we can work or check our mail whenever we want. And they've altered our sense of how we work. I have just about every lesson plan and handout I've ever made stored on my hard drive; this allows me to type the "find" command and search through thousands of files for information on "Hamlet OR Shakespeare." The MacPlus I bought while in the teaching credential program has long since been replaced by a series of computers, the most recent of which was impossible to imagine only ten years ago: it is a sleek four-pound notebook that can connect me to the Internet or play a CD-ROM.

Technology Standards: What Teachers Should Know

Various state and local powers have begun to create staff development objectives, purchase incentive programs, and leadership positions in the area of educational technology. It is such standards that will force the hand of those teachers who remain "unplugged" for soon enough teacher evaluations, school accreditation, and even job requirements will reflect these standards and expectations. Here are a few examples of such standards from the San Luis Obispo County Office of Education, in California:

Level One: Personal Proficiency
Objective: To ensure educators are able to:

1. Use a computer and related software to enhance personal productivity
2. Locate information and conduct research via the Internet/WWW
3. Operate a variety of common media display devices

Level Two: Instructional Proficiency
Objective: Ensure educators are able to apply education technology skills (of at least Level One proficiency) to (1) customize curriculum to enhance its relevance and value to a wider range of learning styles and abilities; (2) improve student ability to improve their education by accessing technologies that will enhance their education; and (3) use technology to meet individual student's needs more effectively.

Performance Standards

The educator is able to:

1. Activate a personal computer and run installed software from a hard drive, floppy disk and/or a CD-ROM.
2. Access and use a word processing application to create and edit a document, save it for future retrieval and print it.
3. Use a desktop publishing, graphics, banner maker program, or other classroom productivity tools.
4. Use a grade program, spreadsheet, or database to assist with classroom record keeping functions.
5. Access the Internet on a dial-up basis or via a school LAN and use a search tool to locate information relevant to his/her personal and professional interests while being cognizant of intellectual property concerns.
6. Send and reply to e-mail messages.
7. Use an overhead projector, VCR, laser/video disk player, LCD panel, and other common media display tool.

8. Be able to use proper file management techniques to save information on a hard drive, zip/external drive, and/or floppy disk. (San Luis Obispo County Office of Education 1997)

Such standards and skills are dramatically different from those expected of teachers entering the class even in the early 1990s. Even as I write this, I am all too aware that technology will have changed still more by the time you read this; yet the "Web" or "Net" would appear to have achieved a stability of form that ensures a common point of reference in the future. It may get faster, better, or more dangerous, but will continue to exist and evolve. Indeed, the fact that as I wrote this book I simultaneously conceived of creating a Web site to accompany it—a sort of Virtual Companion—reflects the fluid nature of information: a Web site allows information to be regularly updated. Which, in effect, is how I imagined my Web site: a means of continuing the conversation begun in this book and adding there to what I am offering here.

Implications for the English Class

Paul Gilster (1997, 1) defined what amounted to a new and essential literacy for all students: "digital literacy." Gilster defines digital literacy as "the ability to access networked computer resources and use them . . . to understand and use information in multiple formats from a wide range of sources. It is cognition of what you see on the computer screen . . . [and] involves mastering a set of core competencies. The most essential of these is the ability to make informed judgments about what you find on-line, for unlike conventional media, much of the Net is unfiltered by editors and open to contributions from all. This art of critical thinking governs how you use what you find on-line, for with the tools of electronic publishing dispersed globally, the Net is a study in the myriad uses of rhetoric. Forming a balanced assessment by distinguishing between content and its presentation is key."

What Gilster calls digital literacy others have termed information literacy; I prefer the former, however, as it includes in it the skills of using computers and navigating the Net, as well as reading critically what one finds on it. This facility with different media tools lies at the heart of what many call "distributed knowledge," a term that refers to our modern, human capacity to use tools to solve our problems. Such tools include a rapidly growing array of technologies, including PDAs (personal digital assistants), cellular phones whose capabilities would make James Bond envious, and pagers that, to most people's chagrin, make them available to their workplace around the clock. Other, nontechnological tools to which one might assign tasks include Post-its and personal planners, which are designed to help us stay afloat in a world that seems only to work longer and harder to do more, make more, sell more.

My revelation that fundamental change had taken place came during final exams for my junior classes one January. Briefly, the assignment called for students to use all they had learned about developing and organizing ideas, analyzing and presenting their ideas in order to persuade their audience. Working in groups, they were required to develop a proposal for a semester-long study of California's history and culture which was, in fact, to be our focus for the next semester. We started working on it the week before the actual day of the final exam, using the library as much as possible. The epiphany came when, on the day of the exam, roughly 70 percent of the students brought in a variety of information that they had gleaned from the Internet or CD-ROMs; those who had not been so organized asked if they could use the Internet connection in my classroom during the exam. Several groups wanted to know if they could create a Web site during the two hours they had as a way of both organizing and presenting their ideas to me. (As I had hoped to find some kids next quarter to do exactly this I was overjoyed by the requests.) Still other groups, led by girls, asked if they could use the computer in the library to create a formal presentation using Microsoft PowerPoint, a multimedia presentation program. It is precisely such work that many have in mind when they speak of such hi-tech tools allowing the creation of communities of learners who are engaged in collaborative critical and cultural inquiries (Cummins and Sayers 1997).

It happens that I know all these software programs, but what about the teacher who doesn't, who may not know anything at all? Some no doubt struggle with what feels like a loss of power or control. The kids don't need you to do these things. You may worry about what they will find in the course of their research. Don't worry about it: you cannot possibly keep up with what your best students know. You can, however, bring your subject matter knowledge to the table and help them learn to evaluate what they find in the course of their info-quest. I'm reminded of the French teacher at my school whom I watched sit with her students as they investigated France: she let them "drive on the information highway," but taught them how to interpret what they saw along the way. What looked like a great resource to the kids, she explained, was a commercial tourist "infosite" provided by a travel agency. Another powerful option is to have those who know teach those who do not know—including the teacher—how to use the computer. This mentoring helps students to develop what Miles Myers (1996) and others have spoken of as an essential skill of the twenty-first century: the ability to teach others.

An activity like the final exam described above—and students' subsequent response to it—exemplifies what California's language arts standards ask for in the following writing standards:

Deliver multimedia presentations that

1) combine text, images, and sound, synthesizing information from a wide range of materials including television, videos, films, newspapers, magazines, CD ROMs, Internet and computer media generated images;

2) select an appropriate medium for each element of the presentation;

3) use the selected media skillfully, including editing and monitoring for quality; and

4) test audience response and revise the presentation accordingly (California Academic Standards Commission 1997).

While my focus here is, appropriately, computers, let me quickly comment on another technology whose use in the English class is potentially profound: video. Though I cannot think of my students' early "video texts" as exemplary of anything other than their ability to hold down the record button and their inability to stand still for three seconds, recent video productions have improved tremendously thanks to new video-editing technologies available in more and more schools. That such texts can demonstrate real insight into a subject and convey this awareness with power was illustrated in a video Lucas and Anthony made as part of their *Huckleberry Finn* Project and presentation to the class. Sam Intrator, a doctoral candidate watching my class that day, wrote in his observation notes:

I was watching Lucas pretty intently. He sort of glowed with nervous pride during the whole video. I also thought of how compelling their movie snippet selections [from *Mississippi Burning, A Time to Kill,* and *Jerry McGuire*] were. Not only were the titles pertinent to the project, but the actual clips were well-selected. In thinking it through, I made the analogy that if a student had written a paper that utilized four cleverly selected quotes from significant novels to make their point I would be exceedingly impressed by their literacy skills. It didn't strike me right away, but their achievement was substantively significant. I also was fascinated and impressed by Lucas's mom [who is interviewed in the video] and his own reflections on racism in his family. You've got these kids being intellectually courageous. It's incredibly powerful to witness.

The brief digression from the larger discussion of computer technology represents the increasing convergence of all these technologies. The Net and its related technologies allow one, given the proper equipment, to integrate video, audio, still images, and, of course, words. Most of these advanced technologies are not present in our schools, however, and it is to those capabilities we do have that I turn now. In my classes, I have had great success using computers for:

- e-mail
- the Internet or databases as brainstorming/topic-refining tools
- the Internet and CD-ROMs for research
- presentations
- writing
- miscellaneous

E-mail. Though sometimes logistically complicated, e-mail offers one of the most engaging and helpful resources in the classroom. It takes your class outside the walls of the room or, similarly, brings the world into your classroom. Using e-mail as part of my interdisciplinary course, we have, at various times, corresponded at length with experts from major universities (e.g., Harvard), an alleged IRA terrorist, a South African journalist (a ten-page meditation to my freshmen about what it was like to live through the transition to Mandela's new government as a white middle-class journalist), and students from various countries. Our quarter-long unit on India benefits every year from an abundant, constant influx of letters from Indians who live all over the world, but join each other on-line for a virtual community that is startling in its vitality. I have found it fascinating to watch the Web provide a worldwide means of arranging marriages for traditional Indian men and women whose professional lives take them far from their native homes but not their values. As we conduct a simulation of an arranged marriage, these Web sites are of great use in the study of their culture. Also, when we have done simulations requiring students to take on characters from different cultures, they have found people from these countries on-line and used their words from the letters as the text of their script. What's more, if they have questions about, for example, what a South African government official would say about something, they can write back to that official they found on-line and ask them directly.

E-mail can also allow students to correspond with each other about the books they read. I offered students this option for several years when they read Amy Tan's *The Kitchen God's Wife*, but only after e-mail caught on did this alternative excite students. (See Chapter 7 for an example.)

E-mail has also demonstrated better than anything else the pressing need to teach students to evaluate information. Because information is on the Net and it is written, perhaps even by someone whose credentials on-line sound impressive, they think it must be true. (See Chapter 13 for a specific example.) A few years back, a group of students were studying the conflicts in Ireland as part of my freshman United Nations Project. They logged onto a newsgroup for Ireland and posted a few questions. They immediately got a few letters back, one coming from a man named Jerry Monahan. Jerry immediately launched into a tirade about the English and how they should all be bombed off the earth. The second message in the list came from someone warning us that we'd be hearing from a Jerry Monahan, who was a "known IRA member" and not to trust a word he said. Soon thereafter a new message popped up, this one from Monahan again. He wanted the kids to know that some people would no doubt write to tell them that what he was a liar; he wanted them to know that what these others said was rubbish and not to listen to them. Subsequent messages from others said that despite the fact that Monahan denied it, they felt honor-bound to tell us that he was, in fact, a terrorist. Mostly we laughed, but it opened my eyes to the absolute importance of teaching them about the truth and how we weigh the credibility of people and what they say.

The Internet or databases as brainstorming/topic-refining tools.   Thanks to the remarkable search engines on-line, users can cast a wide net to catch something related to their topic. However, another way to use this technology is to help you find or refine your topic. Things pop up that you could not have thought about yourself. The range of quality resources I found while writing this book was stunning: I would type in "education and the economy" in hopes of finding Marc Tucker's National Center on Education and the Economy, only to find in Yahoo's list several other sites or ideas I had not imagined existed. Similarly, when my students do a big research project and they are just starting out, I tell them to use Newsbank and other electronic databases as brainstorming tools: type in the word *California* and see what comes up. What you get is essentially a massive list in outline form with categories that can stimulate your thinking. We always work better when we have something to bounce off of; looking at such a list and seeing "sports" might bounce us in the direction of the old Pacific Coast league and lead to a report on the history of baseball in California, complete with poems by Quincy Troupe, whose father played in the California Negro Baseball League.

The Internet and CD-ROMs for research.   The examples I provided above illustrate perhaps the most powerful use of these technologies. Never before have students been able to have access to so much information; in fact, they have access to too much information. This makes it our job to teach them how to sift through it all and recognize what is important and why it is important. Also, it is imperative that students be taught to properly cite the information they glean through such searches. The opportunity to plagiarize is overwhelming and impossible to discover in most cases; we can, however, create topics or assignments that do not lend themselves to such problems. Students in libraries that lack abundant print resources—a source of particular shame in California—can gain access to the best libraries in the world if they have a few Internet connections. Teaching them to use the Internet, requiring the use of the Internet, is essential if the kids are to be prepared for the future that is always getting closer.

Presentations.   Public speaking provides one of the most powerful and engaging opportunities to incorporate technology. Also, it allows you to teach them these skills in the context of a larger assignment. For instance, when my freshman do their huge India/China presentations at the semester's end, students have to create visual aids to help organize and present their information; I take this opportunity to teach them to use both the outlining function and the slide show feature of Claris Works. On other occasions students use multimedia authoring programs like HyperStudio or HyperCard; a few who have PCs at home prefer their own programs and will go as far as to bring in their entire computer to run the presentation at school. In addition to these other programs, presentation software like PowerPoint teaches students the skill of organizing information, "thinking in bullets," and addressing your idea to an audience.

Writing.   I already discussed the use of computers for revision and the general writing process. Other important uses include creating publications, producing poetry anthologies, or allowing special needs students to use these tools to help improve their performance. I have, on occasion, allowed students to write their final exam essays on computers since I share their belief that they write better on the computer; however, they don't let you use computers on the SAT or the state exams, so I waffle on this subject, convinced that students need to know how to sit down and write an essay with a pen in hand, too.

Miscellaneous.   Students use computers for so many different tasks now. Latino students at my school regularly use the computer lab to publish their newsletter *La Raza*. The literary magazine uses the lab for its annual publication. Some of my freshmen, when asked to adapt myths to children's books, create professional-looking books. Still others grab images off the Internet to use in remarkable newspapers complete with period advertisements or articles.

As we move further into the world of the World Wide Web, our students begin to create Web pages for some classes, turning in an index card with a URL and their name on it on the day the project is due. (See Figure 12.1.) Other students, working with classmates or their teacher, create and regularly upgrade a class Web site so parents and friends can see their work and that of their classmates. Other students, using advanced programs such as Microsoft's 3-D Moviemaker, create actual interactive stories about characters who navigate their way through strange virtual worlds. CyberGuides, on-line "virtual tours" of museums, places, or the world of a particular book (e.g., *The Joy Luck Club*), also offer rich opportunities to integrate the computer into your class.

How Teachers Can Use Computers

I've had a computer since I was a student teacher. My master teacher, Pat Hanlon, was way ahead of her time when it came to technology. From the beginning, I was challenged to learn how to use these strange new tools. After many hours of failure, and moments of wonderful insight and

Figure 12.1   *The Web site Rana Kishek created for "The History Project" in her American Literature class. Assignments linked to students' personal interests and talents provide rich opportunities for learning.*

progress, I learned to do what now seems second nature. Here are examples of the primary ways I use my computer on a daily basis:

- Search the Internet to find the full text of *Hamlet* so I can download it and, in my word processor, reformat excerpts to allow students to learn to annotate a text.
- Download Nelson Mandela's speech at the South African premier of *Cry, the Beloved Country* to use in my class while we read the book.
- Create different types of spreadsheets to help me manage conferences, service learning projects, status of projects, or participation in class discussions.
- Download six different translations of Psalm 23 to create a one-page parallel text as part of a unit on the Bible as literature.
- Send out an e-mail query to different listservs or colleagues at other schools asking for ideas about teaching a new novel.
- Create an interactive multimedia timeline of the history of poetry as an exemplar to my students who were then required to create their own multimedia presentations.
- Keep in touch with former students who have gone off to college but all get e-mail accounts.

There are other ways I use the computer, but these represent the primary uses to which I put the machine. I'm pretty sure I could not live—or, more to the point, work—without one. Not only do they save me time—usually—they also allow me to create very professional-looking documents which, thanks to the features of different programs, make my handouts easier to use.

Components of Effective Computer Use/Setup

After soliciting the comments of various teachers who use computers in their classes, I arrived at the following list, which includes those resources and practices common to this work.

- All technology used is related to instructional goals as outlined in your state or local curriculum.
- Learning activities are anchored in the world beyond your class and provide authentic experiences that not only engage students but teach them what they need to know to succeed after leaving school.
- Computers are not used for work that could be done easier and quicker by hand on paper.
- All students have equal and adequate access to machines capable doing what the assignment asks.
- All students have adequate time to learn the program(s) and complete the assignment.
- All students know how to use the programs required for the assignment.
- Teachers teach these programs in context (e.g., how to use the word processor in the course of writing and revising a paper); they can also have students teach other students.
- All computers use the same version of the programs (e.g., Claris Works 4.0) so that a student, returning on subsequent days, can sit down at any computer and continue their work.

- All students spend time using the computer instead of watching one kid, often a boy, do fancy things so quickly no one can learn from them or get any practice themselves.

- Students who know how to use computers well help others learn by being teachers.

- Teachers should always have a backup plan when planning a lesson around technology. Once I watched a "leading innovator from Apple's Classroom of Tomorrow" reduced to waving a CD-ROM around in the air when his elite Powerbook repeatedly crashed. "On this disk," he would say, waving the CD around at the steadily shrinking audience, "you would be able to see these incredible pictures of kids doing these amazing projects."

- Students are responsible for their own data (e.g., backing it up, saving it, keeping it) and should not be allowed such excuses as printer failure, server failure, hard drive failure, father failure ("I don't know what happened, Mr. Burke, my dad was messing around with it and now nothing works and I can't get it to print my paper. I swear, ask my dad!").

- Students must read, discuss, and sign an acceptable-use agreement (AUG) prior to using the Internet; such discussions should include on-line ethics and etiquette. The signing of such AUGs is already mandated by law in many states.

- Students should be taught that style does not triumph over substance: No one ever got an A because they made a pretty cover on the computer; just because they spent all vacation on the Net getting images and creating a really cool-looking HyperStudio stack doesn't mean the resulting project is excellent work.

- Students should always roadtest any presentation prior to the class period when they are to give it; this avoids such last-minute revelations as "Oh darn, this computer doesn't have the same version of the program as the one in the lab," or "Mr. Burke, the overhead doesn't work."

- A classroom should, ideally, have the following equipment:
  - a couple of old Mac SE's (or the like) or 486 machines for simple word processing
  - a networked laser printer (so you can print quietly but also produce quality publications)
  - three full multimedia stations that are also connected to high-speed Internet lines
  - at least one machine that is connected to an LCD panel or a monitor for presentations
  - a secure place to keep all the peripherals and other resources
  - a method for systematic/scheduled file backup over a network or onto a separate storage device (e.g., a zip drive)

Endnote: New Frontiers

Technology is fundamentally changing our notions about the role of the teacher, and our relationship with the text. Several years ago, for example, I began listening to books on tape for my thirty-minute drive to work; this was a transforming experience as it allowed me not only to "read" more, but to try books that I would never otherwise read because I wouldn't take the time. I bring it up because technology raises a simple but essential question we will have to answer in the near future: What constitutes "reading" in a world of so many different texts? If a state reading performance standard demands that students will read a certain number of books or words a year, does a student's two hours of reading Web sites "count" as reading? Does my special education student's weekend spent listening to an abridged version of *All the Pretty Horses* on tape count as a book? When high school teachers are lucky enough to find themselves with a classroom of computers on which their students can write regularly, what new metaphor best captures their role: coach? facilitator? guide? technician? And, perhaps most frustrating to us: if the technology of film provides movie versions for every major book we teach, how will this redefine not only what we teach but how?

And what of the future—which, with technology, seems to get here faster by the day? Here is one speculative view of things to come. Janet Murray, author of *Hamlet on the Holodeck: The Future of Narrative in Cyberspace* (1997), said "The Holodeck is this imaginary entertainment venue of the 24th century that is popular on the *Star Trek* television shows, and it is as if one were in a movie that you could walk into and play a role in the movie. And so I took the Holodeck as part of my title along with *Hamlet* as representing the other pole; that when technologists look forward at what narrative could become, at what all the technologies if they all worked and they all worked together, where they would take us, they think Holodeck, but when literary people think about what we value about literature telling us something about the human condition, we tend to look backwards towards Shakespeare. So I put them together and sat Hamlet on the Holodeck. Is this possible?" The answer to this question is a daunting one, for few things seem impossible in this shifting universe. Several years ago, when one of his advisers asked Deng Xiao Ping to allow China to allow its people access to the Internet, Deng agreed, but said he would like to have a meeting first with the president of the Internet Corporation. "There is no Internet Corporation," his adviser answered. "Well then who is in charge of it?" Deng Xiao Ping wanted to know. "No one," the adviser answered. Sometimes this is how everything feels: like a spaceship out of control, no one at the wheel, with a bunch of teachers bouncing around in the back while a voice comes over the intercom telling us to get out there and take control, do our job, set things right. But the more we use technology, the more we ourselves will be able to chart a course for tomorrow.

REFLECTION

In your journal, write about how you see your own role within the classroom and the curriculum when it comes to technology. What metaphor might best describe how you envision yourself? How do you feel about computers: are they a burden or a blessing—or both? What is one thing you would like to see your students be able to do with computers in your curriculum? How can you help make that happen?

ACTIVITY

Go to the California Language Arts homepage and take a virtual field trip using one of the CyberGuides for a book you teach or just really like. Their Web site is: http://www.sdcoe.k12.ca.us/score/cyberguide.html. While you navigate your way through the guide, think about how you would use this in the class-room and the implications for how you would have to teach if you incorpo-rated it into your class.

RECOMMENDATION

Brave New Schools: Challenging Cultural Illiteracy Through Global Learning Net-works, by Jim Cummins and Dennis Sayers (St. Martin's Press 1997) is a rich combination (in an affordable paperback edition) of practical examples and pedagogical wisdom. The book takes into consideration a range of technologi-cal realities and, most importantly, *all* students and what these global learning networks can do for them as learners and as people.

CHAPTER 13

MEDIA LITERACY
READING THE VISUAL AND VIRTUAL WORLDS

Truth, like time itself, is a product of a conversation man has with himself about and through the techniques of communication he has invented.

—Neil Postman, *Amusing Ourselves to Death: Public Discourse in the Age of Show Business*

[People born before World War II] can't understand how we who were born after the war can read and watch TV at the same time. But we can. When I wrote my book, I had earphones on, blasting rock music or Puccini and Brahms. The soap operas—with sound turned down—flickered on my TV. I'd be talking on the phone at the same time. Baby boomers have a multilayered, multitrack ability to deal with the world.

—Camille Paglia, from a *Harper's* magazine debate with Neil Postman

In 1998 President Clinton and Monica Lewinsky helped usher in a new era for the media. Their affair pushed disinformation to heights (or was it depths?) that would have given George Orwell a nosebleed. The implications for society and education were important, though: people could no longer assume that what they saw, heard, or read was true. Major newspapers, in their overeager effort to scoop the others, no longer worried so much about telling the truth as telling the story. When the "story" became so fragile as to merit caution, they began publishing information on their Web sites so that as soon as the "truth" was deemed false, they could hit the delete button and leave no paper trail of their error. And when the media lacked any new information, they covered their own coverage of the story and considered, at length, the ethics involved in that coverage. The whole event offered teachers a sustainable unit on sensationalism, rhetoric, ethics, and American culture.

Visual truth had become so untrustworthy that *Time* magazine received thousands of inquiries about its cover story on "Bill and Monica." The picture made the pair look so much like a smiling, "legitimate" couple, people assumed that it had been "doctored." Computers had, by this time, taught us how easy it was to create a visual truth from separate pieces of information. During the "Crisis in the Whitehouse," as each radio station dramatically called it at the top of each hour, the Drudge Report emerged as a new and dangerous form of journalism; this on-line report recalled such journalists as Walter Winchell as it took in information it dispensed as public truth only to pull the story by day's end if reality had proved the truth lay somewhere else.

Students logging onto America Online in 1997 found themselves greeted by an increasingly long series of advertisements targeted at the specific user; the advertisements only got more specific as they logged onto the World Wide Web. And the magazines most of my students carried around in their backpacks were so glutted with advertisements, "selling" often seemed the point of the magazine. In addition, students attending schools that broadcasted Channel One in the classroom found themselves watching a series of commercials targeted directly at them. Neil Postman (1985, 160), one of our more important modern social critics, concluded that "the problem does not reside in *what* people watch. The problem is in the fact *that* we watch. The solution must be found in *how* we watch." I take Postman to mean that we must develop in students the same capacities for critical, deep "reading" that I discuss in other sections of this book: asking what the text's author is attempting to accomplish, evaluating how they are doing that, and determining the extent to which they succeed—and why.

Postman opens his book *Amusing Ourselves to Death* by comparing our own society with the one Aldous Huxley envisioned: "As [Huxley] saw it, people will come to love their oppression, to adore the technologies that undo their capacities to think." Though Postman's vision is a dark one, he captures what most English teachers would agree is true to their experience in the classroom and their observations of society:

> What Orwell feared were those who would ban books. What Huxley feared was that there would be no reason to ban a book, for there would be no one who wanted to read one. Orwell feared those who would deprive us of information. Huxley feared those who would give us so much that we would be reduced to passivity and egoism. Orwell feared that the truth would be concealed from us. Huxley feared the truth would be drowned in a sea of irrelevance. Orwell feared we would become a captive culture. Huxley feared we would become a trivial culture. . . . As Huxley remarked in *Brave New World Revisited*, the civil libertarians and rationalists who are ever alert to oppose tyranny "failed to take into account man's almost infinite appetite for distraction."

Reading demands the exact opposite of what Huxley describes: the ability not to get distracted, a discipline fewer and fewer of our students seem to posses. It grows increasingly difficult to teach a book that has not been adapted into a film that students can watch instead. Many English departments, mine included, have begun to include on their summer reading lists only books that have not been made into films. To today's teenagers, the fact that a book has not been made into a film in the first place might signal that it isn't good since it wasn't even worth making into a movie.

Principles of an Effective Media Literacy Program

Given the consumption of visual media—on-line, television, commercials, films, and advertisements—it seems negligent not to equip students with the reading skills necessary to control the effect of different media on them. While my tone may sound somewhat Luddite, I am anything but anti-media or anti-technology; what I oppose is education that does not challenge students to look critically at the world that shapes them. This world, made up of different texts, merits our study and provides exciting avenues for thoughtful discourse about such essential topics as racism, beauty, power, and justice. Renee Hobbs (1998), in her article "Literacy for the Information Age," cites the following five ideas as crucial components of any media literacy program or unit of study:

- All messages are constructions.
- Messages are representations of social reality.
- Individuals negotiate meaning by interacting with messages.
- Messages have economic, political, social, and aesthetic purposes.
- Each form of communication has unique characteristics.

The ideas Hobbs outlines are not significantly different from those we might outline for any printed texts our students study. There are those who argue an intellectual version of the chicken and the egg: which came first, the word or the image? In my mind and for the purposes of the classroom, the answer is irrelevant: both demand to be read and each has specific elements that must be closely examined if the reader/viewer is to understand the intent, meaning, and social context of the message they encounter on the page, screen, or billboard. In this respect, I will offer the following definition of media literacy—adapted from the ideas of many others' writings: literacy is the ability to access, analyze, synthesize, evaluate, and communicate information and ideas in a variety of forms depending on the purpose of that occasion. Language, Hobbs reminds us, is only one of the many symbol systems we humans have created to express and share meaning; today's dilemma—for teachers and students alike—is in deciding which of the many media is best to convey this lesson, this concept, this subject? The ability to make this same decision is yet one more aspect of media literacy: the capacity to use and choose from a variety of tools or, as my father always said, finding the right tool for the right job.

Writing About Film

Just as I start any Shakespeare play by having students read a few sonnets to get them focused on the bard's language, when teaching them how to "read" films I start with a few short films. My favorite is a fifteen-minute film by Alan Davidson called *The Lunch Date*. This and other films, such as *Graffiti* (which is only twenty minutes long and based on the Julio Cortazar short story of the same name), allow us to focus on those elements most common to films:

- the use of music
- the use of the camera
- gestures and speech and how these evoke character
- special effects
- dialogue (or its absence) and language in general
- plot

With short films you watch the entire film, stopping it when necessary to discuss elements or respond in writing, within a single period. If you cannot find short films—my county office has a fine collection of them—you can use excerpts of full-length films that seem to offer the same elements. In Spike Lee's film *Do the Right Thing* (1989), for example, a provocative young man comes into Sal's Pizza to order a slice and the ensuing argument over his overpowering portable stereo culminates in a small riot that has been brewing throughout the film. The language would normally make it impossible to use in the class; turning off the volume, however, offers another powerful means of focusing students' attention on other details and makes them more active participants by forcing them to interpret the film's meaning through their observations.

Once we have introduced such critical viewing, and students' comments—in writing and discussion—suggest that they understand the main ideas, we move into the larger films. You can, of course, work with these films as a unit on films themselves or as a component of your literature curriculum. Generally, I tend toward the latter, but here is an incomplete list of ways and reasons to use film in your English class:

- to complement the study of some printed text (Example: Use Anna Deveare Smith's *Crown Heights* to supplement discussion of race during reading of *Huckleberry Finn.*)
- to provide an initial framework for particularly difficult texts *before* reading them (Example: Any Shakespeare play.)
- to improve observational writing skills (Example: Use short film *Graffiti*, which has only one word in it and thus depends on visual components.)
- to provide an opportunity for me to conference with students on their work or, in the final rush of the semester, as a last resort, to give me time to catch up on any and all paperwork
- to appreciate what a good film is and can do. Sometimes I see a film that is just so good—one I know the kids won't have seen but which works in the context of the course (e.g., *Strictly Ballroom* as a companion to *Romeo and Juliet*)—that I have to make room for it.
- to compare different interpretations of the same literary text by different actors and directors in order to see how meaning and interpretation is negotiated between the actor and the text, or constructed by the director (Example: Compare all the different versions of Hamlet's soliloquy.)
- to contrast the different interpretations of a particular work in different epochs (Example: Conrad's *Heart of Darkness* and *Apocalypse Now* or productions of *Hamlet* set in different time periods.)

Here are some focus questions to help students read or write about films more effectively:

- What decisions does the director face in adapting this story to film?
- What effect did their decision to _____ have on the film?
- What was the director (actor?) trying to accomplish in this film? (Why do you think that?)
- In what ways and to what extent did the director/actor succeed?
- What are the most important differences between the story and the film?
- How is this film version different from other adaptations of the same story (e.g., how is the Brannaugh version of *Hamlet* different from the Gibson *Hamlet*?)
- Why did the director _____?
- What effect did the music have on the film's tone, style, or meaning?
- If they shot it with special effects (e.g., black-and-white, in documentary style) why did they do this—and how did it affect the film's content?
- What assumptions does the director/writer make about you as a viewer?
- Why did they make this film?
- How does this film use the camera and what effect do these uses have on the film?

In *Cultural Reflections: Critical Teaching and Learning in the English Classroom*, John Gaughan (1997) offers a powerful example of how to use film to study both a culture and propaganda. His students study Vietnam through films ranging from the propagandistic *The Green Berets* (1968) to Francis Ford Coppola's *Apocalypse Now* (1979) in order to see how different eras, directors, and writers convey meaning through film about the same event. It is precisely such learning that will enable students to listen and watch carefully when they encounter political advertisements in the future or advertisements that seek to manipulate their self-image.

Movies, advertisements, and all other visual media are tools teachers need to use and media we must master if we are to maintain our credibility in the coming years. Today's youth mistake seeing things with experiencing them; by the time they enter high school most students feel it is insulting to refer to them as kids because this notion of being just a kid contradicts their sense of themselves as worldly. These different forms of media have brought to them, with almost no constraints they cannot easily bypass, adult information that far surpasses any previous generation.

The NCTE/IRA standards refer in several places to "non-print media," which they say students must be able to use and comprehend. Furthermore, at the 1997 NCTE convention, the membership passed the following resolution, On Media Literacy as High School English Courses: "Resolved, that the National Council of Teachers of English affirm that media literacy courses meeting the same academic standards of other high school English courses be counted as English credit for admission to universities and colleges." Students should know how intensely tobacco and beer companies—among others—lobby to provide their products to movies which have become yet another means of advertising. Even the fact that in this day and age so many characters smoke—period: students should be able to interpret that visual manipulation of their beliefs and question the credibility of that text. Only by learning to do so will our students have some sense of power in this era of manipulation. Such power over children—let's not even mention Channel One's foray into the classroom—further confirms that there is a culture of power ruling our minds. Students are particularly endangered by a media that too often still shapes our thinking about gender, race, and culture. Finally, by having students themselves brainstorm and refine the questions the class asks of such commercial media, we help them to develop these critical faculties and give them back some sense of power in the face of such coercion.

Call it what you will—multimedia, media literacy, cultural studies, the new literacies—we stand at the end of an epoch in which what once amounted to being a literate person no longer answers the challenges the world offers. In *Changing Our Minds: Negotiating English and Literacy*, Miles Myers (1996, 1) writes:

> By 1993, three-fourths of the nation's twelfth graders had achieved the goals of decoding/analytic literacy outlined in the nation's standards projects of 1917–18 in *Report on the Reorganization of English in the Secondary Schools* (Hosic 1917) and in *The Cardinal Principles of Secondary Education* (Kingsley 1918). Why all the fuss in the public press about school failure and illiteracy? Because decoding/analytic literacy was no longer adequate. . . . Thus, despite the gains in decoding/analytic literacy, our country, at the national, state, and local levels, was moving toward new definitions of what it means to be literate.

A Clean Well-Lighted Screen: Reading the Internet

Futurist Alan November, speaking at the 1998 California Standards and Assessment Conference, illustrates the point I am trying to make. November's mother was visited by a sixteen-year-old boy who lived next door. He asked her if she knew that the Holocaust never really happened, that it was a legend made up years ago to explain an experiment with viruses that got out of control. She asked him where he learned about this. He said, of course, that he had read about it on the Internet. November suggested that kids now think that if information is on the Internet, it is true, and that if it is *not* on the Internet, it is false (having been rejected by the Internet, that most discerning of editors, I assume).

This neighborhood teenager is not some lunatic, alienated adolescent: he is the son of a highly educated community leader who "should know better." What's more, the author of the "short introduction" is a tenured associate professor of electrical engineering at Northwestern University. This material even appears on his university-hosted homepage, a site that details his passion for "Holocaust revisionism," a subject about which he wrote a book, *The Hoax of the Twentieth Century* (Institute for Historical Review 1976). I include here a few excerpts from Professor Butz's Web site (all italics are mine) so as to further examine the information and its implications for teaching and reading:

> Article published in the *Daily Northwestern* of May 13, 1991, corrected May 14. The links are to commentary and documentation that did not appear in the original article, and *which will be continually updated and elaborated.*
>
> A short introduction to the study of Holocaust revisionism, by Arthur R. Butz. [Note: His title does not suggest any particular slant and thus leads the innocent into the article.]
>
> I see three principal reasons for the widespread but erroneous belief in the legend of millions of Jews killed by the Germans during World War II: US and British troops found horrible piles of corpses in the west German camps they captured in 1945 (e.g. Dachau and Belsen), there are no longer large communities of Jews in Poland, and historians generally support the legend.
>
> Detailed consideration of the specific evidence put forward in support of the legend has been a focus of the revisionist literature and cannot be undertaken here, but I shall mention one point. *The claim of the legend* is that there were no technical means provided for the specific task of extermination, and that means originally provided for other purposes did double duty in improvised arrangements. Thus the Jews were allegedly gassed with the pesticide Zyklon, and their corpses disappeared into the crematoria along with the deaths from "ordinary" causes (the ashes or other remains of millions of victims never having been found).
>
> Surely any thoughtful person must be skeptical.
>
> —Arthur R. Butz is an associate professor of electrical engineering. *Last modification:* 23 September 1997. (Source: http://pubweb.acns.nwu.edu/~abutz/di/intro.html, February 22, 1998, Internet, 11:45 pm.)

First, let's understand why a presumably intelligent sixteen-year-old boy would believe this "legend." If, to quote Professor Butz, "any thoughtful person must be skeptical," students must have some basis upon which to be skeptical. Obvious questions come up right away: Who is speaking? During what historical period are they speaking? To what audience are their remarks addressed? Where do the remarks appear? Unfortunately, Butz's article is hosted by one of our nation's top universities; furthermore, it appeared, as his homepage tells you, in the university's paper, also. If Butz belonged to some lunatic fringe—he does—we would expect him to sound cagey, unhinged by his passion; instead, we hear calm academic prose that could just as easily be discussing how a transformer is built or why electricity works as it does. Finally, within the context of his article, his views make logical sense; by this I mean only that his story works and does not invite, to the uninformed adolescent, immediate cause for suspicion.

How do we teach students to read such a document? One might point, first of all, to the variety of other sources worth consulting to see if his argument holds up. This requires teaching kids how to use various informational resources—print, electronic, digital—to gather information. It also requires teachers to teach, at every step of the way, how to measure truth, how to assess the value of the resources we find along the information highway. Echoing Postman's earlier admonition, November argues that whenever students are taught how to use technology they must also be given serious instruction in how to read and understand the information they find there. Not only should they be taught how to read but how to create and manipulate such information themselves; November goes on to suggest that students in the third grade should learn to create their own Web sites so they can demystify these media tools and realize how easy it is to manipulate the truth through them. Such studies then become as much about rhetoric and aesthetics as they are about reading and comprehension.

A teacher might point out the extent to which Butz's document continues to be revised, which suggests that truth is negotiated, that his argument depends on constant revision. Finally, we get to both his credo—"Surely any thoughtful person must be skeptical"—and his status as a professor at a major university. Using Butz's own standard of skepticism, we need to make sure kids know that authority of a text or an idea does not depend on such external elements as where one works. True, it should mean that certain affiliations (e.g., Stanford or some major corporation) imply authority; usually they do, that's why they are in the big leagues. Still, kids need to know—as we all do in this new era—that credibility comes only after being checked against other, reliable sources.

I did, in fact, teach the lesson I just described, taking a period to explain, discuss, and debrief. It certainly woke students up to the responsibility they have as readers to question the authority of any text they encounter. Christy Upland, a junior, wrote, "Yesterday's lesson taught me something that is very significant in everyday life. Yes, it helped me to distinguish fact from fiction a little better, but most of all it showed me that the Internet and computers are a major power as we are almost into a new century. The most important thing the lesson pointed out was that if the whole world can put their ideas on a computer and share them with each other, then we're going to have to learn who, what, when, why, and how to distinguish if something has the meaning of truth in it or not." Lindsay Hunter, a junior in the same class, wrote, "If I had read that Web site, I wouldn't have believed it because of everything I've learned in the past. However, when I saw that it was written by a college professor, then I started to believe it. It wasn't until you brought up the point that he was a professor in engineering, not history, that I realized this was not a reliable source."

Sample Activity: "Image Studies" Unit

What follows is an assignment I created for my seniors. It asked them to "think visually" about and to critique the world around them. It also provided me the opportunity to bring art and more contemporary visual texts into the class. This is another rationale for the study of the media: it is the world they know and see as their own. To this extent, students are interested in looking more closely at the lyrics, videos, films, and television they watch or listen to each day. Postman (1985, 161) suggests that to get them to ask questions of the media they consume and encounter may be the only possible curriculum we can offer as defense against mindlessness. "To ask is to break the spell. To which I might add that questions about psychic, political and social effects of information are as applicable to the computer as to the television."

Overview.   We encounter an endless stream of images and icons all of which are designed to affect our perceptions of ourselves, of men and women, of what is beautiful and what is ugly, of who is good and who is bad. We find these images in advertisements for Calvin Klein and between scenes of *Seinfeld*; they come at us as we log onto the Web and watch us as we drive down the freeway. What we see, watch, read, hear—these all have the power to exert different, calculated influences on us as people, consumers, citizens. What are you saying, for instance, when you wear a T-shirt that advertises a product (e.g., Calvin Klein)? Shouldn't Calvin Klein be paying you for promoting its product? This unit will require that you look at art, television commercials, print commercials, and, if possible, advertising on the World Wide Web, which is particularly unique because advertisers on the Web can link products to your individual interests.

Requirements

1. Look at five different magazines (not five different issues of the same magazine) and pick ten advertisements that you think are powerful. Provide the following information about each advertisement:
   - The name of the magazine
   - The product advertised
   - A couple of sentences of very descriptive writing that SHOWS the ad: e.g., a white Lexus crosses a wide open, lush green countryside, an ancient castle sitting off to the right on a small hillock. The sun lights everything in warm tones and no one can be seen, as if this is the last person on earth, all alone, driving into the sunset in the world's finest car.
   - What is the advertiser *really* selling (shoes—or power, image, popularity, coolness, performance)? Who is their audience?
   - The ad's location in the publication; what the advertiser hopes to accomplish by putting their ad in this spot.
   - Any significant aspects of this advertisement that you wish to comment on—the depiction of women, the idea, etc.
   - Your response to this advertisement: It is/is not effective because . . .
     - reason one (e.g., it does not clearly identify the product)
     - support (an image with the advertiser's logo in lower corner)
     - explanation (they are trying to associate . . . but . . .)
2. Look at three television advertisements and write up the same analysis. (I realize it is harder with television ads because they don't sit still and let you look at them for a long time, like a page in a book.)
3. Identify the three products most frequently advertised. What can you tell me about these products and their advertising campaign?
4. Read the following articles and write as directed:
   - "The Voice in the Looking Glass," by Maile Maloy
   - "Odalisque," by Elizabeth MacDonald
   - "Ways of Seeing: Men Looking at Women," by John Berger
   - "Mary Cassatt," by Mary Gordon
   - "Just Walk on By: A Black Man Ponders His Ability to Alter Public Space," by Brent Staples
   - "Beauty: When the Other Dancer Is the Self," by Alice Walker
   - "On Being a Cripple," Nancy Mairs
   - "No Name Woman," Maxine Hong Kingston
   - miscellaneous articles on advertising
   - miscellaneous poems on beauty, art (e.g., "Barbie Doll," by Marge Piercy)

5. Show excerpts from the following films and documentaries:
   - *Killing Us Softly* documentary
   - *Absolutely Fabulous/Unzipped*—or some other fashion film
   - *Truth in Advertising* (Dudley Moore film)
   - *American Visions* video with Robert Hughes

6. Complete the Project: A Brief Overview

   Each person or pair will analyze either an artist, photographer, fashion designer, or series of advertisements. You will make a short presentation to the class and write a brief paper in which you discuss your conclusions about advertising.

Obviously this assignment could be done in many different ways or changed to focus on other media. One option would be to recast it as a means of deconstructing the World Wide Web, the students analyzing Web sites and elements of the Web instead of television commercials and print advertisements. It all comes down to a study in rhetoric as used in different genres.

Endnote: The New Marketplace

Various sources calculate that about 85 percent of all books sold in the United States were purchased by women in 1997. Some boys dismiss fiction books as "fake," only to go home to video games, where they live in virtual worlds inhabited by women whose bodies can only be described as fictional. People spent over one billion dollars shopping for Christmas presents on the Internet during December of 1997; 49 percent of these on-line shoppers were women, 50 percent were men. More and more books are purchased on-line; in fact, you may have purchased this book on-line through my Web site, where you might have encountered advertisements for those products or publishers I thought were of interest to you as an English teacher. We live in a labyrinth whose walls are lined with the images we mistake for truths and gods. We must, like Ariadne in the Greek myth, help our students to navigate their way through this media maze and find their way back out so that they can maintain some semblance of control over their lives—and their minds. Otherwise we risk sacrificing ourselves and our culture to the media, which Tony Schwartz (1983) calls "the second god."

REFLECTION

This particular reflection assumes you have done at least one of the activities described in this chapter. Thinking about the different ads you've seen, what concerns you most about what you saw? Why did it bother you? What is it you want your students to be able to do when they encounter such media? Identify the perfect time and place within your curriculum to weave in a discussion of media literacy. Brainstorm a list of movies, activities, or readings you could use.

ACTIVITY

Buy several mainstream magazines your students read, and examine them for their advertising content. Pay close attention to those ads that involve image and gender. Also, watch a couple of shows or listen to a radio station that is very popular with your students and examine these also for their content. For fun and research, check out whatever movie is most popular with your students. Finally, go onto the World Wide Web and surf around for some "teen spots" to see what this digital world looks like to teens; most search engines have a list of popular Web sites or chat rooms for teens.

RECOMMENDATIONS

If you want to read more about media literacy, find a copy of the January 1998 *English Journal*, which was entirely dedicated to this topic. See also *Images in Language, Media, and Mind*. Roy Fox, ed. (NCTE 1994).

CHAPTER 14

INTEGRATING ENGLISH PROJECTS AND EXHIBITIONS INTO THE CURRICULUM

The classroom situation most provocative of thoughtfulness and critical consciousness is the one in which teachers and learners find themselves conducting a kind of collaborative search, each from her or his lived situation. . . . If there is to be a beginning . . . and active learning initiated by those choosing to learn, there has to be an interrogation.

**—Maxine Greene, "Imagination, Breakthroughs, and the Unexpected,"
from *Releasing the Imagination***

So this is the little lady whose book started the Civil War.

—Abraham Lincoln, upon meeting Harriet Beecher Stowe, author of *Uncle Tom's Cabin*

It is hard for most students—and teachers—to imagine that an entire semester could be spent examining just what President Lincoln meant when he spoke these words to Harriet Beecher Stowe. Soon enough, however, students using a range of literacies—cultural, functional, and critical—understand how complicated Lincoln's remark is and that they will have to work long and hard to make sense of it. Pushed a little further, Lincoln's quote easily transforms itself into an "essential question" which can only be answered through a sustained inquiry that requires the active participation of the learner in the quest for understanding.

The Project Method

Thanks in part to the leadership and success of Ted Sizer's Coalition for Essential Schools, the "project method" has enjoyed a renaissance in the last decade. Sizer's call for "exhibitions" that demonstrate mastery or qualify students for graduation redresses earlier criticisms of the experiential or project method. As Miles Myers (1996) and Arthur Applebee (1974) point out, these earlier efforts lacked certain structural elements that critics felt undermined the quality of education. Sizer, as well as other educational thinkers like psychologist Howard Gardner, have helped to provide guidance in the areas of integrated curriculum, project-based learning, and interdisciplinary programs. And further research on the brain has demonstrated the power of organizing students' learning around central ideas or themes through individual and group projects (Caine and Caine 1997; Csikszentmihalyi 1991).

I conducted an informal survey of English teachers to find out what kind of projects they included in their curriculum. Though there are variations—some describe portfolios, dramatic performances, and particular collaborative efforts as major projects—three main types emerged, each one related to the other but different in important ways:

> *Senior Exit Projects*: These projects are sometimes required as part of a larger school program and are not necessarily done in the English class. They may, however, involve the study of literature, for example, or depend heavily on English teachers to teach those skills and help with those parts of such projects that are appropriate to the English curriculum. (See the Champlain Valley Union High School overview of the Graduation Challenge Project following.)

> *Exhibition*: These projects are typically done as part of a class, but represent a culminating activity for a quarter or semester. They are often used as a performance assessment, providing students an opportunity to demonstrate what they know and have learned to do over the course of the term. (See the Social Problems Project following.)

> *Class Projects*: These projects last anywhere from one to four weeks. While they are related to the other two types, they tend to focus on one particular unit of study to which the teacher wants to bring some closure. (See the *Huckleberry Finn* Project following.)

Senior Exit Projects: The Graduation Challenge

The Champlain Valley Union High School Graduation Challenge Project exemplifies not only the kind of project I am discussing here but the process whereby such a project gets developed. It includes people from many domains and continues to evolve over time. Following the overview from their school's handout, I have included a set of questions from parents and students that came from another school (Hillsdale High School in San Mateo, California) during the first year they piloted such a senior graduation requirement.

Champlain Valley Union High School (CVU) "Graduation Challenge"

Overview

Graduation Challenge is a program designed to provide all CVU seniors with a meaningful opportunity to demonstrate that they have successfully mastered the Essential Learning Behaviors, a set of skills and essential behaviors that the district agreed was vital for students if they were to participate and contribute to a democratic community. The guiding principle of Graduation Challenge is that all students who graduate from CVU are able to research and write about a subject of their choice, apply that knowledge, and speak about the experience in a formal setting.

Supported by a CVU Faculty Advisor, each student selects a topic of personal interest to explore through: Tri-search investigation and writing; community experience design and completion, and presentation of his/her learning to a panel of faculty and community members. All three phases of the Graduation Challenge Program must be successfully completed in order for the senior to graduate.

The Letter of Intent.
In this letter, the student communicates his/her program design and Community Consultant selection. It initiates the student into the program.

The Tri-Search Paper.
Students write an 8–10 page paper that combines research, interviews, and personal knowledge. The accuracy of the content of the paper is verified by the Community Consultant.

The Community Experience.
Thirty hours of community time provides each student with opportunity either to apply what s/he learned through tri-search and writing (when the project follows the tri-search) or with opportunity to gain some "hands-on" experience and exploration prior to, or in conjunction with, the tri-search and writing. The student's Community Consultant verifies his/her time spent on the project. Each student also needs to produce a tangible product related to his/her work, which is shared during Presentation time.

The Presentation.
Students present the information they have learned through their research and project to a panel of faculty and community members. The presentation is ten minutes long and is followed by a question and answer period.

Information about these components can be found in the student handbook. A celebration for students, parents and community members is held after the presentations to provide for informal discussion and an opportunity to view the students' work.

As a faculty, we have worked diligently to ensure each student's development of competencies in all the basic, performance, and high order thinking skills needed for successful completion of Graduation Challenge. As an Advisor, if you discover that one of your advisees does not demonstrate competency in all areas of performance required for successful completion of Graduation Challenge, please contact your jury group chairperson or the Graduation Challenge Coordinator; appropriate help for skill development problems or other needs will be located. Advisors also need to maintain a folder of all necessary papers and documentation of meetings, work completed, missed deadlines, and other significant items related to each Graduation Challenge Student's experiences. (Champlain Valley High School 1997)

Questions About Senior Projects.   The following questions come from a parent information night discussion at Hillsdale High School, where they tried to implement a senior exit requirement. I offer them here to help teachers or schools anticipate those concerns parents and students will have about such projects. As a guiding principle, the more regular and open your communication is to both students and parents, the more receptive and supportive they will be. It is, however, essential to know your school community for as some (Mathews 1998) have discovered, affluent communities often resist such reform efforts and will, in certain instances, actively oppose them (Kohn 1998). The actual list of questions from parents was three typed pages; I include here those most likely to be of interest to all teachers:

- If we do not have our own teacher there when we present, how much of our grade is based on the opinion of the teachers who will not know us or have worked with us on this project?
- How will you avoid the problem of different teachers grading differently?
- What if we keep changing our topic and can't find the right one? What can we do?
- What help will be available (and when!) for a student who is behind schedule and struggling with this project?

- What will happen if my son doesn't pass this requirement? Summer school? Resubmit it?
- What are the standards or criteria you will use to assess this project?
- What is being removed from the past school curriculum to make room for this project?
- Are there different standards or requirements for AP students—and if so, what are they and why?
- How does the final project grade get factored into my daughter's English, Economics, and Government grades?
- Why does the information given to the students differ from teacher to teacher?

Exhibitions: The Social Problems Project

Every day I drive by homeless people on my way to Burlingame, a quiet, affluent suburb near San Francisco. Walking to school along Burlingame's serene, picturesque streets, my students find it difficult to imagine the dejected people I see each morning. Confronted with this sharp contrast between home and work, I feel obligated to develop in my sophomores an awareness of those social problems common to our society. Thus each spring semester we embark on a multifaceted project known simply as the Social Problem Project.

How We Begin the Project.   To begin, I ask students to generate a list of "social problems." Walking around the class, I note that several topics are common to many lists: the environment, homelessness, pollution, crime. Scanning farther down their lists, I see that several have listed abortion, birth control, the death penalty; I do not yet point out to them that these are not social problems (but possible solutions to the problems). I give them a few more minutes to come up with problems that are important or of interest to them.

Next we make a master list of topics on the chalkboard (which I ask someone to copy down so we can have it for further reference). I put up whatever they say, not ready to make the first distinction between problems and issues. By the time Brett calls out "gun control," it seems that we have exhausted their lists.

I ask Brett how he arrived at gun control as a social problem. "Well, it seems like so many people are getting killed with guns these days," he says. "So are the guns the problem here, or is there something else going on?" I ask. Andrea points out that the guns are not the problem, but that one problem society faces is a skyrocketing crime rate. "So we might look at the idea of gun control down the line as more of a possible solution to the problem of crime in society," I suggest. Brett nods.

After distributing the project assignment, which includes my expectations and the rubric for the project, I give them time to go over it and get an idea of what they are in for.

Workshop Days: Learning the Necessary Skills.   For the remainder of the quarter—we pursue this project while continuing to study the required literature—I arrange the class into workshops, each with some focus (e.g., interviewing, outlining, summarizing) designed to help them with their current phase of the project. During this phase, the class can sometimes get a little chaotic, but it's "good mess," kind of like a compost pit that has begun to work. Because the project requires different types of work, the students need the opportunity to do many tasks while I meet with them individually or in small groups.

Today Sean and Jim are having difficulty locating articles on the diminishing rainforests, and they expect to have the same trouble finding experts to interview. The workshop format gives me the chance to take them over to the small computer lab and show them how to use the Internet to find experts and other helpful resources. Only a few years before, we would have been doing this by phone book and telephone. Schools who are not equipped with such computer equipment can get around these obstacles by calling toll-free numbers and asking such organizations as the Rainforest Action Network to send them reports and other print materials which are usually free. Another helpful resource is the local newspaper which will often provide class sets of newspapers for a period of time to help with such projects.

When Sean and Jim return to the class, their enthusiasm is obvious. They tell me that they found "some guy" at the Rainforest Action Network who will answer any questions students post to him. All year, these two students have been passive participants in the class as we have studied literature and tried to learn new writing skills. Finding themselves in charge of this project, needing to communicate with "real people," they are engaged and eager to share what they learned with other students who are studying the rainforest. Their work and enthusiasm exemplify what Jim Cummins and Dennis Sayers (1997, 84) say about the power of the Internet in *Brave New Schools*: "The electronic networks not only provide unprecedented access to informational resources, they also, and more significantly, encourage the formation of communities of learning that transcend previous limitations of time and space. [P]articipation in these learning communities can be intensely motivating for students to read more, write more, and ultimately think more."

On workshop days, we sometimes form groups according to topics, so that students can cull from one another's research findings. We confer as a class as needed. In these informal groups, I observe fascinating transformations and transactions in these kids as they learn what it means to collaborate on such "knowledge work."

One day, for example, some students want to know whether they can work together to develop one survey that all can use as opposed to them each developing their own. "What would the advantage of that be?" I ask. "We could get more ideas and organize our efforts to interview more people," they say. Some students in the group have decided to keep their surveys individualized because they want to focus on different aspects of the problem than the rest of the group. Many of the kids are entering into what has been called "flow," a state of full engagement during which time they are motivated by desire, interest, intellectual hunger (Csikszentmihalyi 1991).

Research: How, When, and Where.   The librarian is excited by the opportunity to let the students use her facilities and the new binders of articles (Social Issues Resources—SIRS) on many of the topics they are investigating. Once they begin their research, students submit status reports to let me know they are moving ahead or having trouble. I ask them to find at least two articles on their chosen subject. ("No, a three-sentence blurb in the *Oakland Tribune* does not constitute an article" I say before someone asks.) I also ask for a summary of their articles, which identifies the three main points they will stress. Early on in the project they had to submit formal proposals describing what they would study but also why they wanted to study it and what they thought they would find. This formulation of a focus and purpose was further reinforced by a subsequent outline that explained what they would include; this allowed me to anticipate obstacles, help them see connections, and point them in the direction of resources I knew would help them; furthermore, the outline created a context for all their subsequent reading and thinking. Obviously, such requirements as the article summaries, outlines, or proposals provide helpful checkpoints throughout the quarter so you can catch those errant students who begin to get lost.

When it's time for students to outline their papers, I use the opportunity to teach them how to make a good outline, putting up examples I've prepared for the overhead. After walking through the initial steps to make their own outlines, we brainstorm the attributes of an effective, thorough paper (or good interview, diagram, or Web site). I compile their ideas and mine and give the sheet to them as a handout the next day.

For their interviews and surveys, students must follow the same procedure, summarizing their findings and identifying at least three main ideas to pursue. We spend some time on the mechanics of the process, looking at sample interviews and questionnaires, and discussing the appropriate etiquette. During this part of the assignment, students learn to incorporate information from many sources into one paper to support a larger idea, how to interact with people in a variety of situations, and how to conduct serious discussions about important matters. When Anthony and Lucas, two students doing their project on racism, speak of their interviews with parents and other community members, they say they felt that they were taken seriously, that they felt adults respected them more for asking such serious questions.

Next, the students begin to organize their findings, their interviews, and their own thinking about the subject. After only a month, I hear no complaints. In addition, I am witness to fine work by some previously unenthusiastic members of the class. Most—but not all—are ready to get down to some serious writing. So, cooperating with Jane, the teacher who heads the computer lab, the students begin going to the lab on workshop days to write their papers—which must be, as I told them right off, *typed*. Our use of the workshop format continues to provide the needed flexibility to adapt to the changing directions of the project.

As the unit progresses, I begin to detect a different tone and maturity in many of my students. Suddenly they are aware of problems that concern them, that are significant, and that they can actually do something about. This last revelation is especially important, for the study of large problems can easily lead to feelings of helplessness. However, after plugging into such organizations as Greenpeace, Rainforest Action Network, and local homeless agencies, the students' fears are stemmed. They may not be able to solve these vast problems, but they are learning what can be done to arrest them. Feelings of civic involvement, of the ability to make a difference, abound; meanwhile they have learned many new strategies for writing, reading, organizing, and public speaking.

The Final Phase: Writing the Paper.   Their sense of civic power is further bolstered by the next step in the project. Once they have begun to write their papers, students feel informed enough to write at least one letter. I send a group to the library to gather the addresses of local, state, and federal politicians. By writing letters to these different representatives, they see the power of writing in the real world. Even as young people, they realize that they can have a say in matters that affect them and their community. Such letters have, at one time or another, yielded personal letters from state and federal legislators, the chief of police, and representatives from the United Nations. The belief that one can make a difference must be fed and sustained in teenagers; when Anne Marie du Plessis writes to the Secretary of Commerce to explain her concerns about the killing of dolphins in tuna nets and to outline several alternatives he should consider, she feels a power and potential that teenagers need to taste. In this respect, all such projects provide a rite of passage which brings them into the larger arena of society. My students are no longer safely hidden away in a bedroom community with only one high school. They are writing to Washington about what is going on in the Middle East, to Sacramento about hunger in Africa, to local politicians about the homeless in the Bay Area. And as their research continues, they are able to propose, as Anne Marie did, meaningful solutions, citing reputable sources from magazines, newspapers, and experts to back up their recommendations.

My students are now editing and responding to one another's papers. Because they are well-informed about a common topic, they can make educated appraisals of others' work. They see, for instance, how Shannon, one of the top students in the class, approached a particular problem that many of them initially found too difficult. Or Jake, who still struggled to find information on alternative solutions, could look to the group for advice on where and how to find this information while also getting their feedback on the one solution that he has so far.

D-Day: Celebrating the Arrival.   The end of the quarter nears. Because our sophomore classes emphasize public speaking, the next task my kids face is to present their papers to the class. Very much like a convention of scientists, social scientists, and social workers, the students attentively listen as each person presents their findings on topics that range from transportation to waste disposal, the greenhouse effect to AIDS. As each student leaves the front of the class—a place I have stood in very little in the last quarter—the class offers thunderous applause.

It is the last day. I ask them to write me a letter to accompany the project. I give them twenty minutes to tell me whatever they want to about the project, the experience, the sense of achievement most of them clearly feel. I call them up one at a time and check off their papers—nearly every one of them more than ten typed pages, illustrated with computer graphics or personal drawings. I collect the projects like this so we both know and can celebrate that they turned in a project. One by one, they place their neatly assembled papers on my desk, smiling with pride at a job well done.

When all the projects are turned in, the class sighs in unison. But it is not the sigh of "Thank God, that's done." It is the sigh of satisfaction that comes after hard work. It is the sigh of having done their best work on a problem which, for a quarter, became *their* problem. It is the sound I hope they will make in future years as they walk out of the ballot box or when they write a politician about an issue that is important to them. It is a feeling, that sigh, I imagine them experiencing again and again in the future, as they act as members of a larger community than Burlingame, or even America.

The Huckleberry Finn *Project*

I include here one example of a class project that proved successful with a class of typical high school juniors. I offer this one as a guide to creating your own projects, but direct your attention to the options and the presumption of independence. The same list of options and requirements appears, though with variations, on nearly any project I assign my students. My rationale for this is derived from Gardner's ideas about multiple intelligence and the need for students to demonstrate their "knowing" by those means most available and effective to them.

The *Huck Finn* Project

Overview
While reading *Adventures of Huckleberry Finn* we will use various strategies to better understand the book. We will draw, write poems, discuss, act out parts, and, of course, read and write about the story. It will take us six weeks to read and finish this project. After that, we will have earned our two weeks off. You may propose some projects to be done as a team, but these must be approved. Any project that is turned in as a team and has not been approved by me will not be accepted. Also, my expectations for projects done as a team are higher: two heads are better than one and so should a project done by two people be.

Option I: Jim's Journal.
This option asks you to get in character as Jim and keep a journal as the story unfolds. In other words, you will keep a journal as if you were Jim. The quality of work here will be reflected in the following components:

  • extent to which you inhabit the character (e.g., sound and *think* like he would)
  • overall quality of your writing (note: you may write in the same vernacular style that Twain used, but you must be consistent and effective in your use of this style)

- thoroughness: extent to which your journal reflects on and includes the entire novel
- insight: extent to which your entries show insight into the characters and the story

(Option: You could, if you preferred, write your journal as Mark Twain. Many writers keep journals of what they think while they write their books. What would Twain be thinking and saying to himself about this book as he writes it?)

Option II: Graphic Novel.
This option allows you to use your artistic skills to re-create the story in a graphic novel (i.e., comic book) format. If you are really technologically oriented and want to show off, you could make yours animated and interactive, like *Maus*. The quality of your work here will be determined by the following:

- quality of the art work: it should look sharp—both the pictures and the text
- extent to which your graphic novel includes the entire story of *Huckleberry Finn*
- inclusion of an introduction in which you explain what you tried to achieve through your adaptation of the novel (e.g., "I wanted to emphasize the extent to which they reject society and reveal themselves as rebels in the American spirit. I did this because . . . and showed it by . . .")

Option III: Formal Essay.
This option asks you to choose an idea or character central to the book and examine that idea in depth in an essay. You may also consider taking some recurring aspect of American history or culture, and writing an essay in which you discuss how *Huckleberry Finn* relates to that theme (e.g., the American spirit of independence). Your essay must accomplish the following:

- It must be at least five pages typed (double spaced, 12-point font).
- It should clearly identify the thesis of the paper early on and maintain that focus throughout (see "The Five Principles of an Essay").
- It must examine its subject carefully, substantiating each of its supporting elements with examples from appropriate sources (e.g., *Huckleberry Finn*, your history book, etc.).
- It must be original in its focus so as to avoid questions of whether it was or could have been lifted off the Internet.

(Note: You must approve your topic with me first.)

Option IV: Be the Teacher.
You will teach an entire class period in which you lead a discussion on a particular set of themes or some other focused topic related to *Huckleberry Finn*. During this period you will prepare and be ready to do the following:

- Facilitate a class discussion on selected, important themes.
- Introduce your lesson with some opening remarks.
- Use visual aids—video clips, handouts, posters, overheads—to help the class think about and understand the ideas you present.
- Write a follow-up analysis of what you set out to accomplish, how well you accomplished this goal, and what you learned from the whole experience.

Option V: Publish Your Own Newspaper.
This option asks you to create a six-page newspaper with all of the appropriate elements common to a newspaper of *Huckleberry Finn*'s era. (You can find examples of newspapers on the Web by visiting the CyberGuide for Twain's novel.) Your work will be assessed according to the quality of the following:

- the writing
- the formatting and overall appearance and layout of the paper

- the extent to which the paper shows understanding of and insight into the novel *Huckleberry Finn*
- the extent to which it shows demonstrated mastery of the computer

Option VI: CyberGuides.

This option requires access to the Internet on a regular basis. While you could use the Internet connections available at school, for the moment these are not so easy to use. This assignment asks you to go to the CyberGuide Web site for *Huckleberry Finn* (http://www.sdcoe.k12.ca.us/score/huckcen/huckcentg.html) and, using that site's guidelines and directions, create your own "Cyber-Guide." This idea is very new, but this particular Web site has won several awards and is very "user friendly." I really hope someone will take the opportunity to try this out.

Option VII: American Voices.

This last option invites students to create a project that somehow includes a wide range of "American voices" that discuss a particular subject (e.g., what it means to be "American") or that reflect the complex nature of our society through the range of things they want to talk about. It can be done using audiotaped interviews, which are then edited into one audio interview (see National Public Radio's Teen Diaries Web site at www.npr.org).

Other options for this project might include "My American Odyssey," in which you imagine that you and a companion travel across the country or throughout California gathering "American Voices" and what people have to say about America. Your work on this project will be evaluated based on the following criterion:

- extent to which your project shows insight into the subject you study
- extent to which the subject is somehow related, even thematically, to *Huck Finn*
- overall quality of the text you create—whether spoken, written, or made on a computer (e.g., multimedia project)
- surprise me: this could be a very special and fun project option!

CyberGuides: A Brief Description of the Future?

Among the options on the *Huckleberry Finn* Project you will notice "CyberGuides." These on-line projects promise to be more common and even better in the future. The coordinators of the particular site referenced—Don Mayfield and Linda Taggart-Fregoso, both from the San Diego County Office of Education (SDCOE)—deserve credit for having developed the concept; other educators will certainly follow suit. The SDCOE describes CyberGuides as follows:

CyberGuides are supplementary units of instruction based on core works of literature, designed for students to use the World Wide Web. Most guides are not designed as comprehensive units but as collections of Web-searching activities that lead to a student product. They are designed for the classroom with one computer, connected to the Internet. Each CyberGuide contains:
- a student and teacher edition
- a statement of objectives
- a task and a process by which it may be completed
- a rubric for assessing the quality of the product

The Internet, more than many other tools in the past, challenges teachers and students to connect—both to the larger world through the technology and to the different subject areas they are learning in other classes. As Jim Cummins and Dennis Sayers (1997, 13) write, we must "reframe education around critical inquiry and the collaborative generation of knowledge in such a way that the experience and cultural contributions of all students are valued. [R]ather than passively internalizing the cultural literacy of socially powerful groups, students actively generate their own intercultural literacy through dialogue and collaborative research with colleagues in their own classrooms and in classrooms across the globe."

Projects, of whatever scale, involving just English or all subject areas, provide the means to such deeper learning as Cummins and Sayers describe. Such projects also anticipate the world of work for which students must now be prepared. Schlechty, in *Inventing Better Schools* (1998), identifies several traits of school work that will ideally prepare students for the future, the most relevant of which are:

- The work or activity is product-focused.
- The standards for assessing the product . . . are clear to the students and the students find them compelling.
- The work is designed so that student performances are affirmed.
- Knowledge and information are arranged in such a way that they can be focused on products and problems; that is, they are integrated as opposed to segmented.
- The content presented is rich and significant as opposed to pallid and trivial.

While the comments of such experts matter, providing as they do the rationale for such teaching, it is students who offer the most compelling arguments for the use of projects, the integration of the subjects, the chance to get out into the world and use what they learn. Senior Kristina DeLeuw, remembering when she put William Golding on trial as a freshman, said of the experience:

> Above all other academic endeavors throughout my high school years, the *Lord of the Flies* trial is the most memorable. After reading *Lord of the Flies* in English class and studying important historical figures who made significant contributions to our understanding of human nature in history class, we integrated these studies to produce the mock trial. For the duration of one week, prosecution and defense attorneys interrogated characters from *Lord of the Flies* and historical figures about human nature. The judge ruled over courtroom behavior while the jury decided if human nature is innate or if society is responsible for a person's behavior.
>
> As a prosecuting attorney, I owe my success in the trial to all of the classroom work I had completed prior to the trial. This preparation included classroom discussions, composing essays, analyzing texts, grammar drills, journal entries, reading a variety of texts and taking notes, as well as public speaking. All of these components of my English and history classes aided me as I presented my opening and closing statements, questioned witnesses on the stand, and worked closely with the plaintiff. My responsibilities as a lawyer demonstrated how I could combine everything I learned into a complete piece.
>
> Let's face it—I won't be sitting in a classroom for the rest of my life. What good is it going to do me if I sit in a classroom and write papers and read history books for fifteen years? I need to get out there in the world and gain some experiences. This trial shows how teachers can integrate studies to allow students to show how their knowledge can be beneficial to them in a real life situation.

And Chastity Smith, a junior who, with her partner Rhea Coulter, created an incredible documentary on growing up for the *Huckleberry Finn* Project (see the American Voices option), said:

> When I did my video essay on the theme of growing up, I learned a lot. I learned about the way I think, the way I have ideas that come out of nowhere when I get excited about something. I

also learned a lot about making a video, filming, organizing, and editing. But most of all, I learned that I could make a video that really impressed my peers, my teacher, and, most importantly, myself.

Endnote: The Self as Project

Projects offer students intellectual and, often, very personal rites of passage which they desperately need. I've had students who were abused as children do phenomenal projects on child abuse, an experience that helped them to make sense of their lives. I've had students who examined others' lives—great-grandparents, for example, who survived the concentration camps—and arrived at a new understanding of these people and their own origins. I've had students whose projects were read into the state legislative record at hearings on cancer and others whose actions lead to careers in the fields they studied.

These opportunities provide a means of investigating the world they think they know, but really do not understand. Students can test out their interests against the larger world of available options, an experience they all need as they continue to figure out who they are and what they want to do with their lives. Freshmen, when seniors, often refer back to the different projects I required, saying that they learned things in the process that helped them succeed in school and get some focus in their lives. And, perhaps most importantly, for those critical of such methods, the projects have demanded rigorous academic methods that have resulted in some of the most sophisticated writing, most challenging reading, and most powerful public speaking ever.

They also allowed me to decrease my paper load, since I could handle so much in class through conferences. And, when I did finally have to read them, the range of topics was so broad, the work generally so good, that the reading was a genuine pleasure and gave both my students and me the feeling of achievement we all seek.

REFLECTION

Not everyone feels comfortable with integrating the disciplines or building their class around large projects. Examine your own experience with such approaches, thinking of projects you have done: What did you do? How did it turn out? What did you think of the experience in the end? Reflect on why you do or do not want to work such an approach into your class.

ACTIVITY

Make some kind of graphic organizer—a box with four to eight squares or a cluster will do. Starting with your core English assignment—e.g., a theme or a book around which you plan to organize your class—brainstorm what students could do that involves other subject areas or domains of experience. Example: *Joy Luck Club*: watch documentary; read from Ronald Takaki's *Strangers from a Different Shore: A History of Asian Americans*; visit the Asian Art Museum on the World Wide Web; draw a mandala of the book beginning with the central image of a mah-jongg table with four sides to it; using the idea of Tom Romano's intergenerational paper (see *Writing with Passion*), have them write their own family story. (You might also think about how your proposed activity meets different standards for the English Language Arts.)

RECOMMENDATIONS

If you want to read more about such project-based or interdisciplinary learning, the books to read are:

The I-Search Paper (revised edition of *Searching Writing*). Ken Macrorie (Boynton/Cook, 1988).

The Interdisciplinary Teacher's Handbook: Integrating Teaching Across the Curriculum. Stephen Tchudi and Stephen Lafer (Boynton/Cook, 1996).

Interdisciplinary High School Teaching: Strategies for Integrated Learning. John H. Clarke and Russell M. Agne (Allyn and Bacon, 1997).

CHAPTER 15

SERVICE LEARNING
ITS PLACE AND PURPOSE

If I knew for a certainty that a man was coming to my house with the conscious design of doing me good, I should run for my life.

—**Henry David Thoreau**

The fundamental question we posed, and that was repeatedly posed to us, was how to preserve or create a morally coherent life.

—**Robert Bellah**, *Habits of the Heart: Individualism and Commitment in American Life*

The late 1990s saw a dramatic increase in community service within the school curriculum. Service learning, while similar to community service, requires that service projects be integrated into the curriculum of the class, that the experience serve as the basis for reflection on what these experiences teach students. As with "workplace English," many teachers immediately resist such reforms, seeing them as intrusions on the "real curriculum" they are committed to teaching and which, unfortunately, too many students are equally committed to ignoring. Obviously I am committed to the value and centrality of the English curriculum as traditionally conceived; I am also, however, passionately interested in seeing that each student get every possible chance to find some direction and meaning—and pick up skills along the way—through their education. I also know that while many of my students will not graduate from college, they will all be parents, employees, and citizens.

My original motivation for integrating community service into my curriculum was the same motivation found at the heart of all innovative efforts: necessity and desperation. Faced with the challenge of teaching freshman "Basic English" for the second year (in my second year of teaching), and recalling my previous failure to engage the freshmen, I looked for an opportunity to have these students learn with a purpose they would experience as real and immediate. This work was much easier that year because I collaborated with a special education teacher, as so many of my students were thus identified.

We did not have to look far for opportunities: a wonderful preschool sat just across the street from our high school. We began this adventure by going to the library to get some special training from the children's librarian in how to read and select books appropriate to preschoolers. The first thing I noticed was that many of my students, gang members included, eagerly remembered certain books—"Oh man, *Cat in the Hat!* I loved that book!" During this part of the process they had to all fill out library card applications and answer a few questions. They had to listen—and for a reason. They were nervous about reading to these four-year-olds! Most of them read at about a third- or fourth-grade level. The local paper, which I called to see my students got the attention they deserved, wrote:

> Heather Gamer, 15, hated to read. "I'd just sit there and read a book and get hungry and want to eat all the time," she said.
>
> Brook Morrison, 14, had a library card—somewhere—but it was such a boring place, she only went "when I absolutely have to."
>
> And classmate, Ryann Lynch, 15, found sitting still, staring at some tired words on a page stultifying.
>
> The Castro Valley High School freshmen, however, now speak about reading as exciting, the library as a fun place and sitting still with a good book as an enjoyable way to pass time.
>
> The change for the 35 freshmen in basic English remedial classes [happened when] the teenagers worked with preschool children. The older kids read to the youngsters. (Cutler 1991)

Over the course of the year, these same freshmen would do many other activities that took them into the community to "use" their English, which, of course, helped them to improve these skills, also. In addition to reading to the preschoolers, they:

- published children's books in collaboration with the same preschoolers, prompting the little ones to create stories which my students then transcribed and used the computer to publish
- corresponded with residents at a local retirement community, many of whom were former teachers as it turned out; we ended the year with a luncheon bringing them together to meet and talk
- wrote and published a book of biographies about centenarians for a local hospital; these were based on interviews the students conducted in pairs through the Centenarian Project at the hospital

The local paper, again interested (after my prompting and follow–up calls to make sure they knew how to get to the hospital), wrote:

> When Castro Valley High freshman Alycia Alarcon and Mike Flores were asked to interview a 100-year-old woman for an English class assignment, they weren't sure they'd have a lot to talk to her about.
>
> But they were surprised to learn that Ethel Stensson shared their views on war, that she enjoyed going to dances when she was their age, and that overalls were as much a fashion statement in her time as they are in teen circles today.
>
> "I was amazed she was so sharp and aware," said Alycia, 15. "I used to think old people were all grumps, that their memories were gone, that they were all just dazed." (Strong 1991)

I was not sure that such experiences could be easily replicated in another environment or at another school. Sometimes they seem the product of a rare combination of timing and people. After moving to a new school a few years later, I joined a community organization that included various community leaders, students, and educators from all levels. Listening to the committee throw around ideas for building a bridge between the school and the community, I saw my chance. At the time I was teaching a General English class for a group of seniors who were as likable as they were resistant to doing any work.

Having had no real success in the first weeks of the semester, I snapped at the idea of using my class to publish a community resource directory when someone mentioned it. We worked an entire semester to create the directory. It was our curriculum. Such projects often make me nervous because of the chaos that does not always "look like education": dead time for some kids while I run around helping others, the necessary period of reluctance until they bought in and realized what we were doing.

This reluctance is, in fact, one of the biggest challenges for most teenagers when doing something like this: they don't know what to expect, don't understand what it "looks like." Kids are wary of new experiences until they know it will not embarrass them or promise yet one more experience of failure. There are, however, several steps which can help such projects succeed for both teachers and students:

- Establish clear parameters for the activity so the students know when it will happen; this is particularly important since such projects are woven into the larger academic curriculum, and must not seem to replace such requirements.
- Make the individual or group responsibilities perfectly clear so that each student knows what they should be doing during the project.
- Appoint student-leaders to help edit, manage, or organize the project; this gets them to take their role seriously and diminishes your own responsibilities.
- Do whatever you possibly can to help them understand what their work will lead to or how they should actually do the work; you can do this through rehearsing, modeling, role-playing, or watching videos, after which you might allow for further questions.
- Clarify your own role to both the students and those in the community; for me, this means explaining that I am the director and, in some cases, the designer of the project that the students themselves oversee and implement. The less I do, the more they learn.

What did this group of twenty-three seniors do? Most of them, interestingly, were identified as special education for one reason or another; a few more of them were ESL students who were too old to stay in school anymore, but not yet proficient enough to go into the mainstream after three years of ESL. You can raise the cry of tracking—something I don't advocate—but working with these students under such circumstances allowed us the freedom to do whatever we wanted, so long as it helped those kids learn. When they finished, the school district, in collaboration with the community, published over two thousand copies of their fifty-page directory, something that has been used by real estate agents to point out all the resources that can be found in our community.

Through this work, the students learned many skills and developed many capacities, each of which is anchored in those standards common to any state standards document.

- *Reading*: They read a variety of texts during the course of their research and, by designing and producing a publication, improved their understanding of how such documents actually function.
- *Writing*: They improved their writing skills in all domains by writing letters to public officials, grants to local organizations, and the document itself which, because it was to be published, demanded absolute accuracy of information and mechanics.
- *Speaking and Listening*: By calling local organizations, having meetings with community members and local leaders, students improved their ability to communicate orally and listen carefully.
- *Organizing*: The sheer volume of data, all of it in various stages of development, required that they learn to organize the information so they could find it and use it; they

also learned how to organize information effectively within a document to make it "reader friendly."

- *Collaborating*: Working as a team, these eighteen students, along with a senior citizen mentor, learned to cooperate with each other in their work.
- *Computing*: They all learned to use different software programs—ClarisWorks, Page-Maker, Netscape—to create the document, write the grants, and conduct their research.

With the advent of the Web, such projects and correspondences could be done with even greater ease and success and represents an exciting range of new avenues. It is worth pointing out that such projects represent the kind of product-based activity that organizations love to donate money and resources to help create. They love it for the advertising that you can offer them under the acknowledgments area where it says, "Printing expenses were paid for by the Robinson Foundation."

Service Learning Projects in the English Class

Could such a project as the community directory have been done in a "regular" class? It is possible and, with the advent of the Web, worth considering given the range of high level skills that could be brought to bear on such a product. One might also ask: is it possible—even wise—to *not* offer such experiences given the widespread disaffection among so many teens? What good are the skills of writing and reading if we do not know how to live with each other or find no meaning through our lives as we live them (Goleman 1995)? And though we ask ourselves how we can possibly fit in such experiences in the most challenging classes, books such as Goleman's *Emotional Intelligence* repeatedly emphasize that one's character consistently accounts for success more often than intellectual talent or academic success.

Any effective service learning program should have the following elements:

Integrated Learning: the project's goals are clearly articulated within and arise from the broader curriculum of the course or the mission of the school. It is not added onto but is an integral part of the academic curriculum in that it complements it.

High Quality Service: the service itself responds to an actual community need that is both age appropriate and designed to achieve significant benefits for both the community and the students.

Collaboration: the project is a collaboration among as many partners as is feasible: parents, community, business, school, students.

Student Voice: students actively participate in the choosing, planning, and implementing of the service learning projects.

Civic Responsibility: the service learning project develops students' sense of responsibility for their community and its members.

Reflection: reflection allows students to make thoughtful connections between their experiences and their academic curriculum; moreover, it takes place before, during, and after the project.

Evaluation: all participants, including students, help to evaluate the project to measure its achievement and determine how it can be improved in the future. (Service Learning 2000 Center 1998)

"The Gift of Words": A Service Learning Project

My class of thirty-five juniors established a connection to the neighborhood elementary school kindergarten classes. Every Friday a rotating group of five juniors went over at the beginning of class to have lunch with a bunch of kindergartners and then, after lunch, read to them. My students got themselves over their on their own, on time, dependably. Most weeks they took along a couple ESL students, too, and thereby provided further mentoring to those in their own school community. Nothing pleased me more than the willingness of even the most stone-faced, "tough" guy in the class to go read to the kids. When Chad returned and I ask him how it went, he said only, "It was cool, Mr. Burke." This is big praise from such a young man who the previous day, while we discussed *Joy Luck Club*, had spent the period (without me knowing it until the end) trying to reassemble the neon-green pager that his mother accidentally washed.

D.J. Van Arkel, one of the juniors who helped us by volunteering to go first, wrote:

> I enjoy going to Washington very much. I believe that it shows how well we can behave, but have the kids look up to us as role models. I love little kids. I also believe that a little time between going back strengthens the bond of the class. My best time was the first: I went with Ryan, Anthony, Julia, and Beau. I liked it when Julia asked for kids to go read with her and *all*, I mean *all* the little girls wanted to go with her because she was in her cheerleading uniform. This is a great experience that should happen with all kids so they can feel the love.

Taylor Vogt, another junior in the same class, wrote:

> Going to Washington is a great learning experience. Not only are we helping the kids learn to read and enjoy reading, but we are also learning from the experience. When we are around the kids we have to take on new forms. We really have to watch what we do and say, because our presence will influence and rub off on them. We also get a little taste of parenthood. By reading and being in charge of the kids we can see what it is like to be a parent.

This "magical experience" lead to one of the more impressive extensions of all their work. One of my juniors, Beau Bunch, tossed out the idea of getting books for all the little kids in the midst of a conversation about *Huckleberry Finn*. I could have passed it by easily, dismissed it as an annoying non sequitur intended to distract me from noticing he didn't read the book. But he did read it; in fact, the suggestion grew out of a discussion about helping others in the book. The service learning project that evolved satisfies John Dewey's suggestion that education should always have an aim. Educational philosopher Maxine Greene (1998) picks up on Dewey's idea: Dewey described "an aim as a way of being intelligent, of giving direction to our undertakings. He knew well that there are no guarantees; he was talking . . . about openings, about possibilities, about moving in quest and in pursuit." It was precisely because of the possibilities for personal as well as social and educational outcomes that I stopped the conversation and listened to the proposal. It's almost always easier to say "no"; sometimes we have to find a way to say "Yes!" to risk, to rewards, to the learning we did not know we could look for.

Beau suggested we write a grant to get money to buy books for the kids so each had at least one book of their own at home. Those in the class who participated in the "reading buddies" program (approximately 90 percent of the class) wrote to local organizations such as the Rotary Club and local educational foundations for money to buy books to give to "their" kindergartners. This proposal was one of several writing options for a general writing project. Such work has the added benefit of incorporating multiple literacies: computer use, financial calculation, inquiring about book prices, figuring out how and when to purchase them, and deciding which books to buy. After a week of intense planning, drafting, research, and talking, a group of eight produced the proposal (Figure 15.1).

There is an old chinese proverb that says "I hear and I forget, I see and I remember, I read and I understand"

Our goal is to encourage young students to become more involved in reading. The most effective way to achieve this goal is to encourage the students to read at home. It takes the proper tools to build a child's education. Books are a tool of learning. Won't you help us provide them with the best ones available?

Our program needs to raise $1,200 dollars to buy 80 new hard bound books for the Kindergarten class at Washington Elementary.

Please, make a difference. Take part in the building of our children's minds, by giving generously. We ask your support by giving as much as you can.

What We've Done...

What You Get...

What We Need...

With this goal in mind, we would like you to strongly consider joining us in making the literacy rate increase. We, a group of active students at Burlingame High School, have volunteered time out of our daily schedule to visit our neighboring elementary school, where we encourage children to be more enthusiastic about the joys of reading. Now we are asking you to help us take it one step further.

Why would you be interested in donating money to our cause? Well, other than the fact that your organization will contribute to the future of many youths, your organization will receive a significant amount of positive publicity. To start, your name will appear on the inside of every book that you fund as well as on a thank-you plaque. We are also hoping to have media exposure through many newspapers, so your money won't just help the future of America but will help your organization as well.

As active members in the community we have taken it upon ourselves to raise money to buy books for Kindergartners of Washington Elementary School. We are trying to raise enough money to buy 80 books at 15 dollars a book ($1,200.) These books will be for the children to keep, for as we all know, when something is given to a child by an older peer he admires, it is treated with more respect and used more often than if given to him by an institution.

Figure 15.1 *The grant proposal written by students for "Gift of Words" books for kindergartners. This one page yielded a total of $2300 in donations for books.*

Those who have written such concise documents know how hard you must work to say so much in so few words. It exemplifies E. B. White's thoughts about writing: "Vigorous writing is concise. A sentence should contain no unnecessary words. . . . This requires not that the writer make all his sentences short, or that he avoid all detail and treat his subjects only in outline, but that every word tell" (Strunk and White 1979, xiv). To their proposal I added only a short cover letter before sending it out, providing assurance that it was a real request and that all money would be appropriately spent.

The final result was better than could have been expected. Their proposal yielded over two thousand dollars worth of new books, providing a book not only for each kindergartner, but for every first grader. The dozens of extras went to the library to bolster its collection. The executive director of an international philanthropic organization visited the school to hold a formal meeting with the grant writers, asking them about their experiences with the kindergartners and seeking assurances about the money requested. I did not attend this meeting as I wanted them to learn what the experience would teach them. The following day, I received a letter from the Shinnyo-En Foundation: "On behalf of the Shinnyo-En Foundation, we are delighted to inform you that the Shinnyo-En Foundation will contribute $700 to support the Reading Buddies Program." The letter went on to commend the students for their conduct during the meeting the day before: "Their comments, insights, and reflections on their experience working with the kindergarten students and, subsequently, designing a proposal and raising funds to support literacy efforts were compelling. We were moved by their sincerity, candor, thoughtfulness, and commitment to the program and to engaging in meaningful service to others."

The day of the "Gift of Words" itself—i.e., when the whole class went over to give away the books—was rare. Ben and Jerry's brought ice cream for everyone. The school board president even helped scoop. Reporters came (see Figure 15.2). Parents arriving to pick up their kindergartners came in and watched. Students of mine talked with their former teachers who came

Burke's fourth period turns buddy program into great success

by Jen Spiteri

Jim Burke's 4th period junior English class had a celebration on April 24, to honor the success of the Big Buddy Reading Program called "a gift of words" at Washington Elementary School. The celebration was held at Washington Elementary School last month. Ben and Jerry's Ice Cream sponsored the event giving out free ice cream to all who were there. Each kindergartner and first grader received a brand new hard cover book made possible by a grant written by a few high schoolers.

Last October Burke's fourth period class became involved in Service Learning, a program here at Burlingame that involves students helping other students, also known as PAWS (People Action Work Service.)

Near the end of the '97 school year Burke asked Sue Glick the Service Learning Liaison to help him find a way of incorporating community service into his curriculum. Burke knew that he wanted to work out a "big buddy program" using his students to act as mentors to the elementary school students.

"At another school I used to teach at, I was able to work out a big buddy program one year, and it was very successful," Burke said.

Every Friday a few students from Burke's fourth period class visited Washington Elementary School. From fourth period until the end of lunch the students from his class spent the afternoon with the Kindergarten class eating lunch and then taking them to the school library where each child was allowed to pick out a few books to read to the high schoolers.

"It really surprised all of us to see how many kids would rather listen to

Beau Bunch and other students from Burke's fourth period class hang -out with kindergarteners

us read than to play outside. At first when I heard that we would be reading to them during their lunch break, I thought we would be lucky to get a few kids to come," Beau Bunch said.

"It all started after Mr. Burke taught us persuasive writing skills," Bunch said. That's how Beau Bunch a student from Burke's class came up with the idea of writing a grant to buy new hard cover books for the Kindergartner's and first grader's.

Bunch and several other kids in his class including DJ Van Arkel, Taylor Vogt, Chris Giuliacci, Rhea Coulter, Julia Gunning, Ryan Delehanty, and Anthony Granato got together and wrote the grant asking for donations of 1,200 dollars to purchase 80 new hard cover books for Washington School. Glick sent the let-

ter to various book stores and to other organizations. The grant was very successful and received many responses. "I never thought that we would receive so many generous donations," Bunch said.

Tower Records responded to the students' letter and donated 150 dollars worth of books. The Shinnyo-En Foundation an organization dedicated to human kind has generously donated 700 dollars and the Peninsula Foundation gave 600 dollars towards this program.

"We love to read," said first graders Marnie Hogue, Harley Morgenstern, Elizabeth Hine, and Kelly Dement. The big buddy program at Washington Elementary will continue until the end of the '98 school year.

Figure 15.2   *The "Gift of Words" book give-away was covered by several local papers, including the school's newspaper.*

down to visit and bear witness. The superintendents came and congratulated the kids. Every "littl'un" left with a book and a belly full of ice cream. For my part, I drove home that Friday afternoon feeling a pride in what my students had accomplished, and how they acted on that day swells in me every time that I think about them sitting down reading and giving those brand new books to those kids.

There is room in the English curriculum for such experiences if they are carefully planned and the class maintains its academic focus. The five juniors who went to the elementary school each Friday knew that they needed to make up their work. Their commitment to the Reading Buddy program was measured both by the effort they made to get the class work in and their willingness to give up their lunch hour at school to have lunch and read with kids my son's age. Such learning contributes to and develops capacity for "moral intelligence" (Coles 1997) and instills in them those "habits of the heart" (Bellah et al. 1985) necessary for a healthy individual and a sustainable community.

Were I a parent of one of those kids who came home to boast about their "reading buddy" or their "big friends" from the high school, I would feel a whole lot better about education than the newspapers often allow me to. Were I the parent of one of the high schoolers, I would feel, as they inevitably do, grateful for the effect such experiences have on kids. And the kids? Well, Alex Nerguizian, one of my students, said it best:

> I really like what we did today. I like kids. No, I mean everybody says that. But I really like kids! When I was younger I looked up to the older kids. Older people have helped me become who I am. Now I know that I can be looked up to by younger kids and that's really important. It really feels great. What we did felt meaningful. Older people will still be important to me. Like when I get to college people who take me under their wing will matter to me. That's why I felt good working with those kids today.

Endnote: Extending Ourselves

I have limited myself here to my own students' experiences. There are, however, many compelling examples of exciting work done by English students as part of various service learning projects. Some produce public service commercials for local cable companies. Others publish documents different from those described here. Still other students read to older adults or children in the hospital. I know of some who are just now beginning to create dazzling Web sites to keep the public informed about certain trends, events, or ideas. In the closing lines to his book *The Moral Intelligence of Children*, Robert Coles recalls Henry James's nephew, who as a child, was given the following advice: "Three things in human life are important. The first is to be kind. The second is to be kind. And the third is to be kind." Coles concludes, "The issue here is the hortatory verb, 'be,' as well as the adjective—the insistence that one find an existence that enables one to *be kind*. How to do so? By wading in, over and over, with that purpose in mind, with a willingness to sail on, tacking and tacking again, helped by those we aim to help, guided by our moral yearnings on behalf of others, on behalf of ourselves with others" (Coles 1997, 195).

REFLECTION

Most teachers have experiences that involve working in the community or with others in a communal enterprise. First, describe some of those experiences you or someone you know had, taking time to speculate on the benefits of such work. Then discuss your own ideas about the place of such activities in your English curriculum, brainstorming possible service learning opportunities.

ACTIVITY

Have each student create or find a work of art, and a poem that complements that artwork. Have them create a small (no larger than 11 × 14) poster that includes both the art and the poem; ideally students could use computers to make this, thereby expanding their computer skills in the process. When the posters are finished, put them up around the school as a contribution to the school community. Don't hesitate to be more ambitious: put them up in appropriate places around town.

RECOMMENDATIONS

You can find out more about service learning or get ideas for other projects by visiting the following Web sites for these service learning organizations. Each Web site offers a wider range of print and on-line resources.

Service Learning 2000 Center, 50 Embarcadero Road, Palo Alto, CA 94301; (650) 322-7271
Web site: http://www.stanford.edu/group/SL2000/
E-mail: SL2000@forsythe.stanford.edu

The National Service-Learning Cooperative/Clearinghouse, University of Minnesota, Vocational and Technical Education Bldg., 1954 Buford Avenue, R-290, St. Paul, MN 55108; (612) 625-6276
Web site: http://www.nicsl.coled.umn.edu
E-mail: serve@maroon.tc.umn.edu

CHAPTER 16

SUCCESS FOR ALL
TEACHING STUDENTS
WITH SPECIAL NEEDS

English is not accessible even to Englishmen.

—George Bernard Shaw, from preface to *Pygmalion*

I always think that we should not be timid. We should be courageous to do everything which should be done.

—Fiona Kot, sixteen-year-old ESL student from Hong Kong

You don't know what it is to stay a whole day with your head in your hands trying to squeeze your unfortunate brain so as to find a word.

—Gustave Flaubert

The Human Need for Success

I remember going to my box in late September of my first year of teaching. Mixed in with the adminstrative notices and catalogs was a note from a special ed student in my Basic English class. It was neatly folded into a two-inch square. I will never forget it: "Mr. Birk, I think I'm dum. Can you help me with that?" It was signed, "Your student, Jon." It was a huge admission that reminded me of how I felt when I landed in Tunisia to serve in the Peace Corps with my shiny new college degree and no Arabic. I knew things, knew I was smart (in my own language), knew I could do things (if they were the things I knew how to do). But the culture of the situation made everything feel wrong to me. I remember how angry I felt with all my ideas and feelings bottled up inside me. We have a lot of kids in our schools today, especially boys, that feel this way. They feel this way for very different reasons.

Some of the students in our classes came from other countries as recently as yesterday. They are like I was when I first arrived in Tunisia. And because I had great teachers—I actually had to live with them, surrounded by Arabic twenty-four hours a day!—I learned to think and move between the worlds of Arabic and English so well that I began to take French lessons (from a wonderful woman who began each lesson by making us espresso which we drank in the little cottage out back of her house—ahh, but that's a different story!). Other students in our mainstream English classes have been here long enough to be in "transitional classes" that are designed to support these English language learners in the "regular" English classes. Still other students may have been born here, but at home they speak other languages and so have what some call "second language interference" errors in their English or speak what others would call nonstandard English.

Another group of students consists of those like Jon whose learning difficulties make school hard for them. Some kids have more serious difficulties than others, but the reasons and degree of hardship these difficulties cause them at school varies. Girls like Denise and Shawna, two wonderful kids in my junior class, developed effective strategies and helpful habits early on thanks to fine teachers. And others, like Vince, went to special schools for a time where they were taught a range of strategies by tutors who stayed with them through the years. The big threat for these students, most of whom are identified as "Special Ed" and many of whom do just fine in my classes, is the same threat we all fear: feeling, as Jon said, "stupid." There is no greater anxiety in the school culture. After all, school is about getting and being "smart," right? We have to remember at all times, though, that there are different ways of being "smart" or revealing our intelligence, and in our classes all students need to have access to those opportunities. Only when all our students can walk into the classroom confident of their ability to succeed in that class can we call ourselves a success.

"The Loop": It Takes a Team to Teach a Child

Schools run fast. You have to organize your classes and the school to make sure everyone is "on the bus." Because most departments are distinct and often distant from each other, communication can be difficult. Yet nothing is more crucial to students' success than communication with those who share the responsibility for educating them. This includes parents, counselors, ESL teachers, other specialists who work with these students, or their special ed teacher. That phrase *special ed teacher* is so loaded in the mind of some and that's unfortunate: I used to be one. Later, when I became an English teacher, it was special ed teachers like Teri Jokerst who showed me what could be accomplished with these students in the English class.

Special ed teachers like Teri and ESL teachers like Sandy Briggs taught me about the Loop. They did this by dropping notes and articles in my box; they did it by calling me or stopping by during my prep to ask me if they could help in anyway. Eventually, I learned to do the same, to know I could drop a quick note in any teacher's or counselor's box that said, "I'm having trouble getting Chris to read. Can you give me some ideas or talk to him about that?" Later on, when I became head of the English department, I created routing slips for all department memos that included the special ed and the ESL departments so they were sure to stay abreast of what was happening in English. But the Loop doesn't just involve faculty: it involves the kids themselves.

This is important, for many ESL students and all special ed students have advocates whose jobs are to keep track of them, help them, and, most important to us, help their teachers. The ESL teachers at my school, for example, designate certain ESL students to collect extra copies of any handouts and bring these to the ESL teacher so she can help students with that assignment while keeping track of the class' demands. Sometimes teachers of these different students will stop me in the hall and say, "You know, that assignment that has the big paper? Chuck is going to have some real trouble with that. Can I stop by and meet with you about some ways I can help him with that?" It doesn't always happen that way, but it's wonderful when it does, and makes a huge difference. The Loop is made up of the best intentions of those who live within it and strive to help their kids.

English Language Learners

There are several different groups of students we need to consider in the English class when it comes to ESL:

- ESL students
- transitional ESL students
- non-ESL students whose home language is not English

Those identified as ESL students have a support system (i.e., the ESL teachers/program) which is there to help them succeed by assisting them with work from your class. The third group, those with home languages other than English, often submit written work with observable patterns of error that might be caused by interference from other languages. I find, for instance, somewhat consistent patterns of usage or error among many of my Armenian, Asian, and Russian students. As Mina Shaughnessy pointed out in her essential book *Errors and Expectations* (1977), errors tend to occur in patterns and as such can be taught or addressed more effectively and successfully because there is a sort of "code" that can be cracked.

The ESL department will have information on the student that can help you better assess their ability upon entering your class. This information can be particularly important if you have a student whose performance raises questions about their intellectual functioning overall. Sometimes we mistakenly assume that Sima's struggles are caused by the Hindi that is her primary language; it may be the case, however, that she has some undetected learning disability.

We need a range of strategies to cope with the different students and their challenges. We also need to remember that their challenges are more complicated than just the acquisition of a language. These students are learning about a culture—of both America and school itself—and themselves as they enter your class. We will look at some of the strategies to help these students a little further on in this chapter.

Learning Difficulties

Leaving ESL for a minute, we need to consider the nature and implications of the different learning difficulties that trouble our students. Many of them are specifically associated with language in one way or another. The notion that dyslexia and other such reading disorders are bigger problems today than in the past has gained some public credibility in the wake of a few studies; I side with Jeff McQuillan, however, whose critique of these studies finds no evidence of this climb (McQuillan 1998). Having said this, however, we are left with a very real set of challenges and difficulties in many of our students, some of which include:

- reading disabilities (e.g., dyslexia)
- learning disabilities (e.g., auditory/language processing disorders or attention deficit disorder [ADD])
- speaking disabilities (e.g., stuttering or other problems that can make an English class with all its talking and reading aloud a very threatening place)
- writing disabilities (e.g., visual motor skills, fine motor skills, and dysgraphia)

Other special considerations that might affect performance in an English class include visual limitations (which they had learned to hide), and emotional or psychological problems. One year I had a girl out for months with depression, another girl out for eating disorders that eventually lead to hospitalization, and one out with chronic fatigue syndrome.

"Special needs" is the most accurate term for many of our students these days, because that is exactly what they are. These unique demands involve not only emotional difficulties but psychological and behavioral troubles; they include the linguistic and the neurological problems; many of these special needs have cultural and even political implications (in such states as California where, due to recent legislation school has become a place to fear for some whose parents brought them here from other countries). But they are all in our class, every day, asking us to help them succeed no matter what they need.

Strategies for Success: What We Can Do

While many of these methods benefit all students, some are more helpful with one type of student than another. I have thus organized them into three groups: general, ESL, and special ed strategies.

General Strategies

- Be multimodal, multimedia: it helps all of your students, but the special ed students in particular. Whenever possible, let them hear it, talk about it, see it, and touch it.
- Sequence your activities and assignments logically.
- Provide a weekly assignment sheet to help them check off work they have done or need to do.
- Check frequently for understanding. Do this in a variety of ways (e.g., looking across the room to check in with a student, circling by to look at their work, asking them at the period's end if they understand).
- Discuss learning strategies you think will help them with specific areas or assignments.
- Allow more time for completion or reaction to questions you ask the students.
- Provide additional time if necessary.
- Whenever possible, break up new information into small units, present it slowly and sequentially, and review frequently.
- Be patient.
- Provide immediate feedback whenever possible to help the student measure their progress.
- Ask the student what helps them the most and what is most difficult for them.
- Provide time to practice or rehearse: whether it is a writing test coming up or a speech they must give, be sure to give them time to prepare.
- Use small groups: such groups, if made up of fluent speakers and considerate students, provide the developing speaker with an opportunity to listen more carefully and speak more often without the usual anxiety of raising their hand and speaking when the whole class is listening. One other tip: do not let them huddle together into single-language groups all the time as this will not help them become fluent speakers but do let them help each other by using their primary language to explain things to each other.

- Provide handouts whenever possible. These make it easy for students to follow along; also they help students by giving them directions when they get home to do their work.
- Use the board. For reasons similar to those above, the board provides visual information which the struggling and diligent alike can write down and clarify later. If they don't understand the words they can still get the information written down.
- Do not depend on (but feel free to use) verbal directions.
- Do not talk too fast.
- Provide clear, concise directions.
- Find out if there are audio tape versions of the book you are reading at the local library and suggest that they try these; most states provide books-on-tape for adopted texts at little or no expense through their department of education.
- Recommend that they watch the film version of a book you are teaching, though point out that there might be significant differences in the film version (e.g., *The Scarlet Letter*).
- Make CD-ROMs (e.g., dictionaries, reference works, or encyclopedias) available if you have students that would benefit from such tools.
- Allow them to use Cliffs Notes. Though perhaps controversial in the minds of some, such study aids provide the much-needed support for the student whose language ability makes it hard enough to understand most English readings, not to mention dialects and slang used by writers like Mark Twain or J. D. Salinger.
- Make yourself available outside of class. Many ESL students are reluctant to demand attention until they gain some confidence with their new language; you must then go to them and remind them that you are willing to meet with them if they need the extra help.

ESL Strategies

- Correct their mistakes. Most ESL students give English teachers a different kind of permission to correct their work because they accept that they are learning, and will only learn from having them pointed out; also some of their cultures expect it.
- Assign the ESL student a language partner who is specifically responsible for helping that student understand assignments and words they do not understand.
- Have a dictionary in their native language. Also there are some dictionaries that are specifically designed for English Language Learners (see the *Longman Dictionary for American English: A Dictionary for Learners of English*, Longman, 1983); try to have at least one of these in your class.
- Use gestures to emphasize and illustrate whenever possible.
- Learn what you can about their culture. Have them write you a letter (in lieu of some other assignment) in which they tell you where they are from and what their new life here is like so far. A helpful alternative might be to create a questionnaire that asks them specific questions that will develop a profile of them as a student and a learner (Briggs 1991).
- Allow them, as part of your outside reading program, to read at least one book in their native language.
- Allow them to write first drafts in their primary language as a means of getting their ideas together, then work on the translation and writing in English later.

Special Education Strategies

- Alter the format of written handouts to reduce the amount of material in the student's visual field, or use graphic displays and diagrams to convey information.
- Let them have a partner who understands their needs and is supportive, willing to work with them. I have had girls who were very understanding and supportive of those boys in the class with learning disabilities and provided extra help to them both in and outside of class.
- Enlist the help of a scribe to share note-taking responsibilities; if one is not provided through the student's IEP, look for a student in class who would be willing to help in this area.
- Use graphic or other organizers to help with reading. Even if you are not requiring such tools be used on a particular reading, try to make available some helpful means of organizing the information they will be reading (e.g., quickly review how to make an outline).
- Understand the constraints each students' challenges impose on them and do your best to address their needs by clarifying intended outcomes (e.g., students with ADD typically get very tired by the day's end after trying to overcome distraction and confusion all day).
- Provide clear and logical transitions between ideas and units of instruction.
- Provide lots of concrete examples to illustrate any ideas you are discussing, relating them to the student's background, experience, personal interests (which are usually available in their IEP or student file).
- Seat them up front and away from those people or conditions that would distract or otherwise undermine their performance; usually up front and close to the speaker and away from noise is best.
- Assess their learning style and inform them how they can best learn different types of info, and respond in alternative manners (tape recorder rather than written notes, scribe for tests, computer for writing).
- Establish and maintain high but reasonable expectations.
- Allow them to demonstrate their knowledge through alternative means.

The Elusive Ideal of Success for All

What's real for most of us is that we have classes that are too large to teach the way we wish we could. What I have discussed here are ideal ways to help all our students; school doesn't always cooperate with us, however, as you surely know. As I said above, the Loop consists of everyone's best intentions woven together into the shape of our good will. The ideal is not impossible, though, something we must remember. The willingness of many of these students to work hard strains belief. I've had ESL students come to me at the end of one school year to get the titles they would read the next year so they can read them through once over the summer and be ready to read them successfully the coming year. I've also seen ESL students like Anselmo Chiang enter as freshman unable to speak English and graduate four years later as the valedictorian.

With special ed students it seems to depend on the project. On an assignment like the History Project, Chad, who often struggled even with the help of his special ed teacher and outside tutor, immersed himself in the creation of a remarkable Web site. He spent every "resource period," which is essentially a study period when he can get extra help from his special ed teacher, in the library using the Internet connection to access his Web site so he could keep working on it. He was so enthusiastic about it—it was full of images, animation, and information—he came by each morning to ask me to come down and see what he had added to it. On another occasion, my special ed students collaborated with the local hospital (see Chapter 15) to interview and write the life story of dozens of local centenarians. They brought an intensity to their work in this project that remains a model of engagement. Their final work was published as a book by the hospital and presented to all the centenarians and the kids.

Endnote: The Inclusive Classroom

These projects are all nice, but there remains the challenge of the core curriculum, and the reality of the state and district exams. Many of the strategies above will help students write better, and improve their ability to comprehend the material. When it comes to such official events as state or district tests, I suggest you talk with the teachers in the special ed and ESL departments about the tests. Find out from them what that student's testing options are: Can they have more time? Can the student take the test with his special ed teacher's assistance? Do they even have to take the test? If so, what are some strategies the student can use to perform well on the test?

Sometimes the work of these students raises sticky issues that I still don't always know how to handle. For instance, Josiah's writing in class is just a disaster; but when he gets the chance to work on it at home with his tutor, it comes in nicely word processed and flawlessly written—and obviously not his as evidenced by the vocabulary and grammatical structures. Similar issues arise with some ESL students: I'm thinking, for example, of a wonderful Japanese girl whose homework was always so carefully written but whose in-class final exam was a case study in errors of all types. Issues of grading such work, or providing opportunities for further help and more time, challenge the maturity of your other students (who don't get the same considerations) and the validity of your grading system.

Learning is hard work for all of us. I firmly believe there is room for everyone in the classroom to be together, and ways for teachers to challenge all students at their current level. Projects offer all students the chance to do their very best and push themselves further along the Continuum of Performance (see Chapter 2) toward the confidence we seek to develop in them. When I get discouraged, I think of Jon's note to me, the honesty of it, the way he ultimately woke up to his own strengths when he could tell me what he knew while we worked on improving his ability to write about it, too. That year I had money enough to hire a poet from California Poets in the Schools, a wonderful program that brings poets into the classroom to get the kids to write some excellent poetry. I think of Jon, standing up before the parents and friends who gathered on our Poetry Night in the library, unfolding a piece of paper and reading his poem, taking his applause as evidence of his worth.

REFLECTION

Write about a particular student or two who have special needs in your class. What is your class like for them? How are they doing? What could you be doing that you are not? Consider writing a letter as if you were them, explaining what it is like to be in your class.

ACTIVITY

Take your prep period or lunch period to meet with a teacher from the ESL department one day, and someone from the special ed department another. Write out your questions ahead of time if you can and give them to your colleagues ahead of time so they can prepare for the talk. Go in there willing to be honest about your expectations and frustrations with students. In my experience, both ESL and special ed teachers are some of the most supportive, thoughtful teachers in our profession. They know it can be hard, and will offer suggestions and sincere confirmations that it is a hard situation that you are doing a good job trying to resolve.

RECOMMENDATIONS

I have several books to recommend about these different subjects.

Special Education

Readers with a Difference: A Holistic Approach to Teaching Learning Disabled and Remedial Students. Lynn K. Rhodes and Curt Dudley-Marling (Heinemann 1988). A thorough book that addresses nearly any situation that might arise while trying to help students read and write despite their learning difficulties.

The Learning Mystique: A Critical Look at Learning Disabilities. Gerald Coles (Fawcett Books 1989).

TeachEACH: Classroom Strategies to Teach and Teach All Learners, available free from the Charles and Helen Schwab Foundation, phone: (800) 471-9495.
Web Site: www.perc-schwabfdn.org

English as a Second Language

Between Worlds: Access to Second Language Acquisition. David E. Freeman and Yvonne S. Freeman (Heinemann 1994).

"My Trouble Is My English" Asian Students and the American Dream. Danling Fu (Heinemann 1995).

CHAPTER 17

WHAT GENDER IS ENGLISH?

Henry James could have been a woman. E. M. Forster could have been. George Eliot could
have been a man. I used to be too insistent on this point that there's no sex in the brain; I'm
less insistent now—perhaps I'm being influenced by the changing attitude of women toward
themselves in general? I don't think there's anything that women writers don't know.

—Nadine Gordimer, interview in *The Paris Review*

How Gender Affects Classroom Dynamics

Franco, in his football jersey and the sagging pants, looks out the window while the class talks about Toni Morrison's *Beloved*, a book this advanced American Lit class has been reading for a few weeks. Some of the girls in the class are quick to want to discuss a few key scenes as the conversation gets under way. Franco takes out his pencil and begins to twirl it distractedly; his friend, Jake, is trying to finish his geometry homework which is due the next period. If asked, Jake would say that nothing important is going on; we're just talking, he'd say, it's not like we're actually doing anything important. His buddy across the room, Henry, suddenly perks up, raises his hand, and says in his usually confrontational manner that he thinks this book is totally inappropriate for high school students to be reading. His tone draws the attention of the other two boys across the room; everyone is watching, especially the boys.

Mrs. Estes, the teacher, is calm: she knows her way around the class after twenty years; she knows boys. She grins while she listens, nodding to show she is listening, punctuating his remarks with noncommittal "Uh huhs." Mrs. Estes knows she has several options: give Henry just enough rope to hang himself; crush him since she knows he hasn't done the reading in the first place; let it go where it will and invite the class to respond. Inherently, she realizes that it is too easy to crush him and to do so, moreover, would make an enemy.

He has already asked, on another day, why they are reading Morrison's book instead of Mark Twain's *Huckleberry Finn*. One, he argues is a classic; the other, he says, is just to be politically correct. "We're reading it just because she's a Black woman," Henry charges. He hastily adds that he's not prejudiced, of course; he just thinks that Twain is obviously more important, though if asked he would not know why he thinks this.

Mrs. Estes's response in both situations is to use it as an invitation to the class to discuss the subject. "Well," she wants to know, "why do you think that it's inappropriate?" Henry hardly lets her get the sentence out of her mouth before he starts rambling on about how it has all this violence and these hateful attitudes about men in it; the book is prejudiced against men and just offends him. Mrs. Estes nods and thanks him for his response, then turns to the class where a forest of arms have grown into the air, most of them girls.

The first girl, Gabriella, lights into Henry, wanting to know why he didn't find the rape scene offensive: "Oh, you didn't find *that* upsetting, but it bugs you that she has an attitude toward men?" Another girl, Fannie, joins in, challenging Henry to explain why the scenes where they whipped and beat Sethe, the main character, didn't disgust him. "She [Toni Morrison] won the Nobel Prize for Literature," Maria points out, "what Toni Morrison has to say is every bit as important as Mark Twain." Some girls in the class kept adding to the conversation; others looked on, attentive, interested, unwilling to contribute. Meanwhile, Jake had returned to his geometry, thinking only that the girls were just going at it again, talkin' talkin' talkin'. Qianna raises her hand and asks Henry how much of the book he has actually read; he gets real quiet and blushes a bit, saying that he hadn't really read much of it. At this his friends in class began to give him a hard time, but he only smiles, considering his inquiry a success because it swallowed up nearly twenty-five minutes of class.

As they walk out of class talking about the essay Mrs. Estes assigned, a couple of the boys huddle up in the hall: "Are there Cliffs for this book, Mike?" one wants to know. "I don't know," said Shawn, "but this buddy of mine over at Christian Brothers said there's a bunch of stuff about Morrison on the Web. I'll check it out tonight." "Cool, let me know what you find, all right?" At this they all part, shuffling off to their next class.

As a man in a profession dominated by women, I find myself talking about gender often; that nearly 60 percent of my freshman honors classes consist of girls has forced me to think about it even more. This scenario described above encompasses nearly all the gender issues common to the English class. First, there is the selection of what students read—who wrote it, what it's about, what discussions it will inspire—and why they are reading it. As Applebee writes (1996), "When the quality of a book is questioned, it is usually because of objections to the conversations the book might provoke." That some conversations, particularly about the gender and social equality, inspire resistance confirms what I have previously discussed as the struggle for power within the society. For as soon as you bring one new title (by a woman or nonwhite writer) into the curriculum, you have some contingents lamenting what has been removed, describing it as superior to what has been added. As Liz Whaley and Liz Dodge write, in *Weaving in the Women* (1993), "If you add women authors to the curriculum, if you make sure girls get to speak in class, you are perceived as treating males poorly. It's hard to shake these misperceptions, but I have learned to live with them. Along the way, however, the resistance to reading women authors has vanished."

The previous vignette also points out the complicated dynamics that often make teaching high school so challenging. Today's high schools are home to an increasing number of children from divorced families, adolescents with serious problems, and students from cultures whose attitudes toward women are sometimes complicated by biases that cannot be easily dismissed. Books thrown into the middle of this mix often—and should—stir things up, particularly if the teacher chooses books that open up a conversation about borders—between genders, cultures, generations, and so on. For though many other issues, most prominently race, demand attention in the English curriculum, it is gender that most consistently divides the class due to conversational styles, cultural assumptions, and personal misinterpretations.

Which, in the end, is precisely why it is so important for English teachers to address issues of gender (and ethnicity) in the classroom: our whole curriculum is about communicating effectively with a variety of audiences, considering our audience when writing or discussing, listening to what others (classmates, fictional characters, writers) have to say to us. It becomes our daily responsibility—and ongoing challenge—to confront these biases within the classroom and the texts we use. If we do not, we potentially undermine our students' (especially girls') chances to succeed. Such discussions are, at heart, about power: what it is, who gets it, how you get it, how it works. Peggy Orenstein writes, in *Schoolgirls* (1995), "The boys definitely resent it. They think Ms. Logan [the teacher] is sexist. But you know what I think? I think that it's the resentment of losing their place. In our other classes, the teachers just focus on men, but the boys don't complain that *that's* sexist. They say, 'It's different in those classes because we're focusing on the important people in history, who just happen to be men.'"

What students study shapes what they come to think is important in much the same way as "what gets tested is what gets taught." It is not enough to weave in a poem by Anne Sexton here or a short little essay by Annie Lamott there, especially if these complements to the "core" curriculum are like parsley to the main course. "In the end, what is gained from weaving in the women is the empowerment of students, female and male, the quiet as well as the louder ones. . . . After they've read enough, they can begin to appreciate a culture totally different from theirs so that they can have some idea of what life actually was like for Edna Pontellier in *The Awakening* or for the more reluctant bride in Alice Walker's 'Roselilly.' Their minds begin to wander in preferred directions; they won't stay rigidly on the questions-after-the-story page of the textbook. They want more. Students have more self-esteem because they're taken seriously. They are more willing to take risks, to be vulnerable" (Dodge and Whaley 1993)."

It is precisely this idea of genders as distinct cultures that informs Deborah Tannen's *You Just Don't Understand: Men and Women in Conversation* (1990). In her introduction, Tannen writes that "many frictions arise because boys and girls grow up in what are essentially different cultures, so talk between women and men is cross-cultural communication." Implications for the classroom are serious: if teachers fail to see their class as a place where East meets West, if they do not create and maintain a safe, respectful environment that recognizes and finds ways to honor all sides represented, trouble is inevitable. Some teachers, as depicted in *Cultural Reflections: Critical Teaching and Learning in the English Classroom*, confront the subject head on, making gender itself the focus of an extended course of study (Gaughan 1997). Actually, complexity is inevitable anyway given the classes we have; such trouble, moreover, is healthy and, if absent, a serious sign that something is wrong.

Meanwhile, something *is* wrong in our schools. Mary Pipher, author of *Reviving Ophelia* (1994), describes some of the disturbing realities common to girls in our society, problems that cannot help but affect their performance in school.

> In classes, boys are twice as likely to be seen as role models, five times as likely to receive teachers' attention and twelve times as likely to speak up in class. In textbooks, one-seventh of all illustrations of children are girls. Teachers choose many more classroom activities that appeal to boys than to girls. Girls are exposed to almost three time as many boy-centered stories as girl-centered stories. Boys tend to be portrayed as clever, brave, creative and resourceful, while girls are depicted as kind, dependent, and docile. Girls read six times as many biographies of males as of females. Even in animal stories, the animals are twice as likely to be males. . . . Analysis of classroom videos shows that boys receive more classroom attention and more detailed instruction than girls. They are called on more often than girls and are asked more abstract, open-ended and complex questions.

In short, boys are praised for what will help them succeed and, consequently, afford them greater power than the girls when they grow up.

Honoring Gender

Though a few of the following suggestions come up in Chapter 25, the following provide more specific strategies to help you create a classroom environment that respects all students.

Self-selected reading. Whether for outside or core reading, this option allows students to search for those books by women, for example, that can speak more directly to their experience. You might even do a required project like Whalen and Dodge discuss in *Weaving in the Women* where every student reads the biography of a notable woman, and gives a presentation on her and her contributions to our society.

Writing topics. Topics for papers, journals, and other assignments define what you think is important to be thinking about in your class. In addition to developing their own topics, students should be given topics that will allow them to think privately and seriously about those gender-related issues the conversation in class has raised. The privacy of their journal allows students to risk honesty and sort out the mess of what they really do think about the subject. Mary Pipher writes about the importance of girls keeping journals, and writing poetry and memoirs as a means of reflecting on where they've been and where they are going. She urges young women to ask certain focus questions to help them sort out their thoughts through writing. These questions—about values, goals, changes, strengths, weaknesses, and identity—are designed to give them insight into why they think or feel as they do. Here are a few examples, each of them essential questions for any adolescent:

- What do I think?
- What are my values?
- When do I feel most myself?
- What goals do I have for myself?
- How do my current actions and beliefs help me achieve these goals?

Men read books. Boys need to see that men do, in fact, read. As a teacher, you must model this for them, bringing into the classroom news of what you are reading and why. When my wife and I were expecting our first child, I told my students about all the amazing books I was reading to prepare for that experience. I tell the boys who take shop classes about books I read for construction and carpentry so they realize there are many different types of books for all interests. I always have some magazine or book with me to show them. And when they ask, when they are ready to read, I can pull some book off the shelves in my classroom and put it in their hands in hopes it will find its home in their heart and mind. But if boys think reading is "a girl thing," they will resist it.

The classroom environment. Our classrooms are constantly challenged by elements we find it difficult—if not impossible—to control. In a class of thirty-five students, it is hard to see everyone at all times. Even the nicest kids sometimes write stuff on walls; the things the "rude boys" scratch into the desks or walls offend the freshman girl who arrives in September. Sometimes I catch boys sneaking a look at car magazines which have barely clad women posing next to the muscle cars; when I point out that they are insulting to the girls in the class some boys look at me like I have an extra head: they don't get it. Check out your room: do you have posters of writers or artists on the walls? If so, do you have some women authors—or are the girls surrounded by images of intelligent men? I started decorating my room when I bought a pack of postcards of women authors at an NCTE convention one year. You can get great pictures from magazines like *Literary Cavalcade*, and some bookstores keep posters in the backroom which, if you ask nicely, they will give you for your classroom.

Response to work/ideas. How we respond to students' ideas or writing is always crucial, but more so with some students, particularly girls. Pipher (1994) writes that "offhand remarks can be taken as prophecy, an indictment or a diagnosis. One client decided to become a nurse because her uncle told her she would be a good one." Pipher herself, when in eighth grade, received a poem back from her teacher with the word "trite" hastily written across the top of the paper. It took her, she said, twenty years to resume her plans to be a writer. Men are especially prone to misunderstand the thinking behind girls' responses to questions in class and can, through their response, do great damage to the girls, many of whom will refuse to participate in class discussions after such humiliation (Gilligan 1982).

Use of groups. By working in groups, girls can often take more risks, sharing their fledgling ideas within a more supportive environment and thereby gaining confidence in their thinking. Discussing, for example, how girls might react in the same situation as the boys in *Lord of the Flies*, students have the chance to explore complicated ideas with members of both "cultures." Such smaller groups make room for all students, but specifically those who are otherwise shut out because of the aggressive interrupting that characterizes so much discussion. Secretary of State Madeleine Albright said once, when interviewed, that she never allowed her students to raise their hands but demanded instead that they learn to fight their way into a conversation to make their point, since this is how the world worked. She did this for the benefit of the women in her class who needed to learn how to be more assertive in conversations.

Equal standing. If you introduce works by emphasizing they are written by women, implying that the class is reading it only because it is written by a woman (or some other specific group), it reduces the work's stature by suggesting it is special, different from the other, more serious works you normally read. Instead, just weave in the women, using a variety of texts in different media, to make them a seamless part of the course. When I chose to add Bharati Mukherjee's *Jasmine* and Amy Tan's *The Kitchen God's Wife* to our freshman course, for example, there was little resistance because the context (the study of these cultures) made the reasons for their selection immediately apparent. Furthermore, having my juniors read Tan's *The Joy Luck Club* as part of a quarter-long study of California literature provided a meaningful opportunity to read and discuss the book, an opportunity made all the more welcome given her local status and the local reference points. When boys eventually objected to the portrayal of men in the book, this only provided us new ways to look at whose story gets told and to assess the credibility of the narrator and writer.

Our classes are full of kids trying to figure out what it means to be men and women. This quest for clarity is made more confusing by the adults they see around them, many of whom haven't gotten it right themselves. I've had girls completely fall apart when their father left their mother for other—predictably younger—women. One year I had two young men whose confusion and anger were finally explained when they told me that their fathers had come to terms with their own sexuality, realized they were gay, and left the family with all its pain and confusion in their wake. Each year I have students, particularly young men, whose confusion about their own sexuality makes life particularly difficult, especially if they begin to venture into the gay or lesbian communities, scared to death their peers or parents will find out what they themselves are still not sure they know or understand. Others, mostly freshmen and sophomores, enter into the long winter of discontent with their parents, especially their mothers, in order to find their own awkward and often dangerous way into womanhood. When we read a poem like Anne Sexton's "Pain for a Daughter," the room just swells with angst as they all, for their own reasons, relate the daughter's hermetic silence to their own lives and relationships. Often times their teachers, especially women, only resemble another variation of the mother as an authority figure they are so busy opposing; so they bring in the arsenal of behaviors evidenced in the opening scenario and make the classroom the challenge that it is for us daily.

In *Talking from 9 to 5*, Deborah Tannen (1994) shares her own personal experience of this fear of impotence in the classroom: "I once had a nightmare that I walked into a class to teach, and the students would not look at me or listen to me. They all sat with their chairs turned to the back of the room, so I could not teach. . . . When entering a room in which students are noisily talking to each other, many teachers feel a momentary panic that the students will not stop talking to listen to the teacher. And if they did not, the teacher could not teach, no matter how commanding the performance." More common than an entire class rebuffing a teacher is the individual student who rebels against a teacher. Thus some teachers find themselves in the unfortunate position of feeling they must "not smile before November" as the saying goes, in order to establish their own authority.

Gender and the English Department

In this era of increased collaboration and the ongoing discussions common to the profession, we find ourselves working in close quarters with colleagues. In a profession so heavily populated by women, the dynamics of all discussions are inevitably affected. I've worked with all types of colleagues, department chairs, and administrators, most of them women. Each of us, at one time or another, charges the air with our own gender-based assumptions or remarks which cause greater reactions in some than in others.

Exchanges between colleagues in your average high school are often limited to the few minutes between periods; communication, therefore, tends to be very abrupt, very functional. Such a style can be potentially damaging to some, since miscues can result in misinterpretations that cannot be corrected in the two minutes.

This is not the place to examine the role and importance of gender in the workplace, but I will suggest that you take time to read Deborah Tannen's books on communication between men and women. In particular, I recommend *Talking from 9 to 5: Women and Men in the Workplace: Language, Sex and Power* (1994) for issues related to your colleagues. Her other books, such as *You Just Don't Understand* and *That's Not What I Meant*, while offering invaluable insights into your relationships at work and home, provide very helpful information about the dynamics of your classroom discussions and behaviors.

Endnote: The Mentor

While teaching freshman honors classes opened up my eyes to the biases in our society at large and my teaching in particular, it was only when I found myself mentoring a number of young women during their high school years that I entered into the dialogue about gender seriously. I talked regularly to Andrea, trying to help her decide whether the Army was the right decision for her when she graduated. I began giving Martha my *New Yorker* each week, highlighting the articles I thought she would find interesting. Elissa brought me her latest poems to read; I would then respond to them via e-mail later in the week, telling her what I liked and why. The most intense conversation, however, the one that taught me more than anything, involved Emily Rosenthal and took place during her senior year. This is a young woman I had known since she arrived in my freshman class. As a senior, she was unable to find a class; so I created an independent study humanities class for her which required that she write me a letter each week. I was so immediately engaged by the dialogue that I, too, started writing her letters; by year's end our letters amounted to over seven hundred pages, much of which dealt with the women writers we chose to study for most of the year. Still, she opened my eyes to other issues, as you can see in this excerpt from a letter I wrote to her:

> Our conversation in the office today about the SAT followed me home to the dinner table where my wife Susan and I continued it. She made a couple of very apt and interesting observations. She, too, did only moderately well on the SAT test but then outperformed many of her peers once she got to college. We have a mutual friend, Tamar, who left teaching to go to graduate school at University of Chicago. Tamar said she always hung back when professors asked questions, thinking she wasn't sure if her answer was "right," but the men waded right in, saying that they understood the subject perfectly, that they could do it. (This is a very gifted, intelligent teacher, by the way, a woman who should *never* doubt her answers . . .) However, once in the groups with her classmates, Tamar realized right off that she understood the material—often better than the men. Susan said she had the same experience on many occasions.

In many respects, such relationships are mentorships. Geoffrey Canada writes in *Reaching up for Manhood: Transforming the Lives of Boys in America* (1998), that "there are enough children who need our help that each one of us can find the right match, very likely close to home [in our classrooms], and go to work to build trust and offer support in order to make a real difference in the life of a child." We make that difference most often by using stories—our own, our students', and those of different writers—to help them figure out not just who they are but what they are. Our success is only partial, however, if this "private education" focuses solely on the individual. Rites of passage, whether private or public, are ultimately about taking one's place in a larger group. If we are lucky, the ideas our students encounter in our classes will invite them to think with greater depth about not only themselves but those men and women with whom they share the world.

REFLECTION

If you are currently teaching, try to occupy the mind of one of your students, perhaps one of the opposite gender, and describe what your class is like to them. If you are not currently teaching, reflect back on specific moments in your own education shaped your ideas about gender; these moments can be good ones or bad, or even a combination of both. One other option might be to take a specific incident from your own teaching experience that involved some issues of gender, and to examine what happened and why.

ACTIVITY

If you are currently teaching, give someone (a student, a colleague, or an administrator) a copy of your seating chart, and ask them to put hatch-marks near the names of those you call on or otherwise interact with during the course of a period. When you examine this, pay attention not only to whom you addressed but where they sit in the room. If you want to get real serious, you might consider making up a code to allow for more specific information on the score sheet (e.g., Q = asked them a question; C = called on them; T = talked with them, etc.).

RECOMMENDATIONS

I have included several books here, each one dealing with a different aspect of gender.

Reaching up for Manhood: Transforming the Lives of Boys in America. Geoffrey Canada (Beacon Press 1998). A very moving memoir-manifesto that reflects on what it means to be a mentor and why men need to accept this responsibility, especially in the inner city.

Schoolgirls: Young Women, Self-Esteem, and the Confidence Gap. Peggy Orenstein (Anchor Books 1994). Published in the wake of the American Association of University Women's report (*Short Changing Girls, Shortchanging America*, 1991), Orenstein's book examined the implications of the report for society and schools. Every year a number of girls choose to read this book; they always tell me how much it made them think, and how it helped them to understand some things that had always confused them.

Reviving Ophelia: Saving the Selves of Adolescent Girls. Mary Pipher (Grosset/Putnam 1994). Pipher's book speaks with such insight and depth that it has been translated into nearly every language there is, including two different dialects in Chinese. Her book, while not limited to schools, thoroughly discusses girls' "academic selves" as well as their other personae, considering it all in light of Pipher's experience as a therapist. This book is honest and well-written. It will reveal as much about boys despite its focus on girls.

Weaving in the Women: Transforming the High School Curriculum. Liz Dodge and Liz Whaley (Boynton/Cook 1993). This book offers both background on the subject of women writers and practical activities for integrating these writers into the curriculum. The book is well written, resulting from years of workshops based on their own experience. Its perfection is the result of careful planning and thoughtful research about what to include and how to use it in the classroom, all of it coming from two high school teachers who know what they are talking about.

CHAPTER 18

THOUGHTS ABOUT CULTURE, RACE, AND LANGUAGE

Language is a political instrument, means, and proof of power. It is the most vivid and crucial key to identity.

—James Baldwin, "If Black English Isn't a Language, Then Tell Me, What Is?"

I thought of myself as multicultural. I preferred tacos to egg rolls; I enjoyed Cinco de Mayo more than Chinese New Year. At last I was one of you; I wasn't one of them. Sadly, I still am.

—Elizabeth Wong, from "The Struggle to Be an All-American Girl"

Culture, race, and language combined to feed a wildfire of public debate in 1997 about "ebonics," or Black English. The school board in Oakland, California, suggested that ebonics be accepted as an official language for the purposes of instruction, much as Spanish might be for bilingual education. The rationale was hard to discern amid the firestorm of public commentary that filled the editorial pages for weeks, arguments on one side lamenting the blindness of the other. Theresa Perry (1997) summed up the issue in a special edition of *Rethinking Schools*:

> To say that African-American children were not achieving in the Oakland Public Schools would have been an understatement. Comprising 53% of the students enrolled in the only predominantly Black school district in the state of California, African-American children accounted for 80% of the school system's suspensions and 71% of students classified as having special needs. Their average grade point average was a D+.
>
> These stark, painful realities, reflective of the Oakland school system's inability to ensure even a modicum of academic success for African-American children, are what motivated the school board to unanimously approve the Black Language/Ebonics resolution. Essentially, this resolution maintained that Black Language/Ebonics was a legitimate, rulebased, systematic language, and that this language was the primary language of many African-American children enrolled in the Oakland school system. The board further maintained that Ebonics, the

home/community language of African-American children, should not be stigmatized, and that this language should be affirmed, maintained, and used to help African-American children acquire fluency in the standard code.

Understanding that most teachers have little, if any, accurate knowledge about Black Language, and are likely to harbor negative attitudes about the language and its speakers, primarily because of their socio-political location; and understanding also the relationship of literacy skills to school achievement, the resolution called for the implementation of an educational program for the district's teachers which would focus on the nature and history of Black Language/Ebonics. The assumption was that such a program would address the teachers' knowledge gap about Black Language, begin the process of changing their attitudes about the language, and help teachers figure out how to use the rich and varied linguistic abilities of African-American children to help them become fluent readers and writers. (Perry 1997)

This issue of race and culture was in the news again a year later when two members of the San Francisco board of education proposed that the required reading list for San Francisco high schools be revised to reflect the cultural diversity of its student population. This policy, which was eventually adopted with some changes, met with predictable resistance from those who argued that to change the canon amounted to lowering standards. This objection was inevitable. As Henry Louis Gates, Jr. (1992, xv), writes, "to speak of a curriculum untouched by political concerns is to imagine—as no one does—that education could take place in a vacuum." Gates goes on to say that "the teaching of literature is the teaching of values." In other words, what is *not* taught is not—nor, the omission implies, should it be—valued, respected, honored.

In *Reading, Thinking, and Writing About Multicultural Literature*, Carol Booth Olson (1996) notes that the Hispanic population of California's Orange County grew by 97.3 percent between 1980 and 1990; the black population rose by 54.9 percent during that same period of time; and its Asian and Pacific Islander community swelled by an amazing 177.1 percent during those ten years. Instead of wasting time lamenting or resisting what is, we must clearly work to ensure that *all* our students learn what they need to gain access to the "keys" James Baldwin refers to. Lisa Delpit (1997) writes, "I can be neither for Ebonics or against Ebonics any more than I can be for or against air. It exists. It is the language spoken by many of our African-American children. It is the language they heard as their mothers nursed them and changed their diapers and played peek-a-boo with them. It is the language through which they first encountered love, nurturance and joy." Delpit sums up what we all understand and what James Baldwin also said: what we speak reflects who we are; if we are not accepted as we are then we will turn away and reject that which would deny us our dignity. Cornel West (1994, 14) calls this "black nihilism," which he considers one of the central crises facing those African Americans who live with "the experience of coping with a life of horrifying meaninglessness, hopelessness, and (most important) lovelessness." Kids so stripped of hope and meaning find no reason to care, though I prefer to think that even the coldest ember is just asleep and wants a little wind to light it up.

In fact, according to Keith Gilyard, author of *Voices of the Self* (1991), what has been interpreted as the failure of so many African American students should be viewed as a deliberate act of defiance or resistance: "Black students affirming, through Black English, their sense of self in the face of a school system and society that deny the same." Gilyard goes on to note that studies by Labov show the language of black Americans diverging more from standard English as time goes on. This trend is made all the more confusing to teachers because when looked at alongside the academic patterns of students from other cultures, it can seem an impossible expanse to bridge. It can seem futile for another reason: Asian students' success offers a telling example of the role choice and effort play in school success. Daniel Goleman, author of *Emo-

tional Intelligence (1995), reports that such Asian students are often able to persevere despite setbacks because their effort spawns a sense of optimism that if only they work harder they will succeed.

So what do you do when you walk into class tomorrow and face that room full of energetic statistics you all know by name and love so much? I've just stated the first thing you absolutely must do: see them as human beings not statistics. If I reduce Jaime to a statistic, I pull the rug out from under us both: why bother doing anything if, as my Muslim friends say, "it's a thing in the hand of God"? Meanwhile, Jaime is in my class, comes everyday, appears to listen, and doesn't do any of his work, despite my regular inquiries into the status of his essay, his project, his reading. When, at semester's end, I ask him to explain why he should pass the course, he tells me in a remarkably candid letter that he has read all the books, but just not done the assignments. To prove this, he makes mention of several key parts of the books he liked. He is not pleading so much as trying to quietly prove he has learned and worked—just not as I have asked. He wants me to understand *he* is not an F, that he is not stupid.

His letter entirely redefines—or rather reaffirms—my role as his teacher, part of which demands that I begin by accepting where he is and figuring out how to get him where he needs to be. NCTE's *Position on the Teaching of English: Assumptions and Practices* (1989), says that "students should have guidance and frequent opportunities to:

- read texts by authors of diverse backgrounds: e.g, ethnic, racial, gender, age
- bring their own cultural values, languages, and knowledge to their classroom reading and writing"

The NCTE/IRA standards (1996) urge that

- students develop an understanding of and respect for diversity in language use, patterns, and dialects across cultures, ethnic groups, geographic regions, and social roles
- students whose first language is not English make use of their first language to develop competency in the English language arts and to develop understanding of content across the curriculum. (NCTE/IRA 1996)

All such statements, while important, too often seem remote from the reality of what happens in the classroom. You have your class read Sandra Cisneros's *House on Mango Street* or Maya Angelou's *I Know Why the Caged Bird Sings* only to hear some of the Latino students say *Mango Street* is the most boring book they've ever read or an African American colleague bark that she will never teach "that book" (*Caged Bird*) because she thinks it demeans blacks. Such moments, while the exception, are particularly awkward and upsetting for many teachers who are just teaching what the curriculum requires; the idea that their best efforts might bore the very kids they hoped the book would engage, or actually harm the students the book might otherwise inspire leaves the teacher reeling and hungry to get back to some good ol' grammar or vocabulary where things are neutral, safe, familiar.

Respecting Race and Culture

Start an Engaging Conversation. Arthur Applebee's research (1996) found that students did best in classes where the curriculum was organized to answer a question or foster a conversation about a particular idea that was meaningful to all students or of obvious importance to society at large. Consider the difference between these two introductions for a new book:

> *Scenario One*
> "Okay guys, today we're going to be getting a new book called *The House on Mango Street* by a Latina author. I thought it was really important that we read an author from a different culture since so many students here are Latino."
>
> *Scenario Two*
> (after reading a brief section from Cisneros's book) "So, we've been talking about this whole idea of growing up, about creating an identity for oneself, what it means, how and when it happens. *Huck Finn* allowed us to talk about some important aspects of that whole experience. And Nathan Mc-Call's book told us what it was like for him to grow up as a young black man in the sixties. I thought it would be interesting to see what this other book has to say about the experience since unlike Huck she didn't take off but stayed on Mango Street. I love this book a lot. It took her five years to write this 120-page book. It's like a poem almost, the language and images are so intense."

Clearly, the second scenario establishes a sound rationale for reading the book, and links it to what they have done before. More importantly, the teacher emphasizes the literary merit of the book, and grabs their interest by reading a provocative passage that hooks them before they even know a new book is coming their way. One teacher I interviewed said that when introducing *The House on Mango Street* to a class with many Latino boys (whom she feared might reject the book because it was "about a girl"), she asked the boys to tell her when they were finished if this was a book about a girl or about something else. When they finished reading it, not one boy said it was a "girl book."

Emphasize Similarities.   This last observation leads to another important strategy: the teacher helped them, through lots of discussion and writing, to see themselves in Esperanza, to see the similarities instead of the differences. On my classroom wall is a quote from Terence, who came to Rome as a slave and died a playwright: "Because I am a man nothing can be alien to me." We are teaching in schools where some students drive cars that cost what teachers earn in a year, and other students go home to sleep in cars where they wake to a breakfast of cereal with water. Stories offer the one place where we can meet and, through these narratives, better know ourselves and those sitting at the table with us. But you have to learn how to facilitate such conversations, how to create a conversational space in which students can talk about a common subject despite their apparent differences. Rhea Coulter, speaking about one such conversation which had been lead by her classmate Beau, wrote: "yesterday's discussion [about racism in *Huckleberry Finn* and society today] was a very good one. Beau's thoughts and ideas brought up things in everyone's mind. Each person in the class could relate to the topic. I really enjoyed the discussion because it gave people not only something to think about but a way to vent."

Rhea's response echoes what Martha Nussbaum says in *Poetic Justice* (1995). Nussbaum teaches a class at University of Chicago's law school that requires future judges and lawyers to read such books as *Black Boy* and *Great Expectations* to help them understand the lives of those different from themselves. Nussbaum, summarizing Wayne Booth, writes that "the act of reading and assessing what one has read is ethically valuable precisely because it is constructed in a manner that demands both immersion and critical conversation, comparison of what one has read both with one's own unfolding experience and with the responses and arguments of other readers." This is why such a book as Malcolm X's autobiography can be one of the most memorable books students read: it is a story about someone trying to find his way to the person he is trying to be in this world, a quest all our students share.

Choose and Use Multicultural Texts.   First, I don't like the adjective *multicultural* in this context because it suggests the book is chosen for this reason and not its merit. The same reservation applies to women authors. Most kids resent being subjected to a teacher's politics; however, as Gates writes, curriculum is always political though the classroom should not be. The guiding principle should be balance: between poetry and narrative prose, drama and fiction; between canonical authors and contemporary authors; between male and female authors; and, of course, between white writers and those of other cultural and racial perspectives. What one wants is a conversation, even a heated argument, between the books one reads: have your students read *Parrot in the Oven* and *To Kill a Mockingbird* or *Huck Finn* and *Invisible Man* in order to see what these two books, their authors, and the characters have to say to each other about the same subjects. Some argue that size matters—i.e., balance does not consist of reading novels by white authors and poems by writers from other cultures— and it does; however, nothing allows for a greater diversity of voices than poetry from such anthologies as *Unsettling America: An Anthology of Contemporary Multicultural Poetry* (Gillan and Gillan, 1994) which is organized around such themes as "naming," "uprooting," and "negotiating." Such anthologies are particularly helpful when trying to represent a range of perspectives because the most common criticism—often well-deserved—is that the one text chosen (e.g., *Joy Luck Club* or *I Know Why the Caged Bird Sings*) is not representative of the complex realities of, for example, Asian Americans.

Endnote: The Human Language

One unfortunate consequence of the sociopolitical complications inherent in discussions of culture, race, and language is that we sometimes forget what we are supposed to accomplish in our schools and classrooms. Many African American teachers and parents, reflecting further on the dilemmas inherent in the ebonics debate, feel their children's opportunities in life will be limited if they do not master Standard English. In our stratified society, such worries are justified. These very inequities are blatantly pointed out in Jay Mathews's provocative book, *Class Struggle: What's Wrong (and Right) with America's Best Public High Schools* (1998), where he writes that annually some one hundred thousand students—many of them either black or Latino—are either denied admission to Advanced Placement courses or discouraged from enrolling because schools are unwilling to invest their faith in these students even though their past performance suggests they would likely thrive.

At this point in our cultural history, the struggle for power has focused in large part on language: Should people, whose growing numbers demonstrate increasing political power, be allowed to choose which language they speak? While we educate the heart through the stories we read and the discussions we have, we must also make time to develop in their minds those abilities that will best serve them in their life after school, in their life as voting citizens, as parents, as employees. If we are lucky, the future will see what Rex Brown (1993) calls "thoughtfulness legislation": "What good policy can do is stimulate, legitimate, and sustain healthy conversations and literate discourse. It can assemble people to inquire into the most fundamental matters, to argue about them and use the very skills and dispositions they want to develop in students: problem solving, reasoning, analysis, questioning, collaborating, democratic decision making, and all the rest. . . . Bad policy shuts down discourse, rather than opening it up." Brown's last words answer what remains your final question: "'What should I do differently tomorrow, now that I have read this book?' I have no better answer than this: Get three friends, and ask them three questions raised by [this book]. Follow your answers with tougher and tougher questions, until you all start seeing things differently. You will know what to do." If you don't, try asking the kids: they know things and, if asked the serious questions, will give you serious answers about not just what it means to be black or Chinese or Armenian, but about what it means to be an American and a human being.

REFLECTION

Describe the ethnic community of your school and/or class. In this profile, discuss how people work with each other. What are the most pressing issues you see in your school and its community with regard to ethnicity? What can you do in your class to help address these issues?

ACTIVITY

Take out your grade book and examine your students' performance in the light of their ethnicity. What are the implications for you as a teacher of this info? In other words, if there is no pattern, if your Native American, black, and Latino students are all performing as well as the other students, what are you doing to achieve this? If, on the other hand, all your students in one group are clustered at the bottom, what can you do about that? If you don't know, seek those who do and ask for help.

RECOMMENDATIONS

Of course there are many excellent books out there, but there are two that I find particularly helpful:

Other People's Children. Lisa Delpit (The New Press 1995). A truly important book that looks at the school performance of different ethnic groups and examines how our assumptions about learning do not always include these students.

Reading, Thinking, and Writing About Multicultural Literature. Carol Booth Olson, ed. (ScottForesman 1996). Chosen more for its practical guidance in the effective integration of multicultural titles into the curriculum, this book offers actual lesson plans based on research conducted by the University of California at Irvine Writing Project.

CHAPTER 19

ETHICS AND THE STUDY OF ENGLISH

"Is the bird I am holding living or dead?" the young people ask the blind old woman.
"I don't know," she says. "I don't know whether the bird you are holding is dead or alive, but
what I do know is that it is in your hands. It is in your hands."

—Toni Morrison, from her 1993 Nobel Lecture

Don't ever let me catch you shootin' at a mockingbird, Jem. It's a sin to kill a mockingbird.

—Atticus Finch, in Harper Lee's *To Kill a Mockingbird*

In her book *The Measure of Our Success: A Letter to My Children and Yours*, Marian Wright Edelman (1992) describes her childhood in South Carolina as one built on the foundations of family and church, which was "a hub of Black children's social existence," where "caring Black adults were buffers against the segregated and hostile world that told us we weren't important." Author and doctor Robert Coles (1989) writes of growing up in a household where his father came to his bedside each night to have their usual "brief evening chat" about those dilemmas or problems he encountered during the day. Jill Ker Conway (1989), in her memoir about growing up in the outback of Australia, recalled her father's teachings when, throughout her life, she got confused about the "right" thing to do, thinking often of his advice to "just stand still" if you're lost and think about where you are, where you came from, where you want to go.

These fortunate people enjoyed something too many of our students don't: caring, involved parents who had time to teach them how to live in the world, and communities of faith that conveyed a clear set of standards for ethical decisions. For too many students this leaves the school—and often the English class in particular—as a crucial forum for discussions about values, ethics, and morality. Herbert Kohl (1998), reminding us that "moral development takes place slowly," goes on to say that "we have to avoid blaming children for their moral confusion in a world that adults have been unable to make nurturing or welcoming. What we owe them is time, love, and council as they move toward independence and autonomy." The need for this essential conversation about "moral literacy" has achieved such consensus that both conservative thinkers like William Bennett (1996) and progressive educators like Herbert Kohl can both issue a "call to character" through their respective anthologies of literature chosen for its moral teaching capacity. Ethics or values can no longer be kept out of the classroom.

This became startlingly apparent to me when the Internet came to my school. Almost immediately after installing the Internet in our school's library, a group of boys, several of them top-level students, went on-line and, after finding a Web site with stolen credit card numbers, bought hundreds of dollars worth of CDs. When caught, they expressed shock at the charge that they had "stolen" both information and property; they could not see that what they had done was no different than walking into a music store and stuffing their pockets with CDs. "I would never do that!" one of them said in response to this comparison, as if the administrator insulted him by implying he was a thief. I encountered a more upsetting instance of moral failure later on when a group of boys, who were supposed to be doing some research, went into an on-line support group for suicidal alcoholics and told them to "do us all a favor and get on with it—kill yourselves." I only learned about this particular incident because they happened to be using my personal Internet account—that was the last time I allowed that!—at the time; when I got home and found letters from distraught and angry people in the support group I was utterly dismayed. The next day I made the boys write formal apologies to the group, then we discussed how anonymity can allow us to act in ways we otherwise would not. In such moments the only real good that can be derived is the lesson they learn.

Several factors make the need for ethics in our schools apparent:

- Parents, through divorce, longer hours of work, or their own personal troubles with drugs, depression, or life in general, have lost their place in many children's lives and do not offer such moral guidance as described above.

- Television and movies convey an uninterrupted stream of morally bankrupt images that glorify the use of drugs and alcohol, celebrate physical violence and sex, and give viewers the general idea that it is okay to be rude to anyone, especially those older than you.

- Technology has forced upon us an unprecedented range of ethical problems as illustrated in the previous examples—cheating, stealing, and emotional abuse (through "flaming," or Web sites created to humiliate specific students).

Kids tend to turn to their peers for guidance in the absence of other, more knowledgeable "teachers." This has the predictable results; if given the opportunity to discuss such matters, students themselves will reveal their own frustration about it. If you look around, most kids' lives are remarkably isolated in this modern world. As Mary Pipher said in a talk I heard in San Mateo, California, in 1997, "Our children are being raised by appliances." These appliances challenge their "moral intelligence" (Coles 1997) every day as they encounter information that demands a moral code to help them decide how to act. This absence of mentors in the midst of such inanimate, alienating environments is troubling for "there is nothing more influential, more determinant in a child's life than the moral power of quiet example. For children to take morality seriously they must be in the presence of adults who take morality seriously" (Bennett 1996).

This means confronting reckless thinking in the classroom or in literature when it comes to such issues as prejudice. You can't teach a book like *Huckleberry Finn* without asking if the book is racist, if Twain is racist, if I, as the teacher who invited it into the classroom, am racist. It means stopping the class when the Armenian student hurls the insult at the Turkish student, or when one gender generalizes about another in a hurtful way. It means seeing cheating as an opportunity to discuss moral capacity and personal integrity by explaining how they have diminished the currency of their word in my realm from that point on.

I'm not naive about all this. Just because we talk or I say something doesn't mean anything changes. However, it is the discussion of what is right and wrong, the growth of moral intelligence that counts. We cannot make our students act "better," but we can put them at the center of such essential conversations and, by allowing students to occupy the lives of others—through literature—help them develop the habit of asking of themselves such questions.

These questions involve much more than money and insults. In our diverse society, we must have these discussions if we are to understand the codes by which our neighbors, classmates, and fellow employees live their lives. Such discussions also help us all to recognize the moral dimensions of any decision we make, alerting us to the fact that we should think it through, consider all the ramifications. What might not be a moral dilemma for the Christian student surely can be for the Muslim or the Jewish student; so, too, the boy may not view a particular encounter with a girl as having moral implications, though the girl may well know it is given her own values and dignity. Thus when we talk about characters in stories we should add to it the dimension or idea of *character* as revealed through actions. In their book *A Call to Character*, Kohl and Greer (1995) offer the following list of traits or "virtues" to use Bennett's word: courage, self-discipline, integrity, creativity, playfulness, loyalty, generosity, empathy, honesty, adaptability, idealism, compassion, responsibility, balance, fairness, and love. Bennett's list includes some of these, but offers two that are unique to his list of virtues: work and faith.

I am not advocating that students be given moral instruction that presumes a predetermined outcome; rather I am saying the English curriculum challenges both teacher and student to enter into a conversation about those moral issues that arise within the context of the stories we read together. How can you talk about Huck Finn without examining his moral development or the influence of Jim's teaching on Huck's own moral reasoning? How can you read *The Kitchen God's Wife* without discussing Wen Fu's treatment of his wife, Winnie? What are *Bless Me, Ultima* or *Beloved* if not moral tales inviting the reader not only to think about why people act as they do, but to reflect on how the reader would act in a situation? Toni Morrison has been described as rewriting the Bible for modern times; while I'm not sure about that, it does raise one final question: does the Bible itself have a place in the English classroom? The scholar Harold Bloom (1994) asserts that the Bible's "anxiety of influence" makes it one of the foundations upon which nearly all literature is based. Thus on literary grounds it does have a place within the class to the extent that it helps illuminate other texts.

Once the Bible is opened, however, kids cannot help but marvel at aspects of this strange text that so few, even the fundamentalist Christian students, have read. When my freshmen read *Lord of the Flies*, we read about Cain and Abel, Joseph and his brothers, Jesus and the Sermon on the Mount. Later on, reading *Cry, the Beloved Country*, we are obligated to read of Absalom, for how can we appreciate what Paton is doing if we don't know the story behind his character's name? Discussed as stories, the biblical tales become powerful tools in the teacher's hands that evoke strong and sometimes curious responses from kids. When I introduce the Bible into my class, the first thing I do is play a trick on them by showing them a bunch of passages about Noah, Jesus, Mary, and Moses from the Koran and asking them to identify which of the three texts they came from—the Koran, the Old Testament, or the New Testament. Thus the exercise in cultural literacy doubles as cultural lesson on our similarities instead of our differences.

The conversation about these stories is a means of allowing my well-adjusted kids from the suburbs to understand why the kid sitting next to them, who watched his father get murdered by the enemy of whatever country they fled from, thinks as he does. The conversation invites the boys and girls to talk to each other about their own perceived codes of conduct and, thereby, bring a little more understanding into the world. The guiding question here is "What do *you* think this character should have done—and why?" or "Why do you think they acted that way?" "How would you have acted in that situation?" Such questions offer a foundation to the discussion of many books and, if asked each time, allow the class to compare and contrast the moral thinking of different characters, different time periods, different cultures.

Strategies for Discussing Ethics in the English Class

There are several helpful ways to approach such discussions about ethics and morality, some of which are more involved than others.

Kohlberg's Stages of Moral Reasoning. Using Lawrence Kohlberg's model (which you can find easily on the Internet), have students evaluate the character's moral reasoning, then discuss it as a class. Another option is to have them first develop *their* own stages, then give them Kohlberg's model to compare theirs to before using them to examine the characters. I did this with particular success while teaching *Huckleberry Finn* and *The Kitchen God's Wife.*

Maslow's Hierarchy of Needs. Use Abraham Maslow's principles of human needs as they relate to moral thinking; figure out where on his hierarchy different characters are, then invite them to examine their own moral reasoning by making connections between their own reasoning and Maslow's, or the characters'.

Socratic seminar. Socrates sat under the trees and had essential conversations with anyone who would listen to him. The seminar format is particularly suited for this kind of conversation because students need to listen to what others' say, and have time to find their way into the conversation.

Moral code. Have students develop their own moral code as a means of explaining their own decisions and then have them do the same for different characters—Hamlet, Sethe, Bigger Thomas, Anne Frank. Discussion is essential.

Quotations. I have a variety of quotation and proverb books, all of which have a generous supply of wonderful lines that immediately invite thought—e.g., the African proverb "all that is evil hateth the light." Such quotes challenge students to think about substantial questions that occupy their minds, and with which many students need time to struggle if they are to make sense of the violence and evil they encounter in the world.

Moral dilemmas. Borrowing from the law school case study model, I like to create dilemmas that force deep thinking and promote intelligent discussion. For example, students get into a group and are asked first to define what a friend is. What are the boundaries of this relationship? Are there degrees? I then give them a handout with a variety of examples that range from someone being arrested and asked to identify who else was there to a "friend" asking you if you would mind if they took out your previous boyfriend or girlfriend. They have to reach consensus on each one and then present their arguments to the class during a full class discussion.

Film excerpts. Show the film up to a point then stop it, have them write, discuss, speculate; then watch, and after viewing how the character acted—should the boy have killed himself in *Dead Poets Society*? Should Martin Sheen kill Marlon Brando (aka Kurtz) in *Apocalypse Now*?—discuss it further. Invite them to share their own thoughts about justice, suicide, morality, obligation, and honor.

Writing editorials. Students can take the position for or against some view in a book—e.g., cloning in *Brave New World*—and write an editorial which, if time allows, could be adapted into a persuasive speech before the class or a subsequent class discussion.

Endnote: Moments of Truth

Mark Twain prefaces *The Adventures of Huckleberry Finn* by saying "persons attempting to find a moral in it will be banished," and yet, ironically, it is precisely these moral discussions that the book invites from beginning to end. Students want and need to participate in essential discussions about human rights, dignity, and decency if they are to grow up in and help to create a decent society. These discussions take them seriously by asking them to think about what *they* think and to reflect on why they think it. Through such discussions, "we can bring in the dialogues and laughter that threaten monologues and rigidity" (Greene 1998, 43). Such discussions also bring to mind Robert Coles's memory of childhood when his family inherited forty thousand dollars from an aunt who had spent much of her life volunteering at hospitals. Coles suggested they buy a boat the family had long wanted; his father asked him why he thought that was a good thing to do with the money. "Bobby" said he didn't know and left it to his parents to decide. But they wanted to involve him, to give him the opportunity to watch and practice making such ethical decisions so he would be ready when he entered the world as an adult. I'm not stupid, but I do like to think that discussing those moments when Huck Finn faces a real decision teach my students to recognize such moments in their own lives. Years later, when they, too, face such moments, I hope they will realize there is a decision to make, one that allows for reason and intelligence, one that I hope is based on compassion and decency just as Huck's was when he said, "s'pose you'd a done right and give Jim up; would you felt better than what you do now? No, says I, I'd feel bad—I'd feel just the same way I do now. Well, then, says I, what's the use you learning to do right, when it's troublesome to do right and ain't no trouble to do wrong and the wages is just the same?" It's a moment of learning for Huck—and for our students—that we can't afford to ignore.

REFLECTION

What are some of the most crucial ethical dilemmas in your school or community? What do you see as the most profound influences on your students' thoughts about these issues? Can you think of one example of a real ethical challenge common to most of your students? How do or did they handle this situation? What books or stories do you bring into your class that allow students to talk about these issues?

ACTIVITY

Read Flannery O'Connor's short story "Everything That Rises Must Converge" or Toni Cade Bambara's story "The Lesson." When you are finished, make a short list of the ethical issues each would allow you to discuss in your class. How could you create and sustain that conversation in your class?

RECOMMENDATIONS

The Call of Stories: Teaching and the Moral Imagination. Robert Coles (Houghton Mifflin 1989). A wonderful read.

Releasing the Imagination: Essays on Education, the Arts, and Social Change. Maxine Greene (Jossey-Bass 1998). A collection of powerful essays.

CHAPTER 20

TEACHING ADVANCED PLACEMENT AND HONORS ENGLISH

Jaime Escalante's first rule was to let everyone into Calculus who wanted to try it. His second rule was to cajole or bully into the course everyone else who had the faintest chance of success.

—Jay Mathews, *Class Struggle: What's Wrong (and Right) with America's Best Public High Schools*

Ah, but a man's reach should exceed his grasp,
Or what's a heaven for?

—Robert Browning, "Andrea del Sarto"

This chapter is not about whether such classes as Honors English, Advanced English, or Advanced Placement (AP) English *should* be offered. Rather it is about the fact that they *are* offered, and in more schools all the time: 843,423 AP tests were taken in 1996 by 537,428 students across the country, the AP Literature exam remaining the most widely taken of the different exams available (Mathews 1998). The scores themselves and the number of students taking the AP tests have begun to be used more and more as a measure of the quality of a school's program—"the Challenge Index"—and, if the scores are high enough, they can drive up the value of real estate by as much as several hundred thousand dollars. Teachers in such communities, particularly new teachers, can find themselves under tremendous pressure to issue grades that will keep or get a student in the prestigious honors or AP class for the coming year. Jay Mathews (1998) contends that cheating is common and parental politics notorious given the perceived stakes of university admissions. "If rewriting their child's essay or paying a tutor to correct her physics homework moved the child closer to a good college, then given everything else [these affluent parents] had invested, why hesitate?" Mathews writes. School officials, worn down by the game had, in Mathews's words, come to view such "help" as "positive collaboration."

Enrollment in advanced classes has increased for several reasons. As the cost of college tuition has risen, students, often as a result of parental pressure, have taken AP courses in order to save money. Public schools who find themselves threatened by declining enrollment feel compelled to become more competitive by offering such courses. This trend can be summed up best by the title of Martin Nemko's book *How to Get Your Child a Private School Education in a Public School*. Finally, when universities like University of California at Berkeley receive 14,000 applications for their 1998 freshman class and 4,000 of them have 4.0 GPAs, universities have to do something to help sort through the competing factors; some college admissions directors at major universities cite the AP test as a factor in admissions since a score of 3 or higher signals a student's ability to do university-level work.

The controversy over the AP test stems from who gets to take such classes. Some estimate that as many as one hundred thousand high school students every year are denied the opportunity or encouraged not to take an AP course despite the fact that their performance suggests they would succeed in the class (Mathews 1998). Others, however, point to the success of Jaime Escalante's AP Calculus class as evidence that the AP offers an opportunity for poor or minority students to climb the ladder of success; these educators argue, convincingly, that students are simply not being pushed hard enough, that they are failing because no one expects them to succeed. AP classes offer that opportunity, though it is an opportunity that too often ends up favoring the more affluent students, according to Mathews.

I will assume your school has a series of classes called "honors" classes that culminates in the senior AP English class, though I realize this is not everyone's reality. First, there are two different AP English tests, which means theoretically there could be two different AP English courses: Language and Composition and Literature and Composition, each of which the College Board considers a year-long course.

In the College Board's booklet *Advanced Placement Course Description: English* (for May 1998–May 1999), the following characterize the Language and Composition course:

- students must be skilled readers of prose written in various genres and periods
- the composition curriculum emphasizes expository, analytical, and argumentative writing
- the purpose of the course is to enable students to read complex texts with understanding and to write prose of sufficient richness and complexity to communicate effectively with mature readers
- a consistent emphasis on "stylistic developments" in the student's writing and how professional writers achieve such elements through choices they make

The Literature and Composition course focuses on "the careful reading and critical analysis of imaginative literature" (College Board 1998). The teacher will need to know and be able to effectively teach at a college level such elements of fiction and poetry as metaphor, imagery, style, and symbolism. Within this context students should also learn the range of literary terms while reading from all genres both inside and outside of class. In fact, nothing characterizes the true AP student more than their willingness to read seriously. The AP introductory guide sums this up nicely: "The AP English Committee agrees with Henry David Thoreau that it is wisest to read the best books first; the committee also believes that such reading should be accompanied by thoughtful discussion and writing about those books in the company of one's fellow students." In short, this means that the AP English Literature students will read both the classics and the best of the contemporary authors, all of which is done in anticipation of the exam, and the essays they will write on the exam about these works. The emphasis here is on interpretation, literary analysis, close reading; furthermore, all such critical readings must be explored through subsequent essays whose writing quality must be of the highest caliber if they are to pass the test.

The writing must not only be of the highest caliber but obey certain conventions—literary analysis, prose style analysis, literary vocabulary—with which the teacher must be familiar if they are to successfully prepare students for the AP exam. Many teachers develop these habits of analysis and response in their students through repeated practice with short, dense passages—poetry as well as prose—which students are expected to annotate and explicate. AP teacher Nels Johnson focuses on a continuous series of focused "design model paragraphs" which challenge the students and allow him to respond carefully and quickly to the writing so students get the immediate feedback they need.

Preparing Honors Students

Implications for the teachers in the earlier grades (i.e., those advanced classes leading up to the actual AP class) are somewhat clear. The exact details, however, should be negotiated between the teachers of these courses. If, for example, the AP teacher feels the kids need to come in knowing something about the Bible and its influences on literature, then one of the earlier classes should plan for this. When choosing books for an honors course, those teachers involved may want to consult with the other honors teachers to make sure the readings align themselves with the AP test as best they can. Though I have not taught AP English, those AP teachers I interviewed tend to juggle the obligations to adhere to the AP curriculum with the teacher's need to create their own curriculum. This might mean they teach their curriculum Monday through Thursday most of the year, then train for the AP on Fridays using old tests or practice questions. Many teachers said the course offered by the College Board was instrumental in helping them understand how to do all this.

Not all pre-AP honors classes, however, feel committed to prepare their students for the test. As new reforms have appeared in recent years, certain programs have developed with different goals. Some schools have instituted Humanities courses which, in some cases, become coded as advanced classes since the halls are not lined up with kids saying they really would like to learn more about the Renaissance traditions in art and how those came to affect subsequent literary and musical traditions. Others have created integrated programs that enroll students in both social studies and English, hoping through the accelerated study of both to achieve something that cannot be done in separate courses.

Throughout all these different configurations, a couple questions or issues arise that have direct consequences for students and teachers:

Content. For AP classes, the readings are prescribed—i.e., choose from within a large group—and defined by their consistent thematic and stylistic complexity. Some AP teachers require students to buy their books so they can teach books the school may not have and show students how to annotate their texts.

Quality vs. quantity. The fact is that any such course will require more work, and students in the classes must be able to do it. Students in my advanced freshman class (which is integrated with an advanced World Cultures class), for instance, read at least five books outside of class in addition to their core/required texts for the class. One trait of such a class and its teachers is that students are pushed harder to do better; a culture of challenge pervades the class. The challenge should be intellectual as opposed to quantitative. The standards in such a class—both performance and content standards—should be clearly articulated so as to inculcate in students the highest standards for writing, reading, and thinking. When you send them home to read and explicate Robert Frost's "Birches" and Dylan Thomas's "Fern Hill" prior to writing an analytical essay in which they compare what the two poems say about loss or growing up, you should not hear such predictable questions as "How long should that be?" or "Is this going to be graded?" You most likely will hear them, but since you shouldn't, I suggest you remind them that they are there to work harder and should always do their best work on all assignments.

Pace. This is related to the quality versus quantity discussion above, but with some specific differences. Some books you want to have them read—for whatever different reasons—but given their reading ability you know they don't need to discuss the book much to "get it." Two quick examples come to mind: *The Catcher in the Rye* and *The Kitchen God's Wife*, both books many schools require their students to read. Honors kids don't need that long to read a book like *Catcher*; in fact, to take too long on such a book might seem a waste of time to some. When these kids enter college they will take courses that require them, for example, to read the *Iliad* in three days, complete with notes toward the essay they will write afterwards. High school is not college; however, students in advanced classes should be pushed to read widely and deeply despite the pace. The couple of teachers I surveyed handle *Catcher in the Rye* differently: some require it for summer reading prior to entering the class, while others give the kids two weeks during the school year to read and discuss it, wrapping it up with an essay that might ask them to look at the literary elements such as themes, symbols, or guiding metaphors that recur throughout the book.

Summer reading. All advanced programs require some kind of summer reading to be done prior to entering in September. Some schools do it to weed out the kids who aren't willing to do the work right away in September. It seems silly for the teacher to require an amount of work that will overburden themselves right as the new year is beginning in September. I am intrigued by what Elaine Caret, a colleague of mine, does in her summer reading prospectus. Elaine creates two lists, one classical, the other contemporary writers. The students have to read one off of each list, keeping a reader response log as they go; they also read one common text, which changes every year, so they have a common place to begin their discussions when they return in the fall. This shared text tends to be one that sets a certain tone and theme for the semester if not the year.

Outside reading. They should do lots of it. If it's an AP class, the personal reading should remain anchored in texts from the AP list or books of similar literary merit to those on the list.

Literary analysis. This is the skeleton of the Literature and Composition course and must be directly taught. In recent years some schools have begun to drift away from a strong emphasis on literary analysis as school-to-work and other reforms have made their way into the curriculum. Most teachers of advanced classes refer to and use those literary texts commonly used in most introductory college classes: an anthology like the *Riverside Anthology of Literature* includes not only the readings you will likely require, but also the framework for close analysis.

Endnote: Gifts of the Gifted

My own bias, as with all our classes, is that the teacher absolutely must be reading as much as possible on their own. The AP teacher who can come in and integrate into their discussion the latest feature from that week's *New Yorker*, or the novel the just won that National Book Award, enjoys a credibility unavailable to the teacher who does not read. In most respects, teachers of the advanced classes are those who make the extra efforts to read and write on their own; such classes are not the rewards but rather the consequence of such efforts, and translate into increased professional capacity and credibility.

Funds are often available for AP classes that are not available to other classes or teachers. Special funding comes to the school, sometimes to the GATE (Gifted and Talented Education) program coordinator; other times the money comes to the administrators who oversee the AP classes. This money can pay for materials that help prepare students for the AP tests. It can also be used to pay for workshops and conferences that are designed to help you better prepare your students for these tests. You can say these scores don't matter all you want; the fact remains, however, that every April my room fills with parents whose eighth graders are considering our school, who are deciding whether to buy a house in the community, and whether to send their child to our school, and it all hinges on one factor, a factor that affects the cost of their house and the child's future success (as some would argue): the test scores.

The other challenge common to AP teachers is what to do with the remaining month after the test. This is a serious problem, for the fact is that the kids are spent and graduation is fast approaching. Yet, as one teacher said, "you need to maintain the integrity of the learning environment," and not send the message that school is over. Most teachers I spoke with required of their students some kind of personal project that was both challenging but fun. The team spirit fostered in the months that lead up to the test was thus harnessed for the final stretch as kids came in to class in the final weeks to present their "exhibitions" to the class.

I love the kids I teach in my advanced freshman classes. A group of these kids continues to meet in my room every morning an hour before school even though they are no longer in my class; in my room, they warm up their minds for the day ahead. There is a discernible culture among them which I can only describe as intellectual. Their restless energy for learning and their hunger for books challenges me every day to do more, be better, try new things in the quest to keep them learning and thinking. The irony that I was a terrible student who grew up to be a teacher of these students is not lost on me. Neither, however, is the fact that some of them would have looked down on me as a person for my academic failure if we had gone to school at the same time. Thus questions of humanity and ethics arise in these classes that are not found in other English classes; in other words, at times I feel compelled to somehow remind them that I got Ds in English, that I took Algebra twice, barely scraping by the second time around and even then passing because Mr. Hanks was thinking more about the pigs he farmed outside of school than the grades he gave.

One characteristic of some inventories of "gifted children" is their leadership potential. I take that rather seriously and look for those moments when our discussion can include such subjects as ethics and humanity since these students represent many of our future leaders. I don't want them thinking they live in a different world or are the equivalent of Plato's "gold race," who suffer themselves to share the world with the "bronze and silver" people. These discussions can be, in some schools, all the more important if the diversity in our society is not reflected in their advanced English class. These students honor me with their fine work and the ways they challenge me to learn and teach; as with *all* my students, they are an honor to teach and to know.

REFLECTION

Many English teachers have strong opinions about advanced classes or tracking because as students they were in these classes or were denied access to them. Write about why you think such classes are good and should be offered, including in your discussion what these classes should accomplish. After doing this, write it from the other perspective and explain why these classes should not exist or why anyone who wants should be able to enroll in them.

ACTIVITY

Send away to the College Board or visit their Web site. Request any available materials they offer, including a sample test. Now take this sample AP English exam and see how you fair.

RECOMMENDATION

There really is only one source for information about the AP courses and those that should lead up to them. You can write to them for materials or visit their extensive Web site:

College Board, 45 Columbus Avenue, New York, NY 10023-6992; Phone: (212) 713-8000
Web site: www.collegeboard.com

CHAPTER 21

ENGLISH TEACHERS AND THE LAW

The Law, he thinks, should be accessible to every man and at all times, but when he looks more closely at the doorkeeper in his furred robe, with his huge pointed noise and long, thick, Tartar beard, he decides that he had better wait until he gets permission to enter.

—**Franz Kafka, "Before the Law"**

*"That's some catch, that Catch-22," [Yossarian] observed.
"It's the best there is," Doc Daneeka agreed.*

Joseph Heller, *Catch-22*

Consider these scenarios, all of which have happened in my classroom or schools where I taught:

- A tall young man stands outside the English department office with a crossbow. "Have you seen Mr. Rodgers?" he asks calmly. "Noooo," I say. "We're giving How-to speeches in his class today and I wanted to store this somewhere," he proceeds to explain. I sigh.

- A freshman girl relates that her father is beating her for going out with a boy whom she loves. When I look at her legs in class I see open sores which she tells me at lunch are from a wire hanger.

- A sophomore boy steps up to the podium in his English class to give a speech. "Fuck!" "Shit!" "Goddamn it!" he screams. Then he calmly explains that today he will be discussing the importance of the First Amendment. (In a subsequent speech he will begin to explain how to make napalm; the fact that he was born in Vietnam makes this particular speech all the more disturbing.)

- A junior boy turns in a story in which he describes the mutilation of a dog the narrator allegedly loved; the details are so vivid, the story so disturbing, the teacher cannot finish reading it.

I face legal issues every day. My juniors who go read at the neighborhood elementary school as part of a service learning program must comply with a startling range of laws that govern those who visit elementary schools. These same students must get all sorts of permission papers signed to allow them to participate in this program; if they leave without first signing out, they place the school at risk should something happen. Every time I bring in a poem or article from some magazine, I face the possibility that it will offend a student who might, if insulted enough, file a complaint. When I open up the class for discussion, I run the risk that a student will say something that could lead to trouble: I've had fights in my class over hurled comments, calls from parents inquiring what we were doing discussing the Bible. I take risks in my class, but always provide a clear rationale as to why I am allowing a certain story or image into the room with my students. And if the subject is particularly mature—e.g., portions of Nathan McCall's memoir *Makes Me Want to Holler* contain extreme profanity and violence—I explain what I want to do and why, then ask students for their permission to read it or show it. I then follow the reading with a short survey on index cards about whether it is okay to continue reading a certain story or watching a particular film. As a parent and a teacher, I firmly believe that teachers must always be able to explain the rationale for teaching what they do in a class.

We often think more about how to better teach our students or what we should teach them than whether these two factors can get us in serious trouble. Some laws are obvious and familiar to us: every time you photocopy the poem of some poet you just love, you break the law. When the video guru in your department dubbed three copies of *Hamlet* so you could all show it at the same time, he broke the law; and so did you, each time you showed it to your students. You know these things. And you do them anyway; we all do. And we do it for the right reasons: we want to offer the kids the best we can.

While previous legal challenges focused on books and the occasional film, today's English teachers find themselves under growing legal scrutiny for books and films but also the Internet, writing assignments, racial issues and, most disturbingly, their teaching methods. It is, however, difficult to generalize about these concerns for they are not only regional but local: what is forbidden in the rural areas of Michigan is demanded in the elite communities of California or New England. What is common at one school in a district is considered inappropriate at another in the same district.

Thus when it comes to laws, English teachers should think about them on different levels: district "laws" (i.e., contractual, administrative biases or policies about books or the Internet), state education codes, state laws, and federal laws governing education. This chapter provides a basic overview of those different areas that apply to English teachers; for more information, you should consult your local union, your state NCTE affiliate, NCTE itself, or your state and federal legislators who are there to answer questions you might have.

There is no one way to navigate these shifting waters of public and political opinion; it is essential, however, that we try to explain why we do what we do or to anticipate challenges to our work. This habit of providing a rationale becomes all the more essential in light of the growing momentum of the Parents' Right Movement which seeks to create legislation empowering parents to decide what their students will and won't study within a prescribed curriculum.

I want to first outline the major areas of concern. Following these, I will list some frequently asked questions and try to provide some guidelines to help you resolve these concerns.

Journals. Journals are problematic for two reasons. First, they encourage students to reveal information about themselves or others that can legally bind you to report it. When the freshman girl I mentioned above reported that she was being beaten by her father, she knew I had to report that because I clearly tell them at the beginning of the year that I am required by law to alert the authorities to any abuse. Secondly, the writing prompts themselves can be challenged if they are found to invite personal, psychological revelations similar to those one might find on a psychological examination. This was one of the central arguments against the California Learning Assessment System (CLAS) test in California. Using California Education Code 60650, conservative religious groups and parents argued that the writing prompts on the test resembled those used on a psychological examination.

Movies. Some districts have official policies barring teachers from showing entire films, the argument being that to show a two-hour film cannot possibly be a productive use of instructional time. (For such rules we can thank those individuals, common to all schools, who offer a plug-and-play curriculum.) Other districts restrict teachers from showing any film with even a PG-13 rating; most have restrictions against R-rated films. Legally, it does not matter that Kenneth Brannaugh's *Hamlet* is rated R and that everyone in your class is 17 or older. (This is not to say you shouldn't show it; just beware and know your school's or district's policy.)

Skits/performances. The main concern here is props. Nearly all schools now have strict rules against bringing anything to school that resembles a weapon. This means no cheap plastic or hastily nailed-together swords, and certainly no guns, however un-gunlike they look. This law would, of course, extend to crossbows, also.

Speeches. When I was in high school we all looked on in disbelief as Howard Loftis began his how-to speech by calmly turning over a chair, then carefully removing a condom from its wrapper before methodically applying it to the chair leg. After that incident, all speech topics had to be approved. Speech topics have given me particular trouble, though mostly when I was a new teacher and I did not understand the range of my authority.

Journalism. Many English teachers serve double-duty as the advisor to the school newspaper. Whether this is a class or after-school obligation, the responsibilities are enormous. I did it for one year while the regular advisor was away on sabbatical. I could not believe the range of complaints we received nor the ferocious emotions attached to them. The primary legal issues involve censorship—can the principal kill a story or dictate content in the paper?—and misrepresenting the truth in an article. Though the Hazelwood decision, which protects newspaper advisors from administrative intervention, exists to support journalism advisors, few teachers want the kind of combative relationship with their principal or school boards that the Hazelwood decision would cause if taken to the limit.

Yearbook. Many English teachers also end up in charge of the school's yearbook; some lucky folks even do it in addition to the newspaper. Your primary area of concern here is the accuracy of information and the protection of character. Trouble with yearbooks often stems from art or photos which escaped the advisor's careful eye; another source of such trouble is mistakes made by the publisher. It is important to keep a record of your pages before you send them off to the publisher so you can show what you sent and what they created. This was especially important to one teacher whose homecoming page came back with "Homecomnig" in large letters over the homecoming king and queen, who were both African American. The ensuing attack left the adviser reeling but safe because she could show the mistake was not hers. Another factor in her successful defense was that she had an administrator clearly assigned to the yearbook; this administrator's role was to scan the book for possible trouble and support her should any arise.

Drama. In the late 1990s, an award-winning drama teacher in the Southwest lost her job over the production of a play that was deemed too controversial. In this domain there are several relevant concerns: choice of script, how you perform it, and all the attendant legalities with kids being on campus after hours, during which time they might also be handling power tools and other equipment as part of the crew. Some states now have laws governing those from the community who work on the school site as consultants or volunteers. Find out what your state and local laws say.

Reading materials. No other aspect of the English curriculum is so regularly challenged as what we have students read. People challenge reading material for any number of reasons: language, characterization, religion, culture, sex, racism. We had a formal complaint against *I Know Why the Caged Bird Sings* because of the scene in which the girl does a cartwheel and reveals she has no underwear on. I've had challenges to Amy Tan's *Kitchen God's Wife* because of Wen Fu's repeated sexual violence to his wife, Native American folktales, *Jasmine*, and, of course, *Catcher in the Rye*.

Internet. The obvious legal issue involving the Internet is the fear of what kids will see in Cyberland or, in some cases, what they will do (e.g., find and use stolen credit card numbers). All schools have—or should—Acceptable Use Policies that govern students' access to and use of the Internet. Some parents prohibit their children from using it period and extend this prohibition to the school site.

Copyright. Legally, you cannot photocopy any text and use it in your classroom unless you have the author's permission or it is at least 75 years old, in which case it is considered public domain. The Internet further complicates this issue in the mind of some: "Hey, I found it on the Internet," they say, as if that means it is in the public domain and can then be copied off and used. The same rules apply to film and television media. "Fair use" was introduced some years ago for teachers; according to this principle, teachers can record a show off the television for classroom use so long as it is used and erased within about two weeks of recording.

Special education. Students with special needs are entitled to those adaptations that will help them succeed within their current program. These entitlements and needs are articulated in the student's Individual Educational Program (IEP). It is important for the teacher to know what services or other accommodations the student is entitled to so they don't come into conflict with these obligations.

Instructional practices. In California and other states, curriculum and instructional methods are being legislated, something we have not previously seen. It is hard to generalize what these laws are; it is important, however, to be aware of such laws if they exist in your state, and to know what they mean to the teacher.

Absences. Districts and states have policies and laws about student attendance and the teacher's obligation to the student. In the English class, a student out for prolonged absences through illness or other officially excused reasons (two weeks in Taiwan to visit ailing grandfathers, three weeks for the national tennis championships, four weeks for drug rehabilitation treatment) misses all the discussions and daily writing that take place in your class. Yet we are legally obligated in certain ways to accommodate these exceptions and, as I can attest, if you try to oppose them, you will find yourself under some pressure to change your mind as, generally speaking, you lack any legal argument.

Grading. English as a subject can be sometimes difficult to grade; so many assignments seem to others only vague, impressionistic accountings that can surely be argued, negotiated, especially when it comes to final grades that can affect college admissions. You need a record keeping system that will stand up under administrative scrutiny if your grades of student work are questioned. (See Chapter 11 for more information.)

Public disclosure. Trouble can arise if you use the classroom as a public forum for any issues such as religion, politics, or personal grievances. Especially troublesome examples of this constraint include discussing union business in the classroom or, in some cases, using an administrative memorandum in the classroom to illustrate bad writing. Gay and lesbian teachers face a particularly personal and professional dilemma in this area. If a teacher chooses to tell their students that they are gay or lesbian they need to know the laws—however much they might disagree with them—in their district or state as they pertain to such information.

Bible/religion. The Bible is, according to such major literary scholars as Harold Bloom, the basis of all western literature and art. The nature of the English class has changed considerably, however; literary history and criticism are increasingly marginalized, and the students themselves represent a cultural and religious diversity that demands sensitivity as never before. Some districts or schools require a Bible as Literature unit; others do not require it, but their AP teachers, for example, feel compelled to include such a unit to prepare students for the AP test. It is essential that teachers provide, as prologue to the unit of study, a clear rationale for the study of the Bible in the class, particularly if the class includes students of other, non-Christian faiths.

Assessment. Students, if never prepared for a test whose scores could effect their future, have grounds for a formal complaint. If, for example, a district writing competency test expects students to be able to write an argumentative essay in order to graduate, and a teacher never prepares the students who then do not graduate, that teacher could be considered negligent.

Student conferences. I have never had cause to worry about conferring with students in or outside of class. As teachers, however, we must recognize that any time we meet with students individually outside of class we are taking a risk and must be cautious. This caution is especially necessary among male teachers. To pretend these considerations are inappropriate or do not apply to you is to be naive and reckless.

Classroom libraries. I have more than five hundred books in my classroom and the number always grows as kids bring in new donations or I find others at garage sales. Some books would cost people their jobs in more conservative regions. I have read nearly all of them and know most of the others from a distance. If I see a girl reach for *Bastard out of Carolina*, a book students really love, I let her know that it is a strong story, and suggest that if her parents would object to her reading such a story she should choose another.

Plagiarism/cheating. It happens more all the time. Go to www.schoolsucks.com and download a paper on the symbolism in any novel you teach. Copy and paste any portion of any CD-ROM encyclopedia or Cliffs Notes into a paper and call the words your own. If you are the kind of teacher who gives the same assignments on the same days each year, you should not be surprised when kids start selling their notes and tests to incoming students who then use them to cheat in your class. The one cautionary note I offer has to do with cultural differences. In some countries, most notably those in Central and South America, students' scholarship is apparently measured by the quality of the authors they use in their own paper; thus they often use passages without citing them and are told this is not only acceptable but good so long as the words they "borrow" are the best. Furthermore, when it comes to "cheating," many students from these same cultures collaborate together on homework assignments, doing the work together and thus arriving at the same answers. Punish cheaters; work with the others who are guilty only of trying to do their best for your class.

Questions About the Law

Here are some practical responses to questions you might have at some point in time. Keep in mind that answers may well vary depending on your district or state.

Can I have students buy their own books for class? You can if you obtain their parents' permission. You should also consult your department chair and/or administrators so they know. I know teachers who do not do this; I support their efforts to do what they feel they must to get the best possible books in kids' hands.

What should I do if a book I am teaching is challenged? First, talk with the parents—or the student—and listen to what they have to say. If you don't listen you will be dismissed as an elitist who ignores the views of the parents and their children. If the challenge is organized and aggressive, seek administrative support immediately and contact NCTE. NCTE, along with such organizations as People for the American Way (PFAW), offers immediate support to teachers as the situation requires. You also need to immediately develop for yourself—and the parties involved—a clear rationale for the use of the book in its instructional context. Several options are available to reasonable, respectful people in these difficult situations: offer an alternative book that meets the same ends (e.g., Russell Baker's *Growing Up* in place of *Catcher in the Rye*); suggest that the parent read the book along with their child so as to share with them their concerns about the issues the text brings up. This last option is particularly positive as teenagers and parents have trouble communicating anyway during these years; the book offers the chance to talk about a range of important subjects without threatening the student. I've had several wonderful successes with this option. If lawyers get involved, stop everything, consult your union, school district, NCTE, and PFAW or the ACLU. Abundant resources are available to help you out in such circumstances.

Can I require students to write their papers on the computer? Of course, so long as they have reasonable access to computers at school.

What should I do to avoid problems using the Internet in my classroom? Ideally, your school has something like an "Internet driver's license" that grants the student privileges once they have completed an orientation; the license and all its on-line privileges can then be immediately revoked at the first instance of any transgression. Somewhere—in your class or the computer lab—there must be a Acceptable Use Agreement signed by both parents and students; this protects you in the event that the student breaks the law.

Given the possible problems that could arise, should I have an in class library of high interest books for students? Absolutely. Nothing does more to increase the likelihood that students will read than the presence of books that students or the teacher can recommend to students.

If my district curriculum requires me to teach a book that I find problematic (e.g., Huckleberry Finn), *do I have to teach it?* This is a difficult question and should be negotiated locally. Teachers should be aware, however, that if they defy the school board-approved curriculum they are potentially in violation of their contract and could be subject to certain consequences. I would add that teachers who speak out against the books they teach—I know some who openly confess to their students that they can't stand Shakespeare—undermine their own credibility (and the profession) in the eyes of the students.

Can I teach a book or story in my class if it is not on the district-approved curriculum list? Know your district, know your community. Many teachers do it, especially if they are established and trusted by the parents whose permission should be obtained since you are asking them to buy the books you want to teach.

Can a student legally refuse to read a book, watch a film, or write about a topic, or use the Internet if assigned? Yes. If students have a sound rationale and are willing to satisfy the assignment by some alternative route, they are within their rights to refuse, though it is sometimes helpful to point out, for example, the extent to which they might end up singled out from the rest of the class by reading a different book from everyone else.

What should I bring with me to a meeting with administrators, parents, or community members about a text, grade, or topic? Bring the materials—book, story, grades, assignment, attendance sheets—and an outline of your rationale for choosing the work. Include all handouts that might help to further illustrate why and how you were using the materials in class.

REFLECTION

If you have encountered any of the situations mentioned in this chapter, discuss what happened, why, and how it resolved itself. Assuming you have some distance from the event, consider how else you might have handled it. What did you learn from the experience? If you have not encountered any of these situations, write about how the information in this chapter made you feel about some of the things you do. Will you do anything differently now? What would that be? Why will you make that change?

ACTIVITY

Write down your policy for the following: journals, book selection, and speech topics. Your policies should be succinct but clear. Next time you create a syllabus, consider including these in it. An alternative activity could be to visit the People for the American Way Web site.

RECOMMENDATIONS

Literacy at the Crossroads: Crucial Talk About Reading, Writing, and Other Teaching Dilemmas. Regie Routman (Heinemann 1996). Written in response to events in the early 1990s when attacks on whole language and other methods reached a crisis in some states, this book offers a succinct, insightful set of observations and strategies for responding to different challenges to literacy education. Routman's book reads quickly and is designed for easy reference for the teacher who needs to refer to something fast that they can trust.

Preserving Intellectual Freedom: Fighting Censorship in Our Schools. Jean E. Brown, ed. (NCTE 1994). Jean Brown has been a featured speaker at NCTE's Political Action forum for years, addressing the issues of censorship in a professional manner. This is the one book to get if you need an overview on specific aspects of intellectual freedom.

CHAPTER 22

DEAR NEW TEACHER

It is a journey into the unknown where often you're only conscious of, and what's only visible for you is, that step right in front of you. But you take it and you hope. And when you look up you're reached San Francisco.

Gloria Naylor

The Courage to Teach: The English Teacher's Role

It is a courageous act to teach high school English. I say "courageous" because when you become an English teacher you take on tremendous responsibilities, some you may not realize at the time. Have you ever noticed, after people say "Oh, an English teacher, I'd better watch my grammar around you!" that they just as often say their most influential teacher was also an English teacher, sometimes even the same one who turned them into a lover of language and literature? After thinking about this for some time, I've concluded that we handle the culture's stories and get students to think about their own and how they want those stories to unfold. As psychologist Howard Gardner (1995) found, the most common attribute of powerful leaders is their ability to use stories to unify or motivate people, to make people want to be a part of that story by making it come true. I bring this up because, at our best, that is what we do in our classes: we lead our students.

People often fear English teachers because we have so much power. What kind of power? We have the power, along with our colleagues from other disciplines, to help our students see and know things about themselves and the world around them. We have the power to invest students with the ability to speak and write so well they can persuade people to do things that would not have otherwise occurred to them. And we have the opportunity to challenge them to think with a greater humanity to the extent that we build our class on the foundations of stories and the chance to talk with people about these and their own stories.

If we didn't have power, if we weren't considered dangerous, society would leave us alone, would leave books alone, would leave schools to do as they pleased. I've heard people say they don't want their sons or daughters taught "to think." I've heard people say students should not read *Huckleberry Finn* for every possible reason. And any book that has been suggested in its place has itself been dismissed by another group who thought that book was too dangerous for other or similar reasons. That's why teaching English in American public schools is so exciting: you live at the crossroads of what novelist Ralph Ellison called "the democratic experiment." It can be difficult to teach in the petri dish of public opinion and professional expectations.

The Good, the Bad, and the Cynical: Your Colleagues

So many new teachers arrive at the schools ready and willing only to be greeted by the cynicism of the inevitable teacher who feels somehow obligated to help the new teacher out. When I began my student teaching, I was entirely unprepared for the vast gulf that lay between teachers at this nationally recognized school. Some of the teachers were obvious masters of their craft, people who found a deep satisfaction in their work and in the progress of their students; thankfully, these people were my teachers and it is their example that I have always tried to live up to. But others moved through the office like fog. One man put up 180 Post-Its with 1–180 on them; each day he ceremonially took one down to signal to himself and those who watched that he was that much closer to ending the year. Another man, Henry, shuffled into the office each morning and announced his arrival by dropping his books onto his desk and ritually sighing "Shit. Another day." While out to dinner one night with other teachers, I got a fortune cookie that said "It's not too late to turn back." Henry laughed a good one at that and happily urged me to heed its advice and get out while I could.

Teachers' Teachers: On Mentors and Learning

The problem was that I loved teaching. Even when I failed miserably, when my Nobel Prize-winning lesson plan disintegrated before my eyes, I only found it exciting to figure out what went wrong, what I could do next time to make that great idea work the way I had imagined it. Perhaps this is where my years as a tennis player came in handy: if I could hit five hundred backhands down the line to master a shot, I could surely work harder to "get it right" the next time I tried to teach a poem or a story.

And I had a lot to learn. I didn't get a degree in English, something I've always had a bit of a chip on my shoulder about when talking with some colleagues. "Oh, doesn't that remind you of that scene in Chaucer, Jim?" I don't know, Frances! It might if I had read it. "Jim, do you think I should use that play *J.B.* with my senior AP students; it would go so well with our unit on biblical literature." Gosh, Jack, aside from the fact that those are my initials I don't know what you are talking about. I did, however, have a degree in psychology with an emphasis on learning. This helped me a great deal; how can you be a good teacher if you don't know anything about how we learn, how the mind works, how we think? More important than all the degrees and courses, however, were the mentors.

My mentors came in two forms: people and books. Early on I realized that mentors could show me what was possible and that it was possible. My master teacher, Pat Hanlon, was passionately involved in technology long before most teachers even had their first computer. She didn't teach me about computers or programs; I learned that on my own. What she taught me was much more crucial: she was willing to learn in the presence of her students, to invite them along on her own journey and, by modeling for them, invite them to strike out on their own. She was willing to make mistakes in front of her students and me. What we saw then was someone whom we all respected, coping with the complexity of experience, with what she always referred to as "the difference between what should be and what is." Because she always pushed herself to do better, to learn more, to try it from a different angle, her students and I were willing to do the same.

My mentors have always been those who found the work, despite all its demands, worthy, rich, exciting. Carol Jago and Bill Clawson, two of my most important teachers, always asked me what I was reading, asked me if I had read that week's *New Yorker* or that month's *Harper's*; they kept asking me until I said I had read them, that I did know that poet, that novel. In this way these two mentored me into becoming a reader, something that forever changed my teaching life, for while we complain of all the demands of the work, we forget sometimes why we wanted to be English teachers in the first place: we love words and what they can do. In short, as my friend Peter Briggs says, people find time to do what is important to them.

While many people have been my teachers, have helped me develop the ideas or abilities reflected in this book, no one has taught me more than my students. I don't know how someone can be a successful teacher if they aren't willing to learn what students have to teach you about learning, adolescence, society, schooling. This doesn't mean I try to be one of the kids; nor does it mean I try to be their "friend." Instead I try to be all those things they need me to be, and to learn from them how to recognize what they need at any particular time. English classes are emotional places, after all. I've read poems that have sent students running from the room crying for reasons I did not know. I've had students criticize me for being too mean or critical when what they needed was encouragement and support. But they always know I care about them as people and their future success. This mutual trust and respect enables them to work with me to create a class we can all find meaningful and productive.

Examining Your Roots: Reflecting on the Student You Were

It is helpful to reflect on what kind of student you were—and why. Were you an honors student who just loved school and did all your homework? Or were you one of those kids who refused to read the required books for your English classes but devoured books on your own? Maybe you were like me and hardly read at all and generally did not find school engaging. Such personal examinations are important as they probably shape your own expectations and values when it comes to school. One student teacher I worked with, who had been an honors student, expressed total shock and disappointment when no one in her college prep junior class read the assigned (forty-five-page!) introduction to Arthur Miller's *The Crucible*. It just never occurred to her that her students might not find it as fascinating as she did. But she learned, she changed, and, ultimately, she succeeded; this was in large part because she was willing to let her students teach her what she needed to know about teaching by telling her what they needed to know, what they needed help doing.

Isolation: The Blessing and the Curse

These relationships with students and supportive colleagues are the primary defense against the English teacher's biggest threat: isolation. Some of us teach at campuses the size of small towns. All of us teach at schools that ask more of us than we often feel we have time for, a feeling that contributes to the sense of isolation since we are always on our way to or from somewhere and never too far from sitting down by ourselves (mostly) to plan lessons or grade papers. Through discussion groups, after school coffees with cherished colleagues, and on-line conversations with teachers, however, I have never felt disconnected. Far from it: the work we do connects me to a tradition much larger than myself and which I am proud to be a part of the longer I teach. The inherent isolation, however, can also provide a healthy defense against doing more than you should at times; sometimes we just need to close the door and enjoy a quiet lunch with ourselves while reading the paper or a magazine.

The other mentors I have yet to discuss are the books I've read and the act of reflecting in general. Books about teaching are conversations with others in my field that keep me from feeling alone. I rarely ever read entire books, at least not at a sitting. More than likely you are reading this book in snippets, taking what you need from it as you need it or as it is assigned by a professor. So it is that I picked up James Moffett's *Teaching the Universe of Discourse* early on and "talked with" Moffett, among others, about what I was supposed to be doing in my classes. Later on, when I grew to be more familiar with the books out there, I might pick up Janet Allen's *It's Never Too Late* as a way of just thinking about what was going on with reading in my classes. Perhaps most importantly, however, I never limit myself to books about teaching or education. My friend Carol Jago told me once that Oliver Sacks's *Seeing Voices* taught her more about language than any other book she had read. So I, too, went to this book about the world of the deaf and soon realized how much other disciplines had to teach me about my own. After that I was always looking for the "must read" books in other disciplines—art, science, math, history—so I could learn from them but also, just as important, refer to them in my classes so kids saw that writing came in all forms about all subjects.

Strategies for Survival and Success

At this point there are several things to emphasize, all of which can make a profound difference in your daily teaching life by helping you feel less isolated.

- Find colleagues you immediately recognize as supportive and committed to the habits outlined below.
- Subscribe to at least one professional journal (which should offer a student teacher rate). Depending on what you teach and your particular needs, journals offer guidance and insight into different realms of teaching. The primary journal for English teachers is *English Journal* which is published by the National Council of Teachers of English (NCTE). You should also look into your state or local affiliate English teachers organization to see what help they offer. In California, for example, the California Association of Teachers of English publishes an incredible professional journal (*California English*); local affiliates such as the Greater San Diego County Teachers of English provide readings, coffees, workshops, and books such as their popular *Promising Practices*.
- Follow Donald Murray's advice: "you cannot be a good teacher unless you are reading books, going to the movies, spending time alone, and maintaining a life."
- Enter into a conversation about teaching: do this through one of many on-line "communities" such as NCTE-Talk, joining or starting a bookgroup or discussion group with other (new) teachers where you go to a café once a week to talk about teaching or what you are reading. Look around for a Critical Friends Group, a teacher study group designed to provide a supportive environment for reflecting on practice.
- Read different books on teaching. These help you place yourself in the larger tradition of teaching and realize that no problems are new. These books allow an informal, internal conversation to take place between you and the author, the profession, the book and its ideas. Many books, such as Ruth Vinz's excellent *Composing a Teaching Life* (1996) or Leila Christenbury's *Making the Journey: Being and Becoming a Teacher of English Language Arts* (1994), ask you to come to a better understanding of what you are doing and thinking by reflecting on your practice. This leads me to my last and most important suggestion: keep a journal.

Rough-Draft Teaching: Revision Through Reflection

We don't expect kids—or even ourselves—to write perfect, finished drafts when they sit down to write. Why then should you demand of yourself the equivalent of a finished draft when it comes to teaching? The journal is a place for exploration, thinking, pre-writing, drafting. It is a place to think about things. Ruth Vinz (1996) identifies three distinct types of reflection that can help you improve:

- retrospective
- introspective
- prospective

Vinz characterizes *retrospective* as thinking back on a lesson, a moment, a unit and remembering and examining what happened. This looking backward from the relative safety of the present allows you the critical distance you need to then get *introspective*. The teachers Vinz studied began to look within themselves to understand what happened, why it happened, what they really thought or felt about it. Teacher Sam Intrator created a one-page log sheet for himself that he used at each day's end to provide the following information and reflect on it before returning the next day:

- what I did
- what worked
- what went awry
- what to do next time

This habit of reflection is particularly helpful in the event that you have an unsupportive master teacher or department; like Anne Frank's "Kitty" (the name she called her journal), your journal is an ear that will always listen; the more you write and reflect, the more you will listen—to yourself, to your experiences, to your heart and intelligence. Through this re-vision process, in which you fine tune or change your "vision" of what you are doing, you arrive at sequentially better drafts of your class.

This last phase is what Vinz calls *prospective*. In this phase, the reflective teacher begins to speculate about what would happen if they taught the same material a different way. What if I had them do that in groups—would the same thing have happened? What if I showed them part of the film version first? In this way the teacher begins to use their insights from the introspection and retrospection to improve their teaching; they see the class as a dynamic place and give themselves permission to learn what they must to be a better teacher. According to the Continuum of Performance (see Chapter 2), such a teacher is moving away from insecure and toward confident, fluent. You begin to feel, at least in this domain, more confident and can move on to learn other tasks better. You learn to see your mistakes as rungs on the ladder that leads to mastery instead of the ropes by which you dream your students will hang you.

During these early years you are teaching yourself to be the teacher you will become and, on some days, are. This is important: if you don't establish from the outset the habit of reading for your own pleasure and learning, it is unlikely you ever will. If you don't establish the habit of reflection, you are not likely to pick it up later. You must insist, from the beginning, on a life of your own. Nothing enriches my teaching and further establishes my credibility with my students more than my own reading; I make reference to what I read, to the fact that I read, at every opportunity. And sometimes, doing less "for your students" can translate into better learning for them as illustrated in this moment:

> Late one afternoon [my department chair] found me in the school library looking up background information on Hawthorne. . . . 'Who needs practice looking up the author's background? You or the kids? Who should be doing this work? Who needs practice presenting information in front of a group? You already know how to gather, synthesize, and present material. Your students don't. Make them do the work. You work too hard.' Although I knew Mr. Culley was right, I found it difficult to turn over to my students the responsibility for learning (Metzger 1996).

Available Companions: Who Can Help You?

While you are busy trying to answer that crucial question—what will we do in my American Lit class—you should also ask yourself who can help you do these things. Teaching can be so isolating, particularly if you are new or you don't have a room to call home during the day. One year, in about my eighth year of teaching, I ended up teaching in five different classrooms for a semester. I wandered the halls with my cart, lonesome, disconnected, losing my handouts and papers between classrooms, showing up late, too rushed to feel the calm assurance I was used to. A brief list of allies should—though, unfortunately does not always—include the following people whose job specifically requires them to help you:

- a teacher in your department who is willing to mentor you
- a colleague from a different department
- counselors
- parents
- service learning coordinator
- students
- the administrator in charge of curriculum and instruction
- the custodians
- the department chair
- the principal
- the school librarian
- your master teacher
- your university supervisor

Most important is to keep asking questions, to keep seeing in the work the challenges it offers. Nothing amazes me more than the way teachers in May, so exhausted and ready for summer, already begin making notes about how they want to do things differently next year. Already they are revising their class, thinking about what they want to read that summer to learn more for the next year. Some say things like "I can't wait to get back in September to try this out," or to do it differently. In the meantime, here are some questions I have asked different student teachers I have worked with in the last few years, and which invite us all to think about not just what we do but how and why we do it:

- If writers want their readers to end a story or essay with some particular feeling or idea, what do you want your students to walk out of your classroom thinking and feeling about what happened in there?

- How do you want them to think of you?
- What purpose does your class serve?
- What do you want your students to know and be able to do when they leave your class at semester's/year's end in the areas of reading, writing, speaking, listening, and thinking?
- What drives your class?

Endnote: English Matters

Teaching English has always been a privilege for me. As I write this, school has just finished up and my head still swims with the images of what my students did on their different culminating projects, what they said in their portfolio cover letters where they reflected on the year. I feel very humbled by the achievement of my students when I consider all they learned. As I watched my students stand up in class and speak at length about different topics, as I watched them stand to speak at the funeral of one of my students, and as I watched former students of mine stand to speak at graduation, I was reminded again and again how important our work is. If you find yourself surrounded by people who do not appreciate this, seek your companions in other departments or on-line. Spend your days and the coming years with colleagues who feel the pride we should all feel for helping all our students tell their story even as we are writing and revising our own in classrooms across America.

REFLECTION

Refer to the Life Graph Activity described below. After completing your graph, choose one positive and one negative event, then write about what happened on those occasions. Do you see it differently now from the distance of time? What made it so bad or good at that time?

ACTIVITY

Refer to Chapter 9 to find the directions for the Life Graph. In short, chart out your year's teaching events, dividing them into positive and negative by degrees. Label the events specifically (e.g., –5 for when Bill Robinson canceled the class because I froze up in front of the class the first time I taught) so you can easily refer to them. Try to have as many events as you can and literally graph them out so you see the pattern of your days.

RECOMMENDATION

It's Never Too Late. Janet Allen (Heinemann 1995). Offers a rich blend of personal reflection on her beginnings as a teacher and shows what we can accomplish with even the most reluctant students. In addition to the personal, Allen delivers plenty of the practical to help any teacher not just survive but succeed.

CHAPTER 23

GETTING A JOB TEACHING ENGLISH

You have to remember that nobody ever wants a new writer. You have to create your own demand.

—Doris Lessing

If you seek well, you will find.

—Greek proverb

"How would you distinguish the difference between accountability and responsibility, Jim?" This is a question from my first job interview. I sat in an antiseptic district office, cornered by two muscular administrators in crisp white shirts and power ties. They each had mustaches. It was a Good Cop–Bad Cop situation: one guy asked me these curveball questions (like the one above) and the other would lob me curricular questions. Within ten minutes, though desperate to get my first job, I realized that I could not work in this district. Never mind that I would have had to commute almost ninety minutes to get to work each day.

Interviewing is difficult. I know some teachers who have walked into interviews to find not just administrators and a department chair, but the entire English department. Such interviews were particularly difficult since the teachers knew each of the interviewers had their own biases: grammar, classroom management, writing, classics, poetry. How to answer honestly but effectively? Some of these interviews were followed by subsequent requests to teach an actual class of students; a friend of mine had to read *A Separate Peace* in one night after they called him at 8:00 P.M. to tell him what to be ready to teach!

I have interviewed many teachers and administrators for jobs at all levels, and have suggestions you might find helpful.

Understand the role English plays in the school.   Many parents feel that a school is only as strong as its English department. This is particularly true in today's competitive society and this era of anxiety about students' reading abilities. Another fact to keep in mind: English is always the largest department in the school since all students take English for four years. Most administrators have a bias as to the importance of English teachers given the different roles they often play in a school, and the centrality of reading and writing in all other domains.

Know the school's particular situation.   If it is the second week of the school year, for example, the situation is clear: they need someone desperately to fill those few classes they have. If it is May, they know they have a definite opening and are able to take the time to find the best person; if they don't find someone in this round, they can re-post the position. Thus interviews that take place between May and August are the most competitive and demand careful planning. Call the school in advance of the interview to get certain information to help you prepare—the classes you would be teaching and a copy of the school's curriculum guide. Stop by the school and pick up copies of current or past school newspapers to get a sense of the school's culture. Also, consider calling the head of the English Department to ask them a few questions: Why do you have this opening? How many of your kids go to four-year colleges? Are teachers encouraged to collaborate with each other within or between departments?

Send an excellent, one-page résumé.   When I need to hire a teacher I typically get a stack of résumés and slash through them, looking at each one for an average of about thirty seconds. I separate out a small pile of the most impressive and "file" the others in the recycling bin. An effective résumé is one I can glimpse and get the information from immediately; I primarily do this by reading down the left margin where your previous positions are listed. Figure 23.1 is an example of the format that I find most helpful and effective.

While most districts require you to send a résumé and application to the district office, it often comes down to the department chair to do the interview as it is their department you will be joining. Send them a cover letter and your résumé, too—even if they tell you not to. Show them how well you write; you are an English teacher, after all, and everything you do should convey your mastery of writing and speaking. Make your résumé look very professional—not flashy or gaudy with clip art. In today's world, *professional* translates to mean a résumé and cover letter both of which are nicely formatted, using a computer and printed on a laser printer. Everything you do should convey your familiarity with and mastery of technology.

Send a cover letter with your résumé and keep in touch.   When I began to look for my second job—to get closer to home—I sent out letters long before the schools knew they had a position. The point was to get my name out there and in their minds. So I sent the following letter to all the department chairs at schools where I wanted to teach. Here's the first one, which I sent to them in October:

Dear Burlingame High School:

The school year is only just getting to its feet. So you ask yourself why this young teacher is already inquiring about jobs for next year. I live in San Francisco, and that is where I will stay because we have the good fortune to have a house here. I have taught now for three years in the English department at Castro Valley High School, which has twice been awarded the National Exemplary School Award. During my tenure at Castro Valley, I have distinguished myself through my teaching and contributions to the surrounding East Bay community.

I have included my résumé and a list of my publications as evidence of my commitment to the English profession. I am young and still have much to learn; I am also committed and have much to offer. Let me emphasize that there is absolutely no discontent nor desperation that urges me to leave Castro Valley High School. I like it there and am genuinely proud to be a member of the faculty. I simply wish to get closer to home and to bring to my own community the efforts and contributions that I have given to others. Please consider me should any positions become available for the next school year.

Sincerely,
Jim Burke

Christopher Evans

1422 18th Street • Sacramento, CA 95864 • (916)387.8923 • cevans@aol.com

EDUCATION	**San Francisco State University**
Credential	• Professional Single Subject credentials in English and Psychology, 1995
Certificate	• Certificate in the Teaching of Written Composition, 1994
MA	• Secondary Education, San Francisco State University, 1995
BA	**University of California**, Santa Barbara, 1992
	• Developmental Psychology

TEACHING EXPERIENCE

English Teacher   Rio Americano High School, 1997—present
- Teach freshman Honors and senior English classes full-time
- Chair English Department
- Advise literary and assorted other clubs
- Awarded several grants to create and expand use of technology in the curriculum

English Teacher   John F. Kennedy High School, 195-97
- Designed and implemented team-taught Basic English class for At-Risk Freshman
- Worked with the local business community to develop educational opportunities
- Chaired the Community Involvement Task Force for school restructuring program, 1991-92

Teacher   Deveureux Foundation, 1990-93
- Taught developmentally disabled students in local Arabic dialect
- Established and developed comprehensive curriculum for new school for learning disabled

AWARDS
- Awarded the Sacramento Business and Education Learning Links (BELL) "Bell Ringer Award," May 1991, for efforts to incorporate classroom/students into the community and visa versa.
- Included in Who's Who in American Education, 1997
- Selected to participate in the RJR Nabisco Education Foundation China Breaker Conference, 1997
- National Endowment for the Humanities Fellow, 1996
- National Endowment for the Humanities Fellow, 1999

WRITING EXPERIENCE
- see attached writing credits

POSTS HELD
- Board Member, Sacramento Council of Teachers of English (CATE), 1995-1997
- Creator/Moderator of CATENet, an electronic roundtable linking hundreds of top leaders in English education in California and US via internet 1997-present

RELEVANT SKILLS
- Familiar with all internet and technological tools
- Advanced strategic planning skills
- Write grants

Figure 23.1   *Sample résumé*

This letter yielded a response and encouraging words but no offer. So a few months later I sent them this letter:

Dear Burlingame High School:

Some measure of time has passed since I last wrote you inquiring about jobs at your school. Certainly the educational terrain has grown only more rocky in the months following my query. These difficulties naturally make the hunt more challenging, the desirable job a more elusive prey.

My own situation at Castro Valley High School remains both stable and satisfying; thus I reiterate my previous letter's emphasis that I am not leaving for reasons of dissatisfaction or disfavor. I merely want to work closer to my own home and my own community.

I am enclosing my latest column from *California English*, the bimonthly publication of the California Association of Teachers of English. You will also find an article of mine from the latest *English Journal* which details my work with remedial students at Castro Valley High School. The articles show two things I bring to any school and the students I work with: commitment and professional understanding of those ideas current in English education.

Please contact me if you have any need for qualified, committed teachers at your school. I am distributing my résumé only to those schools where I would be happy to work. I look forward to hearing from you when you have more insight into your school's needs for the coming year.

Sincerely,
Jim Burke

When, a few months later, I learned through a friend that they had an opening—always let people know you are looking so they can look for you, too—I was ready to move and sent the following letter which ultimately got me the interview and, subsequently, the job. Here is the last letter:

Dear Burlingame High School:

Schools are so busy entering into the homestretch of this school year that it hardly seems feasible to consider looking for new teachers for next year. Yet the fact is that your district has many teachers retiring and others taking year-long leaves, so you are ready to look and interview.

I have written on several occasions already to express my interest in teaching at your school next year. Today I am writing only a brief letter to remind you of my existence and to announce that Carol Murphy at your district office has placed my application into the file for active consideration. Thus when you begin in the weeks ahead to interview people to teach high school English—and related areas, including Psychology—please consider me.

Thank you for your time and attention. I hope to hear from you soon.

Sincerely,
Jim Burke

Bring (or send) the interview committee a portfolio.   Even if you are looking for your first job, you have student taught. If you taught well enough you should have at least *some* assignments you can feel proud enough to present. The portfolio impresses people by showing them that you are a professional, reflective, organized, and competent teacher.

Do not submit originals in your portfolio as you might need them later. Instead, go to a copy center and get them professionally reproduced on nice paper (clean white so it's easy to read) and bound with a nice cover page that includes all the information necessary to contact you. If you have enough pages, have them put nice laser-printed dividers ("Lesson Plans," "Student Work," "Classroom Policies") to help the reader easily navigate through your portfolio. Remember that little things often say more than you suspect: e.g., by including your e-mail address on the cover you show that you are computer savvy, something that might immediately set you apart from all the others who *might* be on-line but didn't include their addresses. Your portfolio should include:

- a cover page with all contact information (including fax, e-mail, and URL if available)
- your current résumé on nice paper
- a list of any publications or projects that specifically suggest distinction within the English profession
- any copies of articles or other work you have written
- a sample handout from your classroom that gives an example of you working with writing

- a student sample that shows what you got them to do in response to the handout on writing
- a sample handout from your classroom that gives an example of how you teach reading and literature
- a student sample that shows what they did in response to your reading assignments
- letters of recommendation from your university, colleagues, administrators, or students

As most universities depend on the master teacher at the schools to be the best teachers of their candidates, the letters of recommendations from your on-site master teachers are the most important. They are the ones who know how good you are or will be; their letters will signal if you are ready, often by saying that they would hire you themselves if they could.

The interview for what would be my first teaching assignment was scheduled for 4:45 P.M. on a Friday at the end of May. When I arrived at the office I was greeted by two other friends from my credential program applying for the same job. We acknowledged each other awkwardly. Soon I was shown into the principal's office where I found the principal, the English department chair, and another English teacher, all of whom were so obviously worn out that I immediately realized I had to be careful not to talk too long.

Their concerns were typical. The principal wanted to hear what I had to say about classroom discipline; she wanted to know what else I was willing to do besides teach English full-time; and she wanted to know why she should hire me above all others. These are standard questions and you should be prepared to answer each one of them. According to a guide created for teachers by Stanford University's career center, teachers are most frequently asked questions in the following areas (listed from most frequent to least):

- classroom management
- student teaching experience
- strengths
- teaching philosophy
- weaknesses
- what if . . . (hypothetical situations)
- future plans
- teaching style
- coaching interests
- college courses
- motivational theories
- lesson design
- employment history
- youth-related activities
- curriculum knowledge
- salary
- higher thinking skills/strategies
- college activities
- community activities
- GPA

My future department chair wanted to know what have become fairly standard questions for me when I interview candidates. Here are some of the questions you should be ready to answer:

- My first question is *always*: What are you reading these days? What have you read in the last six months? What is the best book you've read in the last year? If they answer, "I just haven't had time" or "I just mostly read mysteries," the interview is, in my mind, over though, of course, we must follow through. The department head's job is to hire the best teacher they can find. How can I expect you to challenge kids if you don't challenge yourself?
- Tell me about writing in your class: What do you do? How much do kids write in a week? How do you have them work with that writing to improve their abilities in this area?
- What is a book you've taught successfully? Tell me what you did and why you consider this lesson/unit so successful.
- How do you help students improve their reading ability, especially if they hate to read?
- What different methods of assessment do you use with your students?
- How would kids in your class describe you as a teacher?
- Describe your grading and assessment philosophies.
- What role should/does the study of language—rhetoric, grammar, style—play in your class? How do you teach these elements?
- What is your role in the classroom? What would you compare yourself to and why?
- What can you do with computers and what, if anything, have you done with them in your classroom to integrate them into your curriculum?
- What is your responsibility when it comes to preparing students to take the SAT?
- Have you collaborated with other teachers? On what?
- What can you contribute to our department?
- What is your strength as a teacher?
- What is your weakness as a teacher?

These last two questions stall people, but I've argued strongly against hiring a couple people, at least in part, because they could not answer them. Any teacher who cannot identify those areas in which they are strong or need improvement is not asking themselves why they are good and how they can get better. I prefer a teacher who says "You know, I'm still working on how to teach poetry—I find it hard to figure out how to get them into it" to one that says nothing or believes they are fully evolved and are, as a teacher, a final draft.

REFLECTION

List the attributes of the job, school, department, students, teaching assignment you want. Be very thorough and specific. Pay attention to what you have to say: if you want to work with challenging students or want the kind of environment you had in your private Catholic schools while growing up, listen to that. List what else you would be willing to do if asked: e.g., coach, class advisor, etc. Finally, list what you would absolutely not be willing to teach or do.

ACTIVITY

Go to a café with a friend, ideally one who is in education (better if they already teach at the school where you will interview). Using the questions provided here and any other, more local questions, have them grill you. Conduct a mock interview. Then have them critique your answers: e.g., "You were pretty vague about how you handle grammar in your class. What specific example can you give me about what you do in your class?"

RECOMMENDATION

With Portfolio in Hand: Validating the New Teacher Professionalism. Nona Lyons, ed. (Teachers College Press 1998).

CHAPTER 24

ORGANIZING YOURSELF

I love being a writer. What I hate is the paperwork.

—**Peter DeVries**

I was not born organized. In fact, not until I began teaching and faced the river of paper did I force myself to get organized. This need became all the more urgent when overzealous members of the Ecology Club accidentally "recycled" the binder that contained everything—lesson plans, attendance, notices. As a symbol of my new resolve to organize—and to signal to the Ecology Club that this binder was not some kid's forgotten binder—I picked up a very nice binder-sized leather organizer I found on sale for fifteen dollars.

It's important to be able to find documents you create. But as Stephen Covey and many other organizational gurus point out, the organization must serve some greater purpose: providing you time for whatever is important to you. Covey says somewhere that no one ever laid on their death bed and wished they had spent a few more hours at the office. This is serious business for English teachers: you have a right to a life and must learn to achieve that life while at the same time being the good teacher you want to be. Your ability to organize yourself not only helps you find the essential time to be the husband, partner, writer, or golfer you want to be but, equally important, teaches your students this value and these skills through your example. Furthermore, recent discoveries in brain-based research suggest that information presented in a logical, organized manner helps students make a wider range of connections between the new information and what they already know, thus increasing their capacity to learn and remember (Caine and Caine 1994).

One last note before getting down to the basics. The computer is my essential tool when it comes to organization. While some of the ideas I outline here might seem obsessive, this system saved me lots of time and worry once I got it in place; and I spent quite a bit of time working through this system to find the computer programs that worked best for me. This last point is key: my ideas here will not likely fit you perfectly, if at all, but they can help you to find what works for you by giving you something to respond to as you begin the rough draft of your own organizational system.

Papers: Where to Put Them

The Binder

English teachers face certain organizational challenges their colleagues do not. A poem, such as Gary Soto's "Saturday at the Canal" complements my senior curriculum—whose theme is "Where I Am, Where I've Been, Where I'm Going"—very well since his poem is about two kids sitting on the levee in Fresno dreaming of a place where kids know more than a couple of chords on a cheap guitar. The poem is also great to use in my American Literature class, however, when we discuss such ideas as independence and the restlessness of Americans who always want to go somewhere else.

A problem quickly emerges: where do I put this poem so I can find it? Can you possibly have a file for each poem you use during the year? (I probably work in over a hundred poems a year between my classes). Do you keep a "Soto file"? How about an ongoing file titled "Poetry" that holds all the poems you use? And what about the poems I carefully, meticulously annotate, that copy of "Fern Hill" or "Sonnet 29" that I worked so hard on once, swept away with a scholar's joy in searching out all the word meanings and connections? Where do I put that so I won't lose it? In the end, you find that there is no manageable system for keeping so many articles as you would like to, so you create a system that works for you. In this era of computer-using teachers, our need to organize and manage our documents (i.e., back-up, update, revise) grows all the time, especially after a few years of creating lessons.

Though I have changed this idea around a bit from its original format, the credit for this system goes to Clare LePell, a wonderful teacher with whom I first began teaching. It is a common sense approach to organization that, in its own way, adheres to the finer principles of the writing process and portfolios while simultaneously addressing the challenges outlined above.

You need three large (three-inch) binders: one master binder and, assuming you teach two different classes (e.g., freshman and junior English), two archival binders, one for each class. In the master binder, you need divisions for each class ("Frosh" and "Juniors").

Beginning with the first day of the semester, you put in the master binder a copy of every single sheet and lesson plan you create for the class. For example, on day one, I put my prospectus, outside reading, journal, and portfolio handouts in the binder with my day's lesson plan notes on top of that collection of papers. Thus for each day I have the lesson plan and all the handouts that go along with it. If I have a story or poem that I am teaching, and have an overhead transparency or annotated text, I put it right in there. If, as sometimes happens, I use the same poem or essay on the same day in both my freshman and junior classes, I put a copy of it behind that day's lesson plan in each section so I can find it in the future. When a unit wraps up, I take out all those lesson plans and handouts and, keeping them in chronological order, transfer them to the archival binder for that particular class so that I can find them next year when I begin to revise my class. Thus the archival binder becomes a sort of working portfolio of my teaching that year, a collection of papers on which I write various notes to help me teach them better the coming year or to help me remember that I should *not* teach them the next year.

While such a system could be accused of fostering curricular arthritis—"I have my course curriculum all done and in the binder! I'm all set for the next thirty years!"—my point is that you have a draft to work from, but also a foundation on which you can safely build. Such a system is particularly helpful if you suddenly face illness or prolonged absence: you have materials ready even if you can't revise them this time around as you wished. This system saved me when my father was dying and when my second son was being born. The organizational system freed me up to concentrate on what was most important in my life. When my first son was born, I had no such system and ended up calling from the birthing room to tell my colleague what to do in class the next day, drafting a lesson plan over the phone while my wife went into her twenty-fifth hour of labor.

In addition to these divisions for my course, my master binder has divisions for each period, writing topics, and miscellaneous papers such as announcements or student notices that come to me during the day. In the individual period sections, I keep my role sheets, seating charts, attendance scantrons, and assorted notes or reminders for individual students. I also keep a folder clipped into the binder; in here I store miscellaneous papers as well as my lesson plans for subs if I know I will be out ahead of time.

The binder offers several advantages:

- Students returning from absences can be directed to your binder and find everything there to write down (you keep the extra copies of handouts elsewhere for them to take).
- You have a record of what you did on a certain day.
- You have a dependable place to make notes for the future to improve your course, treating the pages as a draft.
- It is surprisingly compact, taking up a total of two binders (one for each semester) which fit nicely on a shelf or can be shuttled between classes if you must.
- Everything is in one place, secured and organized.
- Even if you have everything on the computer, you can keep a hardcopy of it and at least have that to work with should your computer die suddenly (or your house burn to the ground).
- You have an excellent resource to offer to new or collaborating teachers who are teaching a course for the first time and want to study the curriculum to get some ideas.
- A substitute finds an orderly resource to help them successfully run your class in your absence.

The Computer

Recently a friend of mine, a dedicated composition teacher at a high school in California, dreamt that all his files were lost after his computer crashed. He woke up and began madly saving everything to the backup system that he never used. His wife awoke to find him working away before he left for a conference. When he explained what he was doing and why, they both laughed and concluded it was absurd. When his wife picked him up two days later, she had a horrified look on her face. "You know your dream about the computer? It came true last night," she said. Faced with the loss of two years worth of lessons, units, handouts, exemplars, and personal writings of his own, he called a data-recovery service. They said they could recover the lost data for two to five thousand dollars. He had not saved hard copies nor did he have backup disks. Nor, of course, did he have an extra couple thousand dollars lying around. So he lost everything.

Organizing documents on the hard drive.   Within the course of a typical year you can easily generate hundreds of documents: grants, memos, minutes, lesson plans, handouts. The point of doing them on the computer is the ease of retrieval and future use. It can be difficult to find everything, however, after a year or two of teaching. You can use the Macintosh equivalent of Command-F (find) and enter what you think is the key term (e.g., "lord" or "flies") and see if it will find it. This doesn't always work, particularly if you do not have a system for storing your materials.

The system I will briefly outline has served me very well, though it always merits revision as time goes on and more complicated filing needs arise (e.g., writing this book!). The filing system is based on two units: the folder and the file name under which you save it.

I create folders for courses and units so that, like my file cabinets, everything has a place. (See Figure 24.1.) So, for example, in September I will create a folder titled "Junior English 97–98." In this folder I will create such folders as "Independence Project" or "Huckleberry Finn" or "Essay Topics." Within these folders, I will store the files and name them: "TOPICS—Cont. Issue/Driving Laws" or "5CP—HUCK—Study Qs/Chap. 1." (Note: 5CP means first semester of junior English.) This system has the great advantage of allowing you to search easily and successfully in the future. You hit Command-F and then enter "Huck" and know your computer will fish out all your *Huckleberry Finn* files.

Using the computer to plan.   I got tired of losing or not being able to revise my lesson plans every year. I felt like I was reinventing the wheel every year for my first few years of teaching. I would be typing some lesson for *I Know Why the Caged Bird Sings* and know I had written something like this the year before; instead of concentrating on revising and improving, I was focusing on remembering and re-creating. I could have been watching a movie with my wife or reading a book.

Planning has different components: the day, the week, the month, and the semester. Each requires a different way of thinking as each has a different purpose. The daily lesson plan (Figure 24.2) is the script for your day; you may detour but at least you go in with a map. The weekly

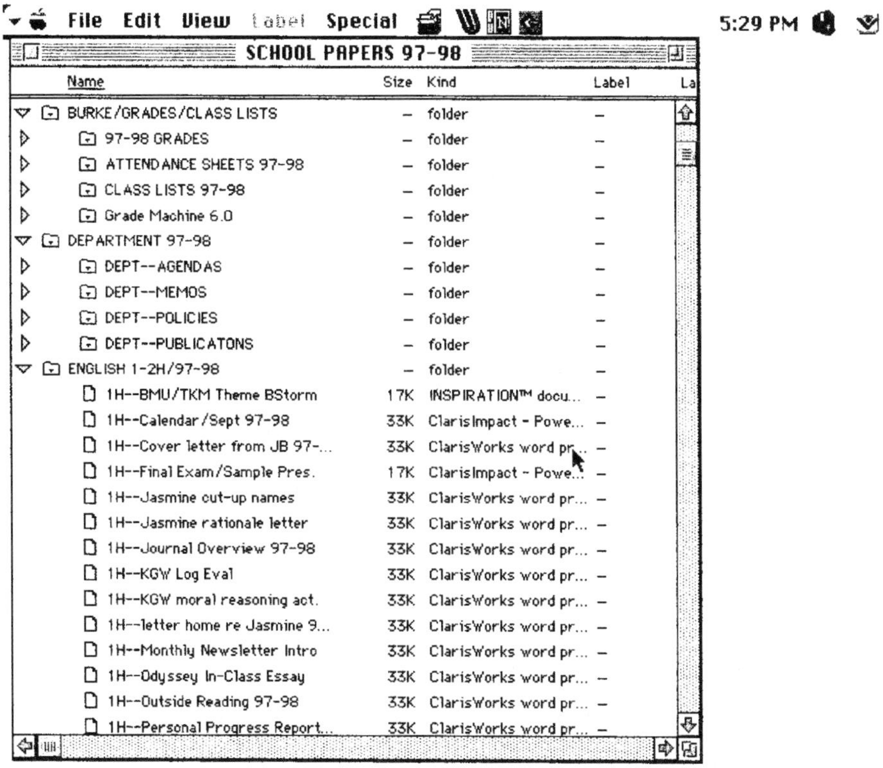

Figure 24.1   *The trick is to be able to find documents: label them by class, book, or unit for easy retrieval.*

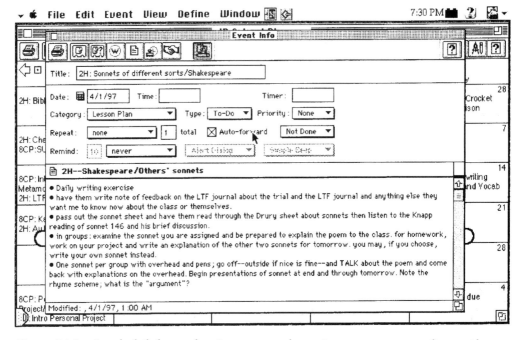

Figure 24.2   *Sample daily lesson plan: I use a personal organizer program to centralize my ideas, plans, and documents.*

lesson plan (Figure 24.3) is the weekly framework, the means of seeing that everything connects in some meaningful way; it also helps you anticipate what materials or assistance you might need so you can order it, reserve it, buy it, or bring it. The month is an important unit because it forces you to think conceptually about the bigger picture; some teachers really nail down the month's schedule (Figure 24.4) while others use it for themselves to just think the month through as a draft.

Weekly assignment sheets (Figure 24.3) I type up in a word processor so I can take advantage of the advanced formatting features like check boxes to make the documents more user-friendly to the students. My students with learning difficulties express their gratitude for these layout features. These computer organizer programs also allow me to run ahead and make notes to myself like "Remember that you have the state tests to prepare for this week." The program helps me centralize all the information I need to manage.

Keeping track of student information.   In this era of different assessments it is hard to know what to recommend since teachers' needs in this area appear to be changing all the time. However, most teachers still have scores to keep track of, and we all have students whose attendance must be kept and names recorded. There are various programs for computers but the one I use (Grade Machine) meets most of my needs and those of other teachers I know. In short, you want to find a program that does the following: allows you flexibility in how you enter and configure student data; generates a dated attendance sheet; produces grade sheets to enter scores by hand; and allows you to set up and manipulate seating charts. I make regular use of this last function—seating charts—as the charts allow me to keep track of groups, student participation, certain assignments, and so on. I can just print up a new seating chart and write "participation in discussion 3/30" on it and put little hatch marks next to their name when they contribute to the discussion. Very helpful, very easy, very quick.

Junior English Weekly Assignments (3.23.98-3.27.98)

Notes • Personal reading--April 13th, done with both books.

☐ Write up a new card and put it in the box on my desk when you start a new book.

☐ You must TYPE up an annotated bibliography of each book on the class computer (so it can be loaded into the website when that is created).

☐ You should notice that I am not requiring extensive reading of *Cannery Row*; this is because I expect you to be reading your personal books also.

☐ *Cannery Row*: This week you will have a variety of assignments that depend on you having done the assigned reading; please keep up so you will do well.

Monday **March 23, 1998**

☐ WEEKLY SENTENCE: parallelism continued (how/why things fit together)

☐ DUE: revised papers on chapters 1-5 from last week. Last chance.

☐ DETERMINE: Who is going to read to kindergartners at Washington this Friday?

☐ GROUPS: create a "magnetic poem" with words provided. Write up when done.

☐ HW: read chapter six for Tuesday; also, read Levine poem "What Work Is" and come in with a one page explanation of what *you* think "work" is and what you think Levine is saying about it. Related it, if you can, to any or all characters in *Cannery Row*. Consider, for example, distinguishing between the words *work*, *career*, *vocation*, and *job*. This should be done on a separate sheet of paper and be ready to turn in Tuesday.

Tuesday **March 24, 1998**

☐ DUE: Levine "Work" paper.

☐ WRITING: find all conjunctions; examine parallel structure.

☐ GROUPS: "The Great Tide Pool": examine parallel between the Tide Pool and the characters in the book; make a statement about view of nature/life and support with examples.

☐ HW: read Chapters 7, 8, and 9 for Wednesday. Write a one-pager about a person to whom you are "indebted" as they all feel they are to Doc. In other words, write a one-two page reflection on someone who you has or has had a real influence on you and why. (Be sure to honor them with a fine piece of writing!)

Wednesday **March 25, 1998**

☐ WRITING: poem to read and respond to; then to connect to discussion: Rodriguez's poem "Speaking with her Hands."

☐ **IMPORTANT:** Next Monday I have arranged for one of the authors of *Burlingame: A City of Trees* to come speak to us during fifth period. We need to do two things:

☐ Brainstorm good questions for him

☐ Arrange for those who wish to field trip out of their fifth period classes by getting a form signed by your fifth period teacher.

☐ DISCUSSION: roundtable discussion about book, people, etc.

☐ INDEX CARDS: reflect on the discussion and the book.

☐ HW: read chapters 10 and 11 for tomorrow. Come in ready to write.

☐ Thursday **March 26, 1998**

☐ INTRODUCE Steinbeck Project: questions, discussion, etc.

☐ CONFERENCES: conference with people re: their Projects. Questions, concerns, approvals (all in groups must get my approval ahead of time.)

☐ HW: read *Cannery Row* chapters 12-15 for Monday. Come in Monday ready to write a short paper at the beginning of class about the different people in the book and how they are all similar.

Friday **March 27, 1998**

☐ Reading Day: be sure to have your outside book with you.

☐ Reading conferences: discussing outside reading.

Figure 24.3 *Sample weekly assignment sheet: This helps me as much as it does the students by allowing us all to plan ahead and see how Monday relates to Friday.*

Endnote: Having a Life

While such a computerized system might seem overzealous, it is actually quite simple and requires only a year's commitment to get a good "draft" down from which you can then work in the years to come. Many computers now come bundled with different organizer programs, most of which are suitable to this task. Also, such a system keeps your paper

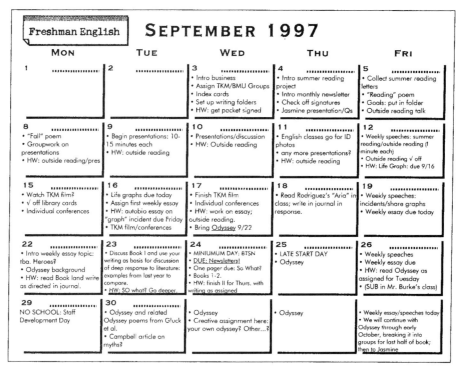

Figure 24.4   *Sample monthly calendar: Some teachers prefer to organize their class by the month instead of the week. I use a computer program to create calendars.*

storage to a minimum, assuming you use the binder and backup your computer regularly for security.

The computer is not our only tool, however, and cannot do everything for us when it comes to keeping organized. English teachers spend years trying to find the ultimate system for storing and sorting papers, transporting them, returning them, and grading them. As a profession, we are obsessed with finding the perfect bag, the one we dream will allow us to store all our gadgets and pens while at the same time providing nice divisions for different sets of papers, magazines, and books we carry around. It's a challenge you will have to solve for yourself. I do think, however, that you should not scrimp when it comes to such tools as a computer or bags. If you think it will work for you, buy it; you're a professional and these are the tools of your trade. So, too, are such tools as organizers, pens, binders, and computers: you will use these constantly so buy professional quality tools that make your work a pleasure and reduce the threat of pain and possible injury.

Many English teachers are walking around with ruined backs from the heavy loads they carry, from the hours spent hunched over papers, from the bad chairs in which they work. I've suffered some symptoms of trouble myself and will say only that the ergonomics of your working environment matter; having learned to use the smallest planner, having purchased a good chair, having learned to keep a copy of heavy texts at school *and* home so I don't have to carry them around— these habits have saved my body from the pain and trouble it began to suffer at one point.

You either learn to organize yourself so you can find time to still do what you love—talk with your spouse, play with your kids, go out to movies, read—or your life is one of quiet desperation and chaos. You owe it to yourself, to your students, and to your family to master this one aspect of teaching; few things will help you to survive the constant demands of the work you love so much.

REFLECTION

Think about your current organizational needs—time, resources, documents— and the system you use to manage these needs. Make a list of those activities— read, exercise, go out with friends—you would like to be able to do regularly. Does your current organizational system help or keep you from enjoying these aspects of your life?

ACTIVITY

If you do not already have a computer organizer, go onto the Internet and download one to try. Most software publishers allow you to download a free trial version of the program; if you like it, you buy it. If you don't have a computer, buy Dorothy Lehmkuhl and Dolores Cotter Lamping's *Organizing for the Creative Person: Right-Brain Styles for Conquering Clutter, Mastering Time, and Reaching Your Goals*, and do some of their recommended exercises to get you more organized.

RECOMMENDATIONS

Stephen Covey's *The Seven Habits of Highly Effective People* offers a compelling argument and practical strategies for using organization to help you achieve personal satisfaction. You don't read a book like this for the writing; this is reading to learn. It is also worth reading for the fact that it is one of the most influential books in the business world and thus helps you better understand what they expect of their employees. The other book I really like, already mentioned above, is Dorothy Lehmkuhl and Dolores Cotter Lamping's *Organizing for the Creative Person: Right-Brain Styles for Conquering Clutter, Mastering Time, and Reaching Your Goals*.

CHAPTER 25

CREATING YOUR CLASSROOM

We shape our dwellings and afterwards our dwellings shape us.

—Winston Churchill

Home is a place of security within an insecure world, a place of certainty within doubt, a familiar place in a strange world, a sacred place in a profane world.

—Kimberly Dovey, "Home and Homelessness," in *Home Environments, Human Behavior and Environment*

Some years ago at Exeter, a philanthropist asked what investment he could make that would significantly improve instruction and student achievement. After careful consideration, the school decided that what they needed were large round tables that would create the opportunity for seminar-style discussions, and lower the number of students in each class. I don't think, however, that it was only the table that made the difference; it was also the environment the table and subsequent teaching created. So it is today, for example, with the computers, which slowly find their way into our classrooms; though these tools in many ways make the world itself our classroom, it is not the computer but the way it challenges teachers to change that makes the difference.

Our "dwellings" or environments have several components that figure significantly in student learning during the time they occupy this shared space we call the classroom. Regie Routman (1994) further confirms the importance of the classroom: "The way we organize our classrooms affects children's views of themselves as readers and writers and has an impact on their attitudes toward school and learning." Today's students, however, are asked to be more than just competent readers and writers; any language arts standards document will further demand that students demonstrate their mastery of multimedia technologies, their ability to give engaging presentations of complicated information, their ability to use the Internet to find information, and their knowledge of how to verify and make sense of this information. Thus the classroom of the modern era is more than just a classroom; it is a lab, a workshop, a community, a studio, a home. Such a classroom has shelves of reference books on different subjects, not all of which are literary; it contains other books relevant to a range of subjects that reflect the increasingly interdisciplinary nature of the curriculum. A computer in one corner serves as a resource for students needing to look up information on those CD-ROMs available to them through the school's server; another computer is surrounded by students searching the Internet for information on a collaborative project between English and Social Science classes. In the standards era, "the standards are everywhere, and the materials in the classroom are selected to match them" (Tucker and Codding 1998). The walls of the classroom show not only students' work, but the state standards against which all such work are measured; the classroom itself is a text that showcases what students know and are able to do right along side of the standards which spell out these same expectations.

The Elements of the Classroom

The classroom is the primary component in all learning by virtue of the fact that it is where students go each day. What they find in that room—joy, despair, action, chaos—is up to the teacher. The class is the blank canvas on which the teacher—and to the extent that the teacher involves them, the student—creates their daily world.

In my classroom, we create this world together from the beginning. The day they walk in they choose where they sit. This simple choice establishes a culture of respect based on clear assumptions about their maturity. I have students who run their parents' businesses or help support their families; to assume they are not responsible enough to sit where they want is insulting. Later, if some student or group of students shows that they cannot, in fact, handle this responsibility then I quickly seat them somewhere else without making a big deal about it. That first day I also clearly establish the obvious rules we all know and understand: no student has the right to insult or otherwise interfere with the work of anyone else in the class. At that point in time, I also go over the prospectus to clarify early on those procedural issues that are important to the class (see Appendix K for the Classroom Self-Evaluation/Checklist).

Finally, I try to always refer to it as "our" classroom, making them feel not only welcome but responsible for it. As the year unfolds, it looks more and more like our classroom as students bring in cartoons they think are worth sharing or somehow related to what we are studying.

The truth is we don't all have our own classrooms and thus do not all have control of our physical environment. We do, however, have the final word when it comes to the intellectual and emotional climate of our rooms and these are crucial to student learning. We are the ones who establish a climate within the classroom where students always feel they are welcome regardless of their beliefs, their problems, their differences. Renate Nummela Caine and Geoffrey Caine (1994) further expand the conception of what a classroom is in light of their research on the human brain, describing it as an "entire learning environment" and emphasizing the benefits of making the classroom itself—through art, words, music—a learning environment.

After thinking about all that it must accomplish, I divided the classroom environment into the following elements, each of which is crucial in the English class:

- physical
- intellectual
- emotional
- personal

The Physical Environment

What the Walls Say.   I assume that, like mine, your room is filled with thirty to thirty-five desks, many of which were probably there when you went to high school. Thus you are left with your walls. My classroom walls end up getting used for everything: bookcases, student work, rubrics (the Six Trait writing rubric), photographs of students working—everything from performing plays to looking studious as they read—and a wide range of posters and pictures depicting things literary. The walls become a text all their own, one the students never seem to tire of "reading" and which yield interesting responses as they ask about a picture, an author, or a certain book. One of my students, D.J. Van Arkel, captures this sense of the classroom as a text when he writes, "The room's exciting. Sometimes I just sit back and read the room, poster to poster, cartoon to cartoon." At least one implication of such an "enriched environment" is the possibility of actual brain growth through stimulation of multiple senses (Caine and Caine 1994).

In her fascinating book, *House as a Mirror of Self: Exploring the Deeper Meaning of Home,* Clare Cooper Marcus (1995) writes, "home fulfills many needs: a place of self expression, a vessel of memories, a refuge from the outside world, a cocoon where we feel nurtured and let down our guard." Marcus captures what has been one of the more satisfying accidents: I shot a roll of pictures once on a whim and put up the photographs only to find that they immediately made my kids feel a sense of community the more the classroom told "their story" through the pictures I kept adding. Now, after nearly ten years, new students immediately sense the room as a welcoming place, the walls giving evidence that things will happen in here, that they and what they do during the coming year will be remembered. Freshman Shannon Ochse, describing my room, wrote: "What helps your mind overflow with memories and ideas for writing is the wall of photos behind the teacher's desk. These photos, some colorless, some vivid, catch your eye and make you remember the times when they were taken in class. With some pictures of his family as well, Mr. Burke provides a small piece of his life outside of school to share with us. I like knowing a little bit about my teacher's life because it helps you understand them. The plaques and awards that Mr. Burke has received are also displayed around the room, helping us learn more about our English teacher." Allegra Conroy, another student of mine, said of the bookcases, "The six shelves of cluttered books are very obvious to me because they show the use that all these books have received over the years. . . . The community of books piled high against each other represent the enthusiasm of students to read and enjoy all books of different kinds."

The Classroom Library.   The presence of these books in the class and their constant use by so many kids—even students from past years will stop by and ask me for something to read—confirms many others' (Allen 1995; Bomer 1995; Krashen 1993; Rief 1992) testimony about the difference the classroom library makes in students' attitudes toward reading. Some teachers pick these books up at garage sales when they see them or after the books have sat long enough on their home shelves. Other teachers get some money from the school's PTA to buy new ones to add to the collection or even solicit publishers. Teachers also get lucky and receive donations from parents who are weeding their bookshelves; this only happens if parents know you are looking. Nothing, however, so radically transforms a room and students' reading habits as the classroom library. Students can't help but see the paperbacks lined up along the walls in my classroom; often a kid will pick up a book and begin thumbing through it. If I see them, I reel them in with an enthusiastic recommendation: "Oh, that's a great book, Florence. I think you'd really like it. He has a new one just out so if you like it you might want to look into it."

One problem plagues the most vigilant of teachers: the books need to find their way home after kids read them. I have pretty good luck in this area, in part because I can remember that I recommended Richard Wright's *Rites of Passage* to Ryan and can follow up with him after I know he's finished it. There are clipboards near each bookcase for students to sign out books on; when they return them, they are supposed to cross off their name. But let's face it: this is not high security. On the other hand, if I had to barcode each book and check it out officially I wouldn't have the library. I solicited hundreds of teachers on-line and found several strategies for classroom library that offered different styles and options, all of which they said worked well for them. Here is a list of ideas for managing your classroom library:

- Tuck a three-by-five-inch card with the book's title into the book. Students checking out that book then write their name on it and return the book to the teacher when they are done with it.

- Have students fill out a three-by-five card at the beginning of the year; they then write on this card the title of any book(s) they check out from the class library. They indicate on this card when they returned the book. Cards are kept in a cardfile box on the teacher's desk.

- Keep a binder with columns—e.g., name, title, date checked out, date returned—which you (or your aide) fills in when students check out books.

- Create a database of all your book titles and then identify genre and subject so students can search a printed or computerized database this way. When the student finds a book they wish to check out, they sign it out on the master database which the teacher keeps.

- Impose time limits on the checkouts; not all teachers do this.

- Label all your books with color coded dots or written labels that identify the genre and/or area of interest.

- Write your own name and room number prominently on all your books; though it detracts from their appearance it ensures they get back to your class if students lose them.

Again, the point is not to create a prohibitively restrictive process that takes your time or keeps kids from checking out the books. When I have had unusually efficient student aides, I have made them the librarian for that period: students checked the books out with them and returned them to that student. These aides, by the way, were also very helpful in keeping my books in working order by reinforcing the bindings or repairing the covers as needed.

Seating Arrangements.   Figure 25.1 shows the layout of my classroom. Desks are arranged so that students face each other. If I had the space, I would arrange them in a "U" shape so it felt a bit more like a circle. This arrangement works well for several reasons. It keeps kids from being able to disappear into the back rows; there are only three seats in any row, so I can see everyone all the time and keep them on track. Another benefit is that students can quickly organize themselves into groups by turning their desks toward each other. It also allows me to move easily around the room and to sit in different places when I am working with them as a class, in groups, or at a workstation. Finally, this classroom structure reflects the ideal of the conversational roundtable so important to my classes. I don't have room to make a circle, but we can approximate that idea by arranging ourselves so we can all feel included in the discussion.

Computers.   One last aspect of the physical environment warrants discussion. While many teachers still lack computers in their classrooms, they are coming whether we like it or not. The "on-line classroom" or "virtual classroom" (Gilster 1997; LeBlanc and Hawisher 1992; Thornburg 1994) raises serious questions about classroom arrangement and instructional practice. When setting up a classroom with computers, be sure to consider the following: access to LCD panels or other projection devices; placement of projection screens and desk

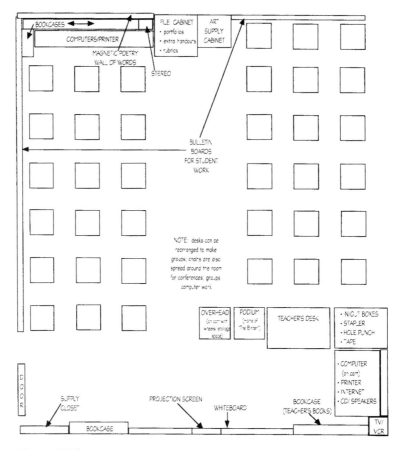

Figure 25.1

arrangements that allow for presentations using these devices; distance from Internet connections; and placement of computers so as to allow students to work in the background without interfering with other work in the classroom. And don't forget about outlets: you can't have extension cords snaking all over your classroom. Ideally your computer will be on a movable cart to allow for greater flexibility of use for presentations and by groups.

The Intellectual Environment

It is not just the physical environment that fosters and maintains this intellectual climate; it is what we talk about, how we talk about it, and why we talk about a subject in the first place. When students walk in and see "Language = Power" on one wall they know they are going to learn something in my class. When they walk in and find groups of kids gathered before school talking, studying, brainstorming at the whiteboard, they know my room is about thinking.

We can do several things to foster an intellectual environment in our class.

- Start class with a short activity—e.g., writing in their journal—that gets them engaged in ways that will keep them attentive throughout the period.
- Constantly push them to "go beyond the obvious," a phrase that will benefit them if it happens to get lodged in their heads. This might mean taking the opening journal en-

Jon, Kristine, and Jessica showing me their multimedia slide show before giving their formal presentation comparing the journeys of Jasmine and Odysseus

tries of a few students who are willing to share and challenging them to write more, or talk about these ideas as an entrée into the "main course" of that day's period.

- Let them, when possible, work where they need to: in the library where it is quiet and they can spread out; in the hall where it is quiet; in the computer lab where they can "write better using a keyboard"; or in a specific place in the classroom (e.g., Janet Allen's [1995] students had comfortable chairs where they could read).
- Clearly establish at the beginning of the year that kids have permission to think differently, to take risks with their thinking; that anyone who criticizes another's ideas is undermining the class community.

One year I had a couple of boys who struggled with the intellectual atmosphere in my classroom. They viewed the world in strictly either/or terms. They often did not try to understand what we were talking about and so did what many students do in such situations: they acted out. We would be in the middle of a great discussion about a poem and Richard would suddenly interrupt our conversation to ask if it was true that when they killed people in the electric chair their heads caught fire and exploded. It was that kind of class. Over time, though, we grew into one of the most family-like classes I've ever taught. And when Richard would begin to say such things a couple of girls who were fiercely maternal would turn around and threaten him, telling him we were having a good class and he "better not say something stupid." While I didn't always approve of their force, the girls and other members of the class came to really value the environment we created and let Richard and the few others like him understand that they did not have the right to undermine that community.

By the year's end, Richard had been forced to accept that the world had changed and that he couldn't get away with reckless thinking in the class. Early on, his common refrain was "I don't need to know about this stuff anyway. I'm just going to be a garbage man." But I never let such remarks pass and would tell him it wasn't that easy anymore. "Garbage trucks only have one guy running them in most communities now, Richard. It's very competitive to get such jobs. They have to know how to do a lot of things they didn't in the past." In this way, creating an "intellectual environment" in your classroom means holding them accountable for their thinking at all times no matter what the thinking is about. Eventually Richard would answer the girls' threats and the wary looks of the class by quickly saying, "No, really, I have a question I want to ask."

The Emotional Environment

Successful and enjoyable learning depends on creating a classroom community where people know they can speak what is on their mind without fear of reprisal or rejection. While the previous example of the girl's reactions to Richard's comments seems to contradict this ideal, it didn't feel that way in that class: the girls were, in fact, enforcing much more forcefully than I could the need for that safety that Richard wanted to deny the class. I don't mean to ignore the very real problem of discipline in the class. A student like Richard can undermine an entire day's success if he refuses to see himself as a member of the team. Most of us quickly—and painfully—learn that nothing is gained by humiliating such disruptive students: that's what they wanted in the first place—to interrupt the lesson they didn't understand. In the second place, they will never forgive you until they have exacted a prolonged revenge for the way you insulted them.

Besides, I just have too many kids these days who could be hurt if they didn't feel safe in my classroom. This includes kids like Richard for whom school had been one long series of harangues from frustrated teachers. It also includes students like the teenage mothers I've had who struggle to return to or stay in school, in part because they don't feel respected. Every year I seem to have more kids, particularly girls, who come in with diagnoses of depression or other afflictions that make them fear criticism. Even fights, something I frankly had not prepared myself to expect, occur in the classroom, one time over something as absurd as a girl's "garlic breath" from a bagel she had at recess. Such elements as physical and emotional safety are essential if deep learning is to occur within the classroom; furthermore, studies have concluded that stress literally impedes the brain's ability to think and, more importantly, learn (Caine and Caine 1994).

Again, certain things in my classroom serve to remind the students that respect and dignity matter and I use these to direct their thinking at times, especially the Roman slave Terance's comment that "I am a man: nothing human is alien to me." This line in particular becomes helpful when discussing certain characters or stories that the kids cannot "relate to." Their Life Graphs (see Chapter 9) or other such personal "graphic stories" cover the walls most of the year, further adding emotional content to the room and our discussions as students see the "lifelines" of their peers surrounding them. Kids who seemed "perfect" suddenly seem "more human" when their peers see they have overcome serious obstacles on their journey. Still other students see that the quiet ones have, as evidenced by their graphic work, done remarkable things, have serious talents that would have otherwise stayed hidden.

Several educators, based on their research, found the following to be the most important components of a supportive classroom environment (Elias et al. 1997):

- free and open interaction among and between staff and students
- high standards of behavior and achievement, including the ability to think critically and make informed judgments about behavior and related consequences
- collaboration, cooperation, and constructive group problem-solving activities

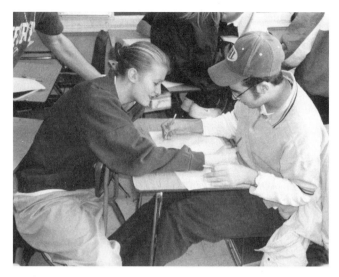

Lindsay and George team up to draw their own conclusions about Robert Frost's poetry. Emotionally healthy environments allow students of all abilities to create meaningful work through effective collaboration.

- equity, fairness, and respect for diversity of race, culture, ethnicity, social class, religion, gender, ability, and other factors
- supportive, positive learning experiences
- strong connections between adults and students, and commitment to the mission and goals of the school

The Personal Environment

While "personal" seems to imply "emotional," there is an important difference that I need to recognize since it has been so crucial in my own class. The personal environment goes back to the idea of the room as "home" to the kids, a place they know they can find shelter on days of rain or despair. I have certain students, for example, who on occasion just get overwhelmed by their emotions or problems and come to the office asking if they can hide out in the room. I will come in near the end of lunch and find them just sitting in the quiet room looking out of the windows at nothing, grateful to get away from the rush for a few minutes. And, of course, there is the "Breakfast Club," a group of some of our school's top students who, as freshman, began gathering in my room before school starts. They collaborate on assignments, surf the Web, goof around, have breakfast, help each other out with math problems and personal troubles; it's a wonderful little community of kids who need a place to go at that hour and I am glad they can find it in my class.

We want rooms that "make you think" about what is important—cultures, careers, good writing, ideas, literature, learning. In fundamental ways, the intellectual and physical environment of the classroom itself sets the standards for what is important in the domain of English. Its walls, filing cabinets, chalkboards—its very atmosphere—should be packed with evidence of such learning and thinking. These public spaces, combined with the private ones—in the mind, on the page, in the heart—amount to a public exhibition and assessment (Wiggins 1998) of what is done in this classroom where we come not only to work but to play, not just to think but to feel, to learn but also to find a home in the world of ideas and chaos.

REFLECTION

Thinking back to your own education, recall those rooms that stand out as exemplary. Who had the "coolest" room? What made it so great? Who made you feel most at home? Who made you feel the most threatened or otherwise unwelcome? What did they do? (My math teacher drew a giant red circle on my forehead to remind me to get my book covered by the next day! She did it before I could react, with the whole class looking on!)

ACTIVITY

Using the Classroom Self-Assessment/Checklist (Appendix K) evaluate your own environment. Consider having some students fill this out to get their perspective; they will either challenge your own assumptions or confirm them.

RECOMMENDATION

If you want to read more about setting up a classroom the book to read is *Time for Meaning*, by Randy Bomer (Boynton/Cook 1995); he has a chapter on this subject that is very useful.

CHAPTER 26

ENJOYING OPEN HOUSE AND PARENT-TEACHER CONFERENCES

Writers must get past the creative process and understand that what they're selling is a product.

—Carol Stacy, publisher

There are several nights each year when high school teachers prepare to meet the parents of their students. While such nights are designed to allow parents and teachers to discuss students' work, teachers should see them as an exhibition of their own work, a presentation of their professional portfolio. Back-to-School Night, for example, typically takes place at the end of September, before fall weather has made its debut, before the first round of grades has been given out, and, sometimes, before teachers have learned all the names of their students. This last item is understandable given that some of us work with as many as 180 students and the opening weeks of school are characterized by a constantly changing roster of students. Another big event is Open House, an evening in the spring when teachers celebrate all their students' learning through exhibitions of their work. Woven throughout the year, depending the community, schools also host exhibitions or, more likely, parent conferences where teachers sit down and discuss individual students' progress with their parents.

Given the politically charged atmosphere of education the last few years, such evenings can be very stressful. If your school is trying to implement certain reforms or experienced conspicuously low scores on such tests as the Advanced Placement exam, the SAT, or the state exams, you might well encounter parents who are ready to question the validity of what you are doing. It is easy to imagine a parent interrupting a teacher these days to ask, "You say that your new literature program will benefit my daughter but what evidence do you have that it will help her do better on the SAT or actually help her read better?" However, beneath all their concern and occasional frustration is a belief they share with us as English teachers: *English matters.* They know that without the ability to read well, to write and communicate effectively, their kids are at a serious disadvantage. Likewise, if you are collaborating with other departments, you might want to prepare a fact sheet or team presentation to answer those questions they are likely to have as to the value of the program.

Parents often come to a school particularly interested in what the English teacher is doing. At my school, such evenings are frequently attended by parents of students who are in middle school but have begun to "shop around"; such parents often come to me first (as the head of the English department) and judge the school by virtue of its English curriculum, teaching staff and, of course, test scores. Many of these parents, coming from professions themselves, believe strongly in the value of the canon and maintain a certain allegiance to titles they consider essential. These parents want to know what classics you teach, what you do when it comes to grammar, spelling, and vocabulary.

There are a few helpful things you can do to make a good impression on such nights, particularly Back-to-School Night, given that parents are forming their judgment of you and your credibility on this night. Most Back-to-School Nights, by the way, ask the parents to follow their child's schedule and sit in the room with their teacher for about 10 minutes during which time their guiding assumption is that you will tell them what you are doing and why you are doing it. Some parents come with the misguided expectation that you will take time to talk to them about their individual child, but this is not possible in a class of thirty-five students—even if only ten students' parents show up. Obviously I don't (nor should you) do all these things; consider them a menu of options that can help.

Have a handout. Many teachers simply run off copies of the course prospectus and use that as a script, casually walking through its policies and reading selections, adding as they go to fill in such blanks as what writing assignments they are doing now. If you send your course prospectus home to be signed by parents, however, then the prospectus is redundant and dull. Consider providing one of the following:

- a letter to the parents to read later
- a newsletter or pamphlet created by that period's students that describes what they are reading, what they have been doing, what they have talked about, what a day in class is like, what books kids are reading outside of class for their independent reading
- a weekly assignment sheet and/or the monthly calendar

Greet parents as they come in. Stand by the door and shake their hands. Look them in the eye and say something friendly like "Hi, glad you could make it tonight. And you are representing. . . ?" I prefer this slightly jovial "and you are representing. . . ?" because I grew tired of saying "Hello, and who are you?" and having them tell me they were "Wilma Fitzpatrick . . . John Crane's mother." These greetings are also your only real chance to personalize the evening: "Mrs. Fitzpatrick, great to meet you. Hey, John did a fine job in our class discussion today. He really understands that book we are reading." It is also a chance to find out what the student tells them by asking as they enter, "Did John tell you what I said about his presentation last week?"

Display student work. This is when the pictures I take serve double duty. On nights such as Open House they become the evidence of all that we have done throughout the year; they are a record of our work and generally show the students at their best. Portfolios are the property of the students; on nights such as these it is not the parents' right to read through their child's portfolio unless the student has given them permission to do so. I usually have some video projects going on the television as well as some projects—multimedia presentations, Web sites, interactive storybooks—up on the computer for parents to see as well. Finally, as many parents cannot get to such events because of work and few relatives (especially grandparents) ever come to such evenings, consider having a couple kids in your class create a permanent classroom Web site to which you can add special projects and information for Open House or Back-to-School Night. One year, parents unable to get to my class to see the video of the infamous *Lord of the Flies* trial could view photographs of the trial on the Web site that the court reporter set up as part of his work for the trial.

Connect what you are doing this year with what you've done in the past. While it is certainly commendable to speak to the parents about the new ideas you are trying out this year, it is also helpful to establish that your class is built on a strong foundation of successful methods. Some teachers have famous units that parents expect their children to experience, for example. For this reason, I mention briefly that we will be doing some interesting new things with the India-China Project or that we will be adding Bharati Mukherjee's novel *Jasmine* to the reading list in order to complement our reading of the *Odyssey*, a unit I've revised and adapted over the years to create a powerful beginning to the year. This sense of continuity and tradition, combined with innovation and experimentation, addresses several of their immediate concerns.

Have parents respond on index cards. This activity is very helpful and interesting. I do my best to collect the cards after a few minutes so that I can quickly flip through them and see if anyone asked questions I can address immediately (e.g., "What are you doing about writing in the class?" or "Will they be expected to read books on their own?"). This parental information reveals a great deal about kids, often helping me understand behaviors or attitudes that had been confusing to me so early in the year. A high schooler might not be ready to confess a major life crisis (e.g., my sister died last month or my parents just got divorced) but parents recognize the importance of this information and will offer it up. The questions vary but here are a few examples of questions I have found helpful:

- What is your name?
- Who is your child?
- What is something I may not know about your son or daughter that might help me to better understand and teach them?
- Do you have any questions or concerns about the class?
- How is your child doing in their other classes?

Emphasize your availability. Some high schools and teachers alienate parents by making them feel unwelcome. This is particularly upsetting to parents who might be coming from a middle school where parents were encouraged to help—in class and around the school. Teachers who communicate a willingness to talk put such parents at ease, make them feel like the teacher has nothing to hide, and is, generally speaking, their partner in their child's education.

Dress like a professional. Most teachers at my school, including myself, dress pretty casually for work. This evening is about your professional credibility as well as your department's; parents want to see that their children are taught by people whom their children can respect.

Do NOT speak critically of a class, a student, or the administration. The parents are, like your students, a captive audience. Unlike students, they can react to what you say by challenging you or speaking against you to the administration or members of the community. It is not a forum for your own problems. They do not want to hear about the lack of support from the department chair or the principal. They want only one thing: to know that their child is getting the best education you can give.

Consider being political. While this seems to contradict what I just urged you never to do, it is different. This is your chance to be an advocate for your profession and your class program. Who knows what services parents in your classes can provide. Tell them that if they have good books laying around the house you'll put them in—or start!—your classroom library. Someone might even say, "I don't have any books but I'll give you some money to buy books so long as they go in the classroom." In California, recent legislation has allowed tax payers to be able to donate to the school libraries through their tax forms, and other legislation has allowed for reduced class sizes in the freshman English classes. If I have time, I try to be sure these assembled voters and taxpayers know what a difference such investments in the schools make by telling them how they benefit their children.

Endnote: Meeting the Parents

I relish these evenings. There is an air of ritual that surrounds the occasion. School gets out around 12:30. After a quiet lunch with a colleague at a nearby deli, I return, put on some music, make some coffee, and begin setting up my room. This activity provides me the time I need to pull back and reflect on just what we have done all year. It is, after all, as much an exhibition of my work as it is of the students'. By the time I leave for a nice conversational dinner with colleagues, my room is alive with the evidence of their work, their growth, their thought. I begin to realize the natural rhythm of the year is moving along, that time is, in fact, passing. I begin to ask myself what we have accomplished this year and what we should achieve and experience in the remaining two months. When parents come in hours later, I feel like an enthusiastic gallery curator telling them about the very interesting, sophisticated work recently done by a young woman named Frannie who just happens to be their daughter.

REFLECTION

Use the handout you create as a means of reflecting on what your students have done so far. As you create this handout, ask yourself what this sheet says about your teaching and their learning; consider it a portfolio of your own work which you will present to your students' parents. What questions might you expect from parents based on what your handout says?

ACTIVITY

Go out for a nice dinner with a few colleagues, and have a nice conversation before the evening begins. I cannot emphasize the value of this enough. We have so little time to talk about what we do and why we love it. Or to talk about the other things important to us—our children, families, hobbies, books we've read, places we want to visit. And make it a nice dinner. Treat yourself; make the night special.

RECOMMENDATIONS

Dumbing Down Our Kids: Why American Children Feel Good About Themselves But Can't Read, Write, or Add. Charles J. Sykes (St. Martin's Griffin 1995). This book allows you to understand what some parents expect from the schools.

Class Struggle: What's Wrong (and Right) with America's Best Public High Schools. Jay Mathews (Times Books 1998). Both of these books put you in the mind of parents as consumers who are coming into your class to evaluate the "product" of your labor on their child's behalf.

CHAPTER 27

THE POLITICS OF EDUCATION
PARENTS, SCHOOL BOARDS, POLITICIANS, AND THE MEDIA

It is impossible to talk about education apart from some conception of the good life; people will inevitably differ in their conceptions of the good life, and hence will inevitably disagree on matters of education: therefore the discussion of education falls squarely within the domain of politics.

—Lawrence Cremin, "Education as Politics," from *Popular Education and Its Discontents*

We should always be able to explain why we do things. Aside from the obvious pedagogical reasons for this (i.e., what is your rationale?), we should be able to account for our choices in texts, our assignments, and our methods. Once, while eating dinner with colleagues at a conference, a college professor said, "Jim, you teach English, so I thought you could tell me whether this is common or if I should worry. Jenny's English teacher had them all lie on the floor, turned out the lights, told them to close their eyes, and then walked around and put a slice of lemon in each student's mouth. Is that a pretty common thing to do?" All the teachers at the table responded immediately, in chorus: "Did she have them write about that?" "I asked the same thing! No, she didn't." "It's nuts. I'd talk to the teacher," I said.

Public Relations: Reaching the Community

English teachers should, by virtue of being English teachers, be masters of communication. We should be able to explain to parents, to community members, or to politicians what we do and why. Yet this is rarely the case, and the "truth" ends up being told by conservative columnists, the editorial letters of cynical citizens, or disgruntled parents sitting in the bleachers surrounded by other parents. It is worth noting that 75 percent of the public does not have children in school, yet many of these people vote on educational initiatives or elect legislators who vote on educational legislation that is based on the testimony of "experts" who assert, as one govern-ment official allegedly did, that "teachers know nothing."

What can we do? This is always the question. My English department has created several documents that help us address parents' concerns, all of which are, in the end, based on their genuine concern for their children, something we do not often allow parents to feel.

Create a newsletter. Thanks to computers they are very easy to make as most programs come with templates for newsletters already laid out; you just need to type in the informa-tion. This newsletter quickly became a means of communicating what we were doing, rec-ognizing our department members' work, or making announcements (e.g., summer reading titles or grants we received).

Create a department brochure. Many schools have occasions for incoming students and their parents who visit the school to learn more about what the year ahead. On such evenings parents have many questions, some of which are easily anticipated and ad-dressed through a brochure that includes test scores, a profile of the department, a general overview of courses (with extra attention paid to freshman English). If you don't know how to use computers to do this, your students do; give teams of students in your class the information, and have them compete to create the document your department will ul-timately use. These brochures can be sent out to feeder schools and made available in the main office, at Back-to-School Night, or Open House.

Daily communication: phone calls, postcards, notes home. By daily I don't mean every day but rather the little moments that merit some more immediate response than a monthly newsletter or published brochure. These communications generally take only a minute and accomplish more than anything else to assert your professional integrity which translates to respect for your department if most staff participate. I have had parents tell me three years later that the phone call I made when Jake was a freshman to just say he was doing some especially fine work lately, or to ask why he hadn't been to school in a week ("No one else called or seemed to care," they would say) or to say he needed to do more work made a bigger difference than anything else. Kids work for those who care about them.

Hold parent-student-teacher conferences. One high school I know faced mounting criticism from parents and the community at large. They decided to take three nights and use the gym to hold conferences where parents and students came to collect the report card. The benefits were stunning and immediate: all complaints vanished; parents began asking what they could do to help their children, the school, the teacher; teachers felt more respected and ap-preciated as it created an opportunity for parents to praise them for the good work they did.

Use your syllabus as a means of communicating with parents by requiring student to take it home and get their parents to sign it.

Use Open House and Back-to-School Night to talk about what you do and why you do it that way; also use it to highlight your students' work which is by far the best advertisement of your own credibility.

Create a school, department, or class Web site in order to regularly communicate to people what you and your students are doing. Students will happily create these for you in case you are warming up to say "I don't have the time." Another option is to consult with your school's Web site development team. Ours consists of a group of students who regularly solicit information—e.g., "Mr. Burke, could you please let us know what books will be on the summer reading lists so we can post them to the Web site?"—and create the pages necessary to house that information.

Educate your principal by dropping a copy of any good assignments or student work in their box; they love to know what is going on so when they speak to parents they can refer to specific teachers and students, and sound as if they really know what is going on in the class.

Meet with the parents group at your school, especially if you are a department chair, to promote the good work your department is doing, taking advantage of the opportunity to let them know how they can help you and your department.

Contact the local or school newspaper to tell them about a particularly impressive project or activity your students are doing. (See Chapter 15.)

Educate your colleagues by talking about what you do and how you do it. Teachers of other departments in your own school can be potentially dangerous critics, especially if they live within the school's community.

Speak at School Board meetings where important issues relating to teaching will be discussed, especially if policies will be created from these discussions.

Invite members of the School Board to visit your class. Like principals, they love to be able to speak specifically about what teachers and students are doing since it gives the impression that they know what is going on in the schools. Here is a letter I received after a visit from a former English teacher who is now a member of our school board :

> Dear Jim Burke,
>
> Thank you for receiving me in your English class. I appreciated the opportunity to visit Burlingame and to experience the activities in your class.
>
> The relevancy of the material the students will use in this assignment makes the class take time on an immediacy that engages the students' interest and enthusiasm.
>
> The outside world in which they live and into which they will disappear soon can be used to produce thinking and writing that means something to them.
>
> It was a pleasure to meet you and see the results of your efforts.
>
> Thank you,
> John Gregory

I am not naive: I know some School Boards or members of School Boards are dangerous and intimidating people. But it is the resistance to having anyone in our classrooms that inspires suspicion of what teachers do. People tend to question what they do not understand. Such efforts to communicate to parents are all the more important in schools where reforms are changing instructional strategies: the parents need to know what you are going to do before they hear it inaccurately reported by their children who are often not very reliable narrators.

Like so many things, these actions I've listed here demand your time and energy, neither of which you have an abundance of; however, if you don't make the investment up front it is almost certain you will eventually lose it later when parents start calling you or your principal or your superintendent. By that time it will be too late and the conversations will be difficult, emotional exchanges that can achieve peace but probably not restore credibility or respect in the short run. Here are some characteristics of effective communication with parents regardless of the form it takes:

- be honest
- be specific
- let parents into your classroom
- provide examples of the success or the problem

- be professional in all speech, manner, and dress
- be willing (to meet, to talk, to help)
- be ready (to explain, to show, to compromise)
- use flawless, articulate language whether speaking or writing

Lights! Camera! Anxiety!

The media defines the public's perceptions of schools. Criticism sells papers; success does not. Low test scores get readers; good scores, generally, do not though there are obvious and welcome exceptions. The teacher who has some moral failure gets written about; the hundreds who taught well, the dozens who changed their students' lives that day get the praise of a quiet, dirty classroom at day's end, a classroom whose walls or In boxes reveal the real success and business of schools. But to ignore the media, to dismiss it as idiotic or absurd is as dangerous as dismissing parents, for while most parents feel good about the school their kids attend, most people surveyed give other schools or schools in general low marks.

Again, it is our professional responsibility to educate the public about what we do. We must tell our story. Whoever tells the story first tells the truth, that's how people perceive it. What follows the first story is only so much defense and distraction. Particularly harsh critiques of the schools—e.g., the teachers do not know how to teach reading—often stir up the greatest furor. My work as the legislative liaison and as moderator of an on-line "virtual roundtable" where many pressing political issues are discussed, has confirmed again and again the fundamental importance of political action. Political trends of the last decade call for more sophisticated, organized responses, some of which I outline here.

Create an electronic mailing list that includes people within your district or community; I did this with all the feeder schools in the wake of criticisms that our school did not adequately inform the other schools what we expected of incoming students. It is easy, quick, and very beneficial.

Write letters to the editor of your local newspaper or any magazines you read that do not tell "the whole story" about a particular educational issue.

Write letters to and call your state and federal elected officials to let them know your views on or concerns about a law or policy that is being proposed. Call NCTE for their Political Action Reference Packet or visit their Web site (http://www.ncte.org) to get helpful guidelines for writing such letters. Also, visit the federal Web site (http://www.congress.org/elecmail.html) for more suggestions about how to communicate effectively with your legislator.

Write a column for your local paper or radio station. Most papers and public radio stations have an open forum spot; many even pay for such columns! I have done both of these over the years and am always amazed to learn how many people hear or read them.

Contact your local newspaper, television, or radio station. If you don't feel like writing yourself then contact them directly and let them know what you think or what your students are doing. They only understand stories to the extent that experts explain them to them; you are an expert. Make it a point to know the name and phone number (or e-mail address) of the local education reporters.

Talk with people at parties and on planes about schooling. As soon as you say you are a teacher many will gladly let you know what they think. Use some of the following questions to help get your point across:

- Why do you think that?
- How did you respond to that?
- What do you do to help your child in a situation like that?
- Can I suggest a couple books or strategies I've found helpful?
- Have you met with the teacher to talk with them about your concerns?
- Have you consulted your child's other teachers to find out if the same thing is going on in other classes?
- Is there anything else going on that might help explain why they are failing or don't want to do this particular assignment?

Join SLATE. SLATE (Support for the Learning and Teaching of English) is the political branch of NCTE. Through a series of position statements and informational papers, they provide quality information about a wide range of current issues to support teachers. This is the branch that addresses censorship issues as well.

Invite your legislator to come visit your school so they can see what schools are really like. Schools are mythic spaces: people think they know all about them because they went through them years before. They will come, given the right occasion; it is, after all, a great photo-op.

Endnote: The Political Context

Becoming a parent transformed my views on the relationship between schools and the communities they teach. Certainly I am a professional and should be trusted to do what my judgment tells me is best for any child. However, to ignore that teaching is a social and political act is reckless, particularly in this era of public scrutiny. The day I sent my oldest son off to kindergarten, I realized what I had never known before: We want to know what is going on with our kids when they are in the hands of others. This anxiety about our children's ultimate success, which can sometimes translate into meddling or even organized opposition from parents, is nowhere more thoroughly examined than in Jay Mathews's *Class Struggle: What's Wrong (and Right) with America's Best Public High Schools* (1998).

I close this chapter by issuing the same challenge to you that NCTE president Sheridan Blau issued to all gathered in Detroit for the 1997 NCTE Convention:

> As teachers of English and the language arts we have seen our subject and our teaching enter the discourse of politics and become the topic for popular discussions about the crisis in public education. We find ourselves caught in a tide of public opinion that is rising against much of what we stand for intellectually and professionally. Politicians, their fingers poised on the public pulse, stand ready to turn popular prejudice into public policy, especially if they can do so in the name of reliable, replicable scientific research. Such challenges require us to abandon our diffidence and, however reluctantly, address the political issues (Blau 1997).

REFLECTION

Make a list of all the different stories you teach. Write about a few books that invite particular concern from the public (e.g., *The Catcher in the Rye* remains one of the most banned books). Why do some parents (or even students) object to these books? How should you respond to such objections? What is your argument for reading any particular book? Consider writing this whole reflection as a letter to a parent who has complained about a specific book you really like to teach.

ACTIVITY

Visit People for the American Way's Web site (www.pfaw.org) and examine the complaints filed against books and teaching practices. Consider visiting some other, more conservative Web sites (e.g., the Eagle Forum) to see how they talk about certain books and what advice they give to parents for dealing with such matters in their children's schools.

RECOMMENDATIONS

Both of these are very clearly written texts and contain helpful information:

Literacy at the Crossroads: Critical Talk About Reading, Writing, and Other Teaching Dilemmas. Regie Routman (Heinemann 1996).

You Can Make a Difference: A Teacher's Guide to Political Action. Barbara Keresty, Susan O'Leary, and Dale Wortley (Heinemann 1998).

CHAPTER 28

JOINING THE PROFESSIONAL CONVERSATION

Do you know that conversation is one of the greatest pleasures in life?

—**William Somerset Maugham**

Regional and National Conventions

As I come off the airplane in Detroit for the 1997 NCTE convention, I see other English teachers arriving from all over the country. Certain hints help to identify them: the way they dress, the bags that bulge with a combination of books and ungraded papers. We all drift toward the baggage area where we find still other teachers and, eventually, our bags. Most don't know each other but recognize in them a fellow teacher and share with them the easy, familiar conversation common to all members of a profession.

Instead of waiting for the shuttle, which will not be there for an hour, people begin grouping up and getting in taxis together. And so we are off, driving into the big city under the encroaching darkness that is punctuated by the evening's first snow. Then we begin talking. It always happens. To come across the country for the NCTE convention is to be interested in what other people do; these other people do the same thing you do in a different place, sometimes in different ways, mostly with the same kids.

By the time I arrive at the hotel forty-five minutes later, I have had a serious conversation with two women from Tennessee about a program they are participating in called Schools of Thought. I am intrigued by the name. I ask them if they have read Rex Brown's book by the same name. "Oh yes, it's a good book," one woman says and goes on to explain that while they are not linked, the program embodies some of Brown's ideas. The other woman, an eighth-grade teacher, works with Apple's Classrooms of Tomorrow (ACOT) program; she has spent much of the last year writing grants as part of a team trying to bring more computers into their schools. Somewhere in the conversation she mentions that their schools, headed by a man who hopes to run for state office the following year, have just bought into E.D. Hirsch's Core Knowledge program for grades K–8, and must teach specific aphorisms and other cultural facts each day as part of the program. By this time, the man up front, who has been asking specific questions about their programs and my work, introduces himself as Peter Smagorinsky, author of *Standards in Practice* (1996), a book I had been reading only two days before. We all begin talking about standards and I talk to him briefly about the questioning strategies for *Huckleberry Finn* that he outlined in the book and which I had used the day before; in fact, thanks to his strategies, my substitute had a good lesson plan which my students—hopefully!—were using in my sixth-period class as we spoke in the taxi.

This is exactly why teachers should go to professional conferences: the Great Conversation. It takes place all over the country and is hosted by professional organizations—NCTE (national), California Association of Teachers of English (state), Greater San Diego County Teachers of English (local). Each gathering has its own style and purpose; some people love regional conferences or Writing Project conferences, but hate big national conventions where as many as ten thousand people come to learn how to be better English teachers.

In my second year of teaching, I somehow found my way to the Asilomar conference in September, an annual pilgrimage to Monterey for many northern California English teachers. I roomed with Bob Chapman, a writing teacher from Eureka, who introduced me to portfolios and talked me into coming to his excellent workshop that weekend. Over dinner one night, I talked at length with Mary Kay Healy and Sandra Murphy—both respected leaders in English language arts education in California—and left with an invitation to write an article about work my freshmen were doing. All this talking gave me some sense of arrival. Here were people who read, who wrote, who never lost their fascination for education and welcomed me into their conversation as an equal partner. Being new and young were not limitations but advantages, part of my knowledge about teaching and education. Sunday afternoon I drove home from Asilomar understanding the concept of *home* and feeling part of a professional community.

There is really only one way to find out about these conferences, and to be a part of the Great Conversation: join NCTE and your state affiliate. Getting away occasionally to a conference is absolutely necessary to your professional survival. One of the most commonly sited reasons for leaving the profession is that teachers feel used up, alienated by working in isolation. One of the most common reasons for not going to such conventions is, understandably, the cost. There are, however, several ways to get money to attend such conventions:

- Request money from the school site professional development committee or other such committee.
- Ask local organizations that offer small grants for teacher improvement.
- Apply for grants from professional organizations like your union, educational organizations (Phi Delta Kappa), or community organizations (Lions, Kiwanis, or local women's club).
- Inquire, through NCTE and its affiliates, about programs, such as Teachers for the Dream, which offer scholarships to new teachers or specific groups, whom they are dedicated to bringing into the conversation.
- Look around your school to see who might have funds through a grant or other program—e.g., technology, mentorships, GATE—that would cover your costs to attend a convention so long as you meet their guidelines (e.g., attend a few sessions on the use of computers in English instruction).
- Write a letter to the director of curriculum or some other department at the district or county office and argue your case.

Your professional organization exists to support your work and enhance your stature as a professional. During the early 1990s, when the national standards initiatives began, NCTE created rich opportunities for teachers to meet and participate in the discussion that lead to the standards document itself. And when censorship arises, it is such organizations as NCTE that can offer the substantial support needed to defend your right to teach as your professional judgment dictates.

Virtual Conversations: The On-Line Community

Obviously not everyone can afford the time or money to attend a national convention. You can, however, participate in these essential discussions through the virtual community found on-line. For instance, the NCTE-Talk listserv generates upwards of fifty postings a day about everything from discussing one's sexuality in the classroom to talking about the role of grammar or value of literature. Such lists further provide a forum for support and inquiry to teachers who live in remote areas and cannot find in such places the professional community they seek. This last reason is of particular importance: if you are reading this book, if you invest in your teaching to try to improve, you may be seeking through such books and journals a conversation you cannot have with people at your school.

I started an electronic roundtable called CATENet (California Association of Teachers of English Network) some years ago to allow for a more immediate, ongoing conversation about issues within the profession. When I entered teaching, I assumed ours was a profession defined by its tolerance, its intelligence, its common purpose: to educate kids. Unfortunately, this assumption ignores our common denominator: we are human and seem to demand some measure of conflict. One of my greatest disappointments has been the realization of how we in our own profession can antagonize each other or our ideas, can pass judgment on others' methods and practices, in the worst cases utterly dismissing each others' knowledge and experience as worthless, meaningless, or even irresponsible.

CATENet, and similar listservs, distinguish the new era of teaching in the global world as one where geography is irrelevant, where the conversation can take place wherever you are and whenever you want. Through e-mail, I have enjoyed a remarkable exchange with educators from all grade levels across the country. CATENet, which has grown to nearly one thousand teachers nationwide, offers us not only a sense of community, but an invaluable professional and political resource. This is best illustrated by this chapter itself: I sent out an inquiry to the people on CATENet asking them about the different conversations they participated in. Many emphasized the advantages of such on-line dialogue as listservs afford, stressing how nice it is to participate in such dialogues when they have the time or feel the need.

The Teacher Study Group

Whether you call it a "study group," an "action research team," a "book group," or "support group," such on-site groups are essential to your professional well-being. Caroline Green, a contributor to CATENet, describes how her group works:

> We have a study group going on using the book *Mosaic of Thought* by Keene and Zimmerman (Heinemann 1997). Through their book we discovered we really needed to look at our own comprehension strategies in order to discover what to teach students. I organized a group at my school site, picked an adult novel (we chose Wallace Stegner's *Crossing to Safety*) and read chapters in each book concurrently. Our focus was on our own comprehending (what we used/did) of the novel. We also discussed what the implications were for our classrooms. Most of the teachers are now teaching

the strategies to their students and sharing rave reviews of things students are talking about and able to do with these strategies! Teachers need to "experience their own processes" of good teaching practices. We have had such a wonderful experience learning about ourselves as readers/comprehenders that we have chosen another Stegner novel and will continue to examine in more depth our own comprehending strategies.

The members of such groups need not be, in fact probably should not be, limited to English teachers unless you are committed to a specific line of research that would not interest others. In his memoir, physicist Richard Feynman talks about having dinner at the table of a different academic department each night while in graduate school; these conversations with other disciplines helped him to think more creatively about his own work in physics. Inevitably the same will happen to you as you talk about learning with a physics teacher, an art teacher, and a few English teachers over coffee at a local café after school.

To ensure the success of such discussion groups, consider some of the ideas outlined below. Also, look around for local sponsors that might even support your group through small collaborative grants in the name of improving education; some foundations have money set aside specifically for such humble but essential projects, and several districts I know offer teachers credits toward salary advancement for such groups. Here are some other suggestions to consider:

- Meet someplace different each time, someplace nice—someone's house, a café, restaurant—and suitable for good conversation.
- Decide on the titles together, so that everyone feels included and committed.
- Have fun with your choices: pick titles that challenge your thinking, that will force a good conversation; also range widely to keep the forum lively (see, for example, Kathleen Norris's *The Cloister Walk* or Daniel Dennett's *Darwin's Dangerous Idea*).
- Invite new people to join.
- Make it a social experience, one that enriches the mind and the soul.
- Establish parameters for your group: e.g., no complaining, no criticizing different ideas, how you choose books.

Endnote: The Great Conversation

You cannot underestimate the value of those friendships that grow up between one or two special colleagues with whom you work and share an enthusiasm for all things English. I have several colleagues that make coming to work exciting because of all that they might possibly teach me that day about books, gender, kids, or life. These mentors, comrades, and friends provide us a sense of community that helps us feel we belong, that we have a place that stands apart from all the bickering and criticism that sometimes gets the better of our colleagues for reasons we all understand too well but must nonetheless resist.

Joining the profession affords you other benefits that you will appreciate. Through such publications as NCTE and your state affiliate publish you find out about grants and other opportunities such as the National Endowment for the Humanities summer institutes, two of which have allowed me to have a much nicer summer with my family than I could otherwise have afforded. Other opportunities come your way, too: publishers need readers, magazines need reviewers. And you are recognized by colleagues and your students as a professional, as someone whose words carry the extra weight of credibility when you say, "You know that's a good question. That came up when I was at a workshop this weekend . . ." and they think, "This teacher is serious: they practice what they preach and are a *professional*."

Welcome to the conversation—and the profession.

REFLECTION

Write about what the word "professional" means to you, using specific examples from your own experience or other fields. Then write about what this term seems to mean to society at large. Are teachers, for example, generally considered professionals in the eyes of the society?

ACTIVITY

Join one of the on-line discussions listed below and give it a try. You can subscribe to a listserv for a few days if you want, and then "unsubscribe" as quick as you please if you don't like what they offer.

On-line forums. NCTE-Talk is probably the most inclusive, far-ranging listserv, as it offers an open forum for anything having to do with the teaching of English. High-volume postings, but those on it appear to enjoy the sense of community it offers. You can find out about other listservs NCTE offers by writing to the following address and putting the word *lists* in the body of your message or by visiting their Web site (www.ncte.org).

To subscribe write to: majordomo@serv1.ncte.org.

RECOMMENDATIONS

The following books came highly recommended by different participants in my on-line discussion group (CATENet). Consider using any of the following books in your study group:

English

The Great Books. David Denby (Touchstone, 1996).

A Lesson Before Dying. Ernest Gaines (Knopf, 1997).

Voices of the Self. Keith Gilyard (Wayne State University Press, 1991).

How to Catch a Shark: Stories About Teaching and Learning. Donald Graves (Heinemann, 1998).

The Schools We Need and Why We Don't Have Them. E. D. Hirsch (Doubleday, 1996).

Teacher Research and Urban Literacy Education. Sandra Hollingsworth and Anthony Cody (Teachers College Press, 1994).

Mosaic of Thought: Teaching Comprehension in a Reader's Workshop. Ellin Oliver Keene and Susan Zimmerman (Heinemann, 1997).

The Discipline of Hope: Learning from a Lifetime of Teaching. Herbert Kohl (Simon and Schuster, 1998).

Changing Our Minds. Miles Myers (NCTE, 1996).

Poetic Justice: The Literary Imagination and Public Life. Martha C. Nussbaum (Beacon Press, 1995).

The Language Instinct. Steven Pinker (Harperperennial, 1995).

The Rise and Fall of English: Reconstructing English as a Discipline. Robert Scholes (Yale University Press, 1998).

Composing a Teaching Life. Ruth Vinz (Heinemann, 1996).

Teaching and Learning *(Across the Disciplines)*

Making Connections: Teaching and the Human Brain. Renate Nummela Caine and Geoffrey Caine (Addison-Wesley, 1994).

Flow: The Psychology of Optimal Experience. Mihalyi Csikszentmihalyi (Harperperennial, 1991).

Other People's Children. Lisa Delpit (The New Press, 1995).

Darwin's Dangerous Idea: Evolution and the Meanings of Life. Daniel C. Dennett (Touchstone Books, 1996).

Surely You're Joking, Dr. Feynman. Richard Feynman (W. W. Norton, 1997).

Creating Minds or Leading Minds. Howard Gardner (Basic Books, 1995).

Cloister Walk. Kathleen Norris (Riverhead Books, 1996).

The Origins of Satan. Elaine Pagels (Vintage Books, 1996).

Possible Lives. Mike Rose (Penguin, 1996).

Results: The Key to Continuous School Improvement. Mike Schmoker (Association for Supervision and Curriculum Development, 1996).

The Reflective Practitioner: How Professionals Think in Action. Donald A. Schon (Basic Books, 1983).

The Fifth Discipline. Peter Senge (Currency, 1990).

A Celebration of Neurons: An Educator's Guide to the Human Brain. Robert Sylvester (Association for Supervision and Curriculum Development, 1995).

WRITING STUDENT RECOMMENDATION LETTERS

Aside from counselors, English teachers write more recommendations than most other teachers. The reason is predictable: students assume we can write well, even persuasively, on their behalf.

These requests do not come with extra time to write them, however, and so we must find effective ways to meet students needs while honoring our own. We need to have time to prepare for the next day's lessons and to play a hand of Go Fish with our own children before reading a little something for our own pleasure. But the letters must be written.

The requests usually begin to come in early October from those students seeking early admissions (which must be postmarked by November 1 in most cases). By November the requests come in steadily and trickle off sometime in late January for most; then a second round of letters for scholarships and awards ensues. Such demands for recommendations are particularly severe for junior teachers as the senior teacher often does not know the students well enough to be able to recommend them, and freshman teachers are seen as too removed from the student's current status to recommend them.

In the *English Journal* back in 1997 a conversation opened up between teachers about the importance of writing honest letters of recommendation and the need to *not* recommend kids who are qualified. The discussion got heated, opening up as it did a philosophical divide. Some teachers cast themselves as gatekeepers to the tower, taking their role very seriously; you might think such teachers were on retainer from the universities and received a dollar for each kid they "weeded out." Those on the other side of the debate argue that kids need recommendations and should be encouraged and helped to go where their desires and dreams take them.

Though I offer my own forms and samples here, they come from other teachers who helped me to be more efficient in this area. Figure A.1 shows the form I give to all students who request a letter or recommendation. If, for some reason, I cannot in good faith recommend a student, I tell them so and apologize (usually, to be honest, telling them that freshman teachers are not seen as valid recommendations). On the rare occasion when I arrive at work and find an envelope full of recommendation forms with a short note

GUIDELINES FOR LETTERS OF RECOMMENDATION

Your name (please include your home phone number)	
I need this letter sent/in my hand (circle one) by...	
What class did you take with me--and what year?	
What grades (F/S) did you earn?	
Why do you want me to write this letter?	
Who am I writing to?	

Put this check-off sheet *on top* of your application or other materials.

The letter should be:

- given to me (the student)
- sent to the university/employer
- other   (explain)_____

Please supply the following:

- A quick note explaining who I am writing to and for what purpose (e.g., "This letter is going to the dean of the College of Engineering which I must apply to separately from the university itself.")
- A clearly formatted list of those points you would like to be sure I emphasize, ideally in order of importance. If it is at all unclear why any of these points is so important you should explain that to me---e.g., "this award/experience is of particular importance because I was the first freshman to ever be nominated...").
- A copy of the school's/organization's guidelines/application that will help me understand who I am writing to and what they might want to hear.
- A resume that is both thorough and nicely done (e.g., done on the computer in proper resume format)
- If appropriate---an envelope with sufficient postage and properly addressed

While some letters---"To whom it may concern..."---can work for more than one school, you may need separate letters in special cases. In such cases, please be sure to follow the guidelines above, but clearly separate the different materials for schools. I ask that you put all the stuff for each school in separate manila envelopes to help me keep all the different papers organized. Wouldn't want me to lose any applications, would we?

If I agreed to write a letter for you, I want to tell you sincerely that I am happy to do it, that I do not do it for anybody who asks. It is a pleasure to recommend you, and I can only hope that the world sees in you all the talent and intelligence I do.

Figure A.1

saying "Please complete the following recommendations for Jane," signed by Jane's mother, I have them sent to Jane's homeroom teacher with a brief note that her mother made an unfortunate mistake. I am happy, in such circumstances, to provide Jane's family with a topic for dinner that night and only occasionally wonder if Jane points out how rude her mother was.

Sample Letter of Recommendation

NOTE: I created various recommendation letter templates on my computer. These allow me to write such letters as the following example quickly and easily. I create two versions of each letter, one with MALE and the other with FEMALE in the file name, leaving room in places to add the personal information for that student. The template function is common to any popular word processing program purchased in the last few years.

To Whom It May Concern:

I have known Brad K——— since he was a freshman in my Honors English class. Brad is one of the most remarkable young men I have had the pleasure to work with in my ten years of teaching. I know him as both a student in my freshman Honors class and a person whom I have continued to speak with often. Within the first weeks of class it was obvious that he brought an impressive range of talents and a level of initiative to the work that are rare in high school students, particularly in young men. To say he is diligent and hard-working is to misrepresent his accomplishment: Brad set a new standard for what I have come to expect in both writing and studying. In many ways his character is best represented by my first impression of him: standing outside my door forty-five minutes before school even started on opening day, pacing back and forth, eager, ready, willing.

Brad's character comes through in all that he does, and in his daily interactions with his peers both in the classroom and around the school. He has grown into a rare type of leader. It is his example, his persistence that wins others over and inspires them. This is a young man who barely made the baseball team as a freshman—despite working out and preparing all year for tryouts—and went on to earn all-league recognition for his fine play in the subsequent years. He works harder than any student I can recall in recent years.

Brad shows "grace under pressure" and succeeds in consistently producing quality work in all his classes that distinguishes itself in both style and content. He consistently challenges himself to write more difficult, substantial papers. His writing and editing skills are sharp, having been honed in the rigorous Honors/AP courses he has taken these past four years. I am thinking in particular of the remarkable work he did on a rather exhausting project in my class, one the freshman have come to see as a rite of passage, called the UN Project. It takes all quarter and asks kids to study in depth a country with a long-standing conflict. Acting as UN representatives, each student must study the history and read the literature of that country; it culminates in a thirty-minute final multi-media presentation of their proposed solution to that country's problems. Students must then hold up under the scrutiny of their peers who can ask them questions about the solution. This kind of work taught Brad to think on his feet and to examine a complex subject. Many seniors I talk to say it was the most challenging and educational project they do in their four years.

In the future, when asked to think about what most distinguished Brad K———, I will say he showed other students that they could truly succeed by virtue of will and a keen intelligence. Through his writing and other activities both in the community and the school, Brad demonstrates a genuine interest in and concern for the world he is preparing to enter.

I recommend Brad K——— without reservation, knowing he will not only do quality academic work, but contribute to your school and its community. I would be happy to answer further questions about Mr. K———'s abilities or character should any arise.

Thank you for your time and attention.

Sincerely,

Jim Burke
English Department Chair

Helping Students Write College Application Essays

It is late October, lunch time, and I am sitting in my room whose windows show the first signs of autumn outside. At the desk next to me sits a young woman from Taiwan who came to the United States specifically to get the best education she could. She is a senior. She wants to go to Columbia. She has asked me, even though I am not nor have I ever been her teacher, to look at her college essay. I immediately notice that my colleague Elaine's comments are on there in her immaculate purple script (compared to my scrawl). I have spent most of my lunches this week meeting with kids to look at their essays. Because the essays are often personal reflections on their journey through the last four years, I find these sessions very informative and often inspiring: the essays show they changed and learned.

This young woman, Helena, wants me to say Elaine's comments are off the mark; she wants me to say, "Oh, Helena, this is just perfect as it is. Really! Here, let me give you a stamp so you can mail it now!" And when I say the same things as Elaine, when I tell her that she should hack out about 75% of it and start over using her concluding paragraph, she looks crushed. She wants me to do her work for her, to give her words, images, a heavy ring of keys that will open up not only the essay but the future she is trying to enter. I don't do that. Honestly, even for kids whose story I know intimately, who deserve to get to whatever next step they want to reach, I won't write their essay for them. My role in this process is to help them see their real subject and let them write the essays.

Strategies and Tips to Write Better College Essays

- Read the topic many times to get clear what it is asking.
- Underline any word in the application that seems essential to the topic: verbs: "reflect," "describe," "examine"; nouns: "person who most influenced you," "an experience that changed you." If you cannot write on the application, make a copy of it so you can.
- Look for those words in the application that the college is likely to use in their scoring rubric: In a *one-page* essay, please *reflect* on *one person* who has had a *strong influence* on

your *development*." Each of the underlined words signals a different aspect of the "story" they are asking you to write.

One young woman I worked with examined the role her voice coach played in her life. The essay said what she *did*, but did not examine the precise ways she had "influenced" her "development." Not only that, but she did not have a sense of her topic: to speak of how someone develops your voice is, frankly, not so interesting or important.

What are they *really* asking? Do they really want to hear about how her voice got more tone and strength to it—or are they interested in her intellectual, emotional, moral growth? Face it, a question like this is asking: what kind of person are you, and are you the kind of person we want at our university? What will you have to offer us? Schools get applications from thousands of kids with remarkable talents and grades; they prefer, in the balance, to give the nod to kids they think have character and will help create a great culture at their school. Penn State, for example, receives approximately sixteen thousand applications annually, 80 percent of whom are qualified for admission based on their numbers alone. However, only 25–30 percent can be admitted. The difference, according to one admissions officer, is *often* their essay because this is a variable "over which they have control." In other words, amidst all the statistics about their performance, the essay provides a chance for the student to really show who they are.

Another admissions officer I interviewed said, "There are three things you don't ever want to watch being made: one is sausage, one is legislation, and the other is college admissions because the process is sometimes so random given the number of kids that come across our desk. I read a thousand applications, each one of which has to have an essay, and I give each application about ten minutes in the first read-through. Anything that kid can do to connect with me as their reader, to make them stand out in that essay, which in many cases is the most important piece of the puzzle, helps me." "When we read them, though the scale is 1–10, we mostly calibrate it to a 2, 5, and 8: two means the essay negatively affects the student's application; 5 means it does nothing to advance their application; 8 means it moves it forward toward acceptance, though other factors are, of course, considered." And this: "Given the assumption that all kids have spell checkers on their word processors, we are now merciless when it comes to spelling errors: we are looking to take 25 percent of all the applications we receive; so even a spelling error can tip the balance against the student in such a competitive environment." Finally, colleges feel insulted and are annoyed by silly essays such as the person who writes an essay about "The Little Engine That Could," in response to the topic "Write about a fictional character that had an influence on your thinking or beliefs."

Your essay should have the following components outlined there:

- *Originality*: What can you write about that others cannot? Even if you are going to write about a topic that invites predictable subjects—"Please write about the book that has had the biggest influence on you"—you must find a way to write differently about it. *To Kill a Mockingbird* is a wonderful book; in fact so many kids think so that any university with such a topic is likely to receive hundreds of essays about Atticus's philosophy of "walking around in another person's shoes for a while." Turn it inside out: write about an unusual character like Dill or the judge. Better still, write about a different book, one that others are unlikely to have read: this will show you are a reader, that you are a thinker, that you don't walk the common path.
- *Correctness*: Your essay must be perfect. Errors are moral and intellectual checkmarks against you in this situation. Each one says you are not conscientious and take no pride in your work.

They want to know several things about you from your essay according to the articles I read:

- what your goals are
- how you prepared yourself for the future while in high school
- how you interact with other people in an increasingly diverse and crowded society
- what you will have to offer their school and its community as a person and a scholar
- that you will succeed and survive at their school (particularly important if you would be coming there from far away, another region and climate: they don't want people leaving because they're too far from home or because it's too cold when they could give the spot to someone who won't have those troubles)
- how will you contribute to the school's diversity and enrich its community
- if you have any links to the college (e.g., relatives who were alumni)
- your extracurricular activities: this includes not only clubs or athletics but non-school related activities like political or church groups, Boy Scouts, or jobs
- if there is an area in which you are, relative to your age, a "master": this is good to show because it suggests commitment to learning and excelling; shows a passion for something which can be transferred into other areas to ensure success and distinction at their school
- if you have an entrepreneurial spirit, to the extent that that reveals a strong character who takes on projects and achieves something you set out to do (e.g., your love of photography in high school leads you to start your own photography business while still in school, and use the money to help pay for the college you will attend).
- if you have "pluck," which, according to one admissions officer, is the gumption to write about something in a way that makes it stand out but not for the sake of standing out. The classic example in recent years is the essay in which a young man lists all the things he has done, exaggerating each one to the extreme—detailing that he has raised a million dollars to help the poor and jumped over tall buildings—but admitting in the end that the one thing he had yet to do was go to college, which he was hoping they would let him do. Such spirit sells you so long as it seems intelligent and a reflection of your character not just a joke.
- You write the story that is yours to write. Not everyone can write, as one student did in their opening line, "I was born in the Alaskan bush on the kitchen table."

Once I accepted the job of reading eighth-grade writing tests for the state exam. About eighty of us came every day for four days to a large, dull-colored room at a suburban high school. It was summer. I knew no one. We could not talk. I could not listen to a Walkman. We could not have drinks on the table with us because, they argued, we might spill them and the tests were legal documents. I read papers for four days, scoring them on a rubric of 0–6. It was hell on earth: each paper was the same as the last one but with different handwriting. And every once in a while, suddenly, I would pick up a paper and it would make me laugh, would make me think, would help me settle into the world a bit more. It was those I remembered at day's end. I can only imagine that college admissions people feel the same way every fall when they get snowed in by the blizzard of papers students send off at midnight.

HELPFUL RESOURCES ————————————————————————————

Essays That Worked. Boykin Curry & Brian Kasbar.

100 Successful College Application Essays. Christopher J. Georges and Gigi E. Georges, eds.

Students will find innumerable sites on the Internet with sample essays to help them. Some essays are for sale through these services. Teachers should warn their students against using any essay they find on-line. College admissions officers keep lists of these essays and immediately dismiss a student's application if they even suspect the student did not write it. Students may, however, find some of these sites useful as springboards for their own essays. Also, some universities provide helpful information about writing essays for their specific university; be sure to consult the university's Web site before writing your essay.

Principles of the Essay Checklist

Thesis

- Write your thesis down. Are you personally committed to this subject?

Focus

- What is the title of your essay? (A title should help you focus on what your paper is about but should not be as broad as "The Death Penalty.")
- Ask yourself as you write: "What do I want to prove?" and "How does what I just wrote help prove my point?"

Concreteness

- What examples do you provide to illustrate your thinking?
- What evidence do you provide to support your opinions?
- If you provide a quote, do you identify who said it and why their opinion on the issue matters?
- When you offer evidence or facts, do you explain why they are important and how they relate to and support your thesis?

Organization

- Did you outline your ideas before starting? (If not, or even if you did, take your rough draft and, using its paragraphs, make an outline to ensure each paragraph has a main idea and that idea relates to the thesis.)
- Does your introduction clearly state the thesis and then effectively elaborate on it to provide a good foundation for the rest of the essay?
- Review your paragraphs and your outline: Do the ideas in the essay follow the clear, logical sequence described in your outline?
- Read the first sentence of a paragraph then, reading the next sentence, ask yourself, "How does that second sentence relate to the first?" If it does not, it may cause your

paragraph—and thus your essay—to lose its focus and organization. Ideally, you will read all sentences and paragraphs, asking at each step, "How does this relate to what came just before it?" *Note:* Sometimes if a sentence does not logically follow the previous sentence it means you have introduced a new idea and may want to begin a new paragraph.

- Which transitional words did you use to provide a smooth progression from one idea to the next?

Mechanics

- If you are using a computer, did you run the spell checker?
- If you are using a computer and ran the spell checker, now re-read your paper and look only for spelling errors, focusing particularly on those words that are incorrectly used (e.g., you wrote *had* but meant to use *has*, or used *to* for *too*) but also looking for other misspellings it did not catch.
- Check all titles and citations: Are they properly formatted?
- Find your longest sentences: Are these complete, properly punctuated sentences—or run-ons?
- Proofreading tip: Read your essay aloud to yourself and listen for language that sounds awkward, phrases that sound too wordy, grammar that sounds incorrect, passages that seem possibly illogical or incoherent.
- Obviously, the more people that read your paper the more likely they are to find errors that your eyes cannot see because you are too familiar with the essay to see them.

103 Things to do Before/During/After Reading

1. **Pantomime** a scene you choose or the class calls out to you while up there.

2. **Dramatic monologue** for a character in a scene: what are they thinking/feeling at that moment--why?

3. **Dramatic monologue** for a character while they are out of the book: where are they? why? thinking?

4. **Business Card Book**: write the story in the most compelling way you can on paper the size of a business card.

5. **Postcard**: write to a friend about this book; to the author; to a character in the book; write as if you were the character or author and write to yourself.

6. **Mapmaker**: draw a map of the book's setting.

7. **Moviemaker**: write a one page "pitch" to a producer explaining why the story would or would not make a great movie.

8. **Trailer**: movie previews always offer a quick sequence of the best moments that make us want to watch it; storyboard or narrate the scenes for your trailer. Focus on verbs.

9. **Billboard**: as in the movies, take what seems the most compelling image(s) and create an ad.

10. **Adjective-itis**: pick five adjectives for the book or character(s), and explain how they apply.

11. **Collage**: create an individual or class collage around themes or characters in the book.

12. Haiku/Limerick: create one about a character.

13. **Cliffs Notes**: have each student take a chapter and, using Cliffs' format, create their own.

14. **Roundtable**: give students a chance to talk about what intrigues, bothers, confuses them about the book.

15. **Silent Roundtable**: the only rule is the teacher cannot say *anything* during the period allotted for class discussion of book.

16. **Silent Conversation**: a student writes about a story on paper; then passes it to another who responds to what they said; each subsequent respondent "talks" to/about all those before.

17. **Fishbowl**: impromptu or scheduled, 2-4 students sit in middle of circle and talk about a text; the class makes observations about the conversation then rotate into the circle.

18. **Movie Review**: students write a review of (or discuss) a movie based on a story.

19. **Dear Author**: after reading a book the student(s) write the author via the publisher (who always forwards them).

20. **Surf the Net**: prior to, while, or after reading a book check out the web and its offerings about the book, its author, or its subject.

21. **Inspirations**: watch a film inspired by a story (e.g., *Franny and Alexander* is inspired by *Hamlet*) and compare/contrast.

22. **Timeline**: create a timeline that includes both the events in the novel and historical information of the time. Try using Post-Its™ on a whiteboard or butcher paper!

23. **Mandala**: create a mandala with many levels to connect different aspects of a book, its historical time, and culture.

24. **Transparencies**: copy portion of text to transparency; kids annotate with markers and then get up to present interpretation to class.

25. **Gender-Bender**: rewrite a scene and change the gender of the characters to show how they might act differently (e.g., *Lord of Flies*); can also have roundtable on gender differences.

26. **Picture This**: bring in art related to book's time or themes; compare, describe, discuss.

27. **Kids Books**: bring in children's books about related themes and read these aloud to class.

28. **Downgrade**: adapt myths or other stories for a younger audience; make into children's books or dramatic adaptation on video or live.

29. **Draw!**: translate chapters into storyboards and cartoons; draw the most important scene in the chapter and explain its importance and action.

30. **Oprah Bookclub**: host a talkshow: students play the host, author, and cast of characters; allow questions from the audience.

31. **Fictional Friends**: who of all the characters would you want for a friend? Why? What would you do or talk about together?

32. **State of the Union**: the President wants to recommend a book to the nation: tell him one important realization you had while reading this book and why he should recommend it.

33. **Interview Question**: when I interview prospective teachers, my first question is always "What are you reading and do you like it?"

34. **Dear Diary**: keep a diary as if you were a character in the story. Write down events that happen during the story and reflect on *how* they affected the character and *why*.

35. **Rosencrantz and Gildenstern**: write a story or journal from the perspective of characters with no real role in the story and show us what they see and think from their perspective.

36. **Improv**: get up in front of class or in fishbowl and be whatever character the class calls out and do whatever they direct. Have fun with it.

37. **What If**: write about or discuss how the story would differ if the characters were something other than they are: a priest, another gender or race, a different age, or social class.

38. **Interrupted Conversations**: pair up and trade-off reading through some text; *any time* you have something to say about some aspect of the story, interrupt the reader and discuss, question, argue.

39. **Found Poetry**: take sections of the story and, choosing carefully, create a found poem; then read these aloud and discuss.

40. **13 Views**: inspired by Stevens's poem "13 Ways of Looking at a Blackbird": each stanza offers a different view of a character or chapter.

41. **Personal Ad**: what would a particular character write in a personal ad for the newspaper? After posting on board, discuss.

42. **Holden Meets Hamlet**: what would one character (or set of them) in one story say to another if given the chance to talk or correspond? Write a dialogue, skit, or letter.

43. **Character Analysis**: describe a character as a psychologist or recruiting officer might: what are they like? Examples? Why are they like that?

44. **Epistle Poem**: write a poem in the form and voice of a letter: e.g., Phoebe to Holden.

45. **Write Into**: find a "hole" in the story where the character disappears (off camera) for a time and describe what they do when we can't see them.

46. **The Woody Allen**: in *Take the Money*, Allen interviews the parents of a man who became a bank robber. Write an imaginary interview with friends and family of a character whom they try to help you understand.

47. **Author Interview**: write an interview or letter in which the character in a story asks the author a series of questions and reflects on how they feel about the way they were "made."

48. **The Kuglemass**: Woody Allen wrote a story in which the character can throw any book into a time machine and it takes you inside the book and the era. What would you do, say, think if you "traveled" into the story you are reading?

49. **Time Machine**: instead of traveling into the book, write a scene or story in which the character(s) travel out of the book into today.

50. **Biography**: write a biography of one of the characters who most interests you.

51. **Autobiography**: have the character that most interests you write their autobiography of the time before, during, or after the story occurs.

52. **P.S.**: After you read the story, write an epilogue in which you explain--using whatever tense and tone the author does--what happened to the character(s) next.

53. **Board Game**: have groups design board games based on stories then play them. This is especially fun and works well with the *Odyssey*.

54. **Life Graph**: using the Life Graph assignment, plot the events in the character's life during the story and evaluate their importance; follow up with discussion of graphs.

55. **Second Chance**: talk or write about how it would change the story if a certain character had made a different decision earlier in the story (e.g., what if Huck had not run away?)

56. **Poetry Connection**: bring in poems that are thematically related to the story; integrate these into larger discussion. Use *Poetry Index*.

57. **Reader Response**: pick the most important word/line/image/object/event in the chapter and explain why you chose it; be sure to support all analysis with examples.

58. **Notes and Quotes**: draw a line down the middle of the page; on one side write down important quotes; on the other comment on and analyze the quotes.

59. **Dear Classmate**: using email or some other means of corresponding, write each other about the book as you read it, having a written conversation about the book.

60. **Convention Introduction**: you have been asked to introduce the book's author to a convention of English teachers. What would you say? Write and deliver your speech.

61. **Sing Me a Song**: write a song/ballad about the story, a character, or an event in the book.

62. **Write Your Own**: using the themes in the story, write your own story, creating your own characters and situation. It does not have to relate to the story at all aside from its theme.

63. **Executive Summary**: take a 3x5 card and

continues

103 Things to do Before/During/After Reading

summarize what happened on one side; on the other, analyze the importance of what happened and the reasons it happened.

64. Read Aloud: one student starts the reading and goes until they wish to pass; they call on whomever they wish and that person picks up and continues reading for as long as they wish.

65. Quaker Reading: like a Quaker meeting, one person stands and reads then sits and whomever wishes to picks up and reads for as long as with wish...and so it goes.

66. Pageant of the Masters: in Los Angeles this remarkable event asks groups to "stage" different classical paintings in real life. People would try to do a still life of some scene from a book or play; the class should then discuss what is going on in this human diorama.

67. Create a Diorama: create a diorama of a particularly important scene such as the courtroom or Ewells' house in *Mockingbird*.

68. Day in Court: use the story as the basis for a court trial; students can be witnesses, expert witnesses called to testify, judge, jury, bailiff, reporter; great fun for a couple days

69. Censorship Defense: imagine that the book you are reading has been challenged by a special interest group; students must write a letter defending the book, using specific evidence from the book to support their ideas.

70. Call for Censorship: in order to better understand all sides to an argument, imagine you are someone who feels this particular book should *not* be read and write a letter in which you argue it should be removed.

71. Speculation: based on everything you know now in the story, what do you think will happen and why do you think that?

72. Questions Anyone?: students make a list of a certain number of questions they have about a particular character or aspect of the book; use these as the basis for class discussion.

73. Newspaper Connection: have students read the newspapers and magazines to find articles that somehow relate to issues and ideas in the book(s) you are reading; bring in and discuss.

74. Jigsaw: organize the class into groups, each one with a specific focus; after a time rotate so that new groups are formed to share what they discussed in their previous group.

75. Open Mind: (some people use a bathtub instead). Draw an empty head and inside of it draw any symbols or words or images that are bouncing around in the mind of the character of a story; follow it up with writing or discussion to explain and explore responses.

76. Interrogation: a student must come up before the class and, pretending to be a character or the author, answer questions from the class.

77. Post-Its™: If they are using a school book in which they cannot make notes or marks, encourage them to keep a pack of Post-Its™ with them and make notes on these.

78. Just the Facts Ma'am: acting as a reporter, ask the students the basic questions to facilitate a discussion: who, what, where, why,

when, how?

79. SQ3R: when reading a textbook or article, try this strategy: **(S)urvey** the assigned reading by first skimming through it; then formulate **(Q)uestions** by turning all chapter headings and subheadings into questions to answer as you read; next **(R)ead** the assigned section and try to answer those questions you formulated; now **(R)ecite** the information by turning away from the text as soon as you've finished reading the assigned section and reiterate it in your own words; finally, **(R)eview** what you read by going back to your questions, the chapter headings, and asking yourself what they are all referring to, what they mean.

80. Brainstorming/Webbing: put a character or other word in the middle of a web; have students brainstorm associations while you write them down; then have them make connections between ideas and discuss or writing about them.

81. Cultural Literacy: find out what students already know and address what they need to know before reading a story or certain part of a story.

82. Storyboard: individually or in groups, create a storyboard for the chapter or story.

83. Interactive Story: if you have a student who is a computer genius, have them create a multimedia, interactive version of the story.

84. CyberGuides: search the Net for virtual tours based on the books you might be studying. Try www.concorde.org.

85. Tableau: similar to the Pageant of the Masters, this option asks you to create a still life setting; then someone steps up to touch different characters who come alive and talk from their perspective about the scene.

86. Audio Books: There are many audio editions of books we teach now available; some are even read by famous stars who turn the book into its own audio performance. Recommend to students with reading difficulties or play portions of them in class.

87. Sound Off!: play a video version of a book you are reading—only turn off the sound while they watch it. Have them narrate or discuss or write about what is happening, what the actors are revealing about the story through their gestures. Then compare what you saw with what you read.

88. Narrate Your Own Reading: show kids how you read a text by reading it aloud and interrupting yourself to explain how you grapple with it as you go. Model your own thinking process; kids often don't know what it "looks like" to think.

89. Magnetic Poetry: if working with a poem, enlarge it on copier or computer and cut all words up into pieces; place in an envelope and have groups create poems from these words; later on discuss using same words for different texts. Heavier stock paper is ideal.

90. Venn Diagram: use a Venn diagram to help you organize your thinking about a text as you read it. Put differences between two books or

characters on opposite sides and similarities in the middle.

91. Write an Essay: using one of the different rhetorical modes, write an essay in which you make meaningful connections between the text and your own experiences or other texts you have read.

92. P.O.V.: how would it change the story if you rewrote it in a different point of view (e.g., changed it from first to third person)? Try it!

93. Daily Edition: using the novel as the basis for your stories, columns and editorials, create a newspaper or magazine based on or inspired by the book you are reading.

94. Read Recursively: on occasion circle back around to the beginning of the chapter or text to keep yourself oriented as to "the big picture." This is especially important if you have questions to answer based on reading.

95. Oral History: if you are reading a historical text, have students interview people who have some familiarity with that time period or the subject of the book.

96. Guest Speaker: if you are reading a book that deals with a subject an expert might help them better understand, invite one in. Try to Veterans of Foreign Wars, for example, if reading about war.

97. Storytelling: After reading a story, pair up with others and tell the story as a group, recalling it in order, piecing it together, and clarifying for each other when one gets lost.

98. Reciprocal Teaching: a designated student or group reads a section of a text and comes prepared to present or "teach" it to the class; follow up with discussion for clarification.

99. Make Your Own Test: have students create their own test or essay questions about the text; this allows them to simultaneously think about the story and prepare for the test on it.

100. Recasting the Text: students rewrite a poem as a story, a short story as a poem or play. All rewrites should then be read and discussed so as to understand how the different genre work.

101. Debates: students reading controversial texts or novels with debatable subjects such as *1984* should debate the issues.

102. Literature Circles: students gather in groups to discuss the text and then report out to the class for full-class discussion.

103. That Was Then, This Is Now: after reading the text, create a Before/After list to compare the ways in which characters or towns have changed over the course of the story. Follow up with discussion of reasons.

How to Help Your Child Write Better

Guiding Principles for Parents
- you must help your child write the best paper they can at this stage; they are the writer, not you.
- you need their permission to work with them or they will resist and undermine your efforts.
- resist the immediate and urgent desire to "correct" their writing; that will not help and they will not want to work with you any more.
- allow them to maintain control over their own writing and your role. If you do this they will value your help and seek it as they need it.

Step One: Clarifying
First, go through the actual writing assignment (e.g., essay topic) and highlight any words that seem essential to the assignment. Look for words like *explain, describe, analyze.* Look for phrases like "...a significant *experience that changed the way you thought* about someone or something," or "...person *who had a lasting influence on your personality.*" Understand what you must write about before you write at all.

Step Two: Before Writing
Try one of these strategies to help your child get started on the assignment. Help them think about what they need to do or what they have to say once they start writing.
- □ *Talk about it* while your child talks about the topic, make notes, ask them such questions as: why do you think that? why is that important? can you tell me more about that? how does that relate to the writing assignment?
- □ *Make a list, cluster, or outline* without worrying too much about rejecting any ideas: just get ideas out of your head for now.
- □ *Write a letter, quickwrite, or quick draft* to get your ideas down before writing an actual draft of the essay

Step Three: Writing!
Write a draft of the assignment, checking the assignment periodically to be sure that you are addressing what it asks.

Step Four: Revising/Rewriting
- □ Use the ending as the new beginning: so often we do not know what we want to say until we reach the conclusion; then we try to bring it together. Take the last paragraph and put it up front in the next draft, then write a new draft of your paper with that paragraph as the introduction.
- □ Ask your child what they want you to focus on when you read it; if they don't have specific directions, read it first without saying or "correcting" anything. Then walk through it *with them,* pointing out those specific problems you can help them resolve by asking them focus questions such as those listed above (see "Talk about It").
- □ Remember: your role *at this stage* is to help them clarify their ideas and address the assigned topic to help them write a working draft of the paper which can then be refined for style, mechanics, and tone.

Step Five: Refining the Writing
- □ *Voice.* Read through the paper and highlight those sentences where the language wakes you up or seems especially effective. Explain *how* these sentences create this effect and help them find places where they can add still more of these details.
- □ *Proofreading.* Read through the paper with *one purpose at a time* to better find errors: e.g., read through only to check punctuation. Don't depend on the spell-check: read it through with your own eyes, specifically looking for words like *to* that should be *too* or *not* that should be *note.*
- □ *Paragraphing.* Read the paper to look at paragraph focus and organization: what is the main idea and how does each sentence relate to it? What examples do they provide to support and illustrate their ideas?
- □ *Style.* Strengthen their verbs and nouns for voice and clarity: go through the paper and identify all nouns and verbs. What can they do to make these nouns more specific, these verbs more active, more precise? Example: change "The dog ran across the field" to "The dachshund waddled across the just-cut wheat field."

Step Six: Finishing
When your child has made their last revisions and fixed their last misspelling, have them print up a final draft of the paper. Encourage them to include all notes and earlier drafts with the final draft, even if their teacher doesn't ask for them; this will show them how hard they worked. (Such evidence of hard work impresses teachers much more than fancy, colorful cover pages done on the computer!)

10 Things You Can Do to Support Your Child's Writing

1. *Create a dedicated, comfortable space* for writing. Preferably they have a desk and decent chair, both of which demonstrate a commitment to them and their studies while sending the message that their work is important. They need quiet; they may also prefer to listen to music that seems impossible to write to: let them listen to it or they will be more distracted.
2. *Buy them books.* Many studies show that reading has profound effects on our writing ability. Reading provides models of style and thinking that help to shape our own voices as writers. Such books are great presents which again show interest in their work; they are also--or can be--random gifts that come during a time when your relationship is going through some serious renegotiations. Also, you must read yourself and let them see this; talk to them about what you read and ask them about what they are reading so they know you are interested in them.
3. *Provide them good reference books.* Every student needs a good dictionary (*American Heritage* is excellent; the *Oxford Desk* is good). Also recommended: *The Synonym Finder* or *21st Century Dictionary of Synonyms and Antonyms.* Writer's Inc. or *Write for College* offer the two most succinct and helpful reference resources for high school students.
4. *Buy your child a computer.* Used models with printer and software are available for as little as $150.00. This investment in your child shows that you are interested in them and that their writing is important.
5. *Ask to read their work.* It shows interest in them and their work; it shows you take them seriously. It allows you to monitor their progress. It allows you to say, "I've got some extra time tonight--d'you want to work on this together a bit?"
6. *Write the assignment yourself.* You can each do the assignment on your own and then compare what you came up with; this creates an opportunity to talk, clarify, or think together, activities that are hard for teens and parents.
7. *Use writing in your house.* The family journal exemplifies this best. Get a nice (but not too nice) journal and keep it near the kitchen table (or wherever your family's central spot it). Write notes, questions, observations to each other to keep talking, to improve communication, to better understand each other, to improve your writing--and theirs! I know people who swear this saved their relationship.
8. *Buy them writer's gifts.* If you are at the office supply store, buy them some colorful post-its, nice paper, a cool pen--anything that will please them and make working with writing more fun to them. Again: invest!
9. *Celebrate their successes.* Movies, special meals, a bulletin board in kitchen...
10. *Play family games that involve language*: Balderdash, Scrabble Magnetic Poetry...

Components of an Effective Presentation or Speech

OVERVIEW

The following ideas are designed to help speak to either one person (e.g., a coach, a teacher, a prospective employer in an interview) or a large group in a formal setting. Speaking in front of people is considered, by most Americans, the most stressful experience imaginable; these strategies can help ease some of that stress by getting you prepared.

PREPARATION

First, clarify your topic. Try the business card test: you have only the side of a business card to state your main idea. Aside from this, the following points are essential, even if they do seem obvious:

- **Preparation**: know your material "cold" so you can worry not about *what* to say but about *how* to say it.
- **Rehearsal**: this might mean walking around your bedroom all afternoon repeating your lines over and over; it might also mean practicing in front of friends, parents, mirrors, even video cameras or tape recorders.
- **Audience**: how you speak, what you include, how you act will be determined by the answers to a few simple questions: To whom am I speaking? Why am I speaking to them? What do they know--and what must I explain? How much time do I have?
- **Tools and Aids**: what, if any, visual or other aids (props, handouts, transparencies, poster board, computer presentation, video) should I use to convey this information to my audience most effectively?

VISUAL AIDS

When your purpose is to convey complex or abundant information to your audience, use visual aids to help them keep track of your main ideas. These aids also let the audience know what to expect; for instance, in the example provided below the audience can relax, knowing the speaker will take questions when they finish their presentation.

Consider using one of the following:

- poster board
- overhead transparencies (with colored pens or xeroxed)
- presentation software such as PowerPoint, HyperStudio, or ClarisWorks
- handout with the same information as displayed on your visual aids so they don't have to take notes but can pay closer attention or supplement your notes with their own

CHARACTERISTICS OF EFFECTIVE PRESENTATIONS/SPEECHES

- Visual aids:
  - are clearly visible and readable to all members of the audience.
  - use large, basic fonts such as Helvetica for clarity and neatness.
  - include minimal text for emphasis and readability.

> - Overview of Presentation
>   - Background
>   - Current status
>   - Proposed changes
>   - Implications
>   - Summary and questions

  - use concrete, precise words that will not confuse the audience.
  - do *not* include graphics or images that compete with the information.
- Effective, engaging speakers:
  - pace their speech so that each word gets the proper enunciation and emphasis.
  - look at their audience as much as possible
  - project and inflect their voice in order to engage the audience and emphasize those ideas they feel are important.
  - use humor or other such devices to engage and maintain their audience's attention.
- Effective presentations
  - provide an overview of the presentation at the beginning.
  - provide a summary of the presentation's main points at the end.
  - provide strong supporting examples to clarify the ideas.
  - follow a logical, coherent progression from idea to idea.
  - avoid any theatrics that will undermine the speaker's ability to effectively convey the information to their audience.
  - anticipate the audience's questions and are ready to answer them.
  - restate questions from the audience to clarify (and provide time to compose a thoughtful response to the question).
  - use transitions to clearly mark where one idea ends and the next begins; these transitions also make for a more fluid, coherent speech.
- Presentation Strategies:
  - **Note cards**: these can contain either cue words or main ideas across the top of the card, followed by ideas or scripts as needed.
  - **Outline**: helpful, abbreviated script that supports but allows you to speak instead of read. Also helpful as check-list of what you've discussed.
  - **Memorize**: if you have time, memorize what you will say, especially if you are presenting your information dramatically. Actors reading off of 3x5 cards just doesn't work too well.
  - **Write your outline or script in larger type and triple-space** it so you don't have to search through the document to find your place.
  - **Have style**: whether this is the handouts, your way of speaking, your humor, or the guiding metaphors and analogies you use to help them understand, make sure your speech engages their attention and their heart if at all possible. Give them something to remember.
  - **Avoid words you can easily trip over** during the course of your speech. This is particularly important for speeches that cause stress.
  - **Monitor your audience**: if you see that you are losing them, adjust your speech, improvise, project yourself more forcefully.
  - **Cue words**: on note cards or outlines, such words, if the speaker is well-prepared, allow the speaker to recall all they want to say about a topic once they see the word. Example: *Implications* signals the memory to recall the list of five different implications for the expanded use of technology in every aspect of our lives.

Sample Rubric:
Presentation Evaluation
Student Name(s):
Period:
Topic of Presentation:

OVERALL QUALITY

NEEDS IMPROVEMENT   GOOD   EXCELLENT

1).   1   2   3   4   5   **Delivery:** includes eye contact, projection of voice, stage presence, clarity of speech.

2).   1   2   3   4   5   **Creativity:** degree to which you show ability to solve the problems the assignment presents; includes originality and honors risks to try different approaches to solve problems.

3).   1   2   3   4   5   **Knowledge/Expertise:** reflects the overall fluency of your knowledge regarding your subject. This is measured by what you say and how you are able to answer people's questions; also by the extent to which specific details reveal the depth of your understanding of the subject. If appropriate, evaluates the quality and effective use of examples to support and illustrate.

4).   1   2   3   4   5   **Visuals/Aids:** this refers to the use and quality of any presentation aids you use. Does not assume you must have a visual or multimedia aid to present successfully; this is meant to assess the extent to which your aids, if you have any, are effectively created and used in your presentation.

5).   1   2   3   4   5   **Insight:** the degree to which your work shows insight into the subject at hand. This is different from knowledge/expertise; if they deal with the what/who, insight deals with the why/how/so?

6).   1   2   3   4   5   **Process:** another word for this is *preparation*: to what extent does your presentation suggest you prepared your materials and speech for this presentation; or does it look like you are making it up as you go along.

7).   1   2   3   4   5   **Benchmark:** quality of this work in relation to your past work and my expectations of what you should be able to do.

TIME_____   **COMMENTS**

GRADE____

APPENDIX H

Conducting Interviews/Surveys

Alice B. Toklas: "Gertrude, what's the answer?"
Gertrude Stein: "What's the question?"
--Stein's last words before dying

STEP ONE: Establish Purpose and Clarify Needs

Before you decide between an interview and a survey--or decide to do both--you must clarify what information your project or paper needs. You can do this by deciding which of the following statements best describes your needs:

1. I need data to prove my thesis (e.g., that teens continue to smoke despite the change in the advertising laws)
2. I want to know what it was like to grow up during the Great Depression

If the first question seems most fitting for your needs--it provides *quantitative* data--you want to do a survey (which is the same as a questionnaire). If, however, the second question is more suited to your purpose--it provides *anecdotal* information--you should prepare to conduct an interview.

NOTE: if you conduct a survey, you must include enough people in your "sample" (of the population) to determine whether or not your findings are significant. If 7 out of 10 kids say they started to smoke after the change in cigarette advertising, this is not as significant as if 70 out of 100 say the same. An interview, on the other hand, achieves depth and insight by asking the right questions of only a few people and getting as much information as possible through these interviews. Also, it is essential that you ask questions in a logical order so one question builds on the next.

STEP TWO: Develop the Questions

- Survey: your questions must be "closed" questions that yield a specific answer: e.g., "yes," "never," "Kennedy."
- Interview: your questions should yield quotes that you can use to illustrate your point or support your thesis.
  - (Lead question) Do you think a woman should have the right to have an abortion?
  - (Follow-up) Why do you think that?
  - Open-ended: What was it like growing up during the Great Depression?

NOTE: Design a survey so people can complete it quickly. Use check boxes or words to circle. Limit your survey to no more than ten questions. If, however, you are interviewing someone, you should limit yourself to about five good "open-ended" questions that will invite the interviewee to speak at length.

HELPFUL TIPS

- Bring a pen and a note pad (to write on your lap).
- If using a tape recorder, check batteries and make sure tape is cued up (with extra batteries and cassette just in case). Same goes for video recording, too.
- Clarify why you are asking them these questions to help them stay focused.
- Thank them and make them feel like an expert on this subject since, for the purposes of your interview, they are.
- Ask permission: to photograph, record, publish, or call on them again to follow-up.
- Prepare ahead of time: know as much as possible about the subject so you can ask good questions and understand what they tell you.
- Listen! You are there to hear what *they* have to say. Don't interrupt. Ask questions to clarify if necessary and be willing to let them talk so long as what they say is relevant. So what if you don't ask all your questions; the point is to get the best information you can.
- Take Notes: try using the two-column method: divide a sheet in half. Put your questions on the left side and take notes on the right side. OR, write your question at the top, take notes on the left, and summarize/make notes on the right side for later use in paper.
- Get Essential Info: to establish their credibility in your paper, get those details you will need: job title, rank, tribe, age.
- Rehearse: for important interviews or if you are nervous, do a mock interview with someone else.
- Road-test Survey: have a couple people try your survey before giving it out; get their feedback about the questions' clarity. If any questions are unclear, revise and try another dry run.
- Make notes on the interviewee's appearance, the setting, their gestures: these can be helpful when writing your report as they allow you to evoke the character of the interviewee.

CITING INTERVIEWS (bibliographic information)

If you quote from an interview, you must cite this in your sources:

- MLA: Junker, Christopher, Personal Interview. 15 November 1998.
- Chicago: Christopher Junker, interview by author, 15 November 1998, Cambridge, Harvard School of Divinity, Cambridge.

QUOTING SOURCES: there are two ways to quote:

- Direct: "People need heroes," said Campbell.
- Indirect: Campbell said people need heroes.

A Helpful Guide to Better Study Skills

LEARNING STYLE/ENVIRONMENT

The best way for me to learn something is to:

hear   see   read   talk   touch

I study best (*check all that apply*):

- ❑ in the morning
- ❑ in the afternoon
- ❑ in the evening
- ❑ by myself
- ❑ in a group
- ❑ a combination: by myself *and* in a group
- ❑ when it's quiet
- ❑ with music on
- ❑ in short segments of time
- ❑ for long periods of time
- ❑ under pressure
- ❑ when I am *not* under pressure

THE IMPORTANCE OF GOALS

Runners compete for their "PB" (personal best) each time they race. Think how much better you will do in all areas if you do the same. Here are the questions to ask yourself when making and trying to achieve goals:

- ❑ what do I want to be able to do or to know?
- ❑ why do I want to do or know this?
- ❑ what must happen for me to achieve this goal?
- ❑ how will I know when I have achieved this goal?
- ❑ what can I do to make sure I maintain this goal?

RAPID RESULT: what is something you can do on this one assignment or in one class this week that will improve your performance and that is achievable? Write this down on your weekly planner under Goals.

REMOTE RESULT: what is something you want to be able to do or learn in each area of school by year's end? Write this down somewhere so you can remind yourself of it.

HOW TO MAKE THE MOST OF YOUR TIME

Try each or any of the following to make better use of time:

- ❑ keep a daily/weekly planner
- ❑ always keep a note pad and pencil with you so you can catch ideas for assignments or make helpful lists
- ❑ make a schedule for each day and week
- ❑ always carry some kind of work on you–a book, a homework assignment, a magazine, a book-on-tape
- ❑ study and read at your optimal hours for best results
- ❑ break your time up into units that work best for you: i.e., if you work best for short periods of time, schedule this

EVALUATE YOUR WORKING ENVIRONMENT

How well we work depends on the conditions of the place where we do our work. You should have the following:

- ❑ a designated space to study
- ❑ a comfortable chair (you <u>cannot</u> learn lying down)
- ❑ a pen/pencil you like to use
- ❑ all necessary supplies
- ❑ no distractions
- ❑ good light (not too bright or too dim)
- ❑ distraction pad: to jot down ideas as they come then return to your immediate work
- ❑ support materials (dictionary, textbook, CD-ROMs)
- ❑ work on the computer; do not study at it: too distracting and too easy to waste time

STRATEGIES TO HELP YOU REMEMBER

- ❑ **Organize information** in logical, efficient ways: (e.g., The seven types of caste are: 1...2...3....)
- ❑ **Cue words**: link the words or ideas you must remember to a particular word (e.g., "Caste") which, upon repeating to yourself, will help you recall other words or ideas.
- ❑ **Create a picture** to help you "see" the idea/word when you need to recall it. (e.g., leg in a cast with different types of caste written all over it)
- ❑ **Make associations** between ideas/words to help remember: caste is like a seven layer burrito at Taco Bell or caste is like a rock group with Brahman like the lead singer....

- ❑ **Mnemonic devices** help you recall words: e.g., "Brahman tastes like Top Ramen..." or you can use a familiar tune "The seven deadly castes: Thou shalt not Brahman..."
- ❑ **Writing**: use writing various ways: to rehearse what to say; help you understand the ideas; to create note cards to carry around or scripts and outlines to study; to summarize all the important ideas or your understanding of a particular subject.
- ❑ **Outlines** help by organizing the information in logical ways that make for easy reference and quick study.
- ❑ **Note cards** allow you to carry them around with you and quiz yourself when you have an extra minute.
- ❑ **Conversations**: talk with someone about the subject; such conversations will not only help you remember but understand the material better.
- ❑ **REFLECTION**: which of these strategies do you use? Which ones work best for you? Why do they work so well?

TAKING GOOD NOTES FOR STUDY AND UNDERSTANDING

- ❑ **Divide and Conquer**: when taking notes, divide the page to create a 1/3-page margin; leave this 1/3 space blank as you make notes. Later, when studying, make notes or write questions in the 1/3 margin to help you summarize, analyze, and organize the information better.
- ❑ **Use an outline format** while taking notes to impose order on the information as you hear it. This makes for more efficient study and easier recall later.
- ❑ **Form and Function**: use the most appropriate form to organize your information: outline, cluster, list, bullets, columns, Venn diagrams, illustrations.
- ❑ **Create Categories**: develop categories specific to the topic and as you take notes, organize the ideas into the appropriate category (e.g., America, China, Mothers, Daughters, Men for Amy Tan's *Kitchen God's Wife*)

READING A TEXT ASSIGNMENT AND MAKING NOTES

- ❑ **First, carefully read the assignment** and underline key words ("summarize") that clarify what you must do
- ❑ **Skim the text** for all headings and summaries to get an idea of what you are going to be reading.
- ❑ **If highlighting**, underline key words–*not* whole paragraphs.
- ❑ **Marginalia**: writing notes/questions in the margin allows you to summarize main ideas or emphasize the location of a specific idea you know you want to return to.
- ❑ **Post-Its™**: if you are using a school textbook that you cannot highlight or make notes in, use Post-Its™ instead.
- ❑ **Review the assignment** to make sure you did all that it asked; put checks next to each requirement to indicate those portions you finished.
- ❑ **Typographical clues**: while reading, play close attention to any words in **bold** or *italics* or <u>underlined</u>.
- ❑ **SQ3R**: when reading a textbook or article, try this strategy: **(S)urvey** the assigned reading by first skimming through it; then formulate **(Q)uestions** by turning all chapter headings and subheadings into questions to answer as you read; next **(R)ead** the assigned section and try to answer those questions you formulated; now **(R)ecite** the information by turning away from the text as soon as you've finished reading the assigned section and reiterate it in your own words; finally, **(R)eview** what you read by going back to your questions, the chapter headings, and asking yourself what they are all referring to, what they mean.

TAKING TESTS WITHOUT ANXIETY

- ❑ Answer those you know first; see if later questions help you answer earlier questions you may have left blank.
- ❑ Rule out those you know cannot be right.
- ❑ Pay close attention to the wording, especially with True/False
- ❑ Use grammatical clues when answering objective questions (i.e., often the correct answer completes the sentence begun by the question).
- ❑ If you have to guess on a True/False test, always choose True.
- ❑ On matching tests, check off each answer after you've used it; saves time.
- ❑ When taking an essay exam, carefully read the topic, underlining key words or directions; half way through, re-read the directions to check.

Source: for more strategies to improve, see *How to Study in College*, 6th ed., Walter Pauk, (New York: Houghton Mifflin, 1997)

🕐 Weekly Planner

√	Assigned	Due	Class	Assignment	Appts./Events	
√	Monday	Tuesday	English	Read Lucille Clifton poem and write analysis	Wed	Game @ 4:15
					GOALS/PRIORITIES	
					YOU MUST DO THIS!!!	
					Register for SAT!	

© Jim Burke 1998

CLASSROOM SELF-EVALUATION/CHECKLIST

Note: The following list does not assume you should have all these things, though they all contribute to an exciting classroom environment. Some, such as stereos, can be found for very little at garage sales or Goodwill.

Physical Environment

- □ Basic Supplies
  - □ stapler
  - □ tape dispenser
  - □ paper clips
  - □ index cards
  - □ Post-Its
  - □ pens and pencils
  - □ art supplies
  - □ scissors
  - □ overhead transparency pens
  - □ computer disks
  - □ chalk or whiteboard pens
  - □ yard sticks and rulers
- □ Technological Equipment
  - □ Computer
    - □ projection device (monitor/LCD)
    - □ printer (quiet one!)
    - □ CD-ROM
    - □ speakers
    - □ Internet connection
  - □ Overhead projector
  - □ Tape recorder (portable) with earphones
  - □ Television
  - □ VCR
  - □ Camera
  - □ Stereo
- □ Physical Space
  - □ bulletin boards to showcase student work, post announcements, cartoons, etc.
  - □ communal board for students to use
  - □ classroom library bookcases
  - □ conferencing space
  - □ regular chairs that can be moved around
  - □ podium or music stand
- □ Organizational Space
  - □ In/Out boxes
  - □ place for extra copies of handouts
- □ Storage Space (ideally lockable if your room is used for summer school or night school classes)
  - □ for works-in-progress
  - □ for portfolios or writing folders
  - □ for art supplies
  - □ for computer supplies
  - □ for your personal things
- □ Academic Supplies
  - □ good dictionaries
  - □ ESL dictionary
  - □ bilingual dictionaries in different languages
  - □ calculator
  - □ thesaurus (or my favorite, *The Synonym Finder*)
  - □ *Writer's Inc.* or *Write for College*
  - □ encyclopedia (e.g., *The Columbia Concise*)
  - □ binders with student exemplars

Emotional Environment

- □ Policies posted, clearly explained, consistently enforced: rules by which we live and work while in this room.
- □ How do you address possible offense caused by some works (e.g., *Huck Finn*)?
- □ Check room regularly for offensive graffiti on desks or walls.
- □ How do you handle the student who says they "can't" or "won't" read a particular book?
- □ Do *a l l* students, regardless of race, gender, ability, or wealth, feel respected and comfortable in your classroom?
- □ Do students feel safe---emotionally and physically---in your class?
- □ What do you do when/if a student offends or attacks another member of the class?
- □ What do students get to make choices about in your class?
- □ Can students describe you/your class as "fair" when it comes to grading and discipline policies and their enforcement?

Intellectual Environment

- □ Do you have a significant classroom library with a range of authors, reading levels, subjects, genre?
- □ Can students say that what they think matters and is heard in your class?
- □ In your class is there only one right answer to the questions you ask?
- □ Do students have, when possible, a variety of ways to demonstrate what they know?
- □ Does your class allow for and validate different views and opinions?
- □ Who asks the questions in your class?
- □ Do your ways of assessing students challenge them to think or try to "catch" them?

Personal Environment

- □ Is this "your" room or "our" room?
- □ Can students meet in or otherwise use your room before school, during recess/lunch, after school?

Traveling Teacher's Checklist

- □ Have a cart if possible; if not, then a crate that is not too big and easy to carry.
- □ *Write for College* or *Writer's Inc.* (one copy)
- □ Master Binder (see Chapter 26)
- □ transparencies and pens
- □ chalk or whiteboard pens
- □ paper clips
- □ Post-Its
- □ class texts needed for class
- □ In/Out box in each classroom
- □ Portfolio/Works-in-Progress storage in each class.

New Teacher Checklist

Note: try to do as many of these activities as you can during your first year. Some are designed to improve your teaching, others are to ensure you stay healthy despite the demands of your work.

☐ Join the National Council of Teachers of English (NCTE)
☐ Join your state/local affiliate
☐ Read as many of the following as you can:
  ☐ Reading: *Mosaic of Thought*, Keene and Zimmerman
  ☐ Writing: *A Writer Teaches Writing*, Donald Murray
  ☐ Grammar: *Lessons to Share*, Connie Weaver
  ☐ Thinking: *To Think*, by Frank Smith
  ☐ Literacy: *Changing Our Minds*, Miles Myers
  ☐ Teaching: *From Communication to Curriculum*, Douglas Barnes
  ☐ English: *The Rise and Fall of English: Reconstructing English as a Discipline*, Robert Scholes
☐ Visit the following organizations on the web:
  ☐ National Council of Teachers of English (www.ncte.org)
  ☐ National Center on Education and the Economy (www.ncee.org)
  ☐ The New Teacher Page: www.geocities.com/Athens/Delphi/7862
  ☐ TeacherNet: www.csulb.edu/~jmcasey
  ☐ Pacesetter English: www.collegeboard.org
  ☐ Center for Learning, Assessment, and School Structure (CLASS): www.classnj.org
  ☐ The Center for Research on Evaluation, Standards, and Student Testing (CRESST): www.cresst.org
  ☐ National Center on Education and the Economy (NCEE): www.ncee.org
  ☐ National Research Center on English Learning and Achievement (NRCELA): www.albany.edu/cela
  ☐ International Reading Association: www.ira.org
  ☐ National Writing Project: www.nwp.org
  ☐ The College Board: www.collegeboard.org
  ☐ The National Board for Professional Teaching Standards: www.nbpts.org
☐ Keep a journal with you and make time during the day or after school to reflect on what you did, how it went, how things are going overall.

Write down the names of five essential companions at school to whom you can go for guidance and support when you need it:
  1. _____
  2. _____
  3. _____
  4. _____
  5. _____

When was the last time you did the following:
  ☐ went out to a movie
  ☐ went out to dinner with friends
  ☐ went away for the weekend
  ☐ exercised
  ☐ took a day off from work to rest or catch up on work
  ☐ went out with colleagues after school for a conversation about books, teaching, life

Do you have the following in place:
  ☐ an organizational system (e.g., planner)
  ☐ exercise routine
  ☐ scheduled breaks from work
  ☐ reading or teacher study group
  ☐ dedicated time for your kids, spouse, interests (e.g., baseball team, woodwork)

☐ What magazines have you read?
  1. _____
  2. _____
  3. _____
  4. _____
  5. _____

6. What books (*not* for school!) have you read?
  1. _____
  2. _____
  3. _____
  4. _____
  5. _____

Finish this sentence: My greatest moment in the classroom this year was...

A Concise Glossary of Literary Terms

Note: After surveying a number of colleagues, I found the following terms and ideas to be the most consistently identified as important for students to know and teachers to teach.

- **Action**: what happens in the story.
- **Allusion**: indirect reference to an event, person, place, or artistic work which the writer assumes the reader knows about; used effectively, the allusion economically links the text to the larger meaning of the other text. When J.D. Salinger alludes to David Copperfield in *Catcher in the Rye*, he is placing his novel in a historical, literary context he assumes the reader should understand.
- **Analogy**: illustrates the idea by linking the current idea to a more familiar idea to better communicate the idea at hand; typically involves the use of an extended simile–Blake's "Tyger, Tyger" in which the industrial plants are compared to a tiger's appearance and danger.
- **Antagonist**: the most prominent of a story's characters who opposes the hero (see Protagonist) in the story; in *Lord of the Flies* the antagonist is Jack who embodies evil and seeks to kill Ralph.
- **Autobiography**: personal remembrance in which the writer tells the story of their own life or a particular event during that life (see Memoir). *I Know Why the Caged Bird Sings* by Maya Angelou exemplifies this genre of writing.
- **Ballad**: a song or orally-performed poem that dramatically retells the story of a popular figure (e.g., Billy the Kid)
- **Biography**: book or story written about the life of someone else; one example would be Justin Kaplan's biography of Mark Twain, *Mr. Twain and Mr. Clemens*
- Blank verse: unrhymed form of poetry; each line composed of 10 syllables in which every other syllable, beginning with the second one, is stressed (iambic pentameter). It is often used in long poems. Tennyson's "Ulysses" (1842) effectively illustrates this form:
     One equal temper of heroic hearts,
     Made weak by time and fate, but strong in will
     To strive, to seek, to find, and not to yield.
- **Cadence**: occasionally used as a synonym for "rhythm" or for "meter." Relates to the rising and falling, the rhythm of speech; often an important aspect of a poet's style.
- **Caesura**: (sometimes spelled "cesura") a pause in a line of verse, often caused by either grammar, logic, or cadence which is similar to the pause for breath.
- **Conflict**: the primary source of tension within a story. Often divided into four categories: the individual vs. themselves (see J.D. Salinger's *Catcher in the Rye*); the individual vs. society (see Ken Kesey's *One Flew Over the Cuckoo's Nest*); the individual vs. nature (see *The Grapes of Wrath*, by John Steinbeck); the individual vs. fate/gods (see Homer's *Odyssey*)
- **Connotation**: the range of further associations that a word or phrase suggests in addition to the primary dictionary meaning (i.e., its denotation).
- **Context**: those parts of the text that precede and follow a passage or event that help to give it meaning; helpful to readers who encounter information they cannot immediately understand.
- **Convention**: an established practice used by authors of literary works. Involves technique, style, structure, or subject-matter; particularly essential to poetry and literature which depend on such conventions as rhyme or the genre conventions of short stories.
- **Couplet**: pair of lines in verse that form a unit; there are several types---e.g., the heroic, open, and end-stopped---and, most notably those that appear at the end of Shakespearean sonnets which form the last two lines and rhyme with each other.
- **Denotation**: the accepted meaning of a word (i.e., the one that appears in the dictionary)

- **Dénouement**: the resolution or undoing of the central "problem" or complications of the story.
- **Dialect**: variation of pronunciation and usage within standard form of speech; typically based on regional, cultural, or social class differences. Best example are the different dialects used by Mark Twain in *Huck Finn*. Another word for this is *vernacular*
- **Dialogue**: conversation carried on between characters in a literary work.
- **Diction**: the choice of words used in a literary work. The writing can be characterized by such features as archaisms, colloquialisms, profanity, slang, trite expressions, or vulgarity.
- **Digression**: temporary departure from the main subject to address a separate idea or event within the story.
- **Dramatic Monologue**: speech in which the poet or character speaks to a silent audience or one or more.
- **Empathy**: the act of placing yourself "in the shoes" of another and forcing yourself to imagine how that person must feel. This is what fiction asks the reader to do.
- **Epic**: long narrative poem or story that tells of the deeds and adventures of a hero. See *Beowulf*.
- **Epigram**: brief, witty poem or thought that often makes fun of the idea it examines. Oscar Wilde raised it to such an art form he became known as an "epigrammatist."
- **Epigraph**: short poem or verse placed at the beginning of a book which bears some relation to the book's themes or subject.
- **Epilogue**: concluding section of a literary work. (see Prologue)
- **Episodic**: a narrative constructed around a series of distinct but related incidents rather than a carefully woven plot.
- **Epitaph**: words or poem suited for inscription on a tomb or gravestone.
- **Essay**: a short written composition in prose that examines a particular subject in depth. There are various "rhetorical modes" for the essay: analytical, reflective, cause-effect, personal narrative, ???
- **Existentialism**: a European philosophy which several authors, among them Albert Camus and Jean Paul Sartre, have adapted to fiction and drama to explore the themes of meaningless, individual freedom, and alienation that plague humanity at the close of the millennium. (for fun, search the Internet for the hilarious "Jean Paul Sartre Cookbook.")
- **Exposition**: writing that makes clear or explains something that might be difficult for the reader to understand; in a play or novel or essay it helps the reader to understand the larger action or subject of the text.
- **Falling Action**: the movement within the story that signals the beginning of trouble or complications for the story or its protagonist. One example would be the point at which Macbeth and his wife commit their first murder.
- **Fiction**: stories which have been created from the writer's imagination or were invented. Novels and short stories are fiction. As novelist Tim O'Brien says, however, just because it didn't happen doesn't mean it isn't true. (see O'Brien's *The Things They Carried*).
- **Foot**: the smallest repeated pattern of stressed and unstressed syllables in line of verse.
- **Foreshadowing**: early on in the story the author gives hints of what will come later in the story.
- **Free Verse:** does not conform to the traditional rules that govern metrical verse; there is no regular meter or rhyme. Such poets as use free verse demand that their reader attend to other aspects of the text such as cadence and imagery. Walt Whitman's poetry exemplifies this form.
- **Genre**: refers to a type of literature specific to its style, form, or content. Examples include mystery novels, epic poems, tragic plays.

continues

A Concise Glossary of Literary Terms

- **Hyperbole**: exaggeration or overstatement of the truth. Holden Caulfield constantly uses this when he describes his own behavior (e.g., lying).

- **Iambic Pentameter:** Since roughly 90% of all verse is written in iambic pentameter it is helpful to carefully define it. An *iamb* is a poetic foot consisting of two unstressed syllables followed by a stressed syllable (e.g., the word *interrupt*). Pentameter means that the line has five feet (or ten syllables) which may or may not rhyme as the poet prefers/intends.

- **Irony**: the writer uses a word or phrase to mean the opposite of its literal or normal meaning. There are three forms of irony commonly used: dramatic irony, verbal irony, and situational irony.

- **Metaphor**: a comparison of two unlike things in which no word of comparison (*like* or *as*) is used. "The river of life...."

- **Meter**: the patterned repetition of stressed and unstressed syllables in a line of poetry.

- **Mood**: relates to the feeling a text arouses in its reader; can shift between scenes but tends to define a work overall (e.g., the mood of *Macbeth is* ominous or heavy).

- **Motif**: a frequently recurring theme or idea in a work of literature. In Amy Tan's *Kitchen God's Wife*, the motif of secrecy runs throughout the story.

- **Narrator**: the person who tells the story; related to this idea is the extent to which the narrator is "reliable." Also, some narrators know more than others depending on the limits the author has imposed on them; for example, some know only what they "see," while others are privy to every thought and emotion of their character.

- **Onomatopoeia**: use of words whose sound defines its meaning; examples include *plop, crash*, and *hum*.

- **Parable**: a short story that illustrates a particular belief or moral; Franz Kafka was particularly interested in the use of parables (see *The Castle*).

- **Parody**: form of literature that mocks a literary work or its style.

- **Personification**: a literary device which describes an animal, object, or idea as if it had human characteristics. "The trees reached toward the sky...." Heavily used in poetry but common to fiction, also.

- **Plot**: it is the "what" of the story: what happens or the action. The plot traditionally contains five elements: exposition, rising action, climax, falling action, and resolution.

- **Point of View**: the perspective from which the story is told. There are several vantage points: first person (e.g., I grew up in Iowa), second person (e.g., "When you grow up in Iowa...."), and third person (e.g., He grew up in Iowa.).

- **Prose**: writing that is not composed according to rules and forms that govern poetry.

- **Protagonist**: the main character or hero of a story. (see Antagonist)

- Pun: word or phrase used in such a way as to imply other possible meanings. Students cannot "get" Shakespeare, for example, if they do not understand and cannot recognize a pun.

- **Rhetoric**: the deliberate use of eloquence to persuade others' feelings and thoughts; the rhetorical elements of a text refer to those aspects of the story that persuade or otherwise guide the response of the readers.

- **Rhythm**: the way in way in which sound is used in a poem; can be used in an ordered or free manner to create a tone and shape to the text.

- **Satire**: used to make fun of or ridicule a human vice or weakness or individual failings; classic example is found in George Orwell's *Animal Farm* which satirizes politics and human nature.

- **Setting**: If Plot is the "what," setting is the "where and when," setting the story in a historical and physical time and space.

- **Soliloquy**: similar to a dramatic monologue; it is a speech a character delivers while on stage alone. The supreme example is, of course, Hamlet's "To be or not to be," soliloquy.

- **Sonnet**: a poem composed of 14 lines written in iambic pentameter, the most commonly encountered in high school being the Shakespearean sonnet; there is another type called the Italian or Petrarchan sonnet.

- **Stanza**: from the Italian word for *room*, the word refers to the number of lines a poetic "paragraph" contains: couplet (two line stanza), triplet, quatrain (four-line stanza), quintet, sestet, septet (seven-line stanza), and octave.

- **Stereotype**: a character is merely a stereotype when they have no individuality to distinguish them from, for example, historical conceptions of their group. Thus Shylock in *Merchant of Venice* or Jim in *Huck Finn* are sometimes considered little more than stereotypes if not read carefully.

- **Simile**: compares two unlike things using *as* or *like*. "She stood in front of the altar, shaking like a freshly caught trout." (Maya Angelou, *I Know Why the Caged Bird Sings*.)

- **Structure**: has to do with the form or organization of the text, particular as it relates to or affects the meaning or action within the story. What purpose is served, for example, by the constant back-and-forth-in-time structure of Bharati Mukherjee's novel *Jasmine*?

- **Style**: how a writer uses words, images, phrases to create a feeling or convey a thought to the reader. It is impossible to discuss some books, such as *Catcher in the Rye*, without examining their style because the style is such a central aspect to the text.

- **Symbol**: person, place, thing that is, in a text, used to represent something else. As Flannery O'Connor says, however, in *Mystery and Manners*, such symbols must first function as intended (e.g., a wooden leg in one of her stories) before it can convey a deeper symbolic truth (e.g., about her character's dependence).

- **Synopsis**: a short summary or précis of a story's plot or themes.

- **Theme**: This is the deep structure consisting of the text's ideas and truths which the writer tries to convey through the action and exposition of the story. Students understand theme when they write "This is a story about alienation," instead of "This is a story about a man who goes to live by himself in the country."

- **Tone**: similar to Mood, it relates to the overall feeling a story creates in the reader.

- **Tragedy**: an outcome which the character could have avoided at any point along the way but, due to certain flaws, chose not to; these errors in judgment lead to their inevitable fall. See Shakespeare.

- **Verse**: consists of a metric line of poetry that has some formal structure to it. Used also to distinguish poetry from prose.

Resources

- *The Concise Oxford Dictionary of Literary Terms*, Chris Baldick, Oxford University press, New York, 1990. An affordable, helpful reference book that has most words you will want to know.

- *Poetry Handbook: A Dictionary of Terms*, Babette Deutsch, Harper Perennial, Fourth Edition, 1974. While the *Oxford* book is helpful as a general reference, you would do better to get this one is you want a book specific to poetry.

- *Princeton Encyclopedia of Poetry and Poetics*–?? check title. I prefer the Deutsch book but this book offers an exhaustive examination of all spheres of poetry and poetics.

- *Writer's Inc.* and *Write for College* (Houghton Mifflin), as part of their encyclopedic resources, both offer a fine little literary and poetic terms section, making them one of the one most useful integrated information resource for your classroom.

The Timetables of Teaching High School English

1600-1900	1900-1929	1930-1939

1600-1900

1600-
1795: Only Greek and Latin accepted as the language of scholarship in American universities.

1751: Benjamin Frankly founds the Philadelphia Academy which features what is arguably the first high school English department and curriculum.

1783: Noah Webster publishes the *Blue-Backed Speller* which is part of his *Grammatical Institute,* a programmatic study of the elements of English.

1795: Webster publishes *An American Selection of Lessons in Reading and Speaking* . It is secular in its content; in light of the American Revolution, Webster's text ushers in new trend: the use of reading to instill in children patriotic values and spirit.

1795: University of North Carolina is the first university to require past study of English for admission to university. When Harvard follows suit, English becomes permanent part of high school curriculum to meet college requirement.

1821: English High School in Boston opens and formally establishes the study of English and creates a complete curriculum (writing, reading, grammar, speaking, rhetoric, diction).

1850s: Role of literature, previously dismissed, revised to focus on importance of national and personal heritage and values; seen as means of protecting the country against eroding values.

1850: Academies began to decline in popularity as country grew and more wanted practical studies not college.

1851: English curriculum of Columbus, Ohio public high schools required 12 separate courses in English.

1895: National Conference on Uniform Entrance Requirements in English held. They release a booklist which students hoping to attend college will subsequently read prior to admission. Results in the College Entrance Exam, a precursor to the SAT. This also introduces a national reading canon.

1892: "Committee of Ten" appointed by National Education Association to institutionalize "English" as a single subject. Report called for five hours a week of English for four years.

1895: Horace Mann argues that novels should <u>not</u> be taught because they appeal to emotion instead of logic.

1896: Appearance of A.B. Hinsdale's *Teaching the Language Arts,* the first book about how to teach high school English.

1896: John Dewey opens his lab school; he argues that the literary canon is too removed from students' experience and thus should be abandoned for a more engaging one.

1897: Jane Addams addresses the NEA on the problem of "Educating the Immigrant Child."

1900-1929

1900: Dramatic increase in number of students enrolling in public high schools

1910: The Army, because of WWI, will develop the first standardized IQ tests which will be used to start "tracking" kids by ability as measured by the Stanford-Binet test.

1902: Percival Chubb redefines the mission of public high school English: the school must adapt to meet the individual student's needs as opposed to the student adapting to the school's needs. Considered first step of the Progressive education movement.

1911: National Council of Teachers of English (NCTE) founded to resist college domination of secondary English curriculum

1913: First NCTE report on English in American high schools.

1913: Commitment to students leads to emphasis on modern writing and thus the inclusion of newspapers, magazines, and dime-store novels into the class in order to engage students more immediately.

1917: NCTE report *Reorganization of English in the Secondary Schools* challenges the assumption that schools' only mission is to prepare students to meet college entrance exams; report calls for new and expanded curriculum designed to provide a wider range of experiences.

1917: NCTE creates Committee on the Economy of Time in English to decide what the "essentials" of English are: these subsequent standards significantly reshaped the teaching of language and composition.

1918: Kilpatrick introduces the "Project Method."

1920: Hall writes that the major justification for the teaching of literature is that it instills in students self-respect, patriotism, reverence, industry, and contentment.

1920s: Dewey and other progressive educators argue that reading a book is having an experience; that exploration of self, society, and past and present worlds is valid course of study in an English class.

1920s: New research suggests silent reading is more efficient and beneficial than oral reading.

1922-24: Scott, Foreman publishes *Literature and Life* anthologies. Provides new common ground to profession and ability to complement core curriculum with more diverse stories, voices, genres.

1924: NCTE creates Committee on the Place and Function of English in American Life" to determine what function the study of English serves. Report further establishes centrality of English to curriculum but marginalizes the study of literature.

1920s: increasing requests to adapt classic texts to make them more "palatable."

1927: Teacher's College study reveals that some students allowed to choose their own books in hopes of increasing student interest; such practice intended to complement core, classic readings.

1930-1939

1932: NCTE conducts four-year study on the benefits of movies on students. Other visual media also introduced into English curriculum. In 1932 NCTE forms "Committee on Photoplay [movie] Appreciation." By 1934 Hollywood producers routinely consult NCTE committee for guidance in making literary classics into movies.

1938: NCTE forms "Ratio Committee" which reports,"censorship of a very discreet sort, is much less valuable than the establishment of a critical attitude in which the good will be properly praised and the bad perceived and--perhaps--avoided."

1930s: Introduction of the "Dalton Plan" or "contract method" for learning. This individualized, goal-oriented approach undermined the previous emphasis on the social function of English.

1930s: NCTE Committee on Research founded. They begin to publish annual survey/report on research findings for that year as a means of informing the profession; committee and report validate the role research is to play henceforth.

1933: Dora V. Smith writes *Instruction in English* after surveying high school English teachers and classrooms across the country; she concludes there are three obstacles to implementation of an effective English program: (1) ineffective teacher training; (2) excessive teacher work load; (3) inadequate book and material supply.

1935: NCTE report, *An Experience Curriculum in English,* promotes a "pattern curriculum" to help establish standards for teaching English. It is, according to Applebee (p. 119), the most ambitious effort to date within the field of English. Most notably, the report abandoned the teaching of formal grammar in favor of "functional instruction." Grammar, the report said, could not be proven to improve reading and writing performance and thus served no function.

1936: *Correlated Curriculum* published by NCTE; the third volume in the series, this report argues for increased integration of disciplines in part because impending budget cutbacks due to Depression threaten to omit certain studies unless they can be subsumed elsewhere in curriculum.

1938: Louise Rosenblatt writes *Literature as Exploration* and ushers in the "reader response" approach; her argument was that no other method allowed for meaningful response to literature. Significant shift: from focus on content of work to student's response to that work.

1939: NCTE publishes *Conducting Experiences* as a companion to *An Experience Curriculum in English* because the left out what students should read and study in the previous report.

1930s: Due to Depression, textbooks become core not complement to curriculum.

NOTE: for the information in this timetable I am particularly indebted to Arthur Applebee's *Tradition and Reform in Teaching English* and Arthur Applebee himself for his suggested corrections to the timetable.

continues

1940-1950

1940-50s: Advent of "general education" as more student stayed in school in wake of Depression.

40s-50s: Armed Services discovered during war a wide spread functional illiteracy so called for new emphasis on "communication skills" for all Americans which resulted in increased use of spelling lists and vocabulary exercises and, most significantly, first serious examination of reading skills in high school.

40-50s: "Life adjustment movement" redefined mission of schools to mean personal development and improvement.

1940: Culmination of 8-year study of high schools which were exempted from standard admission requirements; most notable reforms involved integrated or interdisciplinary studies.

1940s: Shift in subject of literature to adolescent themes, problems, rites of passage. This came about from study by Dora V. Smith which subsequently resulted in creation of "adolescent literature." English Journal endorses trend and begins to include reviews, articles, and research to support the trend.

1940s: Publication of Hayakawa's *Language in Action* and other linguistic books that brought a new focus to language and critical thinking.

1940s: Several major reports from NCTE and Progressive Education Association redefined the English curriculum as including four fundamental language arts: reading, writing, speaking, listening.

1941: NCTE committees releases "Basic Aims for English Instruction in American Schools," listing as its its top priority that language was "the basic instrument of the democratic way of life."

1940s: Development of "developmental reading program" as study of reading reveals how complex it is and how many students struggle with it.

1941 Readers Digest begins to publish a school edition for use in developmental reading classes.

1945 NCTE Commission on English Curriculum redefined mission of English in wake of WWII. NCTE position criticized as too vague as it tries to include and satisfy all sides and thus pleases

1951-1964

1950s General expansion of thematic course of study (e.g., American Literature at 11th grade, British Literature in 12th) Further reflected in anthologies of 50s when "short story" was replaced by such unites as "Understanding Ourselves."

1951 Fund for Advancement of Education creates Advanced Placement test. English test immediately popular; it is heavily influenced by New Critics and thus shapes advanced high school instruction for future.

1955 The "tripod" curriculum introduced: language, literature, and composition

1957 Sputnik launched; American schools considered symbolic of our national failure to be competitive. National Defense Education Act passed in 1958 which makes education a vital national interest. Best and brightest sought. NCTE, in response to emphasis on gifted, forms Committee on English Program for High School Students of Superior Ability.

1958 Modern Language Association (MLA) gets involved again in high school English issues and forms alliances with NCTE.

1959 "Basic Issues in Teaching of English" Conference marks shift away from teacher as expert and toward professors as experts who should be developing curriculum. This culminates in leadership from Northrop Frye and Jerome Bruner in "academic movement" which is a backlash against progressive education.

1959 College Entrance Examination Board creates Commission on English and charges them to create standards of achievement and outline ways of meeting these standards.

1960s Increase in censorship; NCTE begins to offer support for teachers under attack.

1960s Several major studies examine and strongly criticize preparation of teachers.

1961 James Squire, NCTE Executive Secretary, write sand publishes *The National Interest and the Teaching of English* in which he argues that English is essential to the national welfare.

1961 Project English created to conduct serious research on composition, reading, and language skills.

1961 Robert Mager publishes Preparing Objectives for Programmed Instruction which establishes "behavioral objectives" and idea of "programmed instruction." Problem in the end is they do not know what to assess or how best to assess it. NCTE opposed such objectives.

1964 Increased academic focus fosters crisis in urban schools where such study is irrelevant. NCTE forms Task Force on Teaching English to Disadvantaged."

1966-2000

1966 Dartmouth Conference on teaching English. Opens collaboration between England and American teachers about teaching of "English." Two important outcomes are increased use of drama both in response to and as means of better understanding literature and ideas; second was discovery of and expanded use of writing as a tool or process

1970s In response to the calls for "relevance," schools offer elective programs which have no center to them and thus allow all factions—progressive, academics, New Critics, et al—room to implement their curriculum. Academic model was not able to satisfy the needs of such diverse student interests and needs.

1980s *Nation at Risk* report. In response to global economy and perceived threats from Japan and Germany, American Governors Association linked national prosperity and integrity with future educational performance.

1982 Mortimer Adler publishes *Peidea Proposal: An Educational Manifesto*

1983 Publication of Carnegie Foundation report *High School: A Report on Secondary Education in America*, written by Ernest Boyer

1984 Ted Sizer launches reform movement with publication of *Horace's Compromise*.

1987 Publication of E.D. Hirsch's *Cultural Literacy*.

1987 English Coalition Conference. Intended as a 20 year revisitation of the Dartmouth Conference, they sought to answer the question "What is English?"

1990 California Learning Assessment System (CLAS) dismantled after State Board of Education and parents censor certain stories.

1990s Standards movement, which great out of the *Nation at Risk* report and lack of progress toward these goals.

Multi-Media Era: internet, world wide web, TV, cable, movies (of nearly every book read).

1995 NCTE Standards published with no significant consequence. The government had previously canceled their contract with NCTE/IRA when it felt the standards were heading in the wrong direction.

1997 National reading debates: though focused at elementary school level, broad implications for high schools which have increasing number of students who cannot read at grade level. Focused in part on "whole language" which some blame for poor high school

The History of the Relationship between the Text, the Reader, and the Teacher

ERA: Early Civilization	ERA: Socrates' Athens	ERA: Plato's Athens	ERA: Moses, Jesus, Mohammed	ERA: Early Christianity
• VISUAL TEXT: Lascaux cave paintings: earliest "texts"; because they are visual they require no explanation to "reader."	• ORAL TEXT: Socrates and other such "teachers" created an oral text through philosophical discussion--Socratic method--which allowed for direct relationship between text and reader	• EARLY WRITTEN TEXT: written to remember, to express; early literary texts (Homer) which require teacher to explicate and teach; written texts allow for more control in wake of Socrates' heresies.	• SACRED TEXTS: birth of monotheism and debate about meaning of the texts; however, the lives of religious leaders were a "living text" they themselves sought to explicate to followers. Introduces formal narrative as means of teaching.	• SECRET TEXT: Church keeps the Bible a mysterious text in dead language; introduction of teacher (i.e., priest) as keeper of secret meanings and dogmatic reading: there is only one meaning. To imply other possible meanings invites heresy.
Primary Text: "The Story of Art." E.H. Gombrich	Primary Text: "Orality and Literacy: The Technologizing of the Word." Walter J. Ong (1996)	Primary Text: "The Norton Book of Classical Literature," ed. by Bernard Knox (1993)	Primary Text: "A History of God." Karen Armstrong	Primary Text: "The History of Reading," Alberto Manguel

ERA: Early America	ERA: Industrial Era America	ERA: Coming to America, 1900s	ERA: Going to War: Patriotism	ERA: Scientific Era
• "FUNDAMENTALIST TEXT: "Role of education is to instill respect for the Bible." (Kohl, p. 130) • Great respect for books as valuable, expensive and important: Bible and Sears catalog (1880s)	• PRACTICAL TEXT: public asks schools to prepare their children to enter the Industrial Era • Public generally feels a "fundamentalist" education no longer provides what is necessary	• POLITICAL TEXT I: Growing Immigration requires schools to create a curriculum that will acculturate new citizens into American culture; introduces role of teacher as social agent with responsibilities to larger society • Beginning of "tracking"	• PATRIOTIC TEXT: teacher as patriot who is to use curriculum to inspire and prepare students • In wake of Scopes Trial and Communism, new skepticism about teachers •Great Books Program	• SCIENTIFIC TEXT: introduction of textbooks based on "scientific" principles of learning of "facts" which could be subsequently tested on standardized tests; removes teacher from curriculum
Primary Text: " American Education: The Colonial Experience." Lawrence Cremin	Primary Text: How Teachers Taught [1880-1980]." Larry Cuban	Primary Text: "A Fictional History of Public Education." Herbert Kohl	Primary Text: "The Paideia Proposal." Mortimer Adler	Primary Text: "Cult of Efficiency." Raymond E. Callahan

ERA: Reform Era I (60s-70s)	ERA: The Conservative Era (80s)	ERA: Reform Era II (80s-90s)	ERA: Back-to-Basics, late 90s	ERA: The Next Millennium
• NEGOTIATED TEXTS: progressive reforms place student at center of curriculum • In response to 60s, authority of texts is questioned; beginning of negotiated reading which redefined teacher's role as keeper of secret meaning.	• POLITICAL TEXT II: "Nation at Risk" signals "crisis" • "Cultural literacy" movement • Moral Majority begins assaults on texts and teachers	• MULTIMEDIA TEXT: Computerized/TV generation: how can teacher compete with MTV? • Coalition of Essential Schools, et al, begin reforms to meet needs of changing workplace and society	• BASIC TEXT: student performance nation-wide is troubling • Beginning of standards movement which is projected to culminate in state or national curriculum that will be "teacher proof."	• INTERACTIVE TEXT: Distance learning? • Interactive, increasingly visual texts? •Teacher as: "director" or "designer"
Primary Text: "Sometimes a Shining Moment: The Foxfire Experience." Eliot Wigginton	Primary Text: "Closing of the American Mind." Allan Bloom	Primary Text: "Horace's Compromise." Theodore Sizer	Primary Text: "The Schools We Need and Why We Don't Have Them." E.D. Hirsch	Primary Text: "Hamlet on the Holodeck: The Future of Narrative." Janet Murray

Adler, Mortimer. 1982. *The Paideia Proposal: An Educational Manifesto.* New York: Collier Books.

Allen, Janet. 1995. *It's Never Too Late: Leading Adolescents to Lifelong Literacy.* Portsmouth, NH: Heinemann.

Applebee, Arthur. 1974. *Tradition and Reform in the Teaching of English: A History.* Urbana, IL: National Council of Teachers of English.

Applebee, Arthur. 1996. *Curriculum as Conversation: Transforming Traditions of Teaching and Learning.* Chicago: University of Chicago Press.

Applebee, Arthur, and Judith A. Langer. 1987. *How Writing Shapes Thinking: A Study of Teaching and Learning.* Urbana, IL: National Council of Teachers of English.

Baldwin, James. 1988. "A Talk to Teachers." In *Multicultural Literacy: Opening the American Mind,* edited by R. S. Walker. Saint Paul, MN: Graywolf Press.

Barnes, Douglas, ed. 1968. *Drama in the English Classroom.* Urbana, IL: National Council of Teachers of English.

Barnes, Douglas. 1992. *From Communication to Curriculum.* Portsmouth, NH: Boynton/Cook.

Bateson, Mary Catherine. 1990. *Composing a Life.* New York: Plume.

Baumann, James R., and Edward J. Kameenui. 1991. "Research on Vocabulary Instruction: Ode to Voltaire." In *Handbook of Research on Teaching the English Language Arts,* edited by J. M. J. James Flood, Diane Lapp, and James R. Squire. New York: Macmillan.

Bellah, Robert, Richard Madsen, William M. Sullivan, Ann Swidler, and Steven M. Tipton. 1985. *Habits of the Heart: Individualism and Commitment in American Life.* New York: Perennial Library.

Bennett, William, ed. 1996. *The Book of Virtues: A Treasury of Great Moral Stories.* New York: Touchstone.

Bennett, William. 1996. *The Book of Virtues for Young People.* Parsippany, NJ: Silver Burdett Press.

Blau, Sheridan. 1997. National Council of Teachers of English Annual Convention. Detroit.

Bloom, Harold. 1994. *The Western Canon: The Books and School of the Ages.* New York: Harcourt Brace.

Boiarsky, Carolyn. 1997. *The Art of Workplace English.* Portsmouth, NH: Boynton/Cook.

Bomer, Randy. 1995. *Time for Meaning: Crafting Literate Lives in Middle and High School.* Portsmouth, NH: Heinemann.

Boomer, Garth, Nancy Lester, Cynthia Onore, and John Cook, eds. 1992. *Negotiating the Curriculum: Educating for the 21st Century.* Washington, DC: Falmer Press.

Botstein, Leon. 1997. *Jefferson's Children: Education and the Promise of American Culture.* New York: Doubleday.

Briggs, Sandra J. 1991. "The Multilingual/Multicultural Classroom." [*Early draft of an article that later appeared in Phi Delta Kappan Record* (May).]

Brown, Rexford. 1993. *Schools of Thought: How the Politics of Literacy Shape Thinking in the Classroom.* San Francisco: Jossey-Bass.

Bruner, Jerome. 1986. *Actual Minds, Possible Worlds.* Cambridge, MA: Harvard University Press.

Caine, Renate Nummela, and Geoffrey Caine. 1994. *Making Connections: Teaching and the Human Brain.* Menlo Park, CA: Addison-Wesley.

Caine, Renate Nummela, and Geoffrey Caine. 1997. *Education on the Edge of Possibility.* Alexandria, VA: Association for Supervision and Curriculum Development.

California Academic Standards Commission. 1998. *The California Language Arts Content Standards.* Sacramento, CA: California Department of Education.

Camus, Albert. 1955. *The Myth of Sisyphus and Other Essays.* New York: Vintage.

Canada, Geoffrey. 1998. *Reaching up for Manhood: Transforming the Lives of Boys in America.* Boston: Beacon Press.

Champlain Valley (VT) Union High School. 1997. Graduation Challenge Advisor Handbook.

Christenbury, Leila. 1994. *Making the Journey: Being and Becoming a Teacher of English Language Arts.* Portsmouth, NH: Boynton/Cook.

Christenbury, Leila, and Patricia P. Kelly. 1983. *Questioning: A Path to Critical Thinking.* Urbana, IL: ERIC and National Council of Teachers of English.

Ciardi, John, and Miller Williams. 1975. *How Does a Poem Mean?* Boston: Houghton Mifflin.

Claggett, Fran, with Joan Brown. 1992. *Drawing Your Own Conclusions.* Portsmouth, NH: Boynton/Cook.

Claggett, Fran, Louann Reid, and Ruth Vinz. 1996. *Recasting the Text.* Portsmouth, NH: Heinemann.

Coles, Robert. 1989. *The Call of Stories: Teaching and the Moral Imagination.* Boston: Houghton Mifflin.

Coles, Robert. 1997. Newshour Interview. The Newshour. PBS.

Coles, Robert. 1997. *The Moral Intelligence of Children: How to Raise a Moral Child.* New York: Plume.

The College Board. 1998–1999. *Advanced Placement Course Description: English.* New York: College Board.

Conway, Jill Ker. 1989. *The Road from Coorain.* New York: Vintage Departures.

Cook, Jeff Scott. 1989. *The Elements of Speechwriting and Public Speaking: The Essential Guide to Preparing and Delivering Powerful, Eloquent, and Well-Received Speeches, Reducing Panic and Nervousness, and Enjoying All Types of Speaking Engagements.* New York: Macmillan.

Covey, Stephen R. 1989. *The Seven Habits of Highly Effective People.* New York: Simon and Schuster.

Csikszentmihalyi, Mihaly. 1991. *Flow: The Psychology of Optimal Experience.* New York: HarperPerennial.

Csikszentmihalyi, Mihaly. 1996. *Creativity: Flow and the Psychology of Discovery and Invention.* New York: HarperPerennial.

Cummins, Jim, and Dennis Sayers. 1997. *Brave New Schools: Challenging Cultural Illiteracy Through Global Learning Newworks.* New York: St. Martin's Press.

Cutler, Jacqueline. 1991. "They used to hate reading—now they love it." *Oakland Tribune,* March 11, A-1.

Darling-Hammond, Linda. 1997. *The Right to Learn: A Blueprint for Creating Schools That Work.* San Francisco: Jossey-Bass.

Delpit, Lisa. 1995. *Other People's Children: Cultural Conflict in the Classroom.* New York: The New Press.

Delpit, Lisa. 1997. "Ebonics and Cultural Responsive Instruction." *Rethinking Schools: An Urban Educational Journal* 12 (1):6.

Denby, David. 1996. *Great Books: My Adventures with Homer, Rousseau, Woolf, and Other Indestructible Writers of the Western World.* New York: Touchstone Books.

Dodge, Liz, and Liz Whaley. 1993. *Weaving in the Women: Transforming the High School English Curriculum.* Portsmouth, NH: Boynton/Cook.

Edelman, Marian Wright. 1992. *The Measure of Our Success: A Letter to My Children and Yours.* New York: HarperPerennial.

Ehrlich, Jeffrey, and Marc Mannheimer. 1990. *The Carpenter's Manifesto: A Total Guide That Takes All the Mystery out of Carpentry for Everybody.* New York: Henry Holt and Company.

Elbow, Peter. 1981. *Writing with Power: Techniques for Mastering the Writing Process.* New York: Oxford University Press.

Elias, Maurice J., Joseph E. Zins, Roger P. Weissberg, Karin S. Frey, Mark T. Greenberg, Norris M. Haynes, Rachael Kessler, Mary E. Schwab-Stone, and Timothy P. Shriver. 1997. *Promoting Social and Emotional Learning: Guidelines for Educators.* Alexandria, VA: Association for Supervision and Curriculum Development.

Feynman, Richard. 1998. *The Meaning of It All: Thoughts of a Citizen Scientist.* New York: Addison-Wesley.

Fletcher, Ralph. 1996. *Breathing in, Breathing out: Keeping a Writer's Notebook.* Portsmouth, NH: Heinemann.

Flood, James, Julie M. Jensen, Diane Lapp, and James R. Squire. 1991. *Handbook of Research on Teaching the English Language Arts.* New York: Macmillan.

Fulwiler, Toby, ed. 1987. *The Journal Book.* Portsmouth, NH: Boynton/Cook.

Gardner, Howard. 1991. *The Unschooled Mind: How Children Think and How Schools Should Teach.* New York: Basic Books.

Gardner, Howard. 1992. *Multiple Intelligences: The Theory into Practice: A Reader.* New York: Basic Books.

Gardner, Howard. 1995. *Leading Minds: An Anatomy of Leadership.* New York: Basic Books.

Gates, Henry Louis, Jr. 1992. *Loose Canons: Notes on the Culture Wars.* New York: Oxford University Press.

Gaughan, John. 1997. *Cultural Reflections: Critical Teaching and Learning in the English Classroom.* Portsmouth, NH: Boynton/Cook.

Gillan, Maria Mazziotti, and Jennifer Gillan. 1994. *Unsettling America: An Anthology of Contemporary Multicultural Poetry.* New York: Penguin Books.

Gilligan, Carol. 1982. *In a Different Voice: Psychological Theory and Women's Development.* Cambridge, MA: Harvard University Press.

Gilster, Paul. 1997. *Digital Literacy.* New York: Wiley Computer Publishing.

Gilyard, Keith. 1991. *Voices of the Self: A Study of Language Competence.* Detroit: Wayne State University Press.

Goleman, Daniel. 1995. *Emotional Intelligence.* New York: Bantam Books.

Greene, Maxine. 1998. *Releasing the Imagination: Essays on Education, the Arts, and Social Change.* San Francisco: Jossey-Bass.

Greene, Maxine. 1998. "Teaching as Possibility: A Light in Dark Times." *The Journal of Pedagogy, Pluralism, and Practice* 1 (1).

Hall, Donald, and Sven Birkerts. 1994. *Writing Well.* New York: HarperCollins College Publishers.

Harris, Muriel. 1979. "The Overgraded Paper: Another Case of More Is Less." In *How to Handle Paperload*, edited by Gene Stanford. Urbana, IL: NCTE.

Harris, Muriel. 1986. *Teaching One-to-One: The Writing Conference.* Urbana, IL: NCTE.

Heaney, Seamus. 1990. "Seamus Heaney." In *Harvard Poetry Series.* Harvard: Harvard University.

Heilker, Paul. 1996. *The Essay: Theory and Pedagogy for an Active Form.* Urbana, IL: NCTE.

Hillocks, George, Jr. 1995. *Teaching Writing as Reflective Practice.* New York: Teachers College Press.

Hirsch, Edward. 1994. *Transforming Vision: Writers on Art.* Boston: Bulfinch Press Books.

Hobbs, Renee. 1998. "Literacy for the Information Age." *English Journal* 87 (January).

Holbrook, Hilary Taylor. 1984. Qualities of Effective Writing Programs. *ERIC Digest* ED25069484.

Kauffman, Stuart. 1995. *At Home in the Universe: The Search for the Laws of Self-Organization and Complexity.* New York: Oxford University Press.

Kohl, Colin and Herbert Greer, ed. 1997. *A Call to Character: A Family Treasury of Stories, Poems, Plays, Proverbs, and Fables to Guide the Development of Values for You and Yours.* New York: HarperCollins.

Kohl, Herbert. 1998. *The Discipline of Hope: Learning from a Lifetime of Teaching.* New York: Simon and Schuster.

Kohn, Alfie. 1998. "Only for *My* Kid: How Privileged Parents Undermine School Reform." *Phi Delta Kappan* 79 (April):568.

Krashen, Stephen. 1993. *The Power of Reading: Insights from the Research.* Englewood, NJ: Libraries Unlimited.

Lane, Barry. 1993. *After THE END: Teaching and Learning Creative Revision.* Portsmouth, NH: Heinemann.

Langer, Judith A. 1991. "Literacy and Schooling: A Sociocognitive Perspective." In *Literacy for a Diverse Society: Perspectives, Practices, and Policies,* edited by E. H. Heibert. New York: Teachers College Press.

Langer, Judith. 1995. *Envisioning Literature: Literary Understanding and Literature Instruction.* New York: Teachers College Press/International Reading Association.

LeBlanc, Paul, and Gail E. Hawisher. 1992. *Re-Imagining Computers and Composition: Teaching and Research and the Virtual Age.* Portsmouth, NH: Boynton/Cook.

Macrorie, Ken. 1987. Foreword to *The Journal Book,* edited by Toby Fulwiler. Portsmouth, NH: Boynton/Cook.

Manguel, Alberto. 1996. *A History of Reading.* New York: Penguin.

Marcus, Clare Cooper. 1995. *House as a Mirror of Self: Exploring the Deeper Meaning of Home.* Berkeley, CA: Conari Press.

Marzano, Robert J. 1991. *Cultivating Thinking in English and the Language Arts.* Urbana, IL: National Council of Teachers of English.

Mathews, Jay. 1998. *Class Struggle: What's Wrong (and Right) with America's Best Public High Schools.* New York: Times Books.

Mayher, John S. 1990. *Uncommon Sense: Theoretical Practice in Language Education.* Portsmouth, NH: Boynton/Cook.

Mayher, John S., Nancy Lester, and Gordon M. Pradl. 1983. *Learning to Write/Writing to Learn,* Portsmouth, NH: Heinemann.

McCall, Nathan. 1995. *Makes Me Wanna Holler: A Young Black Man in America.* New York: Vintage Books.

McQuillan, Jeff. 1998. *The Literacy Crisis: False Claims, Real Solutions.* Portsmouth, NH: Heinemann.

Metzger, Margaret. 1996. "Maintaining a Life." *Phi Delta Kappan* (January).

Moustafa, Margaret. 1997. *Beyond Traditional Phonics: Research Discoveries and Reading Instruction.* Portsmouth, NH: Heinemann.

Murray, Donald. 1985. *A Writer Teaches Writing.* Boston: Houghton Mifflin.

Murray, Janet. 1997. The Newshour Interview, Public Broadcasting System, Oct. 13.

Murray, Janet. 1997. *Hamlet on the Holodeck: The Future of Narrative in Cyberspace.*

Myers, Miles. 1996. *Changing Our Minds: Negotiating English and Literacy.* Urbana, IL: National Council of Teachers of English.

National Council of Teachers of English. 1989. *NCTE's Position on the Teaching of English: Assumptions and Practices.* Urbana, IL: National Council of Teachers of English.

National Council of Teachers of English/International Reading Association. 1996. *Standards for the English Language Arts.* Urbana, IL: International Reading Association and National Council of Teachers of English.

Nussbaum, Martha C. 1995. *Poetic Justice: The Literary Imagination and Public Life.* Boston: Beacon Press.

Nystrand, Martin, with Adam Gamoran, Robert Kachur, and Catherine Prendergast. 1997. *Opening Dialogue: Understanding the Dynamics of Language and Learning in the English Classroom*. New York: Teachers College Press.

O'Casey, Sean. 1969. *Three Plays: June and the Paycock, The Shadow of a Gunman, and The Plow and the Stars*. New York: St. Martin's Press.

Olson, Carol Booth, ed. 1996. *Reading, Thinking, and Writing About Multicultural Literature*. Glenview, IL: ScottForesman.

Orenstein, Peggy. 1995. *Schoolgirls: Young Women, Self-Esteem, and the Confidence Gap*. New York: Anchor Books.

Padgett, Ron. 1997. *Creative Reading: What It Is, How to Do It, and Why*. Urbana, IL: NCTE.

Perry, Theresa. 1997. "I 'on Know Why They Be Trippin'." *Rethinking Schools: An Urban Educational Journal* 12 (1):3. Guest edited by Lisa Delpit.

Peterson, Art. 1996. *The Writer's Workout Book: 113 Stretches Toward Better Prose*. Berkeley, CA: National Writing Project.

Pipher, Mary. 1994. *Reviving Ophelia: Saving the Selves of Adolescent Girls*. New York: Grosset/Putnam.

Pirie, Bruce. 1997. *Reshaping High School English*. Urbana, IL: National Council of Teachers of English.

Plato. 1956. "Pheadrus." Translated by Jowett. In *The Collected Works of Plato*. Edited by I. Edman. New York: Modern Library.

Postman, Neil. 1985. *Amusing Ourselves to Death: Public Discourse in the Age of Show Business*. New York: Penguin.

Postman, Neil. 1995. *The End of Education: Redefining the Value of School*. New York: Vintage.

Raphael, Taffy E., and Susan I. McMahon. 1997. *The Book Club Connection: Literacy Learning and Classroom Talk*. New York: International Reading Association and Teachers College Press.

Rico, Gabriele Lusser. 1983. *Writing the Natural Way: Using Right-Brain Techniques to Release Your Expressive Powers*. Los Angeles, CA: J. P. Tarcher, Inc.

Rief, Linda. 1992. *Seeking Diversity: Language Arts with Adolescents*. Portsmouth, NH: Heinemann.

Rief, Linda. 1998. *Vision and Voice: Extending the Literacy Spectrum*. Portsmouth, NH: Heinemann.

Romano, Tom. 1987. *Clearing the Way: Working with Teenage Writers*. Portsmouth, NH: Heinemann.

Routman, Regie. 1994. *Invitations: Changing as Teachers and Learners K–12*. Portsmouth, NH: Heinemann.

Ryan, Joan. 1997. Joan Ryan Column. *San Francisco Chronicle*, June 11, A17.

San Luis Obispo County Office of Education. 1997. Technology Certification Proficiencies: San Luis Obispo County Office of Education.

Sato, Kyoko. 1998. "The Invisible Discrepancies in Teaching Language." In *Language Study in Middle School, High School, and Beyond: Views on Enhancing the Study of Language*, edited by J. S. Baines. Newark, NJ: International Reading Association.

Schlechty, Phillip. 1998. *Inventing Better Schools: An Action Plan for Educational Reform*. San Francisco: Jossey-Bass.

Schön, Donald A. 1983. *The Reflective Practitioner: How Professionals Think in Action*. New York: Basic Books.

Schwartz, Tony. 1983. *Media: The Second God*. Garden City, NJ: Anchor Books.

Service Learning 2000 Center. 1998. "Seven Elements of High Quality Service Learning." Palo Alto, CA: Service Learning 2000 Center.

Shaugnessy, Mina P. 1977. *Errors and Expectations: A Guide for the Teacher of Basic Writing*. New York: Oxford University Press.

Sizer, Theodore. 1996. *Horace's Hope: What Works for the American High School*. Boston: Mariner Books.

Smagorinsky, Peter. 1996. *Standards in Practice: Grades 9–12.* Urbana, IL: National Council of Teachers of English.

Smith, Frank. 1982. *Writing and the Writer.* Hillsdale: Lawrence Erlbaum Associates.

Smith, Frank. 1990. *To Think.* New York: Teachers College Press.

Spandel, Vicki, and Richard J. Stiggins. 1997. *Creating Writers: Linking Writing Assessment and Instruction.* New York: Longman.

Stafford, William. 1978. *Writing the Australian Crawl: Views on the Writer's Vocation.* Ann Arbor, MI: University of Michigan Press.

Stock, Patricia Lambert. 1995. *The Dialogic Curriculum: Teaching and Learning in a Multicultural Society.* Portsmouth, NH: Boynton/Cook.

Stone, I.F. 1988. *The Trial of Socrates.* New York: Anchor Books.

Strickland, Kathleen, and James Strickland. 1998. *Reflections on Assessment: Its Purposes, Methods, and Effects on Learning.* Portsmouth, NH: Boynton/Cook.

Strong, Marilee. 1991. "Teens Narrow the Generation Gap." *The Daily Review,* April 21, B-1.

Strunk, William, and E.B. White. 1979. *The Elements of Style.* 3d. ed. New York: Macmillan.

Suzuki, Shunryu. 1988. *Zen Mind, Beginner's Mind.* New York: Weatherhill.

Tannen, Deborah. 1990. *You Just Don't Understand: Men and Women in Conversation.* New York: Ballantine.

Tannen, Deborah. 1994. *Talking from 9 to 5: Women and Men in the Workplace: Language, Sex, and Power.* New York: Avon.

Tchudi, Stephen, and Paul J. Morris II. 1996. *The New Literacy: Moving Beyond the 3Rs.* San Francisco: Jossey-Bass.

Thomason, Paul. 1997. "Maria Callas—in a Class by Herself." *San Francisco Chronicle,* August 17, p. 51.

Thornburg, David D. 1994. *Education in the Communication Age.* San Carlos, CA: Starsong Publications.

Trelease, Jim. 1995. *The Read-Aloud Handbook.* New York: Penguin.

Tucker, Marc S., and Judy B. Codding. 1998. *Standards for Our Schools: How to Set Them, Measure Them, and Reach Them.* San Francisco: Jossey-Bass.

United States Department of Labor. 1991. *Secretary's Commission on Achieving Necessary Skills (SCANS) Report: What Work Requires of Schools.* Washington, DC.

Vinz, Ruth. 1996. *Composing a Teaching Life.* Portsmouth, NH: Boynton/Cook.

Visotsky, Burton. 1996. *The Genesis of Ethics: How the Tormented Family of Genesis Leads Us to Moral Development.* New York: Three Rivers Press.

Vygotsky, Lev. 1994. *Thought and Language.* Edited by A. Kosulin. Cambridge, MA: MIT Press.

West, Cornel. 1994. *Race Matters.* New York: Vintage.

Wiggins, Grant. 1998. *Educative Assessment: Designing Assessments to Inform and Improve Student Performance.* San Francisco: Jossey-Bass.

Wilhelm, Jeffrey D. 1995. *"You Gotta BE the Book": Teaching Engaged and Reflective Reading with Adolescents.* New York: Teachers College Press and National Council of Teachers of English.

Willis, Meredith Sue. 1993. *Deep Revision: A Guide for Teachers, Students, and Other Writers.* New York: Teachers and Writers Press.

Wilson, Edward O. 1998. *Consilience: The Unity of Knowledge.* New York: Alfred A. Knopf.

Wink, Joan. 1997. *Critical Pedagogy: Notes from the Real World.* New York: Longman.

Zehr, Mary Ann. 1998. "Black Students Found Less Likely to Access the Internet." *Education Week,* April 29, p. 9.

INDEX